This is an enlarged version of Professor Cottret's acclaimed study of the Huguenot communities in England, first published in French by Aubier in 1985. *The Huguenots in England* presents a detailed, sympathetic assessment of one of the great migrations of early modern Europe, examining the social origins, aspirations and eventual destiny of the refugees, and their responses to their new-found home, a Protestant *terre d'exil*. Bernard Cottret shows how for the poor weavers, carders and craftsmen who constituted the majority of the exiles the experience of religious persecution was at once personal calamity, disruptive of home and family, and heaven-sent economic opportunity, which many were quick to exploit. The individual testimonies contained in consistory registers entail a wealth of personal narrative, reflection and reaction, enabling Professor Cottret to build a fully rounded picture of the Huguenot experience and of their settlement in early modern England.

In an extended afterword Professor Emmanuel Le Roy Ladurie considers the Huguenot phenomenon in the wider context of the contrasting British and French attitudes to religious minorities in the early modern period.

The Huguenots in England

THE HUGUENOTS IN ENGLAND
Immigration and Settlement
c. 1550–1700

BERNARD COTTRET
Professor at the University of Lille III

Translated by
PEREGRINE and ADRIANA STEVENSON

with an Afterword by
EMMANUEL LE ROY LADURIE

The right of the
University of Cambridge
to print and sell
all manner of books
was granted by
Henry VIII in 1534.
The University has printed
and published continuously
since 1584.

CAMBRIDGE UNIVERSITY PRESS

Cambridge
New York   Port Chester
Melbourne   Sydney

**EDITIONS DE
LA MAISON DES SCIENCES DE L'HOMME**
Paris

CAMBRIDGE UNIVERSITY PRESS
Cambridge, New York, Melbourne, Madrid, Cape Town, Singapore,
São Paulo, Delhi, Dubai, Tokyo

Cambridge University Press
The Edinburgh Building, Cambridge CB2 8RU, UK

With Editions de la Maison des Sciences de l'Homme
54 Boulevard Raspail, 75270 Paris Cedex 06, France

Published in the United States of America by Cambridge University Press, New York

www.cambridge.org
Information on this title: www.cambridge.org/9780521124096

Originally published in French as *Terre d'exil*
by Aubier, Paris 1985
and © Aubier 1985
First published in English by Editions de la Maison des Sciences de l'Homme
and Cambridge University Press 1991 as *The Huguenots in England:
immigration and settlement c. 1550–1700*
English translation © Maison des Sciences de l'Homme and Cambridge
University Press 1991

This digitally printed version 2009

A catalogue record for this publication is available from the British Library

Library of Congress Cataloguing in Publication data
Cottret, Bernard,
[Terre d'exil, English]
The Huguenots in England : immigration and settlement
c. 1550–1700 / Bernard Cottret : translated by Peregrine Stevenson with
an afterword by Emmanuel Le Roy Ladurie.
      p.   cm.
Translation of: Terre d'exil.
Includes bibliographical references and index.
ISBN 0-521-33388-1
1. Huguenots – 17th century. 2. Immigrants – England – History – 17th century.
3. Immigrants – England – History – 16th century. 4. Walloons – England –
History. 5. French – England –
History. I. Title.
DA125.H84C66   1991
941'.008'8245 – dc20   90-43066CIP

ISBN 978-0-521-33388-7 Hardback
ISBN 978-0-521-12409-6 Paperback

CONTENTS

FIGURES

MAPS

TABLES

ACKNOWLEDGEMENTS

Though it deals with foreigners, this is a book about the English and the 'quiet conquest' of England, recently commemorated by a major exhibition in London. At the end of the seventeenth century several thousand Huguenot weavers, craftsmen, whig-makers and artisans – not to forget their betters, pastors and 'gentilshommes' – flocked to Britain to escape the wrath of Louis XIV, in the wake of the Revocation of the Edict of Nantes (1685). Yet the first settlements dated back to the age of the Reformation.

The Huguenot epic, with its emotional appeal and heroic overtones, lends itself to a two-dimensional approach: it was at the same time mythical and realistic, sometimes bordering on the trivial. Even though I have been very careful not to update the phenomenon, yet, in Bolingbroke's words, 'history is philosophy teaching by example' and there was an implicit comparison in my mind between the Huguenot settlement of yore and more recent trends of immigration. Our present concept of a 'refugee' is largely derived from that time.

I have spent some fifteen years with the 'poor refugees' of the past, and I feel particularly indebted to the Huguenot Society of London, and its honorary secretary, Miss Irene Scouloudi, who devoted her whole life to the subject. The Huguenot Library, in Mallet Place, and the French Reformed Church, now in Soho Square, have opened their priceless manuscripts and pamphlets to me, while Miss Anne Oakley guided my steps in the Dean and Chapter Library, Canterbury. I must also thank the staff of all the record offices I have visited: the Guildhall Library, Lambeth Palace, not to forget the British Library – overscrupulous at times, though highly efficient. The Principal and Fellows of St Hilda's College, Oxford, also received me out of term to allow me to study in the Bodleian Library, certainly one of the cosiest libraries. The Norfolk Record Office were so kind as to send me one or two essential microfilms,

xii *Acknowledgements*

while the Bibliothèque Nationale and Bibliothèque de l'Arsenal in Paris contain some interesting pieces on secret intelligence at the time.

Moreover, I have also benefited from the vast knowledge of several scholars. The late Menna Prestwich invited me to her Oxford home, while Professor L. Stone's encouraging remarks were decisive when I wrote the book.

On this side of the Channel, Elisabeth Labrousse read the typescript, and always answered my questions about her own work. Maurice Agulhon directed the French publication with great expertise, while E. Le Roy Ladurie freely discussed the book with me several times.

History is indeed a continuous recreating of the past, and ever since the publication of *Terre d'exil*, I have had innumerable opportunities to confer with other researchers. I should like to mention in particular H. Appia (Paris III), J. Bompaire, former Président de la Société de l'Histoire du Protestantisme Français, N. Bonneuil, from the Institut National d'Etudes Démographiques, A. Cabantous (CNRS), E. Caldicott (University College, Dublin), F. Crouzet (Paris IV), Eveline Cruickshanks (History of Parliament), J. Delumeau (Collège de France), C. Giry (Institut français au Royaume-Uni), Madame Magdelaine (CNRS), Marie-Madeleine Martinet (Paris IV), Roger Mettam (University of London), A. Morvan (Paris III), J.-P. Poussou (Paris IV), J. Tual (Lille III), Dale Van Kley (Calvin College, Grand Rapids) and Roger Zuber (Paris IV).

I should not forget either C. Bruneteau who supervised my thesis on Bolingbroke, or the late Robert Mandrou who literally converted me to history. Neither should I leave unnoticed the friendship of Madame Deconinck, M. Hearn, F. Lessay, and F. Lestringant.

I should also thank Linda Randall, who acted as a freelance copyeditor for Cambridge University Press, and made some very useful remarks.

Finally, I feel much indebted to Richard Fisher who has supervised this English edition which should be read in its own right.

Bernard Cottret
Université Charles de Gaulle (Lille III)

Note on the translation: This translation is, in some measure, from the author's pen, having been reviewed, revised and extended by Professor Cottret.

Introduction

'How to be an alien' reconsidered

Love ye therefore the strangers: for ye were strangers in the land of Egypt.
Deut. 11:19

The true originality of the historian lies in identifying questions.
C. Hill, *Essays*, III, Brighton, 1986, p. 15

Foreigners only exist in the eyes of the beholder. No one would describe himself primarily as an 'alien'. The identity of strangers is – and ever shall be – most elusive and nondescript, not to say paradoxical. There are no foreigners *per se*, and the proudest national may one day become a foreigner, or even feel alienated from his own country, or its system of values.

While the word 'alien' was already in use in the early modern period to describe a foreigner settling in England, other terms have undergone a steady semantic revolution: 'strangers' generally referred to people from another country – though the emphasis was on allegiance rather than soil – while on the other hand a 'foreigner' might well have been an Englishman from a different part of the country, who hence did not enjoy the freedom of a given city. To put it point-blank, 'strangers' were what we would now call 'foreigners', while the same holds true for 'foreigners' who were simply strangers. The legal definition of strangers has been splendidly documented by Miss Irene Scouloudi in a recent publication of the Huguenot Society of London.[1]

Nationality is therefore a legal as well as a cultural phenomenon: since

---

[1] Irene Scouloudi, *Returns of Strangers in the Metropolis. A Study of an Active Minority*, *Publications of the Huguenot Society of London*, 'Quarto Series', LVIII, 1985, pp. 1–17.

the 1948 British Nationality Act, with its insistence on the Commonwealth, Britain has experienced some drastic changes which are closely related to recent trends of immigration from former colonies and to the new possibilities enjoyed by all EEC citizens to enter freely. The 1981 British Nationality Act has now clearly restricted British citizenship to people already legally settled in Britain, or who have one British parent and have been registered abroad at the time of their birth.

The definition of a national has always been a thorny question, which has received different answers in the course of history. In fact, up to the nineteenth century, a third class of persons had been in existence, 'denizens' who held an intermediate status between subjects and aliens. But this distinction was lost in practice when the 1870 Naturalisation Act (33 & 34 Vic. c. 14) allowed aliens to acquire and bequeath land freely.

In the early modern period, 'denization', granted by the Crown, existed alongside 'naturalisation', which depended on an Act of Parliament, though the distinction was often blurred in practice. As we shall see when we examine the reign of Elizabeth I, the concept of 'denization' proved crucial in the experience of Protestant refugees.

The word 'refugee' itself, with its potent emotional appeal, was coined at the time, in reference to the hardships which befell the French Protestants who flocked to England in the 1680s when Louis XIV decreed that Huguenots were simply a figment of the imagination as all good Frenchmen were prepared to joint the Catholic Church *ad majorem Dei gloriam*. But the dragoons, however efficient in times of war, proved poor missionaries; and the problem of the Protestant minority remained unsolved until the 1787 Edict of Toleration, two years before the French Revolution.[2] From then on, the Huguenots were entitled to live and die without any major constraints: the baptism of their children, their own weddings could be registered either by parish priests or local notaries. This brief interlude, at the end of the ancien régime, was in fact a first step towards the complete secularisation of matrimony. In our days, all marriages have to be registered at the *mairie* where a small ceremony is held, apart from the religious celebration if any.

Apart from occasional episodes of unrest, and bouts of economic rivalry on the part of the English society, the Huguenot refugees fared rather well; integration was made easier by a common religious faith which appealed to the Protestant nation at large. Their economic success and cultural assimilation prompted R.D. Gwynn to extol their virtue and sense of self-help in a recent survey of the *Huguenot Heritage*: 'The French refugees were far more important for England's survival in a

[2] A. Encrevé and C. Lauriol (eds.), *Actes des Journées d'Etudes sur l'Edit de 1787*, *Bulletin de la Société de l'Histoire du Protestantisme Français*, 143/2 (1988).

threatening world, and for her future, than either the Catholics or the Quakers of the period.'[3] Yet this blunt overstatement did not entirely convince me. Moreover, Huguenot genetics may never prove a reliable branch of medicine – in spite of Dr Gwynn's final remarks on the 'genetic factors' which 'may have helped determine which French Huguenots possessed the combination of faith, resolution, endurance, and a will to work for a new future which led them to seek refuge in strange lands'.[4]

My own starting point was most different from Dr Gwynn's. Since I was a child, I have always been fascinated by shipwrecks: *Gulliver's Travels* and *Robinson Crusoe* are among the most fruitful of all literary experiences, and were I to be left on a desert island, I would certainly take these two books with me, along with Montesquieu's *Lettres Persanes*. All these titles share the same characteristic: they are about the discovery of the outer world, but the emphasis is always on oneself. Montesquieu's fictitious Iranians provide one of the most accurate and humorous descriptions of early eighteenth-century France. I wanted to apply the same technique in the case of England, but as no Persians were available,[5] I chose the Huguenots. I have therefore followed the peregrinations of my Protestant countrymen in England, our closest neighbour, and, I am afraid to say, our dearest enemy in the past. What has been the result of this journey? How far is it relevant to us today, after more than 300 years?

In the first place, I found that it answered all my expectations. Lucien Febvre – who launched the history of mentality in this century – used to say that there was no proper history without a good working hypothesis.[6] My basic idea, which I have long borne in mind and tested privately before presenting it to the public, is fairly simple: foreigners, settling in another country, are among the best sources of information. Their successes and failures, the pace of their adaptation are certainly worth pursuing in themselves, but, in turn, the question of minorities acts as a sort of social catalyst, shedding light on the hidden feelings and reactions of the majority at large. Hence, cannot we say that the Huguenots, like the English Catholics or Jews – or Quakers – are among the most substantial indicators of English modern history, even though they may have never exceeded 50,000 people in the 1690s?

Like most foreigners, the French Protestants were both the cause and the object of deep-rooted amazement and admiration for their skills and endurance. Fernand Braudel also reminded us that 'estrangement' conferred a privileged perspective, while recently, J.C.D. Clark insisted on the necessity to examine side by side Englishmen and aliens to grasp

---

[3] R.D. Gwynn, *Huguenot Heritage. The History and Contribution of the Huguenots in Britain*, London, 1985, p. 2.   [4] *Ibid.*, p. 175.
[5] G. Lyttelton adopted a similar device with his *Letters from a Persian in England*, 1735.
[6] Lucien Febvre, *Combats pour l'histoire*, Paris (1953), 1965.

more fully the implications of allegiance.[7] The theme was worth pursuing for all those who have crossed the Channel.

In fact, very few attempts have been made yet to answer the apparently simple question, *what is a foreigner*? The issue has now world-wide implications: the labour migrations of our century deserve to hold the historian's attention in their own right. Yet this study may act as a useful reminder that a number of French-speaking artisans migrated across Europe three or four centuries ago; they were either Frenchmen or Walloons – when they migrated from what is now Belgium or the north of France. They would often introduce themselves as Protestants, who had fled their homelands, deeply entrenched in popish superstition, in order to worship God according to the 'true Reformed Faith'. Yet, they were hardly spared economic constraints, and their social integration depended on their economic adaptation. The word 'immigrant' may be misleading, if not anachronistic, because of its present-day connotations of toil and cheap labour.

I have therefore selected England as a particular land of exile. Among other things, this northern country – according to French standards – was often to appear as a bulwark of the 'true Faith' to the Huguenots, in the darkest hours of their history. Moreover, at the end of the seventeenth century, England established herself as a great power, all the more puzzling for the French absolutist state, as after 1688 her unusual brilliance derived from a mixed monarchy. England had long been hailed as a land of revolutions and anarchy by the ambassadors of the most Christian king who strenuously believed in French superiority. Protestantism as such was regarded with awe as a dangerous creed, teaching insubordination and leading people astray to dream of republics.

The Huguenots played a decisive part in relations between the two countries, whether good, bad or indifferent. But the present study is not essentially concerned with international relations, although they inevitably fall within its scope. I have not so much dwelt on the great names of finance or diplomacy, as on those anonymous figures of history – weavers, carders and craftsmen – who came with their pastors to settle on foreign soil.

---

[7] Fernand Braudel, *Ecrits sur l'histoire*, Paris, 1969, p. 59. J.C.D. Clark, *English Society 1688–1832*, Cambridge, 1985, p. 191. My own research on the Huguenots does absolutely confirm the author's analysis of the links between birth and allegiance. Moreover, Dr Clark aptly stresses that 'Not until the Naturalisation Act of 1870 was a procedure for renouncing British nationality laid down.' This shows among other things that philosophical 'contractarianism' – the idea according to which a contract exists between subjects and rulers – is not a safe guide to English institutions, not even after the Glorious Revolution. Hume was among the first to note this discrepancy between Locke's theory and actual practice (*ibid.*, p. 192; B. Cottret and M.-M. Martinet, *Partis et factions dans l'Angleterre du premier XVIIIe siècle*, Paris, 1987, p. 74).

Take for instance the Jean Cornette who appeared on 27 April 1598 before the consistory of the French Reformed Church in London, to be

> severely rebuked for his drunkenness and other unruly conduct, and for showing so little concern to rejoin his wife and children, or support them. Says he is greatly weary of his condition, and wants to go on a voyage to the Indies to put an end to his misery or to his life. Says he somewhat suspects his wife of adultery, and that she was noticed speaking in a strange fashion to a young man passing through Norwich, whose name he does not know.

Or else, on 15 October, the

> wife of William Borne, an Englishman, appeared before the consistory. She was asked how long she had led a life of debauchery with Baudouin Dubois. She replied, about five years, and said she has had two children by him, one of whom died at the hospital in Amsterdam, and the other died also. She said that Baudouin Dubois gave her twelve shillings, so that she could have her first confinement at the hospital in Amsterdam, and that she had sold her clothing to meet her needs.

This realistic concern for trivial matters has the accent of truth. Across three centuries, voices out of the past make themselves heard, spontaneously and with all the immediacy of experience: transient, anonymous destinies, glimpsed in the pages of a register, and then sinking back into oblivion. Hence, precisely, the need to study an extended period of time: birth, life and death, the uprooting of individuals and their eventual assimilation could only be envisaged over a span of several generations. The choice of the century and a half which separates the first official communities of the sixteenth century from the second wave of refugees in the last quarter of the seventeenth century was determined by two considerations. The basic interest of the period extending from the heroic incipient age of the Reformation in Calvin's lifetime, up to the years immediately following the Revocation of the Edict of Nantes, is self-evident. Political, intellectual and religious history, as well as social history, unfold in the course of time. Moreover, the daily pace of adaptation needed to be captured, with its own tone and its changing rhythm – now swifter, now slower. Accordingly, I could not treat time as a mere variable, nor be content with an elliptic typology, let alone with a simple monograph. The Huguenot Society of London – now Huguenot Society 'of Great Britain and Ireland' to please the Irish – have already published a great deal of material allowing genealogists to trace their ancestors. The reader will easily understand that I have neither presented a list of all the pastors nor a complete chronology of each individual Church. Such information may be gathered from the fifty-seven volumes of the 'Quarto Series' of the Huguenot Society, while the *Proceedings* contain a number of articles on specialised subjects. There have been very few general histories of the English Refuge recently, apart from Irene Scouloudi's extensive work, and R.D. Gwynn's somewhat jingoistic approach, which I have already mentioned. Dr Pettegree's study of *Foreign Protestant Communities in Sixteenth-Century London* is deceptive, as it deals mainly with the thirty years from 1550 up to 1580,[8] and involves a certain amount of guesswork. Mark Greengrass' lengthy review article, 'Protestant Exiles and their Assimilation in Early Modern England',[9] may be left out altogether as it seems erratic and possibly pretentious in its concern with what historians should have done – and should not have left undone. In particular Mr Greengrass seems to be determined to revolutionise our approach to Huguenot demography, but he has so far refused to say how.

Of related interest are the contributions to the conferences held in London and Dublin for the tercentenary of the Revocation of the Edict of Nantes in 1985.[10] I was particularly impressed by the book on Ireland:

> The most recent research suggests that some five thousand [French Protestants] arrived in total during the last three decades of the [seventeenth] century, bringing with them the essentially urban skills of banking and finance, trade and industry, the professions and adminis-tration, as well as a tradition – which they were to put to good effect in Ireland – of investment in, or ownership of, land.[11]

I shall spare the reader any well-intentioned, albeit anachronistic, parallel between the refugees of yore and today's displaced persons. Were I to suggest any comparison, I would certainly mention the wave of Jewish emigration which accompanied the forced imposition of Catholicism on the religious minorities of Spain and Portugal after 1492 – a movement which had its Baruch Spinoza just as the French Protestants had their Pierre Bayle, both living in exile in Holland.[12] The perennial character of certain clichés of intolerance, in all their absurdity, is worth noticing; there were Frenchmen, almost three centuries ago, who arrived in England, having endured the *dragonnades*, the persecutions, sometimes the humiliation of a forced abjuration, or else the galleys, or indeed simply the hazards of the journey, only to be accused of having come to 'take the

---

[8] A. Pettegree, *Foreign Protestant Communities in Sixteenth-Century London*, Oxford, 1986.

[9] M. Greengrass, 'Protestant Exiles and their Assimilation in Early Modern England', *Immigrants and minorities*, 4/3 (1985), pp. 68–81.

[10] C.E.J. Caldicott, H. Gough and J.-P. Pittion (eds.), *The Huguenots and Ireland. Anatomy of an Emigration*, Dublin, 1987; Irene Scouloudi (ed.), *Huguenots in Britain and their French Background 1550–1800*, London, 1987.

[11] Caldicott, Gough and Pittion (eds.), *The Huguenots and Ireland*, p. 12.

[12] H. Kamen, 'The Mediterranean and the Expulsion of Spanish Jews in 1492', *Past and Present*, 119 (1988), pp. 30–55.

bread out of the mouths of Englishmen'. But these similarities between past and present are not my chief concern: rather than produce an essay on immigration I wished to write the history of these people in order to bring to life the experience – blood, sweat and tears – of these thousands of men and women whose daily concerns are so vividly described by the consistory registers. Is it appropriate to hail as 'heroes' these men who went into exile 'for the Faith', setting their convictions above all other allegiances, embarking on a journey from which many did not return, and breaking all ties with the past? Anyone who has made a close study of the life of the Protestants in the sixteenth and seventeenth centuries knows how misleading is the Victorian image of the austere Huguenot, characterised alternately as a fearless hero or as a fanatic. I may hold a more dispassionate view of heroism; without denying the moral strength of all those who chose exile rather than renounce their faith, I think it would be a pity to tone down the vigour of their language and confine these creatures of flesh and blood within the mould imposed by an outdated phraseology. The destiny of men of humble condition was as ever punctuated by the problems of daily existence, and the reader will forgive me, I am sure, for having always preferred to draw an authentic picture.

In French usage, a term has been handed down to posterity to refer to the Huguenot diaspora: it is common to speak of the communities in exile as the *Refuge*. In one sense the term is misleading because of its insistence on retreat, exclusion or remoteness. This impression should be mitigated by the strategic situation of the refugees in the history of French Protestantism. Indeed, from the sixteenth century onwards Protestantism became a public, established religion outside France, and expanded beyond the narrow confines of evangelical conventicles to take in the whole of social life. The importance of Strasburg, and later Geneva, as founding cities in the hands of the most illustrious reformers, beginning with Calvin, is well known. Similarly, in the seventeenth and eighteenth centuries, in particular after the practice of the Reformed religion had been prohibited in France, the specific forms of Calvinist worship and social life could exist openly in the Refuge, while, otherwise they were driven underground in the *désert* – or wilderness – where illegal gatherings took place. Therefore, from the very beginning the Refuge Churches acted as a reminder, and upheld, for the 'Churches under the Cross' – i.e. still exposed to persecution or the hazards of the wars of religion – a living example of a society in which the worship of God was reconciled with the service of King and Country. Yet such a dialectic between France and the land of the Refuge gave rise at times to bitterness and misunderstanding: lukewarmness, temporising, compromise, and indeed the excesses of prophesying were all accusations levelled at the Protestants who remained in France.

We need to beware of abstractions; the Refuge, that stronghold of Huguenot resistance, was not a Utopia, or an ideal City. It was made up of individual refugees, of every rank and class, often uprooted, bereft of means, in search of work. From the beginning, indeed, the refugee 'for the true Faith' was far from idle and entered the labour force. The preoccupation with the moral significance of work, which forms so large a part of the Protestant ethos, explains the decisive importance attached to vocational skill and apprenticeship. The Calvinist consistories and their English hosts were equally concerned with sound economic adminis-tration, and both sought to avoid the necessity of prolonged assistance to the poor, thus ensuring that the *minority* never degenerated into a *fringe* group.

But alongside this first sense of the word 'Refuge' was another, which might be called its emblematic meaning. Exile and destitution were sometimes presented, especially in preaching, as a reminder of the divine election of the 'little flock' of the apostolic era of the Church, or indeed as an active commemoration of the destiny of Israel. In 1682, this commemorative aspect of the Refuge, the recollection of the most illustrious precedents in the Bible, were clearly insisted on in a sermon preached at the temple of the Savoy in London. A manuscript copy circulated in France where it was seized by Louis XIV's administration. The following is an extract from this remarkable text addressed to Charles II:

> Your Majesty: It is not I who speak, although it is I who bear the tidings. It is not even our French Church of the Savoy, although it is the Church which very humbly craves audience from Your Majesty; it is your colony of French Protestants whom the tempest casts ashore every day in our harbours. *They are Israelites* crossing the sea to retire into Canaan; they are merchants of the Gospel who have come to seek in our kingdom the Kingdom of Heaven, they are, Sire, the same as these, in some sort. The whole of the Réformed Churches speaks today through my lips, and my words are but the echo of their voice.[13]

The Refuge in time and space

England was a melting pot in its own right as Daniel Defoe observed in a fierce attack on English chauvinism which he published in 1700:

A *True-Born Englishman's* a Contradiction
In speech an Irony, in Fact a Fiction

[13] Paris, Bibliothèque de l'Arsenal, MS 10422.

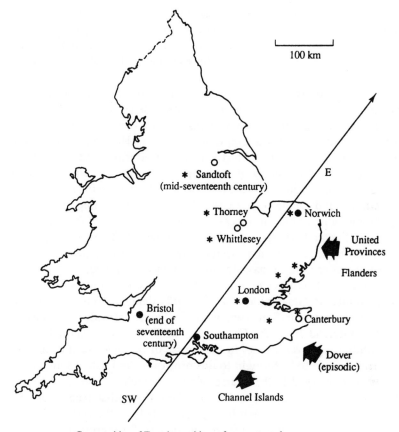

Map 1. Principal locations mentioned in the text

● Communities of French-speaking refugees attested from the sixteenth century onwards

○ Others

✳ Dutch settlements

A Bander made to be a Test of Fools
Which those that use it justly ridicules.
A Metaphor invented to express
A man *a-kin* to all the Universe.[14]

Defoe's potential intention was obvious enough at the time. The Whig pamphleteer defended the Glorious Revolution and William of Orange's

[14] D. Defoe, *The True-Born Englishman* (1700), ed. G. Lamoine, Plan de la Tour, 1980, p. 22.

legitimacy on the English throne against conservative claims. But the examples he invoked were nonetheless convincing, in particular the welcome extended to the Huguenots and the recent waves of immigration of the sixteenth and seventeenth centuries, which all his contemporaries had in mind.

It is difficult to make any precise estimate of these movements of population. The refugees formed a relatively elusive group, with changing patterns of migration, rarely accessible to demographic analysis. A serial approach is worth attempting; where baptismal records are still extant, at least, the pattern of births can be established. Yet one major obstacle remains: the fluidity of these open communities, which were in constant communication with the outside world. Some refugees returned to their homeland, while others either left, or became integrated in the surrounding population, or indeed migrated to another foreign community in England. This instability, although it hampers a proper reconstruction, raises in turn a specific issue: in order to explore this new territory, novel criteria of classification should be adopted.

The presence of refugees in a particular locality was often short-lived: the community at Glastonbury in the 1550s depended entirely on the generosity of Protector Somerset, while in Dover, already the shortest route into England from the Continent, the French Protestant Church was re-established several times in the course of the seventeenth century. Some order needed to be brought to this profusion, and I shall sum up the evidence as it emerged in the course of this research.

If we glance at this century and a half, from the mid-sixteenth century up to 1700, the overall picture is highly contrasted. At the very beginning stands the royal charter, by which the office of superintendent of a Refugee Church established in London was officially conferred on the Polish reformer John a Lasco in 1550. Other foundations took place in the same years: in Canterbury, under the benevolent shadow of Cranmer, several foreigners had met to hold services in the archbishop's palace a year or two before. But Mary Tudor's accession in 1553 was to thwart all these early developments and not until the reign of Elizabeth did the communities begin to flourish anew: Norwich and Southampton had their French-speaking congregations from 1567–8 onwards.

These four Churches, established in the sixteenth century, were to form the backbone of the Refuge for at least a hundred years; other communities were to join them in the next century and a half. There is not, to my knowledge, any exhaustive list of all the Churches, and often among the pages of a register, a new locality is mentioned before disappearing. Thus Hampton, Rye and Winchelsea, at the turn of the 1580s make a brief appearance, but London, Canterbury, Norwich and Southampton, for which we possess lasting records, played a decisive role as the focuses of the Refuge, both in terms of duration and (relative) numerical strength.

Several successive waves of migration may be carefully distinguished. There were at least two separate phases: the first communities struck their roots in the sixteenth century, at the time of the Reformation, but later moves, even more massive in scale, accompanied the *dragonnades* and the Revocation of the Edict of Nantes. The 1680s mark a turning point; the number of the refugees increased virtually tenfold. This gave rise to explosive growth, fragmentation and the conquest of new sites, both in London and in the rest of the country, especially westwards, in expanding Bristol. In the case of London alone, at least thirty different temples were set up in the years immediately following the Revocation, and at the very beginning of the eighteenth century. However, the existence of thirty different locations over a quarter of a century does not imply thirty different communities: new sites and mergers were not uncommon. Likewise, a number of individual families went away to seek their fortune elsewhere. R.D. Gwynn has skilfully drawn the map of the Refugee Churches in the metropolis in the late seventeenth century, and has successfully established the existence of some fifteen Huguenot sites in the provinces during the same period.[15] The precise number of refugees is even more delicate to assert for several reasons: there are gaps and discontinuities in our sources, either because the parish registers have been lost or because some communities experienced a great degree of instability. Paradoxically, then, at the time when the refugees were most numerous – in the late seventeenth century – they are most difficult to pin down in statistical terms. The situation is relatively more simple earlier on, before the great influx of the 1680s and 1690s.

This technical argument is enhanced by another consideration, more ideological in nature, but nonetheless thorny: refugee status is by definition transitory and depends upon social recognition. Was it, for instance, transmitted to the children of refugees? Were they themselves refugees, and how long was this to last? Besides, many French Protestants who settled in England found it difficult to accept the supervision of the Churches, and mutual rejection was nearly as frequent as acceptance. In fact, distrust on the one side, and touchy susceptibilities on the other, poisoned relationships. Tension was at its height in the 1690s (Part II, Ch. 6). The rifts within English society itself also came into play, with the existence, on the fringes of the established Church, of a number of sects which presented possible alternatives to the refugees. Voltaire was later to

[15] R.D. Gwynn, 'The Distribution of Huguenot Refugees in England', *Proceedings of the Huguenot Society of London*, 21, pp. 404–36; *idem* 'The Distribution of Huguenot Refugees in England, II: London and its Environs', *Proceedings of the Huguenot Society of London*, 23, pp. 509–68.

comment: 'This is the land of sects. An Englishman, as a free man, goes to Heaven by whatever path he pleases.'[16]

Let us take the typical refugee of the 1680s. He was exhausted when he arrived in England, having survived a good many perils; in more cases than one, he was separated from his family, and very often he had been driven by threat to recant his Protestant faith, though he was ready to retract as soon as possible. England offered him an extraordinary kaleidoscope of doctrines. He could either remain faithful to the Calvinist discipline if he attended, for instance, the Threadneedle Street temple in the City of London, one of the oldest foundations, or opt for French-speaking Anglicanism as it was practised at the Church of the Savoy, Westminster, or else, of course, once he had learnt the language, attend the services in the nearest English parish – if, that is, he did not sympathise with one of the free Churches. Such competition undoubtedly complicated matters, together with the economic incentives – above all the basic need to find work – which also contributed to geographical diversification.

Should one, then, deduce from all this that the demographic study of the English Refuge cannot be undertaken? That would be to state the problem in the wrong terms; let us assume, rather, that the demography of refugees deserves to be considered in its own right. Such a study extends far beyond the English context, and deserves to be conducted at an international level. A gigantic survey is being carried on by Michèle Magdelaine at the moment. A monumental history of the English population admits that 'many people entered England, for example from the Celtic fringe or in the wake of the persecution of the Huguenots'. Yet their numbers are uncertain in the absence of adequate records.[17]

Provisionally, we may examine some data concerning births, deaths and weddings in the refugee population. Many personal adjustments may prove necessary, so marked were the fluctuations in terms of solidarity or *sense of belonging* during that century and a half.

At times our evidence is relatively scanty. There are no registers of baptisms for London in the sixteenth century, and other types of records should be relied on. Lay subsidies provide lists of aliens, but not in a form which would be useful for our purpose, since they include without distinction Scotsmen, Spaniards, Italians, Dutchmen, Frenchmen and Walloons, and do not specify their religion. Not every foreigner working in England was a refugee – far from it. More interesting are the periodic lists of foreigners drawn up in the Elizabethan period, the 'returns of strangers' Irene Scouloudi has so aptly studied.[18] In the case of London,

---

[16] Voltaire, *Lettres philosophiques* (1734), Paris, 1964, p. 42.
[17] E. Wrigley and R. Schofield, *The Population History of England, 1541–1871, A Reconstruction*, London, 1981, p. 223.
[18] Irene Scouloudi, 'Alien Immigration and Alien Communities in London, 1558–1640', *Proceedings of the Huguenot Society of London*, 25, pp. 27–49.

an estimate would come to the following results in round figures: the total number of foreign residents appears to have risen from 4,700 in 1567 to 5,500 in 1593. The largest single community was the Dutch, followed by the French and Walloons 'born in the lands of King Philip', and finally, far less numerous, the Italians and Spaniards. The population of the communities fluctuated equally; it reached around 2,000 in adjusted figures for the French Church, at the turn of the 1570s (although we have no precise data on the numbers of those who fled to England in the wake of the St Bartholomew's Day massacre), and, conversely, dwindled to its low-water mark ten years later in 1581, with no more than 1,100 persons, thus suggesting a great deal of mobility between host country and homeland. This is clearly indicated in the case of higher ranks. There was, as Schickler thought in 1892, a 'Refuge of St Bartholomew's Day'.[19]

Although the baptismal registers for Threadneeedle Street, London, begin only in 1600, we are on more stable ground for God's House in Southampton, whose registers of baptisms and deaths are the oldest surviving ones starting in 1567 – which is altogether unparalleled. They bear witness to the resilience of this early phase of the Refuge, directly linked to the wars of religion both in France and in Flanders. Hence the speed and vividness with which news travelled from the Continent, to be followed by many prayers and public fasts, beginning on 3 September 1568 for the Prince of Orange, on 6 May 1570 for Condé, on 25 September 1572 in the wake of the St Bartholomew's Day massacre, which was described in these terms:

> a horrible massacre having been committed in Paris on the 24th of August last, in which a great many noblemen and faithful were killed in one day and one night, coming up to twelve or thirteen thousand people, and preaching having been forbidden throughout the kingdom, and the belongings of those of the Religion pillaged throughout the kingdom; for their consolation, and that of the Low Countries, and in order to pray to the Lord for their deliverance, a solemn fast was held.

Thus events in Flanders and in France were curiously interwoven, in accordance with the mixed French and Walloon origins of the refugees at Southampton. Many had come from what is now the north of France – Valenciennes in particular – or nearby Normandy. (On this community, see Dr Spicer's recent thesis (in Bibliography).)

This group – totalling about 500 persons at the end of the sixteenth century – was struck by one calamity after another. They never entirely recovered from the heavy toll taken by the plagues of 1583 and 1604 (see Fig. 1). Again, in 1665, the community suffered the loss of twenty members of 'our little flock'. The fifty or so new arrivals from the Ile de

[19] F. de Schickler, *Les Eglises du Refuge en Angleterre*, 3 vols., Paris, 1892, I, ch. 5.

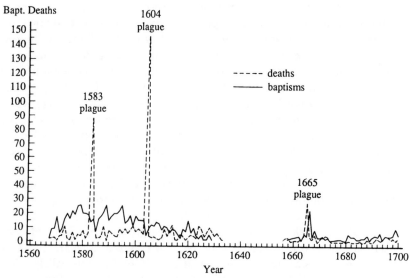

Figure 1. Southampton: refugee population, 1570–1700

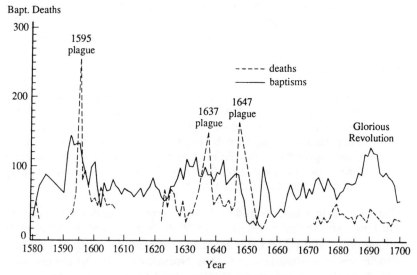

Figure 2. Canterbury: refugee population, 1580–1700

Ré in 1628 were not enough to reverse this long-term falling trend. This is a classical instance of a community decimated by 'ancien régime-type morality', which, in the absence of sufficient immigration to keep it afloat, was slowly disappearing. The trend was reversed with the Revocation of the Edict of Nantes, but even then the community did not recover its former Elizabethan glory. In this respect Southampton typified the early settlements which were doomed to slow asphyxia for want of fresh arrivals. Norwich is also fairly representative of the sixteenth-century Refuge. The number of baptisms (see Fig. 4), declines regularly, following the heyday of the Church at the very end of the Elizabethan period. Slightly different was the situation in Canterbury (see Fig. 2). Here too, the highest point of development was reached in the 1590s, but plague mortality was relatively well compensated by favourable migratory balance rather than natural growth, as other indicators later confirm.

In the case of London (see Fig. 3) more substantial quantitative data is available from 1600 onwards. Thanks to its central position and to the inflow of newcomers, the Threadneedle Street community evinces the slightest fluctuation in population. The first image to emerge from the graph is the succession of periods of expansion and times of fairly sharp contraction, reflecting French history along with purely English events. In particular, the 1630s coincided with a phase of immigration which had rarely been identified as such: this corresponded with the defeat of La Rochelle and the peace of Alès in 1629, which brought all wars of religion to an end. Later on, the disruption of the 1640s and 1650s reflects the turmoil of the Great Rebellion and Interregnum, and reveals the fragmentation of the community along divisive patterns of allegiance. The 1680s were marked by several distinct waves: a first influx occurred at the time of the soldiers' persecutions or *dragonnades* inflicted upon the Huguenots in France, even before the actual Revocation. As far as demography is concerned, the effects of the Revocation coincide with the Glorious Revolution and the accession of William III. The jagged profile of the graph at the end of the century results from two phenomena: very often the Threadneedle Street temple was either a stage before final integration into another community (in London or in the provinces), or indeed departure for another land of Refuge – Ireland, Holland or even the distant prospects of America. All in all, an estimate of the congregation evinces several phases. Initially, the Threadneedle Street community oscillated constantly between 5,000 and 10,000 people, with fairly wide fluctuations – the highest levels being reached in the 1590s or 1630s, the lowest in 1650. The massive immigration of the last quarter of the seventeenth century, beginning *c.* 1681, accordingly represented a complete change of pace and scale, both in quantitative and qualitative terms. This abrupt transformation eludes our observation, in many respects, but the commonly accepted figure of 50,000 refugees may sound relatively convincing. Even so one must take into account the extreme mobility of many of the refugees, who did not necessarily settle in the communities which they passed through. Religious exile on grounds of conscience was often followed by further internal or external migrations, actuated by

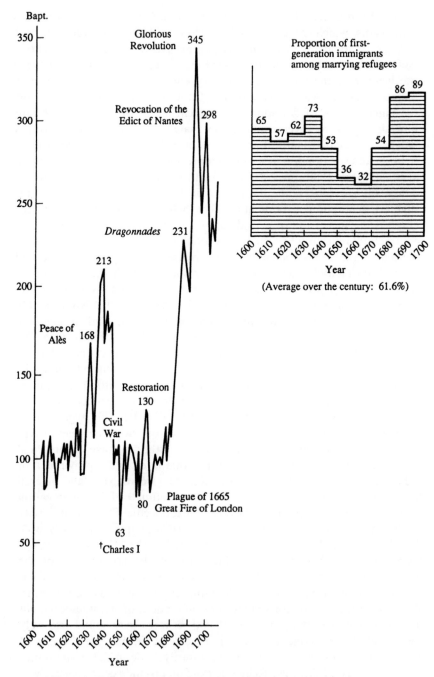

Figure 3. Threadneedle Street, London: refugee population, 1600–1700

economic reasons. The factors governing mobility were varied, reasons of conscience rarely came into play alone.

One fact stands out: here were communities whose very existence depended on immigration; without the infusion of fresh blood from the outside world, they could not effectively sustain themselves. Consequently, new arrivals were a vital necessity, for the odds were that the children of refugees merged fairly quickly into the surrounding population. The natural growth of the foreign communities – the ratio between births and burials – was not sufficient to preserve them. Cut off from immigration, without new arrivals, a congregation began to wane and die. The amplitude of the fluctuations in the graph drawn from the London statistics, its contractions, show the constant reliance on immigration. In other words, only a positive migratory balance, rather than the sheer number of births, could overcome the heavy losses caused by deaths and absorption into the host population. This explains the importance of another trend which the refugees and English authorities were equally aware of: second-generation immigrants behaved differently from their parents, who were still linked to their origins by ties of language and memory. I wondered, initially, if some kind of integration ratio could be established for this second generation. I had to relinquish the idea: such attitudes cannot be expressed in terms of arithmetical averages. However, two distinct sources of statistical data shed some light on this phenomenon.

The first concerns patterns of marriage (see Fig. 3). Indeed, the study of matrimony is most significant in the case of immigration: Jacques Dupâquier has termed it as an important 'mechanism of self-regulation',[20] while Jean-Pierre Poussou wrote that the 'founding of families' played a crucial role, among other things for the study of geographical mobility.[21] Weddings, these acts of independent judgement, rather than baptisms, reflect the individual choice of second-generation immigrants and form the most obvious rites of passage into the surrounding society. This impression is borne out by the constant harassment of young people who deserted the French-speaking Reformed Church for their local English parish. Even when immigration was at its lowest – as in the 1660s for London – recent immigrants still represented a third of all newly married couples.

Secondly, as the reconstruction of individual families is impeded by extreme geographical or religious mobility, I have been led to illustrate the

---

[20] J. Dupâquier, *La Population Rurale du Bassin Parisien à l'époque de Louis XIV*, Ecole des Hautes Etudes en Sciences Sociales, 1979, p. 28.

[21] J.-P. Poussou, *Bordeaux et le Sud-Ouest au XVIII siècle, croissance économique et attraction urbaine*, Ecole des Hautes Etudes en Sciences Sociales, 1983.

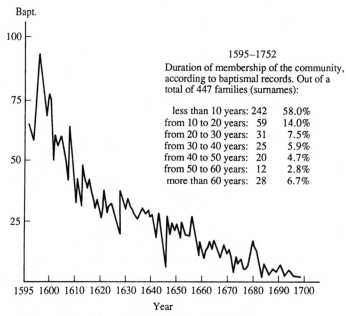

Bapt.

100

1595–1752
Duration of membership of the community,
according to baptismal records. Out of a
total of 447 families (surnames):

75

less than 10 years:	242	58.0%
from 10 to 20 years:	59	14.0%
from 20 to 30 years:	31	7.5%
from 30 to 40 years:	25	5.9%
from 40 to 50 years:	20	4.7%
from 50 to 60 years:	12	2.8%
more than 60 years:	28	6.7%

50

25

1595 1600 1610 1620 1630 1640 1650 1660 1670 1680 1690 1700
Year

Figure 4. Norwich: refugee population, 1595–1700

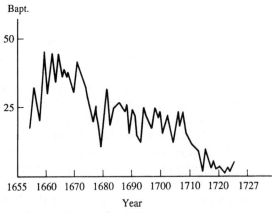

Bapt.

50

25

1655 1660 1670 1680 1690 1700 1710 1720 1727
Year

Figure 5. Thorney, Cambridgeshire: refugee population, *c.* 1655–1725

persistence of family names in the baptismal registers in the case of
Norwich (see Fig. 4).

In this respect another salient fact stands out: the majority of
immigrants deserted the refugee community at the second generation, or
perhaps even sooner. Conversely a small minority of families – around 7
per cent in the case of Norwich – showed a very strong attachment to their

Church, and continued, even for several generations, to attend its services. In other words, choice, rather than any automatic determination, governed individual decisions, and once the family tradition was well established, the tendency was reversed, in favour of staying within the community. Indeed the second generation, when they remained in their native milieu, could aspire to a position of relative eminence, and a seat within the consistory. Their knowledge of the two cultures gave them an invaluable role as cultural intermediaries – reinforced by a complete mastering of English which proved a great advantage in coping with the incessant legal pettifoggery which the refugees were subjected to. In 1634, a letter to Charles I emphasised that

> Although the native born form in some places the greater, and in some others the smaller part of the Church communities: everywhere they are the most important and most considerable part, because they alone possess some property, and by their extraordinarily liberal contributions the Minister is supported, and a great quantity of paupers, who are a charge upon the Churches, are fed. So much so that if they were to withdraw, the pastors would remain without support, the Churches without the exercise of their functions, and the poor without relief.[22]

Accordingly, the second generation often constituted a kind of *major et sanior pars* of the Refuge. Even among those who had successfully become integrated, it was not unusual to show one's benevolence towards the Refugee Churches; Anglican churchmen such as Pierre du Moulin the younger and Meric Casaubon, or a London merchant such as Thomas Papillon, did not scorn their origins.

Dissolution into the English population depended on the surroundings. The history of Thorney, Cambridgeshire, is most dissimilar, not to say entirely different in many respects, from the situations which we have so far considered. Unlike most communities, this was a rural, and not an urban settlement. Moreover, after the initial influx of settlers, it did not benefit from further waves of immigration. The Thorney community is a case in point. The pattern of baptisms (see the graph in Fig. 5) is completely atypical: instead of the sharp contrasts shown in London, or the falling trend of Norwich and Southampton, the number of baptisms declines by slow degrees but without any violent contrasts. The countryside presented fewer alternatives than city life, and therefore the community remained more homogeneous. Conversely, life in towns accentuated the suddenness of arrivals and departures.

This brief survey suggests some preliminary observations. Far from being a zone of stability, with clear-cut boundaries, the Refuge formed a point

---

[22] Canterbury, Dean and Chapter Library, MSS U-47-H-1, vol. 20.

of contact and transition. The consistories' constant distrust of new-comers, reinforced by second-generation pride and prejudices, makes any definitive tally extremely difficult to achieve, and hampers demographic analysis. The well-known French analyst, Louis Henry, was describing the particular situation of immigrants when he wrote twenty years ago: 'in the present state of demography, we do not know how to study open phenomena as such'.[23] The refugees were an open population whether they left for a new destination or returned home, or else became completely assimilated and changed even their names.

At the same time, the status of refugee was an honour, dependent on acceptance by the Churches. At the turn of the 1550s, John a Lasco already expressed his distrust of the unbelievers who, 'being opposed to all Churches, give us to believe that they belong to the English Church, and say to the English that they belong to us, and thus deceive us and the English'.[24]

The colloquy of French and Walloon Churches declared similarly, on 15 June 1582, in its seventh article:

> Since several strangers come here for protection and are received by the benevolence of her Majesty and the Gentlemen of her privy Council on grounds of Religion, though they possess none, and behave in a riotous way in the conduct of their life; and even others who, although they have been admitted into our Churches, nonetheless lead a disorderly life, and scorn all ecclesiastical warnings and censures, it shall be deemed expedient to denounce such persons to the magistrate, so that those who cannot be governed by the Ministry of the Church should be curbed by the authority of the said magistrate, whom God has ordained to this end.

Everything was a matter of perception: where the man in the street saw a French-speaking foreigner, the consistories did not necessarily recognise a coreligionist. Pastor Bulteel – in an atmosphere of crisis – informed the archbishop of Canterbury that there were, in 1634 in London, five French 'papists' for every genuine French Protestant. This rough estimate should not be taken literally, but it evinces the premium of a cultural identity which was defended with great vigilance and caution being that of a minority. Belonging to the community was in no way automatic, but involved in each case a negotiation in which 'letters of testimony' were required, originally issued by the refugee's Church at home, or a recognition of past faults, if not an abjuration of the Roman religion. In practice, the enforcement of strict Church observance, moral control, and various contributions deterred many refugees. Belonging involved a sense of election; social solidarity and religious faith were inextricably

[23] Louis Henry, *Démographie-analyse et modèle*, Paris, 1972, p. 198.
[24] John a Lasco, *Toute la forme et manière du ministère ecclésiastique en l'Eglise des étrangers dressée à Londres*, Emden, 1556, p. 66.

interwoven. The Refuge was surrounded by a fringe of go-betweens and would-be refugees. It included many undisciplined individuals, or independent, wayward spirits, as well as scattered brethren and prodigal sons. Any numerical estimates must take account of this uncertainty. One can never survey more than a part, an important part, undoubtedly, but only a part, of all those who by their social ties or families origins were connected to the Refuge.

I EXILE AND THE KINGDOM IN THE CENTURY OF THE REFORMATION

1   A founding episode: Edward VI's charter, 1550

I see passing across the waves
A great throng of men, and in the harbour a King
Stretching out his hand to pull them ashore
Theodore Beza

In the history of sixteenth-century England, the reign of Edward VI constitutes a kind of impassioned interval. Nonetheless, some threads of continuity unite these six and a half years from January 1547 to July 1553 to the Tudor period as a whole: galloping inflation, all the more threatening since it was left unexplained at the time; poor control of currency; popular riots and palace revolution. While the kingdom remained outside the orbit of Rome, the final episode in the seizure of Church property, which had begun in the reign of Henry VIII, was the dissolution of the chantries. Here was blood mingled with tears, moments of greatness and sudden alterations of fortune. There were rumours of rebellion by factions and patronage. Death on the scaffold threatened men in high places; the king's uncle, Protector Somerset, was to be beheaded in 1552. None of these elements, in truth, is really exceptional. In the preceding reigns the government had often faced the same threats, and endeavoured to check the progress of enclosures which, it was feared, would lead to the depopulation of the kingdom and the 'pulling down of towns'. And yet, these few years have a character and significance of their own, justifying this separate chapter in spite of their brevity.

The reign of Edward seemed to open new vistas: the official religion of State and Church was more protestant in character than at any other time in English history, apart from the Great Rebellion and Interregnum. Edward's reign is a sharp divide between two periods; on the one hand the Henrician schism, which, in its determination to affirm the spiritual ascendancy of the Crown, alternately pursued Catholics and Protestants with aggressive mistrust – Thomas Cromwell, who had conducted the indictment of Sir Thomas More, was to be eliminated in his turn. On the other hand, Mary Tudor was to reinstate Catholicism after 1553. Edward's reign appears as an exception, which, in our picture of the sixteenth century tends to be eclipsed by the epic upheaval of Henry VIII, and the glamorous splendour of Elizabeth.

Erasmus, the 'prince of humanism' who had been greeted by John Colet and Thomas More, influenced the English Church in a decisive way, as J.K. McConica reminded us twenty years ago.[1] His momentous break with Luther – who accused him of lacking piety – made Erasmus a contentious figure; but this did not prevent the English reformers from invoking Erasmus, or at least his writings, in their constant polemics against the Church of Rome.[2] The Erasmian movement had expressed the hope that the Church of all believers would be reformed from within, but events had dictated otherwise: religious and national developments had brought into being two opposed camps, equally divided by doctrinal rigidity.

The early 1550s saw the English Church drift more sharply towards Protestantism, and this move away from Rome was fostered by some of the finest minds among the European reformers, who arrived on English soil at the time. Let us call to mind their names, which should not be buried in oblivion: Martin Bucer, the erstwhile reformer of Strasburg; the Polish nobleman John a Lasco, defender of the faith, restored to its evangelical purity; the Florentine Peter Martyr Vermigli; the Siennese Bernardino Ochino, a former Capuchin; Jan Utenhove of Ghent; Vallerand Poullain of Lille; Pierre Alexandre; or again François Perucel de La Rivière and Richard Vauville, called Gallus, both pastors in London. From 1547 onwards they began to move in at the invitation of Cranmer, the shrewd archbishop of Canterbury who had served Henry VIII with zeal, and had fortunately been left relatively unscathed by his master's outbursts of displeasure.

Favours were showered on these reformers, arriving as they did from the Continent: prestigious chairs of theology were awarded to Bucer at Cambridge, and to Peter Martyr and Bernardino Ochino at Oxford. A prebendary was given to Pierre Alexandre at Canterbury; while Vallerand Poullain ministered the community at Glastonbury, in the West Country, under the direct protection of the duke of Somerset. John a Lasco, for his part, was to become superintendent of the Stranger Church in London. Because of their numbers and regional diversity it would be misleading to ascribe a unified doctrine to these people: although they all advocated

---

[1] J.K. McConica, *English Humanists and Reformation Politics under Henry VIII and Edward VI*, Oxford, 1965.

[2] B. Cottret, 'Traducteurs et divulgateurs clandestins de la Réforme en Angleterre', *Revue d'Histoire Moderne et Contemporaine*, 28 (July–Sept. 1981); on Erasmus: A. Godin, *Humanisme et Patristique. Erasme lecteur d'Origène*, Geneva, 1982.

further Reformation, many issues remained unsettled. Impatience grew with time: the question of *temporising* came to the fore. The 'temporiser' – according to its critics – admitted the outward observance of some rites even though they bore the mark of superstition. In fact the time for a far-reaching regeneration had arrived. In 1550, the Lorrainer Musculus' *Temporiser* appeared in a French translation by Vallerand Poullain, a year after its Latin publication. This feverish climate of expectation, barely tempered by a concern for political realism, explains the reticence of Bucer, who regarded as timorous the liturgy of the Book of Common Prayer of 1549, a still cautious adaptation of a Latin ritual (the 1552 edition was to be the more radical). No unanimous agreement could be reached either on the Lord's Supper: this proved the object of perpetual debate among all reformers and Bucer and John a Lasco themselves were at loggerheads on this issue.[3] These controversies concerning the eucharist involved a complete world picture as I have endeavoured to show in an article.[4]

This survey demonstrates first and foremost that the educated elite of the time were united by a common culture – a legacy, no doubt, of the New Learning strengthened by the all-pervading use of Latin, which created a real community of understanding in spite of linguistic and national differences. Moreover, in England the Reformation was often imposed from above, in conjunction with the twin establishments in Church and State. Therefore, one should not surmise that the English as a whole underwent massive conversion to the 'true faith' – as we know English society was pervaded by doctrinal conservatism at parish, grass-root level.

But the Refuge did not consist solely of a number of high-powered scholars dedicated to the cause of religion: at the same time, a group of foreigners – be they master craftsmen or journeymen, often men of slender means – were allowed more freedom of worship than the population at large. Was this compromise a mere concession granted to a minority? Or was it rather an original experiment which could be extended to the whole of England? The refugees were indeed the 'salt of the earth', and the would-be heralds of a new reforming age which was slow to dawn.

The realm of Jesus and the kingdom of Edward

Unfortunately, there are some wide gaps in our records for these few years; we have neither parish nor consistory registers at our disposal which often prove the best sources for the later social history of the

---

[3] J.V. Pollet, *Martin Bucer – Etudes sur la correspondance*, Paris, 1958.
[4] B. Cottret, 'Pour une sémiotique de la Réforme...', *Annales ESC*, 39 (March–April 1984), pp. 265–85.

refugees. Such archives lend themselves to a different approach with its insistence on anthropological data or on everyday concerns. Attitudes are as important to the historian as doctrines. In the 1550s – contrary to what occurs in other periods – the writings of scholars, although not abundant, are exceptional in their density. What we lose in terms of social history is compensated by our hindsight into the mental set-up of these men or, at least, of their most illustrious representatives. The reign of Edward VI has become the object of reappraisal: a recent collection of studies[5] revises the Whig, rather apologetic, interpretation of the Court, and particularly of the duke of Somerset, whose action had long been envisaged in almost revolutionary terms – as if, for once in the course of history, justice and magnanimity had prevailed. It used to be commonplace to oppose the enticing reign of Edward VI – the child-king who was already grave in intellect and wrote endless dissertation on idolatry under the guidance of his Huguenot preceptor Jean Bellemain – and the 'popish' tyranny of his successor Mary Tudor. A good example of this anti-Catholic commitment is provided by the young king's 'Petit traité à l'encontre de la primauté du pape' ('A small treatise against the Pope's supremacy') which was dedicated to Protector Somerset 'de mon palaise de Ouestmester' ('from my palace at Westminster'), the last day of August 1549. This interesting piece, which has been recently unearthed by Professor J.N. King, is a careful contrapunctual assessment of the difference between the meekness of the Saviour and the pride of the pope:

> Jesus had a crown of thorns, and robe of purple, and he was mocked by everybody: but the pope has three crowns and is honoured by kings, princes, emperors and all estates. Jesus washed the feet of his apostles: but kings kiss the feet of the pope. Jesus paid tribute: but the king receives and has paid no tribute. Jesus preaches and the pope relaxes in his Castel Sant'Angelo...Jesus carries his cross: but the pope is carried. Christ came in peace like a poor man to the world: but the pope takes great pleasure in creating war between the kings and princes of the earth.[6]

J.N. King is certainly right when he emphasises 'Edward's inconsistent use of the historical present' which as a matter of fact 'confuses the distinction...between Jesus's actions in the past and the pope's present practices'. We are therefore left with a dual dichotomy, which is the basis

[5] Jennifer Loach and Robert Tittler, (eds.), *The Mid-Tudor Polity c. 1540–1560*, London, 1980.
[6] J.N. King, *Tudor Royal Iconography*, Princeton, 1989, p. 146. I should also refer the reader to some secondary sources: M.L. Bush, *The Government Policy of Protector Somerset*, London, 1975; J.D. Gould, *The Great Debasement...*, Oxford, 1970; W.R. Heinze, *The Proclamations of the Tudor Kings*, Cambridge, 1976; D.E. Hoak, *The King's Council in the Reign of Edward VI*, Cambridge, 1976; a more classical account: W.K. Jordan, *Edward VI*, 2 vols., London, 1967–70.

of the Edwardian Reformation: present/past, realm of Jesus/worldly concerns of the pope. Yet how could one solve this contradiction? Unfortunately our scarce evidence in the case of the strangers' communities sheds greater light on the common Protestant ideals of the period than on their sociological reality.

These various qualifications lead to caution: the praise of King Edward – quite a common genre, which brought into play both the poetic verve of Pierre du Val or Accasse d'Albiac, and the learned pen of Bucer and Calvin – was not entirely devoid of rhetoric. Very often, if we read between the lines, what is envisaged is not so much England as it is, but England as it should be. The expression of hope outweighs the consideration of actual achievement.[7] The metaphorical title of Josias, first affectionately conferred on the child-king by Bucer and then by countless other writers, invoked the biblical precedent of the pious sovereign of the seventh century BC, who early ascended the throne to become a great reformer. It would certainly be mistaken to speak of prophecy where this image is concerned; we find here an instance of that category of the imagination, the 'future-in-the-past', in which, as recent studies have shown, a reversal of 'the elements of history' serves to express the hope of renewal.[8] In the 1550s, the very concept of time was at stake. Bucer's *De regno Christi* – which was dedicated to Edward – provides a good example of deceived expectations and unexpected delays in the achievement of Christ's kingdom. A good analysis of Bucer's position in England is provided by François Wendel in his introduction to this text:

> Although confined to his academic functions, and only consulted on minor questions, in his private capacity, Bucer had not lost all hope of bringing his influence to bear through the intermediary of Cranmer. He dreamt of an England profoundly transformed in the religious, the social, the economic and even the legal spheres – the vision of a genuine kingdom of Christ on earth. He had adopted a good part of the programme of the 'Commonwealth's Men', for whom, now that Protector Somerset had fallen it might be an advantage to have their opinions propounded by a foreigner such as Bucer, whom no one would suspect of wishing to interfere in English politics.[9]

Bucer's desire for a total reformation, extending to every aspect of men's lives, clearly refers to a Christian Commonwealth; the word may be used

---

[7] Collection of texts relating to the period: A.M. Schmidt, *Johan Calvin, Lettres Anglaises 1548–1561*, Paris, 1959.

[8] Daniel Vidal, *Le Malheur et son Prophète-Inspirés et sectaires en Languedoc calviniste, 1685–1725*, Paris, 1983.

[9] François Wendel, *Martini Buceri, Opera Latina*, xv.2: *Du Royaume de Jésus-Christ...*, Paris, 1954, introduction, p. 6.

in connection with several reformers, among them John Hales, who hoped, in vain, to redress the wrongs of agrarian society.

The Commonwealth so often invoked at the time was equivalent to the Latin *res publica*, but without, as yet, the 'republican' overtones we *associate with rebellion or indeed with the abolition of monarchy, which* took place in 1649. The English word 'commonwealth' had, of course, an emotional appeal which was hardly to be found in its Latin counterpart *republic*; literally, the emphasis lay on the common interest of all Englishmen. Basically, this very old word, which struck its roots in the vernacular, was no doubt less far-fetched and exotic in character than was the term *republic*, in Continental usage.[10]

The idea of a republic does in fact appear in Bucer's text, which was presented to the king as a Christmas gift in 1550; the first chapter lists 'The names of the kingdom of Jesus Christ' – the allusion to Christ's kingdom is no coincidence. The need for a good king (Edward), surrounded by wise counsellors, is strongly emphasised while Bucer's advices even extend to economic life. Commerce, he declares, must be purged of 'superfluities' – the common concern of Christian morality and Classical antiquity which alike condemned luxury as the source of self-indulgence and sloth. Yet Bucer was much more precise in his attacks when he tackled the issue of Church property (Book II, Chapter XIII), which lay at the heart of the economic, social and religious debate concerning the Tudor period. The dissolution of the monasteries, initiated at the time of Henry VIII, met with fairly general agreement to castigate the monks, whose piety Erasmus had already called into question. Nonetheless, many reforming spirits were ill pleased once they came to realise that this gigantic transfer of property did not ensure the spreading of the truth faith but proved a profitable venture for the Crown or its lay purchasers. Might it not have been possible to use this 'ill-gotten' wealth to promote the preaching of the Word or even, more generally, to further the spread of literacy? Landed revenues – long perceived as the true source of licit wealth – might have served to provide for the subsistence of numerous scholars, who could have devoted themselves freely to the Protestant indoctrination of the kingdom. In the years surrounding Edward's accession, this sense of disillusionment was gaining ground: Bucer lamented that 'the property of the Church [had been] thus villainously seized and dissipated', thus echoing Henry Brinklow or Robert Crowley's defence of a truly Christian Commonwealth.[11] The blunt statement of his case gives evidence of Bucer's freedom of expression and determination, even though a foreigner, to intervene in English

[10] Whitney R.D. Jones, *The Tudor Commonwealth 1529–1559*, London, 1970.
[11] Henry Brinklow, *The Complaynt of Roderick Mors...*(1545), London 1874; Robert Crowley, *The Voyce of the laste trumpet...*(1550), London, 1872, etc.

affairs. It also suggests that the relations between Church and State may have been more strained than expected.

But the 'Preface to the King' gives the gist of Bucer's *De Regno Christi*, a book less triumphant in tone, and more expressive of sorrow and disquiet than might appear at first sight. The description of an ideal city – the Christian Utopia of a Messianic kingdom – turns the preface into a manifesto: the circumstances in which the work was composed – 'our time full of darkness, trouble and calamities' – serve to emphasise the distance between the cup and the lip. While Edward VI is compared to a benign and favourable star, this does not bridge the gap which separates Bucer's text from its English context. 'This interplay'[12] suggests that the English situation may have been less idyllic for the reformers than is often supposed. Bucer went on – still in his preface:

> Nevertheless, having set out to deal with certain matters touching the reception, and happy restoration of the kingdom of Christ within this your kingdom, so that it may be known how profitable and necessary it is, both to your sovereign Majesty, and to all the men and estates of your kingdom, to *endeavour with care and to do everything in their power so that the kingdom of Christ be received completely among you* [*var.: among us*], and obtain the preeminent place; and so that it may be known what are the proper and appropriate means of pursuing, in earnest, *this work which contains the salvation and sovereign good of all men*, I shall attempt to show, through the evidence of the holy Scriptures, *what the kingdom of Christ is, and what it is within us, while we yet live in this world of wickedness*, totally repugnant to God, and to assert the nature of true Communion and government. For in these times, a few people understand these secrets pertaining to our salvation, though they keep repeating: 'Our Father, which art in heaven, Thy Kingdom come' [Matt. vi, 10].
>
> And yet I shall treat this matter briefly according to the Word of the Lord, so help me God: first, what is the nature of the kingdom of God within us, and what are its property, communion and government? And secondly, how profitable and absolutely necessary is it for each one of us to apply himself with all his heart to receiving and fully re-establishing within us this kingdom? Finally, by what means is your sovereign Majesty to take counsel, in order to endeavour to labour in earnest to re-establish fully in this your country the kingdom of Christ?[13]

The preaching of the Word seems to summarise Bucer's mission on earth. The author clearly acts as a present witness, thus emphasising the immediacy of his demonstration, reviving the spirit, and the letter, of revelation. Bucer addressed his contemporaries as an envoy of the Lord

---

[12] Louis Marin, *Utopiques: jeux d'espaces*, Paris, 1973.   [13] *Ibid.*, pp. 4–5.

only a few months before his death. This expectation was coupled with the mythical longing for the restoration of the apostolic Church which had been likewise sustained by its faith in the second coming of the Lord. The reader notices Bucer's prolonged hesitation between the Church visible and invisible, the reform of civil society and the mystical union of the faithful. This marks a clear transition between the German and the Calvinist Reformations, and recalls Bucer's connection with Strasburg where a rigorous organisation of the city was being developed, combining a concern for doctrine with moral discipline. Calvin was to remember the case of Strasburg when drawing up his *Ecclesiastical ordinances* for Geneva. Emile Léonard has described the meaning of the word 'Church', in Bucer's usage:

> Not only the invisible Church, the 'kingdom of God', 'Kingdom of Heaven', the 'Holy City', the 'Bride of Christ', the body of Christ still present among men in this world, but also the Church visible, which Bucer wished to see rigorously organised, with its four ministries of doctors, pastors, elders and deacons – a conception which Calvin borrowed from Bucer, more than from any other of his predecessors.[14]

At the same time, the meaning of the term 'kingdom of Jesus Christ', which figures in the title of Bucer's work, is uncertain, at least at first sight. Was Bucer advertising a *millenarian theocracy*, or else, as I am inclined to think, the Utopia of Christian humanism? The idea of a golden age, due to precede the end of time, does not appear, as far as I can see, in Bucer's text, and the king of England does not seem to be invested with any kind of power outside the civil sphere; moreover, his authority is less sacred in character than in the absolutist conception of the divine right of kings. The king must play a part in the conversion of his kingdom; the sword of royal authority may possibly encourage this 'restoration' of Christianity, but cannot take its place (Book II, Chapter V). England is still living through a time of trials, rather than experiencing a second coming, and men utter their prayers – the Lord's Prayer, to which Bucer alludes – without understanding the meaning of the kingdom of God they call for. Accordingly, Bucer's treatise is not so much an expression of approval as an admonition, calling men to repentance in the accents of the gospel according to St Matthew. Let us note, as the end of the long quotation above, that conversion precedes the ideal City, just as faith comes before works. All the difficulty which this text presents – as I have attempted to show, it would be quite pointless to interpret it in a triumphant sense – rests on the very ambivalence of the word 'kingdom' in the scriptural sources of Bucer's thought. The *good tidings of the kingdom* continually brings together two sequences of time – the present and the eschatological

---

[14] E.G. Léonard, *Histoire générale du protestantisme*, 3 vols., Paris, 1961–4, I, p. 172.

perspective. The kingdom of Jesus Christ is already a reality, but at the same time 'it is not of this world'. This dynamic dichotomy, which is already to be found in the New Testament, seems to provide the key to Bucer's own position.

One might indeed apply to Bucer these words of Pierre Chaunu: 'The Church inhabits a dimension of time in which the great and formative moments of her own history are continually recreated. This perpetual reference to the first centuries of the Church is manifest from the opening lines of the great writings of the Reformation.'[15]

The Christian dimension of time is enhanced by the wisdom of antiquity which greatly impressed the men of the Renaissance. In the Republic of Letters, receptive to the humanities, Plato is in the company of Isaiah. But is there not, also, a coincidence between 'salvation' and the 'sovereign good' of philosophers?

In its judicious measure of optimism and reserve – the kingdom is already present and yet still to come – Bucer's treatise reflects, no doubt, the ambiguity of England's position in the 1550s: already following the path of Reformation, and yet outwardly reluctant in attitude.

Bucer also suggested that a new era was dawning on England; the country was living through a founding episode. Not everyone would have agreed with Bucer's interpretation – at least as far as its ultimate religious goals were concerned. Yet Bucer's assessment corresponded to the political and social buoyancy which was sweeping through the kingdom ruled by a child-king.

But could these bonds of friendship between the international elites of Protestantism bear any fruit? And did the position of an individual like Bucer – who belonged, after all, to a minority – involve a genuine exchange between nations?

The experimental Church of John a Lasco

There is indeed a gap between the cup and the lip, and many intellectuals have felt – sometimes to the point of frustration – an obsessive fascination with commitment. This formulation may sound anachronistic and intentionally provocative; but one has to remember that sixteenth-century debates over the Church involved the future of society and not just individual piety. This tendency only grew stronger in the middle years of the century. The strictly spiritual conception of an invisible Church, which might be reconciled with purely outward submission to existing rituals, unleashed Calvin's sarcastic remarks against the 'Nicodemites' who were

---

[15] Pierre Chaunu, *Eglise, culture et société. Essais sur Réforme et Contre-Réforme (1517–1620)*, Paris, 1981, p. 47.

accused of irresolution and laxity.[16] This harsh indictment prevails in times of crisis. The upholding of orthodoxy among Catholics – the influence of Erasmus waned, and his works were soon put on the Index of prohibited books – was paralleled in the reforming camp – Michael Servetus was burnt at the stake in Geneva in 1553. This precipitated an escalation, which Montaigne's 'Que sais-je?' was later to confute.

The involvement of scholars was not always the result of free choice and, far from being actuated simply by the ideal conviction that theory should be expressed in practice, it was often a consequence of situations which they could not altogether keep under control. Thus, the Church was preeminent not only in the formulation of doctrine, and in her monopoly of ideology, established centuries before, but also in terms of careers. Along with the administration of justice, engagement as a preceptor, or the service of the sovereign, what other path was there but the Church, for these intellectuals who were neither fish nor fowl, neither quite a separate estate nor a social class?[17] In the sixteenth century, their ill-defined position already gave rise to a feeling of frustration. Bucer's hopes foundered in England – a situation made all the more bitter by the scholar's linguistic isolation. In *De Regno Christi*, the former reformer of Strasburg cannot help expressing a nostalgia for a total Reformation, no longer restricted to evangelical circles, but extending to the whole of society. These foreign intellectuals constituted a minority within a minority, and depended on the goodwill of the archbishop of Canterbury; they suffered from a kind of splendid isolation which the shared classical culture of the educated elite could hardly have mitigated. Besides, men realised that the conversion of a king would remain precarious, unless his country were converted with him, and one can tell, at a distance, how much the many homages rendered to King Edward – 'lieutenant chosen to order and uphold the kingdom of Jesus Christ in England', in Calvin's words – betray their anxiety about the possibility of a succession less kindly disposed towards the protestant cause. These apprehensions were confirmed when Mary Tudor brought back her country into the fold of Rome.

This peculiar situation explains the interest of the unprecedented experiment launched by John a Lasco, a scholar and theoretician as much as a churchman, who was entrusted with the major task of gathering the 'strangers' of London who agreed into one community of faith. This original experiment only lasted three years. We are able to reconstruct the workings of this Church, despite the loss of its records, thanks to two or three major testimonies, among them that of John a Lasco himself.

The foundation of the Church is related in two complementary texts:

[16] Carlo Ginzburg, *Il nicodemismo*, Turin, 1970.
[17] Robert Mandrou, *Des humanistes aux hommes de science*, Paris, 1973.

John a Lasco's book *Tota forma ac ratio* ... (*The Form and Manner of the Church Ministry in the Strangers Church in London*, published in Frankfurt in 1555); and Edward VI's letter of privilege of 24 April 1550, also quoted in a Lasco (see pp. 271–3). One sees at once that these two texts have a peculiar character, which brings them in line with a written *constitution* rather than with an historical narrative as such. Their common legislative concern is to define *a priori* the role and function of the reformed community of 'strangers' in London; naturally, the two texts are complementary. Edward's charter emphasises the duties of the Christian sovereign, and the place of the Church within his kingdom. But John a Lasco's concern extends beyond England, and his book raises the problem of the Christian body politic as a whole.

These two fundamental contributions should be examined in a critical light; as in the case of Bucer, the ideal predominates over objective description. Disagreements soon became manifest, both among the refugees themselves – who came from different regions or countries – and with the English clergy. In 1552, in particular, the Church of England sought to establish a monopoly in the administration of the sacraments. However, threats of this kind were relatively negligible, at least during the reign of Edward VI. One fact remains: the existence of a separate Reformed Church was an exception to the two Acts of 1549 and 1552 which decreed the religious uniformity of the kingdom. In later years the feeling of competition between different forms of ecclesiastical organisation – Anglicanism and Presbyterian Calvinism as it were – was to take on an intensity which cannot be explained solely by the concern of a few clerics over their parish prerogatives. These two conceptions of the Church involved a political debate on the very nature of civil society; but in 1550 the spirit of conciliation prevailed, and so did the common desire for a break with Rome. Yet if we read Edward's charter properly, we observe a clear refusal – albeit expressed in measured and carefully chosen terms – to allow any kind of osmosis between the two ecclesiastical establishments. A Church on the Continental model constituted an alternative, which provides an original vantage point to the present-day historian.

The charter begins with emphasising the king of England's *supremacy* over the national Church. Edward is the 'supreme head on earth, under Christ, of the Church of England and Ireland', as well as 'defender of the faith'. In matters of religion he enjoys all the prerogatives of a Christian prince: a strong sense of moral obligation and concern for the State imply that 'policy and civil government cannot long endure, nor remain in honour' without the Church. This unruffled pragmatism did not contradict accepted standards of behaviour: civic virtue and the cares of government seemed inconceivable without the help of religion. Lay

conceptions of secular morality had yet to emerge, and for a long time to
come, atheists were to enjoy no degree of tolerance, so clearly did they
seem to constitute a danger to society itself: what trust could one place in
a man who believed in nothing, and could therefore swear to anything?
But were there, in fact, any atheists in the sixteenth century as Lucien
Febvre was wont to ask some fifty years ago?[18] Religion, therefore, was
a matter for the State, as much as it was a matter of State, and the concern
for the Commonwealth governed the explicit wish for a return to the
gospel of Jesus Christ.

Equally – out of concern for Christian charity – we learn of the presence
in England of 'calamitous and afflicted persons, banished because of their
religion'; some of them had been in England for some time already,
having come 'both from Germany and from other distant countries', and
had found in England a 'refuge' – one of the earliest instances of this
word. The mention of Germany is, in fact, deceptive: the term is used,
rather broadly, to refer to the Low Countries; the other refugees were
essentially Walloons; besides them was a small Italian minority. These
foreigners were enabled to flock together, according to their respective
languages and nations, in order to 'treat intelligibly of matters of
religion'; a clear example of the reformers' concern with instruction and
worship in 'native tongues'.

There follow several practical considerations. A temple was provided
for the new Church – the former chapel of the Austin Friars, in the heart
of the City of London. (The Walloons were to migrate before long to
another site in Threadneedle Street, while keeping their claim to Austin
Friars – a source of constant disputes with the Dutch as late as the
seventeenth century.) Four pastors were designated, two for each
community; they were placed under the benevolent supervision of a
superintendent, namely John a Lasco. (This was an institution of an
original kind; in later years, the Reformed Church of London was to be
placed under the superintendence of the bishop of London – as still is the
case today.) The charter constitutes, in fact, a letter of incorporation. The
Stranger Church became 'a body corporate and politic'. It could have a
succession, and strike its roots in the course of time; it now possessed
legitimacy, and could claim tacit recognition from the other corporations
of the kingdom – which also drew their pride from the immemorial
possession of a charter. Society consisted, in fact, in corporate entities,
subject to a network of privileges, laying down their rights and duties. The
kingdom itself was a 'body politic'; the very metaphor of the body, both
physical and social, was to retain its force in political theory, up to Hobbes
in the seventeenth century, though in this particular case, only the

---

[18] Lucien Febvre, *Le Problème de l'incroyance au XVIe siècle, la religion de Rabelais*,
Paris (1942), 1968.

superintendent and the four pastors were named. This conditioned every aspect of social life: religious orthodoxy and discipline were to be strenuously enforced but new arrivals or assistance to the poor were also envisaged. We shall notice the strength of this corporate feeling each time the life of the community was threatened, either by local regulations or, more seldom, by Crown servants. In fact the charter set up a precedent to be perpetually invoked in an age which revered founding episodes, and regarded innovation with awe. Moreover, the image of the body also influenced the forms of social life, as we shall see in the third part of this book.

And yet there are a number of innuendoes in this text. As a sovereign act, decreed by the king out of his 'special grace' – although in keeping with the 'advice of the Council' – it assumed the character of a special favour, wholly dependent on the Crown's prerogative. This gracious expression of royal authority inspired the refugees with unfaltering loyalty to the monarchy till the great Rebellion when the refugees felt divided in their allegiances. Only the Crown could confer an established and recognised status to the Foreign Churches. Often in the course of their history, the refugees were to show towards the established authorities – bishops or councillors – a sort of *loyalty of the defenceless* which was not too personalised in character, and could be transferred without any major damage to Oliver Cromwell, to Charles II or William of Orange, once their position was assured. There were exceptions to this collective behaviour, but nonetheless this deference to the powers that be was not purely opportunistic; in an alien and sometimes hostile environment, it offered the greatest measure of protection.

Edward's charter also expresses its share of divergences from the Refugee Church. The unanimity of the first paragraph, with its allusion to the apostolic Church restored and to the common struggle against the 'tyranny of the Pope', does not imply uniformity, as a final word of caution makes plain. It is right to permit the foreigners to 'enjoy, use and practise among themselves their own manners and ceremonies, and their own particular ecclesiastical discipline, notwithstanding that they do not accord with the manners and ceremonies in use in our Kingdom'.

Yet a genuine difference remained unsolved. Though the charter granted full and complete recognition to the Stranger Church, it did not imply a total identity of view. In many respects, Edward's charter remained ambiguous; the toleration of foreigners did not imply the adoption by England of Continental Protestantism. This reluctance later gave rise to disagreements which, although muted, were nonetheless severe.

Let us take the description of the Stranger Church in John a Lasco's inspired treatise, *Tota forma ac ratio...*, which was published at least two years after the death of Edward VI, 6 July 1553, had brought the experiment to an end. When one examines John a Lasco's ecclesiastical constitution, and sees the assiduous and fervent zeal with which he attempted to rediscover the authenticity of the early Church, one suspects that he was not working solely for the small group of foreigners he supervised. There is something of the apostle in John a Lasco, if not necessarily of the proselyte. His determination to recapture across ten centuries of darkness – as he thought – the pristine purity of the gospel would be incomprehensible unless it aimed at the conversion of the whole kingdom. This impression is borne out by the dedicatory epistle to Sigismund of Poland:

> Since [various] laws of the kingdom prevented us from reforming immediately certain rites of public worship, which remained from the days of popery (and which, for this reason, even the king would have wished to reform as soon as possible), and since on the other hand, I insisted above all on establishing the regulations of the Church of Strangers, we decided finally that the public rites of the Church of England would be reformed gradually, and only in so far as the laws permitted. We decided also that the foreigners, who were less subject to the restrictions of the laws of the kingdom in the form of their worship, would be given Churches in which, in complete liberty and without taking account of the former rites, everything would be reorganised in perfect conformity with apostolic doctrine and observance. *We thought, in fact, that the English Churches themselves, encouraged by this example, would be unanimous, throughout the kingdom, in returning to the apostolic form of worship in all its purity.*[19]

Indeed, just as in Bucer's case, the concept of Reformation rests on a vision of time: the *time of Christ's kingdom* coincides with the *primeval time of origins*. In the early apostolic Church God's revelation and the history of men were closely intertwined. How, across these ten centuries (or more) of darkness – in a Lasco's eyes, the dark ages of the medieval period – can one recapture the genuine spirit of Christianity which came to an end with the decline and fall of the Classical world? John a Lasco shares the common prejudices of Renaissance humanism; but he can be forgiven for sweeping aside, in his artless enthusiasm, these ten centuries which he considers to have been a time of darkness – a point of view which, of course, I cannot share.

The very metaphor of a 'Renaissance' is given literal expression when John a Lasco mentions 'our time in which the gospel has begun to be reborn' (p. xv). The experiment of the Stranger Church in London is not conceivable without reference to Geneva and Strasburg. The Polish baron, born in Warsaw almost with the century, in 1499, was indeed what

---

[19] Schickler, *Les Eglises du Refuge en Angleterre*, I pp. 31–2.

we would now call a European. He had led the life of a travelling cleric from Bologna to Cracow, where he had been awarded the highest distinctions, before breaking with Rome. He then became a minister in Western Friesland, and later superintendent in London, before returning to his native Poland where he died in 1560. John a Lasco, being a churchman with a theoretical bent, was offered the opportunity to achieve his idiosyncratic rigorous ideal, which coincided neither with the Church of England nor with Calvinism proper. In 1974, Father Philippe Denis drew our attention to this specific character of the first Stranger Church, by entitling his research paper: 'The Churches of Strangers in London up to the Death of Calvin, from the Church of John a Lasco to the Establishment of Calvinism'.[20]

This twofold originality explains the deep historical interest of John a Lasco's thought as it explores some of the 'might-have-beens' of the Reformation. In 1550, several diverging evolutions remained possible; this great diversity of forms has not escaped the attention of scholars, from Abraham Kuyper's DD on John a Lasco, published in 1862,[21] to the fine studies of Ferdinand de Schickler. The Frenchman did not conceal his high admiration for the serene faith, and gravity, of an ecclesiology which unites so closely the mass of believers. There were four orders as in Geneva: ministers, doctors, elders and deacons, who exercised administrative functions, covering *four* main areas of responsibility: divine worship, teaching, moral control and, last but not least, the relief of the poor. In spite of apparent similarities with Geneva, the same words here refer to slightly different things. Up to a certain point a Lasco regards these functions as co-extensive: in particular the meaning of *elder* also covers the pastoral ministry:

> Some in the Scriptures are called *priests* (or elders, bishops, prelates and governors), while others (the holders of civil power, and fosterers of the Church of Christ) are what we call *magistrates*. Now, all pastors and doctors belong to this order of priests, but they do not take upon themselves alone the charge of governing and supporting the Church; they do so rather in assembly with the other elders, whom they must endeavour to have in association with them.

Society has therefore a twofold government: *magistrates* who are in charge of the State, and *elders* responsible for the Church. A Lasco's sense of social or ecclesiastical hierarchy seems to be somewhat mitigated by this simplification of titles which only retains two principal authorities, spiritual and secular. The term *magistrate* refers not only to judges but to

[20] Unpublished copy deposited at the Bibliothèque de l'Histoire du Protestantisme Français, rue des Saint-Pères, Paris.
[21] A. Kuyper, *Disquisitio historico-theologica, exhibens J. Calvini et J. a Lasco de Ecclesia sententiarum inter se compositionem*, The Hague, 1862.

all those who govern – kings, councillors or corporations. Likewise, whatever his position in the Church, a bishop or pastor is no more than a lay elder – while exercising different callings. All are alike before the Lord.

The people are given back the 'Christian liberty' (p. xx) which they had long been denied. Imitating the Classics, John a Lasco describes the process of decadence, in a narrative which is more mythical than purely historical: originally the people exercised a sovereign suffrage in the Church. But they were deprived by the magistrates, who gave rise in turn to tyrants, whom no one could resist, while sycophancy prevailed. This is a slightly transformed version of Plato's *Republic*, democracy giving way to aristocracy, and then to tyranny.

John a Lasco clearly envisages some kind of Church democracy, at least in the Classical sense of the word. Democracy does not imply social equality but rather the brotherhood of the saints – or *elect* who have been chosen by God. Christianity constitutes a kind of citizenship, and the new Israel must take part in the election of its elders. Admittedly, the suffrage of the whole people which existed in the early Church, according to a Lasco, seems to him impossible to achieve. Therefore, he opts for a 'two-tier vote', in Schickler's expression – John a Lasco describes the process in his chapter 'Of the Manner of Electing the Ministers'. Having fasted and prayed, all the congregation have a week in which to write to the ministers and elders whom they wish to elect. Then the elders meet, and a further week elapses, during which anyone is free to remove – or attempt to remove – from office the new elder or pastor.

John a Lasco's true originality rests on two heads. He considerably reduced the possibility of mutual choice for presbyters – a procedure often described by the same word 'election'. Moreover, elders and pastors alike received the laying-on of hands. This resulted in a promotion of the laity, which may have offended the clergy of the Church of England. As Ferdinand de Schickler clearly emphasized:

> The principle of an equality among elders, whether they be pastors or laymen – one of the characteristic features of a Lasco's organisation – was well in advance of its time and contradicted the views of the Church of England. Calvin had not gone so far; nor had he instituted the two-tier vote which was observed at each election in the Church of London.[22]

Nonetheless, John a Lasco's treatise should not be interpreted as too radical; it alludes to a minority community, of very short duration. One cannot altogether assert that it referred to an established reality. In this respect, the opposition to the Genevan model should not be carried too far: the scale is not the same. The *experimental* character of John a Lasco's

---

[22] Schickler, *Les Eglises du Refuge en Angleterre*, ɪ p. 41.

Church should be emphasised; could it be applied to society as a whole? John a Lasco does admit one initial divergence from the practice of the early Church: the designation of the pastor directly by the heads of families should be the ideal, though it may no longer be applicable. I have defined this appeal to the people as a *democracy*, with every possible shade of distinction. Yet it is an *exclusive* form of democracy, resting on an heroic conception of the little flock. In other words, the 'people' already implies a certain elite of the faithful which should be defended against the perils of heterodoxy, and of Anabaptism in particular (p. lxvi). Accordingly, democracy can be achieved, provided the Church is not coterminous with the whole of society. Was this a future plan? But in that case, how might John a Lasco's views have evolved? Had they been transferred to a city, or to a whole country, would he not have been led to introduce a further departure from the practice of the early Church? In the present case, we are confronted with an unfinished history; the Refuge of later years was gradually to align itself on the Calvinist model, while Richard Hooker, the theoretician of the Church of England, was to decree the futility of seeking a return to the origins;[23] democracy within the Church, as within the State, was to become the province of sectarian movements.

Epilogue: the end of a Church

Indeed, it is no little thing to be freed from the bishops' yoke. The Lord be blessed forever and ever. Amen.[24]
Jan Utenhove

Jan Utenhove, a Dutch elder and close associate of John a Lasco, is typical of the lay establishment I have referred to. His pungent jests about the prelates are particularly illuminating; he was expressing aloud what many thought silently. Christian charity and diplomacy – as well as the situation of the foreign minority – all restrained considerably any official controversy with the established Church. Yet John a Lasco's ecclesiastical constitution reduced the forms of worship to their bare essentials, and questioned the ecclesiastical hierarchy in practice. He thereby incurred the irritation of some, and the admiration of others. In fact, the Reformation had not yet taken on its lasting form in England, and the correspondence of the Dutch pastor Martin Micronius with Henry Bullinger in Zurich expresses considerable mistrust of the bishops – who are suspected of tampering with the transformation of the Church. The English prelates were not necessarily pleased to be compared with the bishops of the First

[23] R. Hooker, *The Laws of Ecclesiastical Polity (1593–1597)*, London, 1907, etc.
[24] Schickler, *Les Eglises du refuge en Angleterre*, I p. 29.

Epistle to Timothy in order to clip their wings. And yet the attitude of the hierarchy could be ambiguous if we bear in mind the benevolent protection of the archbishop of Canterbury, Cranmer. After all, a little power inspires resentment, but greater power still confers serenity.

Besides, the stranger community was fundamentally heterogeneous in character: individuals from different backgrounds were supposed to rub shoulders and intermingle. This involved a certain latitude from the English Church. John a Lasco's Church was very much at the crossroads of Continental influences: Calvinism could not fail to attract the French-speaking refugee, while conversely some of the Dutch looked towards Zurich rather than Geneva, as Andrew Pettegree recently confirmed.

The Stranger Church did not long survive the death of Edward VI on 6 July 1553, and the accession of his sister Mary Tudor, the Catholic daughter of Catharine of Aragon, whom henry VIII had divorced thirty years before. Though religious history cannot be reduced to the succession of kings – or popes – John a Lasco's establishment could only be confirmed and perpetuated by a Protestant sovereign. The reception of foreigners had formed part of a strategy which intended to use the king's authority to promote a Christian polity. A detailed account of England's return to the Catholic fold would take us far beyond the scope of this book; I shall not dwell upon either received ideas concerning 'bloody' Mary or her false pregnancies which showed the queen's anxiety about the future of the Catholic restoration. The Scottish reformer John Knox attacked the 'monstrous regiment of women' in his own day – and only gained the enmity of the young Elizabeth. Religious conservatism, as well as occasional bouts of indifference to questions of doctrine, were reinforced by sheer loyalty to the Crown. Conversely, Pope Julius III had been careful to intimate that the holders of Church spoils were to be left unscathed.

One of the paradoxes of this deserves to be pointed out: it was as head of the Church of England that Mary Tudor took the initiative of restoring Catholicism. Hence G. R. Elton's admirable formula, 'the devout Queen could only do what she thought right by the exercise of a power she held to be wrong and usurped'.[25] The institutions and practices of Henry VIII's reign proved strangely stable: for instance, Parliament *had* to be summoned to lick its wounds, twenty-five years after the breach with Rome. Oddly enough the shadow cast by this great reign was not easily exorcised, just as the insular distrust of extremes did not favour a complete return to the orbit of the Holy See. The reign of Mary Tudor did not necessarily counterbalance the reign of Henry VIII by the law of gravity. Catholicism itself came to be regarded by the conservative element as an outlandish venture into unfamiliar territory. The Roman faith was good

[25] G.R. Elton, *England under the Tudors*, London, 1955, p. 219.

enough for the peoples of Latin extraction, like the Spaniards or Italians, but inappropriate for Englishmen. The seeds of nationalism and anticlericalism, so cleverly used by Henry VIII, came to the surface, and the queen's Spanish wedding, like the subjugation to Rome, displeased many Englishmen. Besides, by excommunicating Philip II in 1556, and suspending his legate Cardinal Pole the following year, the new pope, Paul IV, made matters even worse.

There were, of course, some pockets of resistance, especially among the nobility in 1553–4, while several Protestants suffered martyrdom. It is generally accepted that some 208 victims were burnt at the stake, Cranmer the protector of the strangers among them.

By a strange reversal of the wheel of fortune, England, once a place of refuge, now became in its turn a country of Protestant emigration as some men left for lands more hospitable to the Reformation. Of the Protestant faithful, 800 went to Frankfurt, Strasburg or Geneva, among them John Knox and John Jewel, the Scottish reformer and the future defender of the Elizabethan establishment in Church and State.

Jan Utenhove has left an account of his exile along with John a Lasco – *Simplex et fidelis narratio…* (1560). On 17 September 1553, about 75 men, Dutch, French, English and Scot, sorrowfully embarked at Gravesend, singing the psalms. On 13 October they arrived in Denmark, and then dispersed towards Frankfurt or towards Emden. In their luggage was a precious document, the charter of King Edward.

Two pastors chose, against all odds, to stay – Peter Delenus and Vallerand Poullain – but the following year they had to flee, when Mary Tudor became betrothed to Philip II of Spain. Meanwhile, Bucer's remains were unearthed, in order to be burnt at the stake, together with his 'impious' works, in a gigantic auto-da-fé.

Not all Protestant foreigners chose the ways of exile; many early settlers, who were already there long before 1550, stayed in England where many ties retained them. Did they attend family worships? We cannot tell. Many of them recanted, if we to judge by later registers, recording their return to the Reformed religion abashed and contrite, once they had a Church of their own again.

Is it appropriate to speak of the end of a Church? The Stranger Churches were to come to life again under Elizabeth; while London would not be forgotten in the communities of Emden or Frankfurt. Edward's charter was handed back to the London Church. John a Lasco's teaching did not disappear completely either; but it was progressively overlaid by a discipline, much more Calvinist in inspiration after 1560. Nothing was to be the same as before. The refugees would no longer find a great reformer like John a Lasco at their head, nor a new King Josias to rule the country. I may lay undue emphasis on certain personalities; there was undoubtedly a generation of the 1550s who believed fervently in the

Christian Utopia of the Kingdom. It would be equally unfair to deny the fact or to lay undue emphasis on purely religious motivations.

In 1553, the expectation of the Kingdom and the eagerness of the early Church ushered in a time of spiritual unease and affliction. Peter Delenus spoke in the accents of Jeremiah to castigate the ingratitude of Jerusalem; the poet Pierre du Val, who became pastor at Emden, wrote his *Petit Dialogue d'un Consolateur – Small Dialogue of a Comforter –* (1555) for the Christians under the Cross in England. His meditation is very much a paraphrase of the Book of Job, in which the obsessive question of the origin of evil recurs. Why do the wicked Mary Tudor and the Catholics succeed, while God puts those whose whom he loves to test?

To conclude this episode, one aspect needs to be singled out: the perception of time. If we are to judge by their writings the Reformed strangers experienced a real obsession with time: the *primeval time of the Apostolic Church*, in the case of John a Lasco, the *time of immediate conversion* for Bucer. These men shared a common refusal to 'temporise' or postpone the advent of the kingdom. They felt they were living at a privileged moment, when the initial time of revelation could coincide with their own. This is precisely the essence of founding episodes.

2 The reign of Elizabeth: charity begins at home

Queen Mary and Cardinal Pole died on the same day – 17 November 1558 – within a few hours of each other. The young Elizabeth, who had been ill-trusted by the deceased queen and relegated to Hatfield House, set out without delay. She was accompanied by her faithful William Cecil, who had shared her past misfortune, and was soon to become one of the chief instruments of her new glory. She made a solemn entry into the City of London on 23 November, and occasioned great rejoicing, in keeping with the spirit of the 'joyous magnificences' so characteristic of Renaissance festivals.

The Elizabethan period is shrouded in a myth, which associates in its baroque metaphors the Virgin queen and the new Astraea, Christianity and Virgil.[1] When discussing the Spanish Armada, Joel Hurstfield used to refer, with Churchill in his mind, to the 'Battle of England'.[2] Yet this all-pervading theme of national unanimity was not devoid of nostalgia and grandeur, from Drake to Raleigh. The importance of a 'code of honour', merging the military and chivalric tradition with the service of the Crown, has been clearly asserted.[3]

The golden Elizabethan legend has only been challenged recently when C. Haigh was able to highlight the discrepancies which existed between 'the idealised queen and kingdom' and reality. The 'rhetorical excesses' of the 'Elizabethan *cult of personality*' do yet deserve our consideration, even though it is difficult to assert how effective they were. One thing is certain: from Camden's *Annales* onwards (1615), 'Elizabeth was praised for the peace and prosperity of her reign; but by the 1610s and after, it was usual to stress the glories of her rule and her patronage of international

---

[1] Frances Yates, *Astraea, the Imperial Theme in the Sixteenth Century*, London, 1975.
[2] J. Hurstfield, *Elizabeth I and the Unity of England* (1960), Pelican, 1971, p. 109.
[3] On this theme, see Mervyn James' remarkable observations in *English Politics and the Concept of Honour, 1485–1642, Past and Present Supplement*, no. 3 (1978).

Protestantism and English sea power.' Moreover, 'the virtues and successes of Elizabeth were...defined by the flaws and omissions of James'. In other words, 'Camden wrote a commentary on the rule of James in the guise of a history of the rule of Elizabeth.'[4] In spite of its appeal to jaundiced Jacobean eyes, the Elizabethan imagery was not entirely new. Some very fine studies on the 'cult of Elizabeth' have clearly identified the early existence of a conscious imagery which 'presents the Queen to her subjects as the sacred virgin whose reign was ushering in a new golden age of peace and plenty'.[5] Yet the image of the queen does not exactly match the contours of the French 'portrait of the king' which recent studies have explored.[6] It fused at least three elements: the learned appeal of antiquity, the Christian tradition and the imperial design. The cult of the Virgin Mary, now lapsed in the wake of the Reformation, was diverted and transferred onto the virgin queen. The Elizabethan incarnation of power – outrageously flattered by the painters – enjoyed a particularly brilliant success, thus illustrating the Western 'feminisation of allegory'.[7]

The reconstruction of the communities

I have insisted on the bright side of the Elizabethan myth because of its lasting potency and emotional appeal. The plight of the strangers offers, if not a contradictory picture, at least a complementary point of view; having returned to London Jan Utenhove wrote a petition on 11 December 1559. He spoke in the name of the exiled Protestants who had been dispersed six years before and asked for the confirmation of Edward's charter. A clear allusion to the Book of Esdras evoked the memory of Cyrus, king of the Persians, who had allowed the Jews to return from captivity to Babylon, and to rebuild their temple in Jerusalem.[8] A striking change of tone had taken place; early on Edward had been considered as a new Josias. But the perspective had since been inverted; what was required in this new context was the queen's benevolence, rather than her active support; the idea of a common Protestant faith had, for the time being, receded altogether.

The first weeks of the reign were still full of disquiet for the reformers, who remained doubtful about the religious outcome of the succession – a clear sign of the times. One of the first decisions of the new queen, the proclamation of 28 December forbidding all preaching, was deeply

---

[4] C. Haigh, (ed.), *The Reign of Elizabeth I*, London, 1984, p. 9.
[5] Roy Strong, *The Cult of Elizabeth*, London, 1977, p. 114; M.-M. Martinet, *Miroir de l'Esprit dans le théâtre élisabéthain*, Paris, 1981.
[6] Louis Marin, *Le Portrait du roi*, Paris, 1981.
[7] Maurice Agulhon, *Marianne au combat*, Paris, 1979, p. 7.
[8] State Papers, Domestic series (hereafter SP Dom.), Eliz., VII, 63.

resented by the remaining members of the strangers' communities who found this apparent attack incomprehensible; in fact, it derived from Elizabeth's obdurate wish to resolve the religious question by a political settlement. The first Parliament of the reign was summoned, while a reluctant Church assembly of Marian bishops was convened in Westminster. Parliament, as ever, reaffirmed the fundamental principles of the royal supremacy (1 Eliz. i c. 1).

Only then did the queen take measures to authorise the communities of strangers officially; we know that they had already gathered together beforehand. On 24 February 1560 the queen enjoined the marquess of Winchester to let the Austin Friars Chapel again to the 'strangers' – with the restriction, however, that 'no rite or custom contrary to law take place there'.[9] The office of superintendent was also maintained, but it was no longer in the hands of a foreigner – as formerly in the time of John a Lasco – but was taken over by the bishop of London. The second step in this reconstruction was the appointment of new pastors. On 18 March 1560, the French Church applied to Calvin, in a carefully drafted letter, signed by the two consistories, and by their superintendent Edmund Grindal, bishop of London.[10] They deplored the scarcity of 'learned men', who would be 'apt' to the ministry. Above all, they did not want to scandalise the English. With some timidity, they raised the possibility of receiving Theodore Beza as minister, or Nicholas des Gallars, who finally set out in the spring, bearing a missive from Calvin to the bishop of London, dated 15 May. The reformer expressed his regrets that the course of the Reformation in England had been delayed – a portentous change of tone since the reign of Edward.

Nicolas des Gallars, Sieur de Saules, had been born in Paris in 1520. He was not to remain in London for very long; in 1562 he accompanied Theodore Beza to the Colloquy of Poissy, and returned only briefly to London – where he aroused hostility – before spending the remainder of his life in Geneva, Orleans and then in Bearn. And yet his stay had a decisive influence; it marked the alignment of the French Church on the Calvinist mode. A new discipline was issued: *Forme de police ecclésiastique instituée à Londres en l'Eglise des François* (*Form of ecclesiastical polity instituted in the French Church of London*) (1561).

Some elements of John a Lasco's constitution were preserved. Communion was held monthly, more frequently than in Geneva. Appeals could be made against judgements by the consistories of either Church to the *coetus*, an assembly composed of representatives of both communities

---

[9] *Ibid.*, xi, 24.
[10] Paris, Bibliothèque Nationale (hereafter BN), MSS Dupuy 102, fols. 137 ff; quoted in Schickler, *Les Eglises du Refuge en Angleterre*, iii, pp. 44–7.

– Walloon and Dutch. Last but not least, 'prophesying' described an inspired reading from the Scriptures, given by a pastor or elder.

Where the participation of laymen was concerned, a distinct regression can be observed; elders and pastors were now clearly separated and, contrary to former practice, only the latter received a laying-on of hands. As for the choice of ministers and elders, it became entrusted to the consistories; the *people* now intervened only to ratify their appointment. Should this be regarded as a more oligarchic, less democratic, concept of the Church than in a Lasco's lifetime? Nicolas des Gallars emphasised knowledge rather than fortune. Spiritual authority and study were to be rewarded while the most learned were supposedly the wisest. They knew where the true interest of the community lay. This donnish defiance and self-consciousness displeased many of the congregation and betrayed an obvious fear of religious instability. Was there not a risk that Anabaptists, antitrinitarians or simply laymen of an unconventional turn of mind would seize the lasting opportunities offered by John a Lasco's ecclesiastical discipline? Thus, the outward praise of strength and authority often concealed weakness. Indeed, two ideas of the Church were at variance throughout the history of the English Refuge. A tension emerged between a hierarchical vision of the Church, resting on an elite of learning or fortune, and a more egalitarian outlook which insisted on the participation of all laymen. The opposition was perhaps even sharper than in the Reformed Churches of the Continent, owing to the proximity of the Church of England, which, with its comforting sense of hierarchy, attracted some and deterred others.

The third stage in this reconstruction consisted in reclaiming the morals of the congregation. They were suspected of having acquired bad habits during the years they had spent without adequate pastoral guidance. Indeed, neither Ebrard nor Pierre Alexandre, who had been in charge of preaching before the arrival of des Gallars, were to enjoy his esteem and respect. Ebrard was strongly advised to return to his beloved studies, before leaving to become pastor at Amiens; but Pierre Alexandre proved tougher, and nearly had himself elected titular pastor. Finally he was granted permission simply to preach at one o'clock in the afternoon every Sunday and on alternate Thursdays. The bishop of London had to intervene before peace was restored – although the holy pulpit war between Alexandre and des Gallars continued with increasing fury at each sermon. Shortly before his death Pierre Alexandre, a former Carmelite, crippled with gout, pronounced a resounding lecture which went beyond the bounds of propriety and decency. We find it reported as follows, in the consistory register for 29 July 1561: 'I was a monk, Martin Luther was a monk, and so were Master Bucer, Peter Martyr and others of whom everyone knows whether they were good men or not ... he also said that he indeed had more to say, but that it was better to leave children with their noses dirty than pull their noses off.'

This rather indelicate allusion thoroughly displeased the new consistory, and although the parties involved were summoned to appear before the bishop, this evidently failed to calm them, for the consistory register disappeared, probably removed by a supporter of Pierre Alexandre, if not by Pierre Alexandre himself, and did not surface again until three years later. This conflict between the two men – an anecdote clearly coloured by ill-feeling – illustrates, with pronounced overtones of a psychological and affective nature, the lingering reservations which surrounded the pastor from Geneva. Indeed, the re-establishment of the Church was accompanied by tightening control in the field of doctrine or discipline. Countless numbers of the faithful who had 'adhered to idolatry' under Mary Tudor flocked to their Church in droves to disavow their errors. Thus, on 14 July 1560, Pierre Maubert 'confessed to *having done as others did* during the persecution in this kingdom, and that having gone to Dover to flee from them, he returned and then went back to his parish priest at St. Thomas''. The dwellers of each parish were methodically summoned; St Catherine, Westminster and Templebar on 15 October; Whitechapel on the 18th; St-Martin-in-the-Fields on the 22nd. The most sincere of the past sinners were admitted to the first Communion held on 10 November. One is struck, however, by the number of renegades among these refugees 'exiled for their faith'. I am not passing judgement on these men but I simply wish to observe that in the sixteenth century economically motivated immigration – which did not come to a halt under Mary Tudor – did not necessarily coincide with clauses of conscience. This is often confirmed by the mutual suspicion which permeated the Churches themselves, especially in times of crisis or renewed immigration. In the heavy atmosphere of the 1560s which followed the Marian visitation, John a Lasco's optimistic constitution no longer corresponded with the spirit of the time: heterodoxy, the contagion of Anabaptism, or adherence to the pernicious doctrines of Servetus, had to be mercilessly eradicated among the refugees. On 22 October, Casidor, a Spaniard, admitted having heard that 'as for the word Trinity ... there is no such word to be found in the holy Scriptures'. By means of denunciations, whole networks – possibly entirely fictitious ones – were unravelled and dismantled. There was a paranoid element in sixteenth-century suspicion of heresy, as there was to be in later years in the fear of conspiracy. And God's little flock, however predestined to salvation, could be led astray and needed its good shepherds to preserve it from the dangers of contagion. Several affairs were to arouse the detective skills of the censors. Adrian Hambstede, a former Dutch pastor, was excommunicated by the bishop of London, in front of the two assemblies gathered together at Austin Friars. Although he did not share the Anabaptists' ideal, according to him they nonetheless deserved the name of Christians. At the end of the decade Corranus, a native of Seville, was to be harassed on account of his antitrinitarian views sympathetic to Castellio.

The English Refuge remained relatively resistant to the Calvinist form of organisation – not only in theological matters, but also where the system of elections was concerned. And the schism which shook the Dutch Church permitted Nicolas des Gallars' successor, Jean Cousin, to emphasise forcefully the danger of choosing elders or deacons 'by a plurality of votes', given the people's immoderate inclination towards 'factions' and 'intrigues', as he complained to Calvin on 1 May 1568. According to Cousin, the invocation of 'Christian liberty', this term which we have met in John a Lasco's writings, became, with the appeal to 'conscience', a pretext for disorder and laxity.[11]

Refugees and/or strangers

The communities claimed to consist of men 'all in exile for their faith': newcomers were scrutinised, lest they might be Catholic or even Anabaptist. But immigration did not necessarily follow the waves of persecution of the Continent. Except in the case of massive movements individual mobility, it should be stressed, did not necessarily involve ideological motivations. Thus, alongside strictly religious inspiration, the pinch of necessity and economic factors developed a logic of their own: settling in a particular community could be made easier thanks to a reputable relative or cousin, who was already on the spot. And why not also admit the attraction of novelty? Hence the periodical accusations of hypocrisy, which the English at large would immediately resort to, in times of conflict or competition with the immigrants. Whether the original motive for immigration was religious or not made little difference once in England. It was then necessary to become integrated into a world where employment was strictly codified by various corporate regulations. Like other countries, sixteenth-century England was not a free-for-all society. The 'immigrant for the sake of his faith' discovered, sometimes to his cost, that in the eyes of the law he was only a foreigner. In the language of the period, he was a *stranger*, and did not enjoy the full rights and privileges of the subjects of the realm. This abstract legalism, which confronted generation after generation of fugitives, met with resistance – beginning with the petition in Flemish of 29 January 1560, which was repeated in Latin six months later for the Refuge as a whole.[12] The

---

[11] Schickler, *Les Eglises du Refuge en Angleterre*, III, pp. 69–73.
[12] J.H. Hessels, *Ecclesiae Londino-Batavae Archivum*, 3 vols., Cambridge, 1889–97, II, pp. 40ff.

refugees complained of the humiliations imposed by the English on their Continental brethren. They deserved the particular consideration of their hosts because of their faith, though they were treated like any other foreigners in the kingdom. In the years after 1558, and in particular after the taking of Calais by the French, even Parliament had been affected by xenophobia; a law decreeing the expulsion of all Frenchmen had barely been rejected by a few votes. The often spontaneous distrust of foreigners could assume violent forms, and everyone would call to mind May day 1517 when the festive merriment of the London apprentices had turned against Flemings, Frenchmen, Italians and Hanseatic Germans. The riot had been suppressed with terrible severity. No doubt this 'evil May Day' acted as a useful reminder; in these centuries, when no one pretended to believe in the good nature of our species, the strangers knew that the sovereign authority of the king or queen, or of their servants, provided the best protection against popular resentment and pettiness.

And so in the long run each of the refugees found himself confronted in his individual existence by his alien status which remained virtually unchanged until the nineteenth century. Not until 1844, and more particularly 1870 (Naturalisation Act, 33 & 34 Vic. c. 14) could aliens acquire real property in England. The concept of a genuine English subject, as opposed to a stranger, had evolved under the pressure of the movements of population which accompanied the advances and withdrawals of the troops during the Hundred Years War. As one might well imagine, several adjustments proved necessary in the years between the reigns of Edward III and Queen Victoria. In particular, the debate gained prominence at the very beginning of the seventeenth century, when a Scottish king, James VI, came to the throne. What rights did his Scottish subjects now possess in England? The king, the subject and the property of the realm: these are the three terms of the controversy which ran through the centuries and rebounded with the Protestant refugees, who were often foreigners against their will. I have attempted, following the best authorities, among them one recent work by a French scholar,[13] to establish a table of the various forms of citizenship (see Fig. 6).

A number of observations should be made. In the first place, the intricacies of a legal definition do not exhaust by any means the complexity of actual practice. The Jacobean lawyers – to whom I shall refer, for the sake of convenience – attempted to rationalise an ancestral custom, fortified as they were with the innate sense of law and precedent which permeated the century. Can one safely transpose their analyses further back to the 1560s and to the reign of Elizabeth? Once these

---

[13] R. Marienstras, *New Perspectives on the Shakespearean World*, Cambridge, 1985, in part ch. 5: 'The near and the far: the Calvin affair and the status of foreigners under James I of England', pp. 99–125.

LEGAL STATUS	MANNER IN WHICH ACQUIRED	PRIVILEGES			TAXATION Double taxation (Subsidies and customs duties)
		Protection	'Personal property'	'Real property'	
(I) SUBJECT – Born subject	Allegiance from birth to the king of England	YES	YES	YES	NO
– Naturalised	Parliament	YES	YES	YES	NO
(II) DENIZEN – Adoptive subject	Letters patent from the Crown	YES	YES	YES (transmission restricted to children born in England)	YES
(III) Foreigner ('alien', 'stranger', 'peregrinus') – Friend	Subject of a prince at peace with England	YES	YES	NO	YES
– Enemy	Subject of a prince at war with England	NO (except safe-conduct)	NO	NO	?

Sources: BM Harleian MSS 444, fol. 376 [? (n.d.)]; Howell, *State Trials*, II pp. 559ff: 'The Case of the *Postnati*…'(1608) contains the opinions of Edward Coke and Francis Bacon; J. Cowell, *The Interpreter*, Cambridge 1607, articles 'alien' and 'denizen'.

Figure 6. The forms of citizenship

reservations have been accepted, several facts emerge for our consideration. The status of a refugee did not exist as such – it emerged as an ethical notion rather than as a purely lawful concern. Some actual remedies existed: one could decide, for instance, to naturalise the refugees and turn them into subjects of the realm. This was to assume greater significance still with the Revocation of the Edict of Nantes in the 1680s. In addition, whereas we would think naturally of two categories, Englishmen and strangers, there was in fact a third group of people, the *denizens*. Though they enjoyed extensive rights, denizens were not Englishmen. Like subjects they had access to property, but in other respects they remained separate, in a class of their own, and had to meet heavier fiscal pressure. And even once they had been *naturalised*, the label *denizen* was still indiscriminately applied to many refugees in common parlance at least until the seventeenth century. We have to note that this carefully drawn division between subjects, strangers and denizens came into conflict with deep-rooted patterns of behaviour. The alternative remained to belong, or not to belong, to a Stranger Church. Their offspring, when they had been born in England, were technically English, but they had not been cut loose from the many ties still linking them to the immigrant communities. We must beware of the anachronistic risk of individualist concerns: in the early modern period, one could hardly distinguish the individual from the group, or divorce him from his lineage, his household or indeed from his kith and kin. In fact present-day social anthropologists are familiar with the specific problem of the second generation. In our next chapter we shall see how the 'native born' encountered the increasing suspicion of the Establishment. This legal maze has therefore a purely indicative value. Let us sum up its compass by citing Maitland, writing in 1887:

> An act of parliament might of course turn an alien into a subject, and until lately acts having the object of naturalising this or that foreigner were not uncommon. A statute, however, was necessary; it seems to have been established at an early time, certainly before Coke, that the king without parliament could turn an alien into a subject for the purposes. He might for some, but not for all. This doctrine gave rise to the class of persons known as denizens – intermediate between subjects and aliens. The denizen was so made by the king's letters patent, i.e. by an act done by the king without parliament. The limit to the royal power (as a I understand it) was this: the person whom the king made a denizen of his realm became capable of acquiring lands by purchase or devise, or of holding them when acquired, and in general he became a subject of the realm, but the king could not make him capable of inheriting.[14]

---

[14] F.W. Maitland, *The Constitutional History of England*, Cambridge (1908), 1977, p. 427.

The legal status of strangers, or indeed of denizens, suffered from a fundamental ambiguity when one considers the informal mass of artisans or journeymen who composed the refugee population. The stranger was envisaged essentially in relation to *the law of property* rather than *employment* – there was an obsession with transfer through inheritance. This evidently reflects the persistence of a concern with the king as master and protector, to whom each tenure ultimately belonged. Accordingly, unless one were at least a denizen, it was impossible to transfer even the smallest part of this territory to one's posterity lest it should enter into the allegiance of a foreign sovereign.

The pervading influence of a feudal concept of men's loyalty, in part the legacy of the Hundred Years War, explains the inadequacy of existing jurisdiction and, while the law expressed the conservatism of world pictures and attitudes, the daily encounters with the corporations and Livery Companies called for constant readjustments. The law of tenure, and the gracious protection of the sovereign, were ill-adapted to massive migration and large-scale settlements: the propertyless stranger, who was often a townsman, or had come from the crowded world of Flanders, was not encompassed in the narrow scope of an already partly archaic definition. And so, from at least the fifteenth century onwards, the English authorities resorted to restrictive measures, preventing any hasty identification of the denizens with the natural subjects.

The air of the cities

Finally, restrictions of a second kind bore upon the refugees. The definition of the foreigner in national terms – as an individual bound by allegiance to another king or queen – proves inadequate. There were two respects in which one was a foreigner – in relation to the kingdom, but equally in relation to the cities or boroughs, endowed with charters enunciating long-standing privileges. The fugitive found himself confronted by this ancient body of law, by labour constraints, and by the weight of past customs and habits. Yet in spite of all these restrictive elements, he nonetheless experienced a new sense of freedom, especially in the field of religion. In the language of the time two distinct terms were available: the *stranger* was alien to the country as a whole, while *foreigner*, contrary to present-day usage, denoted the newcomer to the city. In this respect the refugee was a foreigner by virtue of his national origin, but also in relation to the town in which he found shelter. If, indeed, 'the air of the cities makes men free', as the proverb says, the freedom in question was relative by nature. The *freemen* of a given city were its citizens. The status of freeman, with its sense of respectability, defined an institution rather than a social class, an established sense of belonging which could be acquired only through descent or marriage, apprenticeship or merit. This pseudo-genealogy remained a factor of conservatism rather than of innovation: the ancestral honour of each trade, the native dignity of the craftsman bequeathed by his fathers, whether real or adoptive, a lengthy apprenticeship in the city constituted so many obstacles for the newcomer who resented his estrangement and yet came to share, by slow degrees, the native pride of the host society. We might read John Evans' description of the situation in seventeenth-century Norwich, the site of one of the most flourishing strangers' settlements:

> The all-important dividing line among townsmen was between freemen and non-freemen. Freedom of the city involved both privileges and obligations as set down in local ordinances and enforced in the Mayor's Court. The effect of these ordinances was to provide the freemen, or citizenry, with a virtual monopoly over both political and economic affairs in Norwich. Only freemen could hold civic office and only freemen could vote in municipal and parliamentary elections. Non-freemen and 'foreigners' were prohibited from taking on apprentices.[15]

John Evans goes on to point out that the non-freeman was increasingly affected in the course of the seventeenth century by a ban on all mercantile activity. He also admits that it is difficult for today's historians to tell if this rigour, backed by fines of various descriptions, was efficient in deterring 'foreigners' from illegal activity. The residents who did not enjoy the freedom of the city included not only those in receipt of poor relief but also servants and members of the professions – not counting the few aristocratic families who took up their winter quarters in this regional capital. In 1690 the freemen accounted for perhaps 30 per cent of the adult male population in Norwich.

And yet it would be mistaken to deduce, from this rather elusive stratification, any lack of dynamism, vitality or initiative. Being a land of transition and tradition, England seized the opportunity to enrich her cities with the influx of artisans from the Continent – and so did Norwich in particular from the sixteenth century onwards. Like Colchester and the whole of East Anglia bordering the North Sea, Norwich benefited from exchanges with Flanders, that great purveyor of men and ideas. In 1564, Thomas Sotherton, the mayor of Norwich, addressed the insurgents of the Low Countries directly. Those people, who were so harshly persecuted by the duke of Alba, were also endowed with priceless technical skills, and he invited them to settle in his city, which had been struck by economic decline. He thereby hoped to give new impetus to textile production and enhance its quality. Having listed the consequences of the crisis, and emphasised the dangerous idleness of the unemployed, the mayor of Norwich explains:

[15] J.T. Evans, *Seventeenth-Century Norwich...*, Oxford, 1979, p. 7.

> After many consultations and devices what trades might be practised to redress this poor state, [I] was given intelligence that diverse strangers of the Low Countries were now come to London and Sandwich and got licence of the Queen's Majesty to exercise the making of Flanders commodities made of wool, which strangers came over for refuge against the persecution then raised against them by the power of the Duke of Alba, principal for the king of Spain. And because the poor here might be exercised in their spinning and woolwork a motion was made to Thomas, then duke of Norfolk, then lodged at his house in this city.

The duke of Norfolk interceded on behalf of the city of Norwich when he went to London. As a result,

> the Queen's Majesty having compassion of the poor state of this her highness' city, did tolerate and admit to be and inhabit within this her highness' City of Norwich thirty master workmen, to have either of them ten servants to exercise the making of those commodities with warrant to the Mayor and citizens to permit them so to do[16]

A letter patent authorised thirty Flemings – with their households – to settle in the country. For the Low Countries, the 1560s corresponded to what Solange Deyon and Alain Lottin, in a recent work, have called the 'spring-time of the *beggars*' – or radical insurgent.[17] Queen Elizabeth, in spite of her sympathy for the 'true Faith', was also wary of subversion and she interpreted this appeal as an economic gesture, in agreement with a well-established tradition of privileged connections with Flanders. One cannot sufficiently emphasise this special relationship which had had a decisive influence from the Middle Ages onwards even though the English always had mixed feelings towards the Dutch. Often a partner, sometimes an adversary, the man from Flanders alternately aroused fascination and disquiet. In Elizabethan England the memory of the strategic alliance with the house of Burgundy lurked in people's minds, but who was the true heir to this tradition, the Spaniard Philip II or his rebellious subjects? Bruges, which had been famous in 1475 when Caxton had printed there the first book in English, gave way to Antwerp, and its gigantic warehouses and financial market, where Thomas Gresham – who had aptly said that 'bad money drives out good' – enjoyed credit enough to borrow considerable sums for his mistress Queen Elizabeth.[18] It is true that the *Magnus Intercursus* of 1495, which granted England favourable trading conditions at Antwerp, noticeably lost momentum. But there is no need to enter into details here, and in spite of all its uncertainties, this Anglo-Flemish

[16] R.H. Tawney and Eileen Power (eds.), *Tudor Economic Documents*, 3 vols., London, 1924, I, p. 298.
[17] Solange Deyon and Alain Lottin, *Les Casseurs de l'été 1566*, Paris, 1981.
[18] G.D. Ramsay, *The City of London in International Politics at the Accession of Elizabeth Tudor*, Manchester, 1975.

connection remained, for better or for worse, a point of contact between the two nations. In the sixteenth century, indeed, men rather than tools were the *principal vectors of technology transfer*.

According to a local census, there were nearly 4,000 aliens in Norwich, about a quarter of them of Walloon origin, in 1571. The primary characteristic of this relatively massive immigration, by sixteenth-century standards, is that it retained the character of a self-contained community, grafted onto English society – a concentration of men and skills which aimed at the effective transposition and successful adaptation of the 'New Draperies'. Lipson's lasting contribution depicted the situation of Norwich in the following terms:

> The most important event in the industrial history of the sixteenth century was the coming of the Dutch and Walloon weavers. Their immigration constitutes the second great landmark in the history of the English cloth trade, just as the influx of Flemish weavers in the fourteenth century was the first... The exiles were welcomed by the English Government both as religious refugees and as a valuable accession to the economic resources of the country for they established in this country a new branch of the woollen industry. This was the manufacture of the finer fabrics, known as the 'new draperies', many of which were either unknown in this country or were beyond the technical skill of English textile workers. Among other centres the strangers settled in Norwich, whose prosperity was declining owing to a succession of epidemics and fires and the migration of craftsmen into the country districts.[19]

We should stress that society was not the sum total of individuals, or the aggregate of their desires and enterprise; such a conception had no place in the thinking of the sixteenth century. Society was an association of corporate entities, with a strong sense of hierarchy, and all negotiations concerning the labour force were expected to take place between one community and another. All this goes without saying; yet it is worth insisting that the economic freedom which is characteristic, to a greater or lesser extent, of our time did not exist in the sixteenth century, but are the ultimate implications of the phenomenon always understood? There was no labour market in which producers and entrepreneurs confronted one another – or at least it remained as yet an entirely peripheral phenomenon. Even in theory, the 1563 Statute of Artificers entrusted the local oligarchies – justices of the peace or mayors – with the fixing of maximum wage-rates. The Crown thereby intended to take account of soaring price levels in order to forestall the social curses which Tudor sovereigns constantly strove to exorcise – hunger riots, the uprooting of individuals

---

[19] E.Lipson, *The Woollen and Worsted Industries*, London, 1921, p. 21.

or the depopulation of the countryside – which epitomised instinctive fears of rebellion or unrest. Such measures were indeed a good illustration of the Elizabethan world picture; yet did they promote any effective control of economic life? The question lies outside the scope of the present enquiry. In any case, economic historians agree on an overall decline in purchasing power, constantly lagging behind the rise in prices, but differ as to its extent.[20]

The effect wage control had on real earnings certainly varied from county to county and from town to town. Likewise, supply and demand may have exercised a surreptitious influence in spite of all regulations. We are yet in a better position to appreciate the considerable distance which sets the sixteenth-century refugees of yore apart from the immigrants of later centuries. Neither did they constitute an industrial reserve force in Marxist terms, nor a population of small shopkeepers, since they had in theory no access to the retail trade. Their lot remained relatively happy and a certain spirit of mutual help may have worked to their advantage. I do not claim that past centuries knew nothing of the exploitation of men by men. Yet Peter Laslett's thesis that England was a 'one-class society', however provocative, is not altogether ill-founded, in spite of its nostalgic mood; the kingdom conceived of itself as one great body politic, in which each organ had its specific function to perform.[21] But this was only one of the facets of a changing reality which presented multifarious aspects, and in which localism often prevailed. There did not exist an altogether transparent and undivided community of interest between the refugees and their hosts – indeed the strangers aroused constant popular suspicion and they were spared neither economic rivalry nor even competition – but it was always the group rather than isolated individuals who were the targets of popular resentment. The gregarious instincts of the crowd should not surprise us, though a comparative study of the communities of foreigners illustrates the paradox of stagnation and mobility in Elizabethan England. How can one withhold a feeling of admiration for the wisdom and cleverness of the English who took advantage of the religious persecutions abroad in order to benefit from a fortunate transfer of techniques? But this praiseworthy empiricism and openness were not the only elements at play. The age was suspicious of *innovation* – the term still retained derogatory overtones, even in the next century – while accepting *de facto* novelty. They yet remained as short-sighted as some present governments. What future was there in store for the immigrants? What would their children do? This overwhelming question was not even raised. Why should the future be different from the past? We have since changed

[20] F. Mauro, *Le XVIe siècle européen, aspects économiques*, Paris, 1966, p. 126; D. Woodward, 'Wage Rates and Living Standards in Pre-Industrial England', *Past and Present* 91 (May 1981), pp. 28–45.
[21] P. Laslett, *The World We Have Lost*, London, 1965–71.

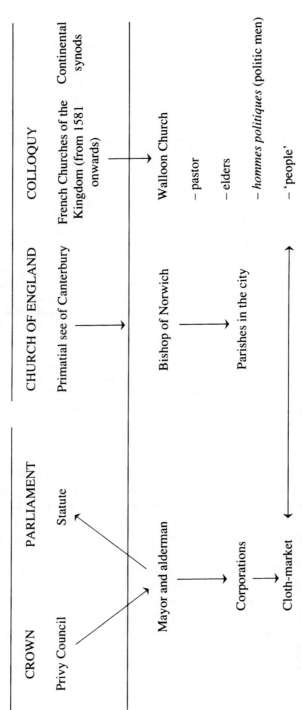

Figure 7. The principal authorities in charge of the strangers' community in Norwich

Figure 8. Principal privileges of foreigners in Norwich

Duties towards the mayor	Newcomers to be presented, with certificate, within ten days, lodging permitted at an inn; *private individuals forbidden to accommodate them for more than two days* (*five shillings*), denunciation encouraged. Eight Flemish 'hommes politiques' – politic men – and four Walloons to be presented for the keeping of order within the community.
Duties towards the English parish church	Payment of parish rates (a rate of one penny in the shilling levied on property).
Duties towards the city watch	According to lot (?) (threepence); *not to go out half an hour after curfew.*
Economic duties	
(1) Trade	To declare imported goods (twopence on Flemish cloth, etc.), *contraband* (*according to value*). Tailors, butchers, cobblers, shoemakers, etc., to trade only with other foreigners; *opening of shops prohibited, premises not to open directly into the street.*
(2) Production	Inspection of merchandise produced, essentially various kinds of serge, by an official who checked the quality of the cloth and of the dyeing before affixing his seal (twopence per bale); *in case of contravention* (ten pence). Sale of cloth permitted only at the cloth-market, from one o'clock to five every day (one penny per piece of cloth, or gratuity). Permitted to send cloth to London or other cities, *excluding villages, towns, markets and fairs.* *Forbidden to buy leather from unauthorised traders.*

Note: infractions given in italics; duties, taxes or fines incurred appear in parentheses.
Source: Norwich, Norfolk Record office, MSS NRO 17/D, Book of Orders for Strangers, fols. 76ff: letter from the Privy Council, dated 25 April 1571.

perspectives, and duration for us involves change more than repetition, while this was meaningless for an Elizabethan. In fact, the idea of *assimilation*, which has now become commonplace, was practically unknown, and when the Crown attempted to assimilate the strangers in the 1630s it encountered the worst possible opposition on the part of the refugees. I am not pretending that the aliens did not become integrated in the end, but they did so imperceptibly – as it were, surreptitiously. The absence of assimilation as a practical concern hinges on a concept of time different from ours. Time was envisaged as a succession of generations bound to the identical repetition of actions and conditions, following the slow rhythm of work, and of passing days. In theory, the only possible outcome for the strangers was a separate evolution. This never amounted to apartheid, or racism; neither was there the least element of fear or exclusion on either side: wisdom and common sense prevailed as in most domestic concerns. The absurd doctrine of 'blood purity' – *limpieza de sangre* – which poisoned Spanish minds in the same period[22] had no counterpart in England, and the division of labour alone dictated this separation between foreigners and Englishmen: the strangers were to develop the textile production to the best of their long-established ability, without encroaching upon the privileges of the guilds.

The Dutch and Walloon communities in Norwich constituted neither a distinct nor a separate class. They centred on their Churches, which were the depositories of their linguistic identity just as much as spiritual authorities. Moreover, the Churches were supposed to keep law and order, though this involvement may have caused some concern and was entrusted to a body of *hommes politiques* or politic men – as it were – distinct from the elders and pastors (see Fig. 7).

This diagram emphasises vertical relationships for the sake of clarity; but many intermediary stages should be mentioned, like the possibility of appeal to the mayor or bishop, the benevolent protection of the Crown, or the constant and dignified invocation of privilege. Purely individual initiative was extremely rare and on the verge of indiscipline – hence this ingrained sense of hierarchy which acted as a constant reminder that solidarity went hand in hand with constraint. Yet life cannot be reduced to a diagram, though some kind of institutional framework may prove useful to the reader.

Likewise, the conditions of employment, which were sometimes incredibly strict, have led me to present a final list to the reader (Fig. 8). Several conclusions may be drawn, without going into endless details. The title which I have adopted may sound surprising; I have used the word *privileges*, and yet this is a purely negative list of duties and constraints, with corresponding fines and punishments: the strangers were not supposed to engage in retailing, nor were they allowed to receive visitors for more than two days – a clear incentive against illegal immigration. In fact, privilege was the everyday form of the law, which was given far more to exceptions than to universal declarations on rights in the abstract – a notion difficult to envisage in this urban setting, where distinctions and titles merged into tradition. Besides, this list of privileges in which restrictions and impositions abound (the difficulties in lodging newcomers, the numerous checks and controls, incessant taxation, the prohibition of retail trading) was less coercive in reality than it appears. At all events, these regulations were not perceived as arbitrary at the time, neither did they prevent the foreigners in Norwich from prospering. In fact, there was nothing vexatious in these clauses: they did not raise the indignation which such laws of exception would provoke today. Even in Canterbury, where a large Walloon minority was to be found, similar measures were adopted. For example, in November 1574 an officer was appointed to affix

[22] B. Bennassar, *L'Homme espagnol*, Paris, 1975, p. 175.

his seal to woven fabrics, while in 1579, trading in the foreigners' commodities was limited to one specific hall, where only freemen of the city were allowed to buy.[23] On 26 October 1574 the London Common Council forbade tradesmen to take as apprentices anyone who was not the son of an Englishman, on pain of losing their rights as freemen of the City. This severe threat may serve to indicate the wide possibility of infringement. But above all, it confirms the above-mentioned reservations concerning the theoretical status of the second-generation immigrants: they were English by birth, but still foreigners in the eyes of the beholder.

However, there was a difference between London and other cities. At the end of the sixteenth century, the population of Norwich amounted to less than a fifteenth of that of London. With at least 200,000 inhabitants around 1600, London was the only real metropolis and acted as a sort of 'magnet' for the country at large: while one in twenty Englishmen lived in London around 1600, this proportion doubled in the course of the seventeenth century, amounting to one in ten in 1700. Roger Finlay has aptly described the situation: 'London was thus of great importance in English society and economy, not only because such a high proportion of the total population lived in the metropolis; but also because the high mortality rate meant that the population of London was unable to replace itself.'[24] Therefore the element of mobility, which characterised the strangers' communities, is to some extent comparable to the developments of early modern urban society: in both cases, the new immigrants were necessary to raise, or, indeed, to maintain, the figures of a population which could not rely solely on its natural increase. There is yet a major difference between the refugees and an ordinary sample of seventeenth-century Londoners. Two factors intervened to reduce the levels of population in the case of the refugees: one was the death rate, the other was sheer dilution through assimilation with the English.

The overall concentration of strangers was much higher in Norwich or Canterbury, where they often made up nearly one third of the population. Indeed, there were specific implantations in certain London wards, and the density of foreigners also varied from one street to another. However, in Norwich and Canterbury only did there exist a kind of autonomous police force, made up of strangers.

The boundaries of these religious minorities remained unsettled: the Protestant strangers could not be distinguished at first sight from other foreigners. Thus, the freemen of London's grievance in 1571[25] mentions merchants and craftsmen from other nations, and complains of various tricks: dishonest control of the market; retailing; illegal export of precious

---

[23] Dean and Chapter Burghmote Minute Book.
[24] R. Finlay, *Population and Metropolis. The Demography of London 1580–1650*, Cambridge, 1981, p. 7.
[25] R. Marx (ed.), *Documents d'histoire anglais*, Paris, 1971, p. 76.

metals, a classic mercantilist argument; covert agreements; monopolies; and illicit exercise of forbidden trades. Accompanying each point is a reminder of a number of restrictive laws, dating from the fourteenth century onwards, which had quite evidently been flouted. This text provides two major hints. In the first place, it confirms that aliens, even when they had become denizens or had been born in England and were technically English, remained foreigners in the eyes of the population (article 6). 'They are a commonwealth within themselves... though they be denizens or born here amongst us, yet they keep themselves severed from us in Church, in government, in trade, in language and marriage.'

In addition, the freemen wanted to revive an ancient law, according to which every foreign merchant had to reside with an English host, who had to keep an eye on his guest. Before we come to the practical outcome of this request, five years later, one further point needs clarifying: our concept of the police, as a professional body, had not yet come into being. The few constables, elected or appointed by the justices of the peace, cannot be regarded as an organised force. The majority of prosecutions, from accusations of high treason[26] to minor economic infractions,[27] fell within the public province; a number of informers – some of them highly specialised – hoped to benefit from the intelligence they supplied, and often received a reward out of the fine imposed. As the police were nowhere to be found, constant watchfulness prevailed among neighbours. Gossip and hearsay, denunciation or slander conferred on these times the instability of mercury, conducive to irrational bouts of sudden fears. But, after all, denunciation was only a consequence of this well-knit world of lasting solidarity, and the forced residence of strangers, advocated by the citizens of London, was just another form of hospitality. However, it would be misleading to insist only on the dark, repressive side of the coin. The multifarious restrictions, which in theory at least bore upon the foreigners, should not always be taken for granted. Should this gap between official declarations and practice escape our attention, our perception of Tudor England would be distorted into an unduly authoritarian image; with few exceptions, the age was only too glad not to conform to any systematic consistency.

And so, in 1576, 'the office of hostager and host' of all foreign merchants in the kingdom was entrusted for twenty-one years to William Tipper, a freeman of the City and a grocer by trade, who in fact acted as a proxy for Sir Christopher Hatton, the famous Elizabethan courtier:

> His proposal was to revive the ancient laws of 'hosting' or 'hostage' of merchant strangers, which had long fallen into disuse. By hosting was meant the obligation of a foreign merchant coming to England to lodge

[26] G.R. Elton, *Policy and Police*, Cambridge, 1972.
[27] M.G. Davies, *The Enforcement of English Apprenticeship*, Harvard, 1956.

with an English merchant who was called his host. In this way the trading communities of London and the other cities could ensure that foreign merchants did not infringe the laws by which English trade and industry were regulated, and could also keep a check on the foreigners' activities.[28]

There were exceptions to this rule in the case of Italian or Hanseatic merchants and it is difficult to disentangle the strictly financial motive from the determination to maintain effective control. Disapproval from more than one quarter was immediately expressed: the measure met with the immediate opposition of Sir Thomas Smith,[29] the great Elizabethan councillor; then the Flemish towns and in particular Antwerp expressed their worst fears which are later confirmed by the emperor's brother. This humiliating regulation does not seem to have been very successful or efficient among foreigners. While the Spaniards and Portuguese were exempted, William Tipper – still advised behind the scenes by Hatton – very quickly turned to other sources of profit, cochineal or maritime ventures.

On the whole the concern for good management, however insular in character, predominated over discrimination or expulsion. For this was a society of management and thrift which bewailed the loss of bullion while securing social peace by the most ruthless of all systems of poor relief.[30] This sense of accounting, rather than feelings or emotions, explains the favourable welcome extended to the refugees. Unfortunately, we are not in a position to assess the extent of the financial contributions levied on foreigners. But the most unpopular of all was certainly the double rates the strangers had to pay to their local English parish church to which they only belonged in a fictitious way, and to their own community – in order to provide for the upkeep of their chapel. The pastor's stipend, the poor-fund, and other charges were regarded with growing suspicion and unease. According to an estimate of 1578,[31] the budget of the two Foreign Churches in Norwich amounted to £100 per annum. The foreigners were said to lend money to the English at very advantageous rates (there is even mention of loans without any interest, which may well have been the case). And finally, their presence had led, apparently, to a beneficial increase in rents. We know, however, how sceptical one has to be of such approximations. Moreover, money matters were not, if I can put it that way, strictly monetary; the circulation of species often took on an additional, symbolic value within the community (see Part III). Nonethe-

[28] E. St. John Brooks, *Sir Christopher Hatton*, London, 1946, p. 223.
[29] SP Dom., Eliz, cxxx, 25: MS appeal against the measure, by Thos Smith, dated March 1579: 'The Prosecution of William Tipper's suit to the Lord Mayor and Aldermen of London for the hostage of merchant strangers'. The author declares the measure to be contrary to the 'Magna Charta Angliae' and to humanity.
[30] J. Pound, *Poverty and Vagrancy in Tudor England*, London, 1971.
[31] SP Dom., Eliz., cxxviii, 81.

less, in the Elizabethan period the strangers' presence proved profitable for the English.

An issue between nations

> But the number of the ungodly hath gotten such power, there is now no place left in the whole world, which they have not tried to corrupt with their most wicked Doctrines. Amongst others, *Elizabeth*, the pretended Queen of *England*, a slave of wickedness, lending thereunto her helping hand, with whom, as in a Sanctuary, the most pernicious of all men have found a Refuge.

This is an extract from the bull promulgated in 1570 by Pius V, *Regnans in Excelsis*..., which constituted a real 'declaration of war'[32] against Queen Elizabeth on the part of the papacy. In this passage England is indeed regarded as a 'sanctuary' and land of 'Refuge', a hotbed of international subversion according to Rome. Protestant migrations were properly speaking a question of geopolitics, to borrow the language of contemporary analysts. This view calls for qualification; the craftsmen whose steps we have traced had other concerns than to act as the agents of some secret international confederacy. Serious history has always disproven theories of massive conspiracy. Migratory phenomena, however, interfered with the complex strategy which drew England to the forefront among the Protestant belligerents. In 1570, the hostilities between London and the Holy See emerged from cold war, and took an offensive turn; the most prominent feature of these times was to be the Anglo-Spanish rivalry, across a theatre of operations already as extensive as the ocean. In what way, then, were religion and politics interwoven? The question underlies any examination of the period, and the answer cannot be too straightforward. Admittedly England was directly involved in two series of phenomena: an ideological conflict, and military rivalry. These two threads only partially coincide. At the height of the confrontation with Spain, and in particular in 1588 when Philip II armed his Invincible Armada, an intensification of religious propaganda occurred on both sides. The English could not fail to see the hand of God in the Spaniards' defeat, caused in part by disastrous weather conditions. This atmosphere of ordeal, the invocation of providence, undeniably coloured the most prominent episodes in the conflict with the Catholic powers. And the Huguenot epic, steeped in the themes of the 68th Psalm – 'Let God arise...' – was piously to record the English victory over Spain. As late as 1639, the poet Lobeau evokes 'the year fifteen hundred and eighty-eight',

---

[32] G.R. Elton, *The Tudor Constitution*, Cambridge, 1960, p. 411.

and the victory of the 'great living God' of the 'Everlasting' over the false gods of popery:

> Their relics and false gods
> Their beads, drones and spears
> Could not defend them;
> Nor could their saints,
> Whom they invoke with hands clasped
> Ever hear their clamour
> Or their cries...[33]

Is the poem referring to the *Invincible Armada*, or else to the more recent confrontations of that year 1639, which saw the Dutch and Spaniards in conflict? This makes little difference; we are immersed in a mythical time sequence, and the titanic confrontation of Faith and Error, of religion and superstition, takes on a cosmic aspect in which the very natural elements are involved:

> The sea, in great wrath against them
> Would suffer not one of them
> Within itself to stay,
> But spewed them forth in its tide
> As men saw when it returned,
> Breaking them, belly and back.

Without any undue realism, or excessive debunking, one can readily imagine that international politics rarely attained this sublime character, and that behind-the-scenes negotiations were not the province of chivalrous and virtuous heroes alone. In reality, there was not strict chronological coincidence between religious policy and the confrontation with Spain, except in the 1580s. One should therefore recognise a clear separation between ideology and practice in accordance with the teachings of Machiavelli. Despite Pius V's bull, it was only with some reserve that England became engaged in the theatre of operations, having tried in vain, as late as the 1570s not to inflame the disputes with the Spaniards, who aimed at holding the mastery of the seas. It took some time for the rebellious Low Countries to rally Elizabeth to their support;[34] conversely, how is one to disentangle the part played by calculation in the goodwill which England showed towards the Huguenots?

Nonetheless, although there was no strict alignment of behaviour on religious convictions, the intensification of international antagonisms was

---

[33] Isaye de Lobeau, 'Chanson nouvelle touchant la Mémorable Victoire obtenue par les Hollandais et Zellandois contre l'Armées Navalle du Roy d'Espagne aux Costes d'Angleterre, l'An 1639', *Proceedings of the Huguenot Society of London*, 1, pp. 313–23.

[34] Charles Wilson, *Queen Elizabeth and the Revolt of the Netherlands*, Berkeley, 1970.

to have a damaging effect on the Catholic cause in England, and a favourable influence on the Refuge. The great new feature of this period is *the identification of Protestantism with English national consciousness.* This was largely an after-effect of Pope Pius V's bull, which antagonised the English, but that feeling was reinforced ten years later. In a sense, the English Catholics' situation was the opposite of the exiled Protestants'. Often enough, suspicion of the papists resembled the distrust shown towards foreigners; hence the wish expressed in Parliament, in March 1585, to impose double taxation on HM's Catholic subjects, depriving them of their native rights to treat them as mere strangers who were submitted to heavier fiscal pressure. The definition of citizenship derived from the allegiance to the king or queen rather than from purely territorial considerations. This explains the isolation of the English Catholics, soon entertained by Jesuit would-be martyrs who proved more serviceable in the salvation of souls than in the emancipation of the papists. The heroic fathers unwillingly buttressed the idea that every Catholic was an agent of a foreign power, an instrument of Antichrist and an emissary of the Great Whore of Babylon. The Catholics were to be charged continually with holding a dual and irreconcilable allegiance; how could one be a lawful subject to the king or queen, if one owed obedience to a pope who had absolved him from his natural duty of obedience? The fascinating question of English Catholicism cannot be fully explored here. I shall simply mention the attempt at compromise over the heads of the Jesuits, which marked the end of the reign. What matters to us here is not the actual Catholic, but his fictitious counterpart in an imagery which values the Protestant refugee while castigating the native papist. Ideally the Protestant foreigner, even if the subject of a hostile sovereign, was more to be trusted than the English Catholic. This transfer of allegiance considerably complicated the situation. Some reservations emerged. The Protestant international was often as fictitious as newfangled ideas about international cooperation. Henceforth, alongside its economic or religious role, the Refuge also answered international considerations, while providing semi-official diplomatic links alongside pastoral contacts with Geneva. Huguenot military leaders such as François Hotman or Philippe Duplessis-Mornay travelled to England. The reader should be reminded of the unmistakable epic flavour which surrounded the defence of the 'true Faith' in the second half of the sixteenth century. The service of God was often another name for the service of arms, and the great knightly cavalcades, the adventures on the seas were just as important for the men of the time as pious considerations. In France, this was an age of wars of religion. And, although the image of England as a land of refuge and a bulwark of Protestantism seems to be on the whole justified, it should be to some extent mitigated: the refugees had to experience a few episodes of unrest, even though protection from above prevented any serious escalation at their expense.

Let me take up the thread at the very beginning of the reign. The resentment at the fall of Calais, a few months before the death of Mary Tudor, justified the occupation of Le Havre by Warwick's troops. The Norman port, rechristened New-Haven, passed out of English hands in July 1562, after the Huguenot military leaders had withdrawn their support – Condé in particular had signed the peace of Amboise with his king. These hostilities were accompanied by seizures, detrimental to the foreigners: merchant vessels were impounded on both sides. Several refugees were affected, and the mayor of London, Thomas Lodge, turned to the Privy Council. On 2 August any proceedings against these peaceable communities of law-abiding denizens or Englishmen by birth were to be stopped. Undoubtedly, a great deal of circumspection was needed to ensure that these friendly refugees did not become the hostages of popular ill feelings.

But worse was in store, and a major source of tension arose in the 1570s; assisting William of Orange–Nassau and the Dutch rebels would have amounted to an open declaration of war on Spain, and Queen Elizabeth wished to avoid an escalation. The English were very sensitive to the unleashing of anti-Protestant feelings on the Continent; there was a flow of refugees in the wake of the massacres of St Bartholomew's Day in 1572, and the English court was in mourning to greet the French ambassador, La Mothe-Fenelon. Yet in April 1575, the Crown forbade the Prince of Orange and the Dutch rebels to enter the ports of the kingdom; despite the advice of councillors such as Walsingham, the queen reaffirmed her attachment to peace in March 1576. Tension rose and was further exacerbated by the memory of several Dutchmen's expulsion a few months before. An English ship returning from Antwerp was even detained off Dover by the Zeelanders. We may readily understand the anxiety of the refugees when they were officially summoned to meet the costs of detainment of some Orangists among their number. A petition, issued on 23 June, is to be found among the records of the Walloon Church in Canterbury:

> The following resolution was approved, namely that we thought it right to thank her Majesty and the Gentlemen of the Council both for their past and for their present favours, with prayers and supplications for their safeguarding and protection against popular tumults, considering our innocence and blamelessness in the matter. And moreover that we are much aggrieved at the division which, we understand, exists between Her Majesty and His Grace the Prince of Orange; and chiefly that he is said to have been incited by some of our party to speak ill of the English, a thing unknown and repudiated among us.

The organic metaphor of the 'body politic' was highly suggestive at the time. Between peace and rebellion lay the half-way zone of febrility and instinct, destructive of neighbouring relations; the mask of courtesy or indifference could drop, ushering in an era of suspicion, distrust and perhaps even outright violence. The mob, like the body, had its overflowing humours and passions. Aliens had cause to dread the crowd, whenever international politics sustained xenophobia. Contemporary sociologists may not so readily accept this transfer of individual psychology to that of the crowd; yet the odium cast on foreigners gave prejudice the force of popular consensus. This kind of assumption, though often implicit, underlay representations of the 'body politic' which only the wisdom of the king or queen could temper in its excesses. Allegiance and loyalty were born of fear, which, as Jean Delumeau has brilliantly established,[35] was omnipresent at that time. Hence, the dissociation of loyalties produced the most acute unease: were the refugees to make a clear choice between William Nassau, who fought for the 'true Faith', and Queen Elizabeth, who was unwilling to cooperate with the rebels?

How could they choose? The consistory of Canterbury settled the matter when it decided with the wisdom of Solomon to invoke the duties contracted by strangers towards the foster-country. And, joining the action to the word, they argued that Pierre de Brusle, who had wanted to help the Low Countries, was to be suspended from Holy Communion, following 'our promise and the Court's order that no help be given at the time to any officer of His Grace the Prince'. Neither perjury nor foul play were to be expected from the refugees.

Evading an oath would have called into question any working relationship within society, and while conflicting loyalties were one of the springs of tragedy on the Elizabethan stage, the invocation of honour provided the only adequate response. The odds are that the communities suffered from contradictory demands: international solidarity with the Protestants of the Continent had to be mitigated by respect for royal decisions at home. Now, as ever, good refugees are not supposed to meddle in politics. In the early modern period, foreign Protestants acted as constant reminders of Catholic fury abroad. Yet it would have been prejudicial to international relations in the century of Machiavelli to let the bewailing chorus of charitable lament muffle the powerful voice of Reason of State. And yet the Elizabethan period contrived to avoid all excesses; at the most difficult moments, in 1563 as well as in 1576 when international involvements contradicted religious fellowship, the Crown kept the situation under control and never did popular resentment against strangers degenerate into riot.

[35] J. Delumeau, *La Peur en Occident, XIV–XVIIIe siècles*, Paris, 1978.

I should like to draw the reader's attention to another, associated aspect which often placed international relations between the devil and the deep blue sea. The coasts and even the ports were the scene of perpetual confrontation between sailors – sometimes politically inspired, but often the sheer result of chance or haphazard encounters. The fearsome Wooden-Leg, a French privateer of the 'true Faith' but nonetheless a privateer, chilled the popish seamen with fear. Indeed, if England did not officially confront Spain until quite late in the century, there were constant skirmishes, beginning in the 1560s when Hawkins defied the servants of Philip II in the distant Americas. Subjects of contention accumulated among seafaring men, whose ways were often 'somewhat rough', to borrow the conventional understatement. It was easy to find a convenient *casus belli* among them, but even when uncalled for, they could inflame the international situation. The damaging effect of the conspicuous exploit of a few Zeeland privateers in 1576 has already been alluded to; such skirmishes irritated merchants by their disruption of seaborne trade. Similarly, in 1586 a good Protestant captain from La Rochelle, protected by Condé, demanded the return of his ship, the *Bonne Aventure*, which had been captured at sea by Drake. The English had taken advantage of the weakness of the crew, decimated by disease – no doubt scurvy.[36]

Often enough tensions accompanied economic grievances, but the continuous litigations relating to the insecurity of the seas necessarily affected the communities of foreigners. Indeed the Churches tended to centralise information and in turn they served as staging posts in the spread of news. The London congregation followed with interest the progress of Henri IV, 'the first of the race of Bourbon destined to succeed to the crown, and the first king of that country to be of the reformed religion, which he professes and has professed since his youth' (21 September 1589). Likewise, Le Maçon de La Fontaine, a London pastor at the end of the century who held a close correspondence with Duplessis-Mornay, was to play a role in the negotiations between Elizabeth and Henri IV. The queen of England's bitter disappointment and diplomatic frustration at the news of Henri IV's abjuration led her to write an inimitable letter in French, beginning with these words: 'Ah! What sorrow! And what lamentations I felt in my heart at the sound of such news!'[37]

Refugees and Puritans

Protestant unanimity was a political instrument rather than an efficient cause, although this rule suffered many exceptions in times of peril. The

[36] SP Dom., Eliz., Add. xxix, 170.
[37] *Bulletin de la Société de l'Histoire du Protestantisme Français* (1858), p. 263.

Church of England presented a singular aspect in comparison with the other brands of the Reformation. One may assert the influence of Calvinism upon its theology, although Richard Stauffer has emphasised the need for the greatest of caution.[38] But in the sixteenth century, without denying doctrinal niceties, the chief accusation levelled at the established Church concerned episcopacy. Many a tart remark against *prelates* emphasised their propinquity with Roman Catholicism. The Marprelate controversy gathered momentum between 1587 and 1589, when the Spanish threat and the fear of an invasion were at their height. That the Reformation had been left unfinished was to be a Puritan motto in the years to come: but what was a *Puritan* exactly? Let us beware of later connotations: Puritanism was not so much a matter of moral rectitude as genuine faith. A radical *purification* of ritual, ceremonies or creed had been long overdue. The Puritan was not yet necessarily a separatist; as far as he could, he worked within the established Church, but was to be subjected to increasing pressure.[39] The Foreign Churches in England adumbrated a more profoundly reformed Christianity: bishops could be ultimately replaced by *synods* or *classes*, in which pastors and laymen both played a part. Without radicalising Calvinism to the extreme – for Calvinism, too, could be conservative – this type of ecclesiology constituted potential danger for the Church of England. This became all the more threatening when the Puritans began to invoke the example of the Reformed Churches on the Continent to illustrate the backwardness of the English reformation. Would-be reformers did not fail to implore the arbitration of Geneva to advocate a purification of the liturgy. Of course, this was not necessarily a good thing for the stranger communities; willy-nilly, they demonstrated both England's attachment to the Protestant camp, and her detachment from the Reformation. At least this paradoxical, albeit pithy, interpretation of the situation loomed large in Puritan minds. The ominous tension between the advocates of a complete break with the past and the conservative elements, who favoured continuity, initiated one of the most important debates in early modern England: the question of gospel truth and authentic Christianity often served to disclose conflicts of a social nature.

The identification of Puritanism with the French-speaking Reformed Churches never became an established fact – Calvin himself had accepted the role of bishops in the English Reformation. This leniency may surprise the reader who knows the Puritans' unquestionable attraction for

[38] R. Stauffer, 'Les Enjeux théologiques d'un ouvrage récent', *Annales* ESC, 38 (1983), pp. 536–48.
[39] P. Collinson, *The Elizabethan Puritan Movement*, Berkeley, 1967; *idem*, 'The Elizabethan Puritans and the Foreign Reformed Churches in London', *Proceedings of the Huguenot Society of London*, 20, pp. 528–55.

Calvinism. But such sympathy did not apply exclusively to the Puritans at least prior to the 1630s; many enlightened clergymen, without any clear Puritan inclination, followed with devotion the developments of Continental Protestantism, sharing its affirmations and hesitations in matters of doctrine, such as Communion or predestination. The Puritans were not alone in England in studying the legacy of Calvin, but it remains true that their desire for a more complete Reformation – one which, far from being confined to questions of doctrine, would embrace the actual organisation of the Church – had much to infatuate the refugees. Patrick Collinson has drawn our attention to this shared benevolence in the Elizabethan period: 'As Calvinists, the strangers must have enjoyed some fellowship with their English co-religionists, even if these contacts were restricted by barriers of language, English insular prejudice and the inward-looking tendencies of the refugee group.'[40]

Again in the 1590s, pastor Jean Castel's correspondence with Theodore Beza shows the growing divergences between Geneva and the English form of Protestantism twenty-five years after the death of Calvin.[41]

> [26 August 1584] We have also to provide for posterity, so that men be not deprived of our labours through which they may know the truth, and do not let themselves be drawn back to the bad customs of former times.

> [22 July 1590] I think it expedient for the glory of God and for the peace of the Churches that you should maintain the friendship [of the Archbishop of Canterbury], without giving him any argument of which he might take advantage, lest under the pretext of our authority he does even greater injury to those *who desire a Reformation*. These poor people are much molested at present. A good part of them are in a pitiful predicament. I am far from excusing them entirely but [the authorities] are demanding a vague oath [the *ex officio* oath] that they will answer any questions put to them, and make use of the magistrates' power under civil law, and of the example of Geneva.

> [12 August 1591] ...[of] hope in this country there is none now, and it is a scarcely believable thing to see the change and alteration of men's hearts...Their affections are entirely alienated, their former pity and charity are almost completely extinguished.

Occasional sympathy, then, between Puritans and French-speaking Calvinists was stimulated by similarities, but this feeling did not imply complete identification; in the most troubled times of the next century the equivocal interplay of affinity and denial was to operate with some force. Birds of a feather flock together. This saying is largely true: yet English Puritanism and Continental Calvinism did not entirely coincide. The

---

[40] *Ibid.*, p. 529.
[41] Schickler, *Les Eglises du Refuge en Angleterre*, I, pp. 139, 143, 147, respectively.

bonds which united Puritans and Huguenots remained ambiguous and could be subjected to changing political events or individual encounters, while good relations between the English Church or State and Huguenot leaders were also to be preserved.

Charity and policy

Policy without charity is impiety.[42]
Anonymous speech in Parliament, 1588

First, charity must be mixed with policy.[43]
Francis Moore, speaking in Parliament, March 1593

What exactly were the relations between *charity* and *policy*? This was no doubt a thorny question which the refugees' presence on English soil raised forcefully. In fact, the two quotations which I have singled out both appear in the course of the parliamentary debates on the extent of the strangers' economic rights and privileges. Five years elapsed between the two speeches, delivered in the same place, but not exactly before the same men, in 1588 and 1593. In the meantime, Parliament had been dissolved and summoned anew. They express, besides, contrary opinions: the anonymous speech, preserved among the records of the Cecils – a detail worth mentioning as will soon appear – takes the foreigners' side; the second, on the contrary, wishes to limit their abilities. And yet, while their conclusions differ completely, the two statements reveal a strict parallelism and likewise refer to policy and charity. Which of the two, policy or charity, held the last word? Which consideration was to prevail?

This leads in turn to a new type of question, if we move, as it were, from the *terms of the problem* to the *problem of the terms*. Why policy? Why charity? Why refer precisely to these two schemes of values? The history of mentality is no stranger to the phenomenon: contradictory theses can be buttressed by identical systems of reference. The deep-seated unity of thought of the Elizabethan elite outshone petty divergences. This conceptual framework, which the friends and foes of the refugees held in common, should not be left unexplained. The word 'policy' still belonged to scholarly language; it referred to the affairs of the 'city' in the Greek sense of the word or 'body politic', to use an English equivalent. On no account should we attribute to the word a restricted sense – for 'policy' was the opposite of partisan confrontation, and was indeed too serious a matter, in the eyes of an Elizabethan, to conform to the dissentient

---

[42] John Strype, *Annals of the Reformation...*, 3 vols., Oxford, 1824, III (part 2), p. 568.
[43] Sir Simonds d'Ewes, *The Journals of all the Parliaments during the reign of Queen Elizabeth...*, London, 1682, p. 505.

motives of rival factions. Policy, on the contrary, consisted in the higher interest of the nation. 'Policy' was a term of consensus, and in one sense, one sense only, the strict opposite of what 'politics' means today.

Conversely, the equivocal nature of Elizabethan charity will strike the twentieth-century reader. The prime motive of charity, however spurious or genuine, was not primarily the commiseration which a few worthy souls have at all times evinced towards the unfortunate. Poor relief acted as a check on potential disorder rather than as a means of economic redistribution, as in our present welfare schemes; its main purpose was to prevent social unrest. Qualified benevolence aimed to deter idleness, begging and other disorders. The masterpiece of Elizabethan legislation were the successive poor laws which drew a lasting distinction between relief, rightly understood, and the encouragement of vice among 'sturdy beggars'. Charity, then, denoted the social treatment of pauperism as much as Christian fellowship. This rather blunt realism, which the refugees themselves commended, contributed to humanise, for all its obvious paternalism, the conditions of the most disadvantaged in all the hardships of life. Total reprobation and whipping gave way to more lenient considerations. Charity gradually moved out of the ethical, into the economic sphere What were to be the effects of immigration on the organisation of labour?

This was the main issue in the parliamentary debate of March 1593, which envisaged debarring foreigners from 'selling by way of retail any foreign commodities'. I have previously mentioned (Fig. 3) such restrictions in the case of Norwich. In 1593, the issue was whether or not such a regulation should be more widely applied and become statutory. The bill was to be defeated in the Lords, having passed through the Commons. Yet the debates as recorded by Sir Simonds d'Ewes[44] deserve our consideration. They allow us to grasp beneath the surface two opposing lines, each of which had its protector: the protectionist English nationalism strenuously advocated by Sir Walter Raleigh met the broader, international outlook and readiness to welcome foreigners, defended by the Cecil clan. Indeed, in the session of 23 March, Walter Raleigh and Robert Cecil confronted each other directly.

These clashing personalities express complementary aspects of Elizabethan England: on the one hand stood the valiant Walter Raleigh, the adventurer of the seas. The reckless fighter was to be sacrificed in the following century to friendship with Spain, without having achieved his dream, the discovery of Eldorado. On the other side, Robert Cecil was the frail champion of behind-the-scenes negotiations. The shrewd politician had inherited from his father – whom he succeeded as chief adviser of Elizabeth and then of James I – an excellent sense of mediation and

[44] See also E. Bourcier (ed.), *The Diary of Sir Simonds d'Ewes*, Paris, 1974.

compromise. This opposition between two men sums up the period, with its judicious measure of passion and reserve, prudence and pugnacity, devotion to the Queen and State.

The case of the strangers again discloses the divisions of the host society. The debate had been initiated at the request of the City of London, represented by Francis Moore, a well-known lawyer who complained of unfair competition on the part of aliens, whom he held responsible for unemployment. 'Unemployment' is partly misleading: idleness, indigence, impoverishment, and their outcome, poor relief – such were an Elizabethan's terms of reference when describing, in a language whose concepts were not as concise as those of the political economy of later times, the effects of immigration on the movements of prices and labour. Let us sum up his argument: foreign commodities were of better quality, and produced at lower cost. This created a fierce competition, which the English could not match. The religious argument, which was quickly invoked – 'the strangers who have come to find religious Refuge and assistance' – did nothing to alleviate the effects of adversity, though it may be difficult for us to come to a fair estimate. Still, Francis Moore provides us, at the same time, with a valuable indication of the refugees' area of settlement in London, when he mentions the district of St-Martin-in-the-Fields. This former ecclesiastical sanctuary, even if now a thing of the past, made the area propitious for an economic freedom of action and *laissez-faire* which paid little heed to City regulations. A new bill was read, which aimed at prohibiting foreigners from carrying on the trade of shoemaker. Our chronicler found this argument so absurd that he regarded this as a piece of provocation, or even a hoax, intended to pour ridicule on any restrictive measure.

Several speeches then followed, either *for* or *against* the foreigners and their economic activity. Henry Finch, who sat for Canterbury, described them in eulogistic terms, and expressed the wish that a plain distinction be made between 'those of the Church' and their compatriots who had come simply for reasons of convenience:

> We ought not to be undesirable, but this must be the Rule, none must so relieve Strangers, as by it to beggar themselves. But for their riches, it groweth chiefly by Parsimony and where they dwell I see not that the Nation is so much grieved at them as here in *London*, for they contribute to all Scots and Lots as we do. Though they be a church by themselves, their Example is profitable amongst us, for their children are no sooner able to go, but they are taught to serve God, and to flee idleness, for the least of them earneth his meat by his labour. Our Nation is sure more blessed for their sakes. Wherefore as the Scripture saith *Let us not grieve the Soul of the stranger*...
>
> But as I am for the strangers of the Church, so not against any Law that should be made against such strangers as be not of the Church, but

> here only for Merchandise; and those who have come here for conscience sake only, may again (the fire being quenched) safely return into their own Countries.[45]

This is an invaluable testimony, in particular as far as the Walloons at Canterbury were concerned. Moreover, it seems to be relatively accurate: moral rigour and the sanctification of work did indeed correspond to the avowed ideal of the Calvinist Churches. Yet I would still insist, as I have done previously, on the difficulty of drawing a strict boundary between refugees and aliens. Henry Finch seems to have been inspired by common sense when he eventually pointed out that the complexity of the retail trade would technically hamper any legislation. Profane wisdom met the prerequisites of Christian charity. Doing good to others is to guard oneself against the future possibility of adversity or deprivation: 'In the days of Queen *Mary*, when our Cause was as theirs is now, those Countries did allow us that liberty, which now we seek to deny them. They are strangers now, we may be strangers hereafter. So let us do as we would be done unto.'

Thus, Christ's injunction 'love thy neighbour as thyself' combined with the lessons of recent history to eulogise solidarity among God-fearing Protestants.

The debate was adjourned until Friday 23 March, while a commission examined the bill. We may now turn to Sir Walter Raleigh's speech on that date. With characteristic vigour, he forthrightly declared his irritation:

> Whereas it is pretended, that for strangers it is against Charity, against Honour, against Profit to expel them; in my opinion it is no matter of Charity to relieve them. For first, such as fly hither have forsaken their own king; and religion is no pretext for them, for we have no Dutchmen here, but such as came from those Provinces where the Gospel is Preached, and here they live disliking our Church. For *Honour*, it is Honour to use strangers as they use us; and it is a lightness in a common-wealth, yea a baseness in a Nation to give a liberty to another Nation which we cannot receive again.

This glib oratorical display only drew a very timid reply from Robert Cecil, who invoked his personal conscience.

There was, besides, a tide of mounting xenophobia as the 1593 London plague was followed by several bad harvests between 1594 and 1598. In times of crisis the endemic distrust of strangers gathered momentum and came to the surface. Immigrants or minorities are natural scapegoats in times of hardship. That same year, a violent text was directed against all strangers, including the Protestant refugees:

[45] D'Ewes, *Journals of all the Parliaments*, pp. 506–7, for this and the following quotations.

> Doth not the world see, that you, beastly brutes, the Belgians or rather drunken drones, and fainthearted Flemings; and you, fraudulent father, Frenchmen, by your cowardly flight from your own natural countries, have abandoned the same into the hands of your proud, cowardly enemies, and have, by a feigned hypocrisy and counterfeit show of religion, placed yourselves here in a most fertile soil, under a most gracious and merciful prince, who hath been contented to the great prejudice of her own natural subjects, to suffer you to live in better care and more freedom than her own people? Be it known to all Flemings and Frenchmen that which follows: for that there shall be many a sore stripe. Apprentices will rise to the number 2336. And all apprentices and journeymen will down with the Flemings and strangers.[46]

The text is self-explicit. Its frenzied character and ominous mention of the number of apprentices, though derisive in themselves, contained a real threat. A typology of city mobs would certainly show the importance of particular age-groups in early modern hooliganism: the world of apprentices was no doubt permeated by its specific tokens of identification and its sub-culture may often elude us. But at the time the portentous May Day 1517 still lingered on in the vision of 'the world turned upside down'; the apprentices could suddenly become a devastating crowd. Was xenophobia a misdirected class struggle? Or was it an irrational escalation? Both, no doubt, and we have much to learn from the study of fear and specific fears.[47] Not that one should pay too much attention to these manifestations of vindictiveness in Elizabethan England. They remained exceptional yet they had to be mentioned in passing, for they are the dark side of a fruitful experience. The welcome extended to strangers was indeed of good omen for the future of the country.

[46] Strype, *Annals of the Reformation*, IV, p. 234.
[47] Delumeau, *La Peur en Occident; idem, Le Péché et la peur, la culpabilisation en occident, XIII – XVIIIe siècles*, Paris, 1983.

II SPLENDOURS AND MISFORTUNES OF THE SEVENTEENTH CENTURY

3 From religious loyalty to political exasperation: 1603–1642

The world is not reborn with each century; rarely does the end of a reign coincide with a radical transformation of the country at large. The caesura of the year 1603, marked by the decease of Queen Elizabeth on 24 March, is no exception to this rule. And yet, in the absence of any conspicuous break with the past, the accession of James I provides a convenient subdivision. Indeed, the two reigns are joined by strands of continuity which had long been underestimated and minimised by jaundiced historians: the 'Glorious sixteenth century' of the Tudor sovereigns was often idealised to the detriment of the 'Dark seventeenth century'. In the 1730s, Bolingbroke introduced the period in these terms:

> The scene we are now going to open will appear vastly different from that which we have just closed. Instead of an uninterrupted, pleasing harmony of government, we shall meet with a perpetual, jarring dissonance; instead of success and glory abroad, disappointment and contempt; instead of satisfaction, prosperity and union at home, discontent, distress and at last civil war, will present themselves to us in all their horrors.[1]

Bolingbroke went on to deplore the fact that James I had not followed the example of Elizabeth. Lord Bolingbroke's impressive burst of eloquence expresses the common concern of his enlightened age for public virtue; but later historians did not fail to educate their contemporaries when they used to emphasise the sharp contrast between the two periods. Besides, Bolingbroke, who has often been treated with contempt in his approach to history in spite of Voltaire's eulogies, had at least the merit of echoing the common wisdom of his time. G.R. Elton has disapprovingly

---

[1] Bolingbroke, *Remarks on the History of England* (1730–1), *Historical Writings*, Chicago, 1972, p. 275.

commented upon Bolingbroke's role as 'a purveyor of mostly tedious commonplaces'.[2]

We shall be wary, then, of received notions. Elizabeth I's love affair with her subjects was marked by occasional episodes of litigation, rightly emphasised forty years ago by John Neale's study on the different Parliaments of the reign. The criticism of monopolies, which was to bedevil the Jacobeans, had already embittered the last years of Elizabeth's reign.[3]

Basically the statistical approach permeating contemporary studies of price movements or the reconstruction of past populations as well as the history of mentality has tended to invalidate the ascendancy of such or such a king or queen upon the destiny of their country. This bloodless revolution in the hands of peaceful historians tend to obliterate the personal role of the monarch. Though in the observer's eye any division into periods is relative, this point of view calls for some qualification. Life has none of the regularity of a mechanism; the succession of kings, with their episodes of splendour or affliction, are the natural landmarks of remembered experience. Accordingly, the reign of James I deserves a separate treatment: the image of the Protestant defender of the faith underwent contradictory developments. While some of the best Continental pastors praised him, James I aroused the condemnation of the Puritans. The first half of the seventeenth century witnessed the close-knit association of blind devotion to the king and political exasperation which I retained as the title of this chapter. The phenomenon was certainly far from new, but James I's emphasis on the *divine right* of kings gave it wider currency. The political philosophy of the new dynasty did indeed mark a break with the England of the Tudors, and for once the term *absolutism* may sound appropriate. A few words of explanation are necessary: the unflinching authority of the Tudors is not open to question; yet from James I onwards the sacred character of the king made him 'God's lieutenant upon Earth'. The king's power came from the Lord and, conversely, God was to be the sole judge of his actions, good, bad or indifferent. It is difficult to give a fair appraisal of James I's reign. Generations of historians have endeavoured to show the unwarranted nature of absolutism in England, by stressing undue influences from other countries: the dynasty's Scottish origin or the contamination of French modes of thought were equally blamed. I shall not dwell upon this debate here, except indirectly; but I should like to show, using the testimony of the refugees, that Jacobean absolutism possessed an unusual degree of coherence, and constituted in its own right an original, albeit unpopular,

---

[2] G.R. Elton, *Modern Historians on British History*..., London, 1970, p. 181.
[3] J.E. Neale, *Elizabeth I and her Parliaments, 1559–1601*, 2 vols., London, 1949 and 1957 . To be supplemented by T.E. Hartley, *Proceedings in the Parliaments of Elizabeth, 1558–1581*, Leicester, 1981.

response to the twofold challenge of the Puritans' opposition at home and the Catholic threat abroad.

The Jacobean peace, *c.* 1603–*c.* 1625

The dark sides of the Jacobean era have been grossly exaggerated. The good tidings of James I's accession reached London in an atmosphere of sanguine expectation, as a recent work reminded us:

> His advent was welcome. Queen Elizabeth had long outlived men's affection, if not their fear and respect, and after fifty years of petticoat government (since Mary I's accession in 1553), they welcomed a male ruler, and the end of female tantrums, sulks and irrationality. James was a highly intelligent man who had found time in the hurly-burly of Scottish politics to publish several volumes of quite creditable poetry and biblical exegesis, as well as his more notorious political treatises, the *Basilikon Doron* (1603) and *The True Law of Free Monarchies* (1598). The two last were published in England on his accession, and his forthright insistence on the Divine Right of Kings did not at this stage frighten his new subjects as much as it did the Whig historians.[4]

J.P. Kenyon's sarcastic remarks on the reign of Elizabeth may not be altogether inappropriate. The mistrust of women and the high praise of manliness were well-established features at the time, and the reader will certainly remember the exasperation of John Knox, fifty years before, at the 'monstrous regiment of women', i.e. Mary Stuart and Mary Tudor. Theodore Beza in Geneva insisted that the reign of a queen was no more than an exception, and should be regarded as a mixed blessing, 'seeing that the Lord, to chastise the cowardice and the effeminate hearts of men, has often favoured such dominations of women'.[5]

The interview at Greenwich, 23 May 1603

The Refuge joined in the celebration of the manly virtues of the king. Out of his concern for his image abroad, James I received a delegation led by pastor Le Maçon de La Fontaine at Greenwich on 23 May 1603, barely five days after his arrival. The envoys extolled the new king, and their eulogies hinted at 'the faith of Abraham, the chastity and foresight of Joseph, the benevolence and fidelity of Moses, the victories of Joshua and David, the riches and wisdom of Solomon, the sanctity of Hezekiah and Josias'.

[4] J.P. Kenyon, *Stuart England*, Pelican, 1978, p. 48.
[5] T. Beza, *Confession de la foi chrétienne* (1560), quoted by R.M. Kingdon (ed.), *Du droit des magistrats*, Geneva, 1970, p. 71.

This list of names should not be left unexplained: the biblical allusion took on an allegorical value which bestowed upon the new reign the fictious legitimacy of God's elect and chosen ones. God's design and the history of men were thereby supposed to coincide, a common literary device in the Scriptures. This lineage, borrowed exclusively from the Old Testament, emphasised the manly figure of the patriarch with Abraham, of the lawgiver in the case of Moses, of the sovereign – David and Solomon – without forgetting the power of the sword with Joshua, or the reforming spirit of Josias – so dear to the refugees' hearts. At Greenwich, the aspirations of the time of Edward, of happy memory, were revived and we may discern between the lines the ideal of kingship: power, justice and faith. Not counting the chastity of Joseph which, while avoiding the dissemination of arrogant royal bastards had, in fact, its disadvantages: the ascendancy of favourites, their fortunes and lavish expenditures which were taken to the extreme at the end of the reign by the mercurial Buckingham, brought the Crown into considerable disrepute.

But the adoption of this biblical code answered another objective still. Everything in this carefully regulated ballet of homage to the king shows an evident familiarity within his thought. For here was a sovereign who prided himself upon his theology; his immoderate inclination for *belles lettres* along with a versatile talent and genuine intellectual curiosity had led him to publish two or three treatises infused with (nearly) the same biblical allusions. Le Maçon de La Fontaine had certainly read James I beforehand, and much to his advantage it was, for the king was highly receptive to his message, based on the mutual recognition of the throne and the pulpit. The Churches' role was to legitimise such an auspicious reign while the king was expected to grant his benevolent protection in return.

James I was delighted and he replied:

> Messieurs. Although you have never seen me until now, nonetheless I am no stranger to you, nor unknown. You know, as to my religion, who I am, not only by what report you may have heard of me, *but also by my writings*, in which I have truly expressed the affections of my heart. For this reason, I need not use many words to express my goodwill towards you, who have taken refuge here for Religion's sake. Two things, as I perceive, made my late sister the queen renowned throughout the world; one was the desire she always had to maintain and further the service of God in this kingdom. And the other was her hospitality towards foreigners, the praise of which I wish to inherit. I know well, by the testimony of the lords of this kingdom, as you have told me, that you always prayed for her, and that you have not gone beyond the bounds of your duty. I know also that you have enriched this kingdom with several crafts, manufactures and politic arts.
>
> If there had been opportunity, while I was still far removed in another corner of the world, I would have shown you the affection I bear towards

you. But since I have never attempted or wished to encroach upon the property of any Prince, and since also it has now pleased God to make me King of this country, I assure you that if anyone should molest you in your Churches, if you address your grievance unto me, I shall avenge you. And although you are not my own subjects, yet I shall defend you as much as any Prince in the world.[6]

The address – translated here from James I's French – presents few difficulties apart from its slightly allusive character. The 'lords of this kingdom' include the 'lords spiritual' – or bishops – but the refugees' highest protection probably came from Robert Cecil, the architect of the Jacobean succession, who was held in high esteem at the time. Moreover, James I referred in passing to the late queen's moderation, and promised to show greater ardour for the Protestant faith than she had done, granting the refugees really effective help against their enemies. James I was indeed a new Josias, at least in his speech and later drew considerable advantage from the astute friendship of the Reformed Churches, which buttressed his authority. His political philosophy was to be absolutist in inspiration, but its avowed authoritarianism was only the counterpart of the humiliation endured, for so many years, at the hands of the unruly Scottish noblemen. The Greenwich interview marked a turning point. A mature king of thirty-seven, already experienced in matters of State, pledged his full support to the foreign Protestants – this was to involve a lasting collaboration both at home and abroad, which we will need to examine more closely.

From loyalty to loyalism

A persistent misunderstanding opposed Calvinism and monarchies. This was not so much a matter of doctrine – for why not give back unto Caesar what belongs to Caesar? – as of legitimate suspicion: the son of Mary Stuart had long resented the outspoken reforming zeal and activism of his compatriots. The Scots derived some of their inspiration from Theodore Beza, Calvin's successor in Geneva. Nonetheless, James I was determined to use the Huguenots to the best of their abilities, both to isolate the Puritans at home and to foster his Protestant image on the Continent.

Jacobean absolutism has often been niggardly disparaged and would certainly deserve a complete reappraisal, in the light of the new king's attitude to the French Protestants. In fact, both sides needed to buttress their cause. The times were ripe for reconciliation between Calvinism and kingship: from 1598 onwards, the Edict of Nantes offered the hope of a peaceful settlement in France. The image of the king was the cement that

[6] Schickler, *Les Eglises du Refuge en Angleterre*, I, pp. 369–70.

bound together erstwhile enemies. The Huguenots were granted a number of privileges by Henri IV, himself a former Protestant, which guaranteed their military might and right to worship freely in certain specific areas, to avoid all conflicts with the surrounding Catholic majority. (On all these aspects, see E. Le Roy Ladurie's Afterword.) A concern for the situation in France bore quite unmistakably upon the refugees' celebration of James I: they seized the opportunity to vindicate themselves of the charge of seditious republicanism. While James I's primary concern was to affirm the authentically Protestant character of his own brand of absolutism, genuine Protestants were all too keen to show their loyalty towards kings. Elizabeth Labrousse was among the first to examine the grounds of this change in Huguenot sensibilities in the early seventeenth century: 'The Edict of Nantes had been imposed on the French Catholics by royal authority and, in France at least, the rule of civil tolerance could proceed only from the sovereign pleasure of the King.'[7]

We might even say that absolutism as such was a new idea. The word has met with the disfavour of numerous historians, especially in England. Yet the identification which soon became cumbersome, of King and State, was a necessity, at least in the case of France, to heal the wounds of the wars of religion. In addition, James I's somewhat innocuous theological affectation resulted in a number of carefully penned treatises which mark a turning point in the history of ideas – as they tend to bridge the gap between philosophers and kings. In the meantime, the French Protestants themselves had 'incorporated predestination in the sphere of the state'[8] – thus confirming the sacred character of kings. The resolute destroyers of idolatry, who had advocated the worship of God alone, came to adopt the same pulpit oratory as the Catholics when speaking of kings. In France the divine right of kings became the stock-in-trade of ordinary preachers of all persuasions.

Another aspect of this celebration was the sustained and vivid memory of the wars of religion which brought to mind relentless images of disorder, carnage and bloodshed. Submission to the sovereign and his authority were the only possible means to cope with fallen human nature and metaphysical evil, an obsessive memory. A few years later, Hobbes was to draw similar conclusions from the English civil wars. In this context, the glorification of the king was not simply sycophantic; it was born of blood and tears. Nor was the refugees' loyalty to James I simply dictated by circumstances; it followed a coherent political plan. The refugees' need for royal protection has already been emphasised, but this attitude, common to most minorities, was not the only element at play. The vindications of James I were more than dutiful formalities. There

---

[7] E. Labrousse, *Pierre Bayle, hétérodoxie et rigorisme*, The Hague, 1964, p. 495. See also Solange Deyon, *Du loyalisme au refus*, Lille, 1976.
[8] D. Richet, *La France moderne: l'esprit des institutions*, Paris, 1973, p. 56.

existed a genuine and profound *sympathy*, between the French Protestants
and the king of England, more evident than in the reign of Elizabeth, who
had been too astute a politician to commit herself too much on their
behalf.

This was a question of sense and sensibility: the young James VI of
Scotland had expressed unbounded admiration for the Huguenot poet
Guillaume de Salluste, sieur du Bartas, which brought him, in return, the
gratitude of the author of *La Semaine* – a best-selling epic on the
Creation. Likewise, in 1610, Isaac Casaubon, a renowned scholar who had
received a pension from Henri IV, encountered the warmest of welcomes
in England. This learned layman, devoted to patristic studies, found the
Church of England most congenial to his temperament. He was confirmed
in his piety by a royal pension of £300 and a prebend at Canterbury. At
his death in 1614, he deserved to be buried in Westminster Abbey; his son
Meric, a confirmed Anglican, as we shall see later in this study, also
expressed his affection for the Church.

But it was Pierre du Moulin who gave this privileged Anglo-French
relationship its greatest lustre. Two of his sons, Pierre and Louis – as it
happens, radically opposed in their convictions – settled in their turn
across the Channel, and distinguished themselves in controversy. Pierre II
du Moulin, so called to avoid confusion with his father Pierre I, became
one of the fervent mainstays of the *Ecclesia anglicana* which his
independent brother vilified. This famous ecclesiastical lineage – which
shows the existence of true Church dynasties – illustrates the links which
apparently dissimilar Churches forged under the benevolent eye of James
I. This ideological proximity between James I and Continental Protestants
at the very outset of Puritan disavowal, raises anew the fundamental
question of the relationship between political authority and religion. The
image of the confederate Huguenot, who was supposed to be rebellious
and seditious by nature, was a lasting concern: the best answer to the
suspicion of *republicanism* was the friendship of a king like James I. One
of the strategies of Catholic propaganda, even in England, was to claim
'that Catholics are better friends to monarchies than Calvinists', to quote
a secret correspondence with the French ambassador in the 1620s.[9]

It must be added, to atone for this distrust, that during the French wars
of religion, about 1570, Theodore Beza, Duplessis-Mornay and Hotman,
or even Buchanan in Scotland, had clearly advocated open rebellion
against a sovereign who had turned a tyrant. The possibility of putting the
despot to death, the question of *tyrannicide*, greatly preoccupied men's
minds in England, where the execution of Mary Queen of Scots gave the
debate a timeliness reinforced by Shakespeare's *Julius Caesar*. Was it
permissible to kill tyrants? In the sixteenth century, there was nothing

<hr />

[9] B. Cottret, 'Diplomatie et éthique de l'Etat', in *L'Etat baroque*, Paris, 1985.

innocuous about this ominous perspective. The precedent of Moses'
insubordination to Pharaoh, a passing allusion to the Acts of the Apostles
– 'we ought to obey God rather than men' (5:29) – the suitability of
biblical imagery in various circumstances, all conferred a freedom of
expression which challenged all objections to the contrary. This mastery
of scriptural reference, the precise knowledge of verse and chapter, this
Canaan dialect, reflected a sincere faith, but they also proved extremely
efficient, thanks to their rhetorical strength. The most daring allusions to
the present were thereby fully justified.

James I was no stranger to these scathing rejoinders. The former pupil
of Buchanan, who had inauspiciously insisted on the covenant which
bound the magistrate to his people, was to retain throughout his life an
understandable distrust of his mentor and of all Scottish reformers. He
frowned upon the 'tribuni plebis', advocating a 'democracy' in Church
and State which led up to the execution of his mother, Mary Queen of
Scots. Though a Protestant at heart, he regarded some of the reformers as
extremists. In fact, in his moderation, James I had everything to gain from
the official recognition of the European Reformed Churches. As king of
England, he absolved them from the accusation of republicanism, while in
turn they comforted his public image as 'defender of the Faith' and even
sustained his theological ambitions. Who were most to be feared of
Catholic or Protestant subjects? Each camp had harboured its zealots; yet
the assassination of Henri III, the French Catholic League, the
Gunpowder Plot, the murder of Henri IV, tilted the balance unfavourably
towards the Catholic side. The Jesuits and their enduring hostility to
James suited the Protestant cause: they seemed to confirm Rome's scant
regard for kings, while forbidding loyal, lawful subjects to take an oath of
allegiance which English Catholics favoured. James I's retort, levelled
directly at Bellarmine and Pope Paul V, was translated into French, Latin
and Dutch with the help of pastor Le Maçon de La Fontaine. Between
1607 and 1609 this *Triplici nodo, triplex cuneus, or a Vindication of the Oath
of Allegiance* expressed James' wrath. He called all the Christian Churches
to the bar to indict the virulence of the papacy. This parallel between
Catholics and Protestants, who both harboured fanatics and supporters of
King and Country, tended to blur all clear-cut distinctions and gave
greater cogency to James I's absolutist claims. The Jesuits, as well as the
Calvinists, had advocated in turn the rights of people and the dignity of
kings. Robert Parsons S.J. had recognised in 1594 that election, as much
as birth, could legitimise the succession of kings to the detriment of the
fiction of divine right.[10] The absolutism of James I can be partly explained
by the Jesuits' challenge. In short, whether Protestantism or Catholicism,

[10] Dolman [Robert Parsons, S.J.], *Conference about the Next Succession to the Crown of
England*, 1594.

no religion whatever extended its unqualified blessings to kings. Neither were Catholics necessarily absolutist nor Protestants dyed-in-the-wool republicans.

Pierre du Moulin, James I's Calvinist supporter

I shall dwell a moment here upon a striking destiny. Pierre du Moulin (1568–1658) has left a most remarkable autobiography displaying his keen devotion to England.[11] The son of a pastor, he narrowly escaped the massacre of St Bartholomew's Day in his youth, saved by a woman 'of the opposite religion, but who bore affection to us'. She hid the four-year-old child under the straw while the attackers attempted to exterminate the whole family. His mother died of exhaustion six months later. The orphan passed his childhood between Soisson and Sedan. At twenty, he went up to Paris, but owing to the uprising of the Holy Catholic League could not remain there; finally, putting his trust in God, he crossed to England. The year was 1588, the time of the Invincible Armada. And naturally, he came into contact with pastor Castel in London, but once again he owed a great deal to the friendship of a Catholic, an Englishman named Constable – 'this gentleman, although a Papist, nonetheless showed me kindness and wished me well'. He received news from France; his brother Eleazar had been buried alive in the religious struggle. Violence, banishment, bereavement and cruelty lurked in the minds of the generation who were to embrace absolutism in early seventeenth-century France. Nonetheless, in the midst of discord, disconcerting manifestations of human solidarity emerged; Pierre du Moulin remembered with gratitude his Catholic servant and English host.

Then, thanks to the protection of the countess of Rutland, Cambridge opened its doors to him: he was awarded a scholarship to become a pastor. In 1592, aged twenty-four, he moved to Holland, and first taught 'Greek, Music and Horace' at Leiden, and eventually philosophy. All in all, he tells us, 'all the time of my residence in foreign countries amounted to ten years, and during all that time God showed me the favour of never being bedridden for more than three days'.

France, England, Holland: a century before the Revocation one of the principal axes of Protestant migration was already fixed. Pierre du Moulin's disconcerting mobility from one country to another or from Cambridge to Leiden was, indeed, a lasting idiosyncracy of the Huguenot elite. But it also extended to other social strata, especially in times of large-scale persecution and migration.

[11] 'La vie de M. Pierre du moulin, ministre de l'Eglise réformée de Sedan et professeur en théologie, escrite par luy-même', *Bulletin de la Société de l'Histoire du Protestantisme Français* (1884), pp. 170–83, 333–44, 465–77.

Appointed pastor at the age of thirty, Pierre du Moulin performed his ministry at the Temple of Charenton, which from 1605 onwards was attended by the Protestant community of Paris. This illustrious office, brought him into contact with the great families of the capital; but despite this respectable, established position, he made frequent moves to Alsace, Lorraine, Vivarais or Dauphine, according to the demands of the various synods, and owing to human encounters. In 1614, he published a treatise against Cardinal Bellarmine, *De monarchia temporali papae*, which brought him a gift of several hundred pounds from James I, and an invitation to England, in February 1615. James I bestowed upon the French pastor endless tokens of his generosity:

> This king received me very kindly; I usually stood behind his chair at his meals...He had me preach before him in French in his royal chapel at Greenwich. He also wished me to take the degree of D.D. at Cambridge. There a public disputation was held, in which the king himself proposed some arguments. I spent three months on this journey, and took my leave of the king at Midsummer...He gave my brother Jean a golden chain worth two hundred crowns while I was granted a prebend at Canterbury, with a fine house. Later he also gave me a rectorship in Wales. The canons of the chapter at Canterbury, at my reception, wanted to oblige me upon oath to conform to the laws and customs of England. But this I would do only on condition of doing nothing prejudicial to the obedience which I owe to my king and to the ecclesiastical discipline established in our French Churches; and this was granted to me.[12]

The good terms he established with James I, whose unflinching esteem the pastor regards with gratitude, did not undermine the specific identity of French Protestantism, or the subject's loyalty to his native kingdom. And yet Pierre du Moulin remained under close scrutiny, and after each stay in England, in 1615 or ten years later in 1625, he was briefly detained. Likewise, no Frenchman was allowed to attend the synod of Dordrecht in 1618. The Frenchman eventually accepted a chair of divinity at the Academy of Sedan in 1621, a mark of caution on the part of one of the most conspicuous polemicists in the international Protestant movement. The opponent of Bellarmine or François de Sales would rely on the Word rather than on the sword to spread the 'true faith'. The formidable controversialist put his pen at the service of James I and wrote the *Remonstrance of the most gracious King James I – for the Right of Kings and the independence of their crowns. Against an oration of the most illustrious Card. of Perron...*, Cambridge, 1616. Originally published in French in 1615, it appeared in an English and Latin edition in the following year. This treatise was directed at Cardinal Du Perron, one of the most prestigious orators of the French clergy, and at his speeches in

---

[12] *Ibid.*, p. 343.

the Estates-General of 1614–15. James I astutely shifted the debate from the strictly theological sphere to the political domain: all subjects owed absolute loyalty to their king who required their oath in exchange for his protection. Thus Gallicanism and 'Anglicanism' – as it were – showed a common concern for national autonomy; in the last instance, the power of the pope amounted to a challenge to all nation-states. But the most compelling argument was the recent assassination of Henri IV, an ominous sign to which no reader could remain indifferent.

James I's motives and inclinations to use the talents of the French pastor and append his signature to the fruit of their joint endeavour may be foreseeable. Yet what did du Moulin expect in return? Honours would be a trifling answer; the clergyman had a greater plan in mind: as early as February 1615, he informed Duplessis-Mornay that he intended to work towards the unification of the Churches.[13] His aim was to bring about a close cooperation between Calvinists, Lutherans and 'Anglicans' – to use a slightly anachronistic term. During his stay in England, Pierre du Moulin seemed to be filled with elation. But his was a mercurial temperament, subject to phases of exaltation and occasional bouts of 'melancholy', that ailment of the age which scarcely spared him. In the spring of 1615, the future seemed radiant; a remarkable document was sent directly to the provincial synod of the Ile-de-France in 1615: 'Preliminary measures towards the union of the Christian Churches which have thrown off the yoke of the papacy, and towards resolving the differences which have already arisen, or might arise in the future'. The king of England was invested with a particularly illustrious mission, 'being the greatest and most powerful and moreover the most clear-sighted and the most favourably disposed of all sovereigns'.[14] The outcome of this association should have been the constitution, with the help of James I, of new Reformed Churches, incorporating the former 'Lutherans, Calvinists and Sacramentarians'. Moreover, though Pierre du Moulin was more sceptical on this count, why not eventually contact the Church of Rome?

Our author's disappointment ten years later, when he described his 'atrabilious' humour, may be explained by his frustrated expectations. But why set such high hopes on the English monarchy? This reminds us of Emile Leonard's caustic, albeit justified, observation: 'having become the adversary of the Roman pontiff, James I would gladly have played the Protestant Pope'. Conversely, Pierre du Moulin would have been an

---

[13] Letter received in March 1615, *Bulletin de la Société de l'Histoire du Protestantisme Français* (1858), p. 402.

[14] Pierre du Moulin, 'Escrit de Monsieur de Moulin envoié de Londres par luy mesme au Synode Provincial de l'Isle de France...', in David Blondel, *Actes Authentiques*, Amsterdam, 1655, pp. 72ff.

excellent Calvinist bishop, and as no bishoprics were available at home, the French pastor, who according to a recent study had 'not at all grasped the Anglican niceties', applied for the see of Gloucester in October 1624. Secretary Conway, who answered his letter, insisted that he wrote in the name of 'God's best Lieutenant on Earth' – i.e. James I – and addressed du Moulin as 'one of the most remarkable Lights of God's church'. Yet the good councillor decently avoided to mention his correspondent's immodest proposal and preferred to concentrate on lesser transactions of a few hundred pounds, namely a present of £200 and a Welsh prebend yielding £100 per annum. The presents topped the gifts the Frenchman had already received ten years before on his first visit, including a canonry in Canterbury, which passed on to his son after 1660.[15]

A genuine form of absolutism

How is one to explain James I's particular prestige for a Huguenot? Indeed, seventeenth-century style is often hyperbolic, yet that reverence went beyond conventional rhetoric. Besides, the community of interests and esteem, the loyalty of Protestant subjects or the depth of James I's convictions shed an unusual light on the period. What was the philosophy of the Crown? How could it prove acceptable to Protestant consciences? Three principal ideas emerge from James I's writings: the emphasis on the Scriptures, the idea of *adiaphora* or 'indifferent things' and last but not least, a striking obsession with the law.

The insistence on the Bible provides a thread of continuity or inspiration, with Le Maçon de La Fontaine's address at Greenwich. The Old Testament served to justify royal power: James I insisted on the figure of the priest-king, in order to counteract the pretensions of the pope, if not of clerics of all persuasion. The royal priesthood – which rested on the example of David and Solomon – enabled James I to say to his son in *Basilikon Doron*: 'your office is likewise mixed, betwixt the Ecclesiastical and Civil estate: For a king is not mere *laicus*, as both the Papists and Anabaptists would have him, to which error also the Puritans incline over far'.[16]

A century ago, J.N. Figgis' work on the divine right of kings clarified our understanding of Jacobean phraseology whose practical aims are too often ignored. Having established that James I personified the doctrine of the divine right of kings, the Victorian historian revealed that one of the aims of this absolutist claim was to reduce the pretensions of the clergy.

---

[15] Léonard, *Histoire générale du protestantisme*, II, p. 178; E. Labrousse, 'Great Britain as Envisaged by the Huguenots of the seventeenth Century', in Scouloudi (ed.), *Huguenots in Britain*, pp. 143–57. The correspondence between du Moulin and Conway is in the Public Record Office, SP 78/73, 254 and 277.

[16] *The Political Works of James I* (1616), Harvard, 1918, p. 45.

This emphasis on the divine right of kings, however repellent for true-born Englishmen, was not a mere flight of fancy, nor was it purely an effect of bigotry: it served both to defy the pope and to reassure the established Church by dismissing the claims of Catholics and Puritans alike.[17]

The second, and most original, feature of this absolutism was its insistence on the concept of *adiaphora*. The term *adiaphora* may sound relatively technical, though we can all understand that some articles may be held necessary to be saved, while others are regarded as indifferent. Thus faith alone, the free gift of God, conferred justification, and it was readily opposed to the outward demonstrations of piety. This distinction, between necessary and incidental beliefs is associated in particular with the irenic teachings of the Lutheran Philip Melanchthon, who endeavoured to conciliate the different Christian confessions. According to recent studies,[18] it seems that Melanchthon, who was concerned in the tradition of Erasmus with the precepts, maxims and wisdom of Christianity, simply gave weight to an accepted idea. All plans for Christian unity are bound to involve an assessment of the basic tenets of Christianity, transcending individual variations. Pierre du Moulin expressed the hope that universal agreement might be reached on the fundamentals of revelation. James I conferred a truly political dimension upon this distinction between things necessary and things indifferent, when he extended it to the whole of social life. 'Indifferent things' are among the guiding themes of the *Basilikon Doron*. They justify an extremely virulent indictment of the Puritans. The latter longed for total purification of the ways and means of the Church in accordance with the Word of God. James I explained that they failed to grasp the practical necessity of prescribed rites. For the sake of uniformity, the Crown could enforce certain rules which, albeit indifferent in themselves, acted as a useful reminder of national unity; such were, for instance, the sign of the Cross, or the distinctive vestments of the clergy. In every country strict discipline was to be enforced: some common practices depended either on the sovereign's decree or on the lasting manners and customs of the people. The Puritans did not share this functional concern for tradition and deep-rooted memory. They wished to transform, in the name of the absolute, forms of piety which custom had sanctioned if not sanctified. They were therefore guilty, in James I's eyes, of mental confusion. But worse was in store: they could even rebel against the magistrates' ordinance. They were led astray as the Anabaptists had been before them and failed to distinguish the particular case from the general law. Their narrow-mindedness, disproportionate attention to detail and fear of idolatry

---

[17] J.N. Figgis, *The Divine Right of Kings*, Cambridge, 1896; republished with an introduction by G.R. Elton, New York, 1965, p. 257.
[18] Bernard J. Verkamp, *The Indifferent Means*, Ohio Univ. Press, 1977.

taken to the point of austerity undermined royal authority, impaired the irresistible attraction of ceremonies and thwarted the legitimate desire of the king to determine, for the greater good of his people, if not the articles of faith, at least the outward forms of devotion:

> But learn wisely to discern betwixt points of salvation and indifferent things, betwixt substance and ceremonies, and betwixt the express commandment and will of God in his Word, and the invention or ordinance of man; since all that is necessary for salvation is contained in the Scripture: for in anything that is expressly commanded or prohibited in the book of God, ye cannot be over precise... But as for all other things not contained in the Scripture, spare not to use or alter them, as the necessity of the time shall require.[19]

The third bone of contention was the king's relation to the law. The meaning of term *magistrate* in Protestant thought is self-explicit: the word applied indiscriminately to all those who held civil power. Every king was thus a magistrate. The theme of the judge-king – borrowed from Solomon in the Bible – was decisive for James I. The king was *the* great lawgiver – a situation which in England was tempered by increasing competition: in the course of the century Parliament and common lawyers attempted to defend an alternative concept. In 1607, James I declared forthrightly to his Parliament, in a curious mixture of English and Latin, and with conspicuous priggish pedantry: '*Rex est judex* for his is *lex loquens*.'[20] This judge-king, who interpreted the law, had the solemnity which divine vocation confers, for being the judge of men, the king cannot be judged except by God.

Did this argument win over the aforementioned acceptance of the French Protestants? They did not contradict it, as far as we know. Apparently the Refuge did not hesitate to support the Jacobean theocracy which had the merit of showing that appeals to the sole Word of God could be reconciled with monarchy. According to James I, the authority of the king and the authority of the Scripture were all one. The authorised version, 'appointed to be read in Churches', rests on this dual authority. Yet this official translation was not only a contribution to the religious unity of the kingdom; its avowed claim was to limit the influence of Geneva. At the Hampton Court conference of January 1604, the new king and his clergy had confronted one another. The idea of a new English translation emanated directly from the royal person; James had clearly expressed his strenuous opposition to the Geneva Bible whose notes were deemed, in the king's own words, 'very partial, untrue, seditious and savouring too much of dangerous and treacherous conceits'.[21] In fact,

[19] *The Political Works...*, p. 17.   [20] *Ibid.*, p. 299.
[21] William Barlow, *The Summe and Substance of the Conference...at Hampton Court*, London, 1604, p. 46.

what comes to the surface is the obsession with tyrannicide, or more simply with disobedience to the king, should his hardened heart – like that of Pharaoh – know nothing of clemency.

This led James I to issue a twofold recommendation: 'first, that errors in matters of faith might be rectified and amended. Secondly, that matters indifferent might rather be interpreted.' Reason of State demanded an established form of worship, dispelling endless local variations: the doctrine of the *adiaphora* provided a guiding thread. But paradoxically, the recognition of *indifferent things* did not lead to toleration; on the contrary, it justified constraint, by entrusting to the Crown the determination of lawful forms of piety. The heterogeneous expressions of faith, the manifold diversity of the Churches, the decline and fall of medieval Christendom were justified, in so far as they coincided with sundry kingdoms. If one pursues James I's reasoning, each country was left to establish its own Church without permitting dissent.

On that same occasion, James I also expressed his deep aversion for Puritanism, which 'as well agreeth with a monarch, as God and the Devil. Then Jack and Tom and Will and Dick shall meet, and at their pleasures censure me, and my Council, and all our proceedings.'[22] The allusion was hardly favourable to the presbyters. But several English Puritans drew their inspiration from the Scots, and how can one overlook the affinity which linked native Presbyterianism to Calvinism as a whole? James I was adamant on this point: a national Church must maintain a powerful hierarchy, based upon the bishops. Hence an often quoted declaration; turning to the bishops, raising his hand to his hat to salute them without uncovering his head, the king exclaimed; 'But if once you were out, and they [the Presbyterians] in place, I know what would become of my Supremacy. *No bishop, no king*, as before I said.'[23]

The analogy of religion and politics, which Puritanism forcefully asserted, proceeded, then, from the *initial theological claims of the English Crown*, and its annexation of the Church. In the sixteenth and seventeenth centuries, the episcopalian question took on the dimensions of a national debate; and in fact the abolition of the bishops was to be one of the revolutionary demands of the 1640s. Our estimate of James I's reign needs, however, a fair amount of reappraisal. Every aspect of the king's bold assertions and his avowedly absolutist plan were apparently at variance with received ideas of Calvinism. The Reformed faith was equated with a form of democracy, perfectly at odds with the monarchic design. And yet the king's protest of friendship towards the Refuge seems to me unfeigned.

The support of England could hardly be disregarded for tactical as much as for strategic reasons in a troubled international context. In the

---

[22] *Ibid.*, p. 79. [23] *Ibid.*, p. 82.

early seventeenth century, the future seemed to lie with monarchies. We have already traced the itinerary of Pierre du Moulin, which is so typical in this respect. Moreover, in the course of the century, many French Protestants were to express their growing distrust of the Puritans.

One should not exclude altogether the prestige of the Church of England, which many of the refugees subsequently joined. An established Church did present a few compensations compared to the minority status of the Huguenots at home. The *doctrines* of Calvinism were often more congenial to English churchmen than its *discipline*. At least this situation lasted till the reign of Charles I and the Armenian counter-offensive which was to bear heavily upon the Refugee Churches in the decade preceding the revolution. But, until that crisis the Calvinist organisation of the immigrant communities was accepted as an exception rather than as a credible alternative for the Church of England. It was admittedly a precarious equilibrium which will collapse before our eyes.

Finally, the greatest caution is required in our picture of Jacobean proto-absolutism. James I delighted in boisterous declarations and gave full vent to his dislike for the Puritans. But in practice, several degrees of conformity coexisted in the English parishes, as Claire Cross has shown in a remarkable study.[24] The first quarter of the seventeenth century did indeed mark the 'consolidation of Protestantism' in England – an impression largely confirmed by the history of the Refuge, which benefited from the king's lenity.

'Royalist oratory', 'the defence of civil peace'

This recent vindication of Henri IV,[25] after the turmoil of the French wars of religion, explains the growing support of absolutism in enlightened Huguenot circles. Kings were the best protectors of peace. Besides, what other hope was there for a minority than a strong authority entrusted to a king, provided he was favourably disposed? James I fulfilled these two conditions as he officially claimed to be a Prince of Peace. At the end of his life, as the Thirty Years War set Germany ablaze, his sullen moderation and lack of involvement were scorned by jaundiced Puritans. While Sir Walter Raleigh fell a martyr to the Spanish 'unnatural' alliance in 1618, the hatred of new-fangled courtiers and upstarts found a scapegoat in Buckingham, the new lord admiral who could not match any of the feats of arms of the sixteenth century. The recollections of the Elizabethan epic embittered the end of the reign, together with the economic slump of the 1620s.

[24] Claire Cross, *Church and People 1450–1660*, Fontana, 1976.
[25] R. Descimon, *Qui étaient les seize? Mythes et réalités de la Ligue parisienne (1585–1594)*, Paris, 1983, p. 44. See also Arlette Jouanna, *Le Devoir de révolte*, Paris, 1989; D. Crouzet, *Les Guerriers de Dieu*, Seyssel, 1990.

And yet pastor Primerose, James' fellow-countryman who ministered to the French congregation in Threadneedle Street, emphasised the merits of the king in sincere, albeit highly commendatory, terms *c.* 1623–4:

> If any one among us would be quarrelsome or contentious, let him understand that our God is the *God of peace*, that *he has called us to peace*, and that *he hates him who sows discord amongst his brethren*, and let him cease his turbulence, so that he may not disrupt the peace of Church and State which we enjoy.
> – Indeed, is not peace admirable? Consider the political, ecclesiastical and economic state of this kingdom: everywhere there is peace, while elsewhere there is nothing but disorder and war: let us observe with admiration how all is well between our good, wise and pacific king and his subjects; between the grave, learned and vigilant pastors and their congregation; between religious parents and their obedient children; between masters and servants...
> – Having considered it aright, it seems to me that this concord, within your families, within the Church, and within the State, is a foretaste of the happiness of the life to come, that it is a Paradise on earth, whereas discord is a hell, and turns all delight to bitterness...
> – Let us pray also that God may bring such a peace to the Churches of Germany, France, and the low Countries, which are variously afflicted with schisms, heresy and bloody persecutions.[26]

'Church', 'State' and 'family': these three themes were constantly interwoven and could not be separated according to Primerose. This harmony seemed to characterise England in the eyes of refugees. The eulogy may sound excessive, yet at that very moment France and Germany were the scene of violent turmoil. Immediately below God was the king, the father of his people and a man of wisdom, after the examples of David and Solomon – who were constantly invoked. James I dispensed liberally that peace which he alone could guarantee.,

This conventional imagery conjures up both the limitations and the attraction of all topical similes. A commonplace may either express a deep-rooted conviction or be a mere ornament. The role of the family, which has been recently reassessed by anthropologists and demographers could hardly be overemphasised. Robert Filmer's arch-Royalist *Patriarcha, or the Natural Power of Kings*, written during the Civil War and first issued in the 1680s, insisted on the father image assumed by all titular authority, from Adam onwards. Yet Filmer's mythical vision of history since the creation has too often been treated as a silly fiction, following John Locke's onslaught in the *Two Treatises of Government* (1690), later echoed by Jean-Jacques Rousseau. However, this negative approach is undergoing steady revision in our days.[27] Though he may not have been

---

[26] Schickler, *Les Eglises du Refuge en Angleterre*, III, pp. 163–4.
[27] F. Lessay, *Locke et Filmer*, PUF, forthcoming.

a first-rate philosopher compared to Hobbes, Robert Filmer epitomises the lasting links between kinship and kingship. In his recent synthesis on the period, Derek Hirst insisted on the role of the fifth Commandment, 'Honour thy father and thy mother', which 'despite its reference to both parents' was 'the most frequently cited justification of obedience to political authority in the seventeenth century'. Society was perceived as an 'organic whole, and interdependent family' in which 'paternalistic values' served to buttress an attitude of deference to rulers.[28] Received opinions and the common wisdom of a time often hold greater depth than one might suspect. Thus, the perennial association of 'Church', 'State' and 'family'. The whole problem for refugees – or indeed for religious minorities as a whole – is to strike a balance between these three terms. In times of crisis, let alone of persecution, the family may act as a useful counterbalance to majority rule. *Church, State and family*: fifteen years later, the disruption of their association was to mark the end of an era for the Stranger Churches.

The end of an era: the reign of Charles I

You are the defender of that Faith, whereof they make profession ... 300 families continually pray to God for your prosperity.[29]
Henri de Rohan to Charles I, 12 March 1628

This martial declaration was issued when the Huguenot party were driven to surrender their military might in the late 1620s. It testifies to the continuing friendship with England – cooled, to be sure, by the unreliability of international politics in the previous decade, which can only be alluded to here.[30]

Under Charles I, Protestant unanimity suffered its worst setback: the Churches of the Refuge, already exposed to suspicion, lived through their darkest period *c*. 1634–5. The very existence of these foreign communities, as religious and cultural entities within a centralising Church–State, appeared doomed by forced assimilation. Not that one should unduly emphasise the importance of reigns; in fact the crisis had been latent from the beginning. But the concept of the body politic entertained by an Elizabethan, or even a Jacobean, was too steeped in entrenched particularism for the idea of assimilation to predominate. The alien communities were a symptom of the host society and reflected its image to a large extent. Their rights and privileges, as well as their economic

---

[28] D. Hirst, *Authority and Conflict. England 1603–1658*, London, 1986, p. 50.
[29] London, British Library (hereafter BL), Stowe MSS 151, fol. 136.
[30] B. Cottret, 'Solidarité protestante et assistance: l'aide aux marins rochelais de juillet 1621 à octobre 1622 en Angleterre', *Bulletin de la Société de l'Histoire du Protestantisme Français* (1978), pp. 392–8.

function, were partly exogenous; they were the legacy of piecemeal legislation and countless adaptations. Yet in turn the refugees had handled their situation in cultural terms and had become attached to their identity, lending additional value to their minority status.

The day-to-day existence of the Churches went back in essence to the sixteenth century. Why grant these foreigners a perpetual right of asylum? Some unkind spirits here and there could not understand why the status of refugee, by definition transitory, should now become permanent: those who had been persecuted for a time could well go home. This simplistic argument had certainly been heard in England from the sixteenth century onwards. In the Caroline period, however, the French and Walloon settlers, as well as their Dutch brethren, deeply resented the relentless opposition of Laud. No xenophobia or racism were involved but rather as a matter of Church policy, William Laud wished to eradicate Calvinism in England.

Grace abounding? Puritans vs. Arminians[31]

> There come here from abroad men stricken with the plague, and sectaries of Arminius; as for the former ... we cannot prevent them, and leave that to the magistrate. As to the latter we shall notify the Bishop of London, our Superintendent, in order to determine how we should conduct ourselves towards them.
>
> London, consistory, October 1617

Each age has its truths, each century its heretics. The seventeenth century as a whole saw a succession of contradictory writings on grace everywhere in Europe: admittedly, these theological controversies are often highly technical. Yet they had considerable implications for England. Nicholas Tyacke has underlined the secular and religious connotations of the word 'Arminian'. Indeed, if 'religion was a major contributary cause of the English civil war',[32] the 1630s were a time of crisis for the Calvinist refugees. This does *not* mean that the Dutch divine Jacobus Arminius, who had died in 1609, should be held responsible for the ominous measures which threatened the survival of the Stranger Churches in England. The Arminians themselves had been persecuted in the Low Countries. Yet a new body of doctrine, which rejected the tenet of Calvinist predestination and insisted on the 'hierarchical nature of both church and state,'[33] fuelled the Laudian reaction. From the Low Countries

---

[31] The reader is referred to two collections of essays: Rosemary O'Day and Felicity Heal (eds.), *Continuity and Change. Personnel and Administration of the Church of England, 1500–1642*, Leicester, 1976; and *idem, Princes and Paupers in the English Church*, Leicester, 1981.

[32] N. Tyacke, *Anti-Calvinists, the Rise of English Arminianism, c. 1590–1640*, Oxford, 1987, p. 244.   [33] *Ibid.*, p. 246.

the contagion had spread to England, much to the displeasure of James I, who had expressed orthodox positions at the time of the synod of Dordrecht, which condemned the heresy outright in 1618–19. Hence the use of the term Arminian to characterise English anti-Calvinism which was soon associated in beleaguered Puritan minds with a revival of Roman Catholicism. But, if the accusation of 'downright popery' does not seem justified – with the occasional exception of Buckingham's flirtation with the 'old' religion – it remains true that English Arminianism became associated with a genuine cultural counter-revolution. The term *Arminian* is equivocal: in practice, a learned position on the question of salvation – which no one has ever been able to solve – was linked directly to the issue of power. In the beginning, a minority movement in Holland, Arminianism was to become increasingly identified in England with the Church and King party. From 1633 onwards William Laud, then archbishop of Canterbury and Charles I's main adviser, displayed his strenuous opposition to Calvinism. We shall not dwell on the doctrinal features of Arminianism. Let us simply note how closely the consistory of London associated, in one succinct commonplace, the germs of pestilence and those of heresy.

The Stranger Churches had everything to fear from adverse theological positions. And yet Arminianism incurred their reprobation, not so much by its denial of the doctrine of predestination – which only affected the most pious of the refugees – as by its political implications: the growing emphasis on the bishops' role at the expense of the clergy, and the widening gap between clerics and laymen. Arminianism, in its Laudian form, contradicted one of the most fundamental aspirations of Protestantism: the promotion of laymen. As Lucien Febvre has aptly put it:

> by restoring the Word, the divine message in its entirety, to the layman, [the Reformation] clearly displayed its fundamental anticlericalism. This anticlericalism was so strong, in the wishes of the mass of the people, so welcome and popular that many of its advocates, finding that the original leaders were not pursuing it far enough, rebelled against the latter's hesitations – against the remnants of sacerdotalism which they (Luther, above all) strenuously preserved in public worship.[34]

Clericalism, anticlericalism: let us beware of the most recent implications of these terms especially in French history. The emphasis on the laity should not be equated with disbelief: it remained profoundly theological in its demand for the sacralisation of social life, and distrust of intermediaries, which alike culminated in the rejection of monks, friars, celibacy and the monastic *fuga mundi*. The Laudian reaction should be set

---

[34] L. Febvre, *Au cœur religieux du XVIe siècle*, Paris (1957), 1968, p. 49. There is also a fine study by René Rémond, *L'Anticléricalisme en France de 1815 à nos jours*, Paris, 1976.

in its proper European context: it revived a pyramidal conception of the Church which had often been flouted in a recent past by the 'priesthood of all believers'. This aggravated the opposition between clerics and laymen, high clergy and low clergy, ministers and preachers, which the English Reformation had never entirely solved. *Uniformity* and *conformity*: the two terms are not interchangeable. They run through all the religious history of England, continually confronting the historian with their ambiguity. Conformity could be occasional, and accommodate individual variations in piety, while uniformity was more definite. It aimed at the unity of the kingdom, disregarding the Puritan claim for further Reformation. From 1619 onwards the Churches of the Refuge anticipated the rising storm; at least, the conference registers contain a very explicit mention of their fears:

> Article II: (proposed by the brethren of Norwich) *How far can we have recourse to the authority of the bishops and their officers, without prejudice to our discipline?* So that good order be observed in our Churches, it shall not be permissible either for an individual members of the Church, against another member, or for the Consistory against its pastor, or for the pastor against his consistory or Church to appeal to the bishop, or to his chancellor or even to disclose our contentions. But rather they will apply to the consistories, and to the other Foreign Churches of our language in this kingdom.[35]

To illustrate this fear, on the part of the Norwich community, let us mention John Overall, then bishop of that city, who was in close correspondence with Vossius and the Dutch Arminians. Basically, the Stranger Churches dreaded the possible rivalry between their consistories, which included a number of laymen, and the bishops. This insistence on non-interference, one of the symptoms of the incipient crisis, shows the increasing concern of Calvinist refugees. Moreover, this testimony is extremely interesting as it proves that the impending conflict with Arminianism preceded the Laudian offensive of the 1630s. Clearly, one of the most remarkable issues in Calvinist anthropology is the secularisation of time and place, while Arminianism wanted to reinstate deference in Church. Indeed, we learn that the bishop of Norwich demanded that communicants should stand, and not sit as they were wont to do; later, he even commanded that they should kneel.

The response given by the conference is a plain refusal, skilfully formulated: let everyone rely on his consistory – specifying that in London they shall follow 'those forms which are customary in all the French Churches in this kingdom'. This was no empty formula, but involved a specific reassertion of Calvinist modes of worship, with their insistence on

---

[35] A.C. Chamier, *Les Actes des colloques...*, Lymington, 1890, p. 58.

plainness extending to the Lord's Supper. The gestures of Communion were extremely codified. The Lord's Supper involved prescribed rites and the codes of deference appeared less strict in Calvinist worship. In their *determination to avoid idolatry, French Protestants even today* ostensibly refuse to show too much respect for the bread and wine of Communion. In the seventeenth century, gestures played an essential part: attitudes, dress and head gear made up a close-knit web of social differentiation. This fascinating territory has been uncovered in a recent paper devoted to the medieval period.[36]

In this particular respect, Protestant attitudes involved a distinct break with the past. As Pierre Chaunu has aptly put it, the Reformation proscribed

> all gestures which were held to be idolatrous... And by the same token European Protestantism established the significance, in religious matters, of antigestures. For French Protestants and Puritans, this entailed the rejection of the sign of the Cross; for Quakers, the refusal to uncover one's head even before the king – as opposed to the Lord. Among the Anabaptists, it was the refusal to bear arms. All these were negative or anti-gestures.[37]

The Arminian insistence on kneeling provoked a passionate reaction because it seemed to interfere with private conscience. One was not expected to stoop before the bread and wine of Communion, while the Huguenots viewed the Arminians' sense of distance as a return to error, in short, an *innovation* compared with the 'true Faith'. Besides, the social function of the 'beauty of holiness' was to isolate the clergy by accentuating the divide which separated them from the congregation. Thus, the choir was set apart in churches – a development emphasised by William Laud.

Gestures, space and alienation: these are the basic ingredients of acting. If 'all the world is a stage', the pervading sense of drama and representation was characteristic of the age, both in Church and State. This baroque element, which culminated in the Counter-Reformation abroad, may partly explain Puritan reactions against the stage.

The Laudian enterprise: innovation, or reaction?

Time is the greatest innovator[38]
Francis Bacon, *Essays*

---

[36] J.-C. Schmitt, 'Le geste, la cathédrale et le roi', *L'Arc*, 72, in honour of Georges Duby, pp. 9–12.
[37] Pierre Chaunu, *Eglise, culture et société. Essais sur Réforme et Contre-Réforme (1517–1620)*, Paris, 1981.
[38] F. Bacon, *Essays* (1597–1625), London, 1906, p. 74.

Clearly, we cannot avoid semantics. Our categories are the reverse of those of that century: many of our contemporaries tend to scorn the old, and revere the new. How, then, is one to avoid the risk of sophistry? 'Innovation', in seventeenth-century usage, was a negative assertion; the label was applied to William Laud, not to defend him, but to indict him, and the most progressive elements were those who claimed to be the most backward, perpetually invoking a past which we know, in any case, to have been altogether fictitious. The argument is somewhat misleading; yet William Laud interfered with the refugees in his massive onslaught on their cherished privileges. While he aimed at their assimilation, they turned a deaf ear to his predictions. He foretold the future; his opponents retorted with the past. But in the end *he* was to be defeated. What a splendid paradox on the irreversibility of time!

The brilliant archbishop's disputes with the Refuge occupy an impressive number of pages of close-packed arguments, the interest of their subject-matter being fully equalled by their astonishing irascibility. The Church, the State, and a civil and religious minority of aliens – a brilliant formula for an intractable situation!

But before we relate the impassioned confrontations between Laud and the Churches of the Refuge, let us examine the type of documents which the past has handed down to us. *Prima facie* evidence is overshadowed by numerous commentaries. They are carefully written, though, and skilfully arranged to indict William Laud.

We shall first refer to a pamphlet by Bulteel, the Walloon pastor at Canterbury. In 1645, during the revolution, he issued a relation of the afflictions of the Walloon and Dutch communities of Kent – the closest to the primate's see.[39] I am inclined to think that the printed version of the text succeeded an incipient manuscript document which incorporated the main elements of the later book from *c.* 1634–5 – the time of Laud's encroachment. This is further demonstrated by the existence of a Dutch manuscript, now at the Guildhall Library in London. Timotheus van Vleteren puts forward the same elements, with a few exceptions, for the public's consideration.[40] This should indicate the existence of an early compendium intended to advertise the confrontations with William Laud, both for the benefit of the aliens and of their English brethren – Bulteel's text was indeed in English. A third version is extant in Canterbury: it is an English manuscript, written by pastor Delmé. This text is contemporary to Laud's impeachment in 1640–1 and may have influenced the charges

---

[39] John Bulteel, *A Relation of the Troubles of the three forraign Churches in Kent, caused by the Injunctions of Wiliam Laud Archbishop of Canterbury, Anno dom. 1634 & c.....*, London, 1645.

[40] London, Guildhall Library, MSS 7430, Timotheus van Vleteren, 'De histoire vent synode, An. 1635...'.

levelled at the prelate who was to be executed in 1645.[41] A few lines will be devoted to this affair in the next chapter, but I wished initially to show how much we are dependent on an unfavourable view of Charles I's evil counsellor. Indeed, the issue of the refugees took on the tones of a public campaign, which was carefully staged by the Foreign Churches in the 1630s and later revived, like certain press files at the present day, to incriminate Laud at the time of the revolution. Having become a *cause célèbre*, the strangers' fate threw a disturbing light on the uneasy atmosphere of the time. All Protestants of Europe were called upon to witness the misdeeds of the archbishop and of the Court party, who encountered the same insuperable resentment. It was tempting, for a man of the seventeenth century, to stigmatise the prelate, and regard him as the persecutor of the 'true Faith'. Laud's failings towards the 'poor' refugees only served to blacken his image. Indeed, was not the memory of Wolsey shortly revived to castigate the new prelate?

Yet propaganda, however biased, deserves to be considered in its own right. But I should like to correct this immediate interpretation of the event by contemporary observers and suggest an alternative view. Again the coherence of a political system, namely that of the absolutist State, should be invoked. Coherence is the catchword of historians. Whatever our sympathies or exasperations, let us admit that causes which are not any longer ours nonetheless obeyed a logic of their own, which deserves a proper assessment.

William Laud – who was more authoritarian than tyrannical, and arbitrary rather than capricious – showed remarkable statesmanship when he put the question of immigration, in his rather blunt manner, in terms of integration. Until that time, the only logic which men recognised had been that of exceptions rather than rules. *Assimilation* was not yet a concept, even for an Elizabethan; the status of second-generation immigrants remained ambiguous: though they were English by birth they were often regarded as aliens in fact. Only a statesman could so insensitively apply to an intractable situation a remedy even worse than the complaint. Thus, the issue hinged on the definition of the king's subjects.

State/family, kinship/citizenship

We may here follow John Bulteel's relation. Its introduction summarises a few facts which accepted interpretations confirm: George Abbot, William Laud's predecessor at Canterbury, showed genuine attachment to Protestantism, and did not interfere with the privileges of the Foreign

---

[41] Dean and Chapter Library, MSS U-47-H 1, fol. 30, 'A summarie Relation concerning the prosecution of the Archbishop of C[anterbury]...'.

Churches. Certain bishops had already tried to restrict their freedom of action as was the case in Norwich in 1619. But these were mere skirmishes compared with the Laudian offensive, which, by its very timing, constitutes an involuntary prelude to the revolution. In 1634, scarcely eight years before the Civil War, while he had been archbishop for only a few months, William Laud attacked the foreign Churches directly:

> Yet as soon as William Laud was warm in his archbishop's seat, he endeavoured with tooth and nail to suppress and abrogate our Privileges and Immunities granted to our foreign Churches by his Majesty and his Royal Ancestors, to introduce the Book of Common Prayer in our churches, and subject us to the English Liturgy translated into French, etc., and to withdraw from our churches those of the first and second descent, to have them go to the English Parishes, as may fully appear by this Relation.[42]

In fact, these measures of exception – or rather this attempt at alignment with the rest of the kingdom – fell, at least originally, within the scope of a pastoral visitation. Sir Nathaniel Brent, the vicar-general, summoned the foreign pastors of the diocese to a memorable interview, on 14 April 1634. John Bulteel and Philippe Delmé represented the French and Walloons of Canterbury, while Jan Miller and Gasparus Nieren stood for the Dutch-speaking communities of Sandwich and Maidstone. They had to answer loaded questions, which clearly indicated in themselves the turn of events:

1 What rites were in use? Had the English liturgy been translated?
2 How many of the congregation were 'born-subjects'? We would say, in present-day terms, what was the proportion of second-generation immigrants?
3 Would the 'born-subjects' confirm?

In his reply, John Bulteel used a skilful formula, which had already proven its efficiency in the disputes with the bishop of Norwich: 'though those three foreign churches were *in* my Lord Archbishop of Canterbury's Diocese, they were not *of* his Diocese'. (This is a clear paraphrase of Jesus Christ's answer to Pilate: 'My kingdom is not of this world': St John 19:36.) Undoubtedly, this distinction borrowed from the gospel is not merely topical: it sets a clear limit to the prerogative of ecclesiastical authorities. This timely opposition – being *in* the diocese without being *of* the diocese – marks the adoption, in a defensive spirit, of one of the forms of exposition favoured in the gospel according to St John: the contradiction between being *in* the world, as a messenger of God, and being *of* the world in the sense of the darkness of sin. John Bulteel's remark certainly deserves this interpretation which enhances the Christian

[42] Bulteel, *A Relation of the Troubles*, p. iii of the introduction, 'To the Christian reader'.

identity of the little flock who refuse to conform. *Asylum now became exile*, and the Arminian apostasy of Calvinism, as it were, demanded a new alignment. The minority became a besieged citadel, an impregnable stronghold bearing witness to Christian authenticity, which once again was called into question. In the face of this new challenge, self-defence lay not in frosty withdrawal but in the invocation of a right to differ, sanctified by the most renowned of scriptural allusions.

Sir Nathaniel Brent, nonetheless, in front of this surge of indignation, remained unruffled and faced the storm with bureaucratic equanimity. Besides, he never proved a fanatical Laudian; having already been in office at the time of George Abbot, he was later to turn against William Laud when necessary.

The pastors in dismay sent the questionnaire to the Coetus in London, which acted as a kind of regular council of the Foreign Churches, French and Dutch. We no longer have the register for this period, at best a few letters are still extant. But Bulteel's text provides us with the information; the response was contained in three points:

1 The Churches reaffirmed their attachment to their reformed discipline which had been in force in England, as well as in France and in the Walloon Churches of the Low Countries. The English liturgy had indeed been translated, but there could be no question of its being adopted.

2 They estimated that only one third of the heads of refugee families belonged to the second generation; this confirms the demographic assessment of the introduction.

3 If the 'born-subjects' were to join their parish Churches, this would mark the death of the Stranger Churches, for human as much as for economic or financial reasons. Moreover, religious conformity would also create linguistic disarray. But above all, families would be disorganised.

Who can describe, in all their complexity, the obscure links between the family, as a basic social unit, and the nation at large? That relationship was certainly ambiguous and allowed constant transliterations: the image of the king as father of his people was often offered to the filial devotion of his subjects. Here we have a symmetrical phenomenon, the Crown supplanting ancestral solidarities, and imposing a new status which contradicted the sentiment of an inherited identity. This alternative strikes its roots in the household. It was decried by the spokesmen of the refugees, who valued the integrity of the family which they duly regarded as the focus of their minority culture and faith as always, but especially in times of crisis. Yet we may assume, as I shall try to prove in the third part of this book, that English society offered many attractions to prodigal sons, determined to throw off paternal authority. By encouraging defectors, the host society and its Church made it possible to escape from the all-pervading constraints of the Refuge. For these sons of Huguenots, merging with the English meant a new sense of freedom. This was common knowledge, and the consistories often incurred the blame for their excessive moral regulations. The host society may be regarded as a frontier which favoured the dissolution of the group, should a conflict arise. This *permeability* of the refugee communities, which Laud encouraged, is worth emphasising.

The interview with Laud, or Moses and Pharaoh

Precedents were the best of arguments. We have noted the deference of the Refuge for Edward VI's charter which marked its foundation. Thus, when they were called upon to send the document to Laud, the refugees only passed on a copy in order to retain the original. But the decision seemed irrevocable in this month of December 1634. The communities received the order to submit at the end of the year, by March at the latest. The matter was made very clear: the 'born-subjects' were to join their respective parish Churches; as for the others, they were to worship according to the English liturgy, translated into French.

The refugees then addressed themselves directly to Laud. He received the deputies of the Churches in great state, perched upon his throne, and subjected them to one vexatious gesture after another: he interrupted them, cut them short and protested loudly his zeal for the Crown. At one point he took from his pocket the copy of Edward's charter with contempt, and referred sarcastically to the practice of receiving Communion in a sitting position, 'as if drinking in a tavern or an inn'. He pointed out that the reformed discipline was not 'according to the Gospel' – *secundum Evangelium* – but that on the other hand, the bishops were *jure divino*, by divine right. And finally he remarked angrily that the refugees were like the Jews of Egypt, seeking to establish a 'State within the State'.

This scoffing flippancy which Bulteel put into the mouth of Laud became a subject of pride for a Protestant consciousness sustained by biblical references. Even insult was praise at a time of trials, and identification with Israel a mark of God's election. I even wonder if Bulteel's relation has not accentuated the charge against Laud, his Pharaonic character contrasting with the dignity of the pastors which reminds one of Moses. The message is clear: *the host society became a land of captivity*.

In the winter of 1634–5 the situation was at a deadlock. The basic issue in this conflict was the State and/or the family. Being concerned with the transmission of a cultural and financial inheritance, and the perpetuation of its specific rites, the micro-society of the Refuge tended to set the greatest of value on its tutelary character. This claim clashed with the development of absolutism and its concern for unity in Church and State. The foreigner was identified, for William Laud, with that portentous figure in European consciousness, the wandering Jew. A mark of scorn for some, this fictitious assimilation was indeed in its turn to be claimed as an honour for the new Israel.

The hidden king

What remained to be done once all endeavours had failed? As the king's servants proved inflexible, the refugees appealed to Charles I. French historians have emphasised the identification of King and State in the seventeenth century, following Louis XIV's spurious statement: 'I am the State.' Yet this identification remained ambivalent: although he was the figure that represented the State, the king was the best defence against the excesses of bureaucracy. A common fiction developed: the king did not know, he was misinformed about the discontent of his subjects. His evil counsellors who kept him from the truth bore the brunt of this obloquy. The omnipresence of the Crown, the ubiquity of its effigy[43] rested, in fact, on the remoteness of the monarch's person. The king, the State: the State and its double. This functional duplicity may explain the lasting success of monarchies, and their adaptability – as it also explains the hatred of favourites and bad ministers. Laud and Strafford were to be sacrificed ten years later, just as ten years before, the dashing Buckingham had borne upon his shoulders the weight of an execration which did not yet dare – at least officially – to look directly at the Crown.

The king was unaware of the malpractices of his archbishop, he suspected nothing of his iniquity – the refugees adhered to the myth and tried to inform Charles I of their lot. He alone could re-establish a right which had been disregarded by his servants, even though the benevolence shown towards Protestantism by successive kings of England, since Edward VI, was a token of continuity. This fiction – that the king did not know, and that all the blame rested with his evil counsellors – was still alive in the 1640s. Pastor Delmé then collected evidence against William Laud, whose hostile intrigues were presented as 'contrary to His Most Gracious Majesty, and his ancestors of happy memory, since Edward VI'. This convenient rhetoric, 'all the harm comes from evil counsellors', seems to have been relatively common in ancien régime societies. Similar arguments were resorted to in France: Mazarin, like Laud and Strafford, was to be vilified and lampooned at the time of the Fronde. Favourites, ministers and confidants provided the first of scapegoats absolving the king from suspicion. Yet how persuasive and convincing was this rhetorical commonplace? I am inclined to think that the years 1634–5,

---

[43] Louis Marin, *Le Portrait du roi*, Paris, 1981.

though they did not coincide with the total disappearance of all loyalty to the Crown, marked a genuine crisis of confidence, if not a more profound desacralisation of the king's image in the ranks of the refugees. William Laud's invocation of divine right for his own office of archbishop tended to depreciate the currency of absolutist reference and reverence. This constant symbolic transfer, from Church to State, and then from State to Church, far from strengthening the clergy, was in fact to provoke a resurgence of anticlericalism.

The synod which met in London in February 1634, 'on the occasion of the injunction issued by Archbishop William Laud', defined the necessary tactical steps to approach the royal person. My sources here are the accounts given by Bulteel and Delmé, as well as the actual proceedings of the synod.[44] Two main moves were planned: a first operation was to be entrusted to Benjamin Soubise, who was the younger brother of Rohan, a famous military leader and Huguenot seaman who lived in exile and maintained his own aristocratic oratory. Rohan was not a member, in the strict sense of the word, of the Threadneedle Street congregation. At the same time, the refugees discovered an ally within the Privy Council itself: Sir John Coke, a former servant of Buckingham and of King James, now in his seventies, and exposed to the sarcasm of Francis Windebanke twenty years his junior, who tried to eclipse the old councillor and was eventually to oust him on the eve of the revolution – just in time to see a favourable situation turn to his disadvantage. It is not always easy to disentangle the interplay of personal antagonisms between courtiers from religious convictions or disinterested benevolence. Sir John Coke certainly left behind him the memory of his real devotion to Protestantism, whereas the reputation of Windebanke was to remain associated, in the eyes of posterity, with the Crown's secret transactions with Gregorio Panzani, the emissary of the pope.

On 12 February 1635, a petition was submitted to the king. An unverified gossip spread in Court circles and this aristocratic form of rumour caused some disquiet among the refugees. Charles I seemed to show scant concern for this people of hard-working strangers who neither awakened nor deserved any particular attention on the part of His Majesty. The king received in writing the text of a speech which they had wished to deliver aloud to him in person.[45] Their whole address evokes the risks of a new exile for the 'little flock' who had believed that they found in England 'a place of Refuge, a sanctuary of the holy temple'. Tradition was invoked, but also the defence of Protestantism, and its place in the world. This proved a decisive argument in my opinion, and even Laud was too shrewd a politician not to consider the use that could be made of the

[44] Reproduced by Chamier, *Les Actes des colloques.*   [45] SP Dom., Ch. I, 279, 5.

Protestant banner in foreign policy. As long as Calvinism was practised outside Britain the prelate did not care! International pressures could be used to buttress the refugees' claims.

Two ministers, Primerose and Bulteel, were despatched to John Coke. I shall turn for a moment to the main figures we shall meet among the defenders of the Churches. Delmé, pastor at Canterbury, was born in England of refugee parents; Primerose a minister in London, was of Scottish origin. We may well imagine what forced conformity would have meant for them. Coke received in person the fundamental documents of the Churches, or at least copies of them. Starting with Edward's charter, all the official texts were regarded by the refugees as binding precedents. These included various declarations by successive sovereigns, and Orders in Council concerning equally the Dutch and Walloons since 1550.

Time was short; the decision was to come into effect in March. The intervention of Soubise was related in a few lines: 'The duc de Soubise, spoke to the king on the Churches' behalf as requested, and now reports that the king said that *we show more fear than we have cause for*, and that his intention concerned only the first proposition, namely the born-subjects.'[46]

One can tell that Charles I was irritated by these fears and did not feel any compassion for the refugees. And yet a definite improvement appeared: uniformity was to apply only to subjects in the strict sense of the word, i.e. those born within the realm. On 7 March, William Laud received a delegation from the Churches with unusual civility:

> The said Lord Archbishop declared that his intention was to reduce everything to *uniformity*. And as for the second injunction to receive the English liturgy, he told them that his intention was never to compel the strangers to do so, and that he had given no such order. Consequently the strangers might keep their own liturgy, and the kingdom would always be a place of Refuge for those who came here, being persecuted for religion's sake.[47]

What a change of tone! Charles I's goodwill, underlaid by his haughty indifference, justified Laud's evolution. He followed his master's example, while John Coke, for his part, was reassuring: 'You will find the king very graciously disposed.' The good tidings were received with sighs of relief. The English liturgy could still be laid aside for this time. The fateful month of March elapsed without any incident. The refugees congratulated themselves: unlike Caesar, they had passed the ides of March without any misfortune. They expressed their thanks profusely, while John Coke modestly retorted; 'I have done no more than my duty.'

This serenity, however, was not destined to last.

---

[46] Chamier, *Les Actes des colloques*, p. 69.   [47] *Ibid.*, p. 70.

The ways of disobedience

The planned and systematic extinction of the foreign communities was indeed the aim pursued by the Crown. The political philosophy of the pragmatic archbishop, which was shared by the king, distrusted all intermediary bodies and lasting particularisms. The existence of schisms within the Church and of factions within the State took on the value of a premonitory obsession only a few years before the outbreak of the revolution. However, it was of no avail. In his fine book on William Laud, H.R. Trevor-Roper pointed out:

> The idea that any church, corporation, or district should be exempt from his jurisdiction was hateful to Laud, valuing as he did the idea of equality before the fact of individual liberties and privileges, and while Brent was carrying his policy into every diocese in his province, Laud was striking at another group which claimed to be independent of his authority – the French and Dutch Protestants who had found a refuge in England from the triumphs of the Counter-Reformation abroad, and who had settled there under their own ecclesiastical constitution.

Continental Calvinism was not the archbishop's concern. Laud was more preoccupied with his own country than with any quixotic aim to spread theological Arminianism abroad. H.R. Trevor-Roper went on:

> When they settled in England he required them to become subject in all things to the English government, and in religious matters to the English bishops, lest by their exemption they should provide a permanent example of independent ecclesiastical jurisdiction, and attract to their Puritan services all those local English Puritans who could understand their languages.[48]

Up to 1635, the Refuge appeared unanimous in its loyalty to the Crown. The confidence to be placed in the monarchy, the supreme role of the Crown as an ultimate bulwark against intolerance, the king's arbitration – even when necessary, against the severity of the State – had long remained unquestioned. In April, this vision of the world began to crumble.

On 13 April the ecclesiastical court of Canterbury took up the case: the born-subjects were to leave their native community. As for the rites in force in the *temples*, the court strongly recommended that they be replaced by a French version of the English liturgy. This judgement was to be immediately implemented, and publicly announced. Conversely, the English parishes were charged with receiving the second-generation immigrants.

---

[48] H.R. Trevor-Roper, *Archbishop Laud 1573–1645*, London, 1940, p. 197.

Now began a period of resistance, facilitated by the slowness, inefficiency and possibly lack of zeal of the local parishes. The result of these measures is difficult to gauge for the historian. Laud's official correspondence with Charles I seems to support the idea that conformity was established within a few months in the case of the born subjects. Yet, as we all know, administrators are apt to overstate their ability whenever they wish to claim that their natural and sovereign authority subdues all resistance. In fact there were no significant changes in the number of baptisms after 1635, as if demographic trends were unaffected by this population transfer. The Civil War, five years later, was to prove a greater factor of dissolution than Laud's injuctions. On the contrary, Laud's antagonism may even have strengthened ties between refugees. Many intermediaries reacted slackly to an authoritarianism which was not taken altogether seriously. Can one ever emphasise sufficiently that mainspring of human societies, the force of inertia? The corporation of Canterbury did not wish in the least to see its working population streamed according to new criteria. The Stranger Churches had quite healthy finances, they took care of their poor, provided work and permitted no begging or idleness. The Crown's contention that all of HM's subjects should flock together in the same parishes had little to inspire active cooperation on the part of the English population. Indeed, either one did not like strangers and did not wish these sons of foreigners to be accepted as Englishmen, or one sympathised with their cause but then why not let things stand as they were? The only justification to force the refugees to comply would have been doctrinal; but the Church of England was not composed solely of devout Arminians. Brent, the vicar-general, met with general indifference from the parishes, which balked at the prospect of accommodating the strangers. The attraction of gain was occasionally played on. The churchwardens of the parish of St Margaret's, Canterbury, extended a friendly invitation to their foreign neighbours on 15 April 1639, though the care of souls may not have been their primary concern. The 'Note for those of the French and Walloon congregation of the parish of St Margaret's in Canterbury that are householders, and masters of families' contained an impressive list of all the new duties which the refugees were expected to perform:

> We hereby signify that we have assessed you of the French and Walloon congregation, and that are strangers inhabiting in the parish, whether lately come over, or of the first and second descent for their time to pay for the reparations and adorning of our church and necessary ornaments thereunto belonging the sum of £5/10 sterling which we desire you to collect amongst yourselves (because you best know your own estates) and pay to us churchwardens before next Saturday night at six of the clock, and if this you neglect to do, then we give you notice to appear in

the North chancel of our church next Lord's Day immediately after evening prayer.[49]

Moreover, the brethren of the second generation were also supposed to pay for their pews, the churchwardens insisting on their proper accommodation: 'On Saturday night next we desire the names of all married persons in your congregation of the second descent that are inhabitants in our parish, that we may take order for decent seats for them, as you shall signify their estates and qualities to us.'

Likewise, bachelors and spinsters were required to 'resort to our church' if they were of the 'second descent' while 'those of sixteen years old and upwards' had to receive the sacrament on the next Lord's Day, unless they had already communicated at Easter. Moreover, all children, and 'servants under sixteen' were to be 'catechised according to the order of our church'. This formal injunction was accompanied by the threat of proceedings against defaulters. Should we then say that Laud succeeded in his policy of 'thorough' anglicisation? Not all Englishmen were prepared to endorse his move; 'among those of hotter understanding amongst the English brethren these proceedings against the strangers' churches have wrought rather pity than a change to worse in their neighbours' affections and behaviour'. Yet some there were, especially 'among the vulgar', who rejoiced at this petty despotism. In 1639, the most likely attitude was at best outward conformity. The children of the refugees, at least in theory, could no longer hear 'the word preached as used from their very infancy'. Moreover, the strangers had an ingrained feeling of superiority: they resented the poor quality of the English parish services 'where for the most part is no preaching'.

But this cultural change was also detrimental to morality, as some refugees could be tempted 'to live at will and pleasure', away from the control exercised by their elders. In practice, this could lead to 'great faults and scandals'. As a matter of fact, the gravest threat was posed by the behaviour of young people who ran the risk of 'disorderly, rushed, and sudden marriages without or against the due consent of parents'.

On the other hand, the beleaguered minority were tempted to highlight their religious importance:

> If such things be done to the foreign churches who have patent privileges and immunities and promises from such great Princes for themselves and their prosperity, in regard to their discipline, exempted from the subjection of Archbishops and Bishops: what can the English churches expect, subjected to the power and authority of Prelates? Nay, what can they not expect but multiplication of ceremonies, innovation in rites,

[49] Dean and Chapter Library, MSS U-47-H 1.

introduction of Popery, Socinianism, Arminianism, profanation of the Lord's day, new Canons and oaths; persecution, banishment and branding, suspension, imprisonment and fining of those holy Pastors that will not submit their necks to that slavish yoke of Babylon, and drink of the cup of abominations of that purple whore of Rome, and enchantments of *Jezabel*.[50]

Written, or at least published, in 1645, Bulteel's relation does not abound with polite understatements. Before the revolution, the tone had been more shrewdly cautious, but basically Bulteel's diatribe, with its full-blown rhetoric, emphasises what was essentially at stake for the refugees in the Laudian persecution. In the years immediately preceding the revolution, administrative centralisation and social or religious innovation conflicted with the wisdom of privilege and ancestral precepts. They were perceived as threats from an absolutism which drew none of its justification from the past, but was turned towards the unconceived horizons of the future.

Citizenship in Church and State

That a country or a State should permit more than one religious denomination would now seem self-evident. Even if occasionally religion still sanctifies certain great acts of public life, it belongs essentially to private conviction. Observance, belief and *a fortiori* faith are a question of conscience, as most would agree. For the man of the seventeenth century, the situation was altogether different. Wherever he turned his gaze, the religion of the subjects was that of the State, and the religion of the State that of the King. Special dispensations from this principle, *cujus regio, ejus religio*, were practically unknown. France alone, of all the great territorial entities, presented a different face, as it allowed the existence of a large Protestant minority, at least until 1685. The English Catholics did not enjoy any such legal advantage. As to the United Provinces, which from 1615 onwards publicly accepted the presence of banished Iberian Jews, they were undoubtedly an exemplary centre of tolerance throughout the century, despite inevitable tensions. But we cannot dwell here on the complex situation of Judaism, which in England was still officially excluded.

In the years of crisis immediately before the revolution, the history of the refugees permits a better understanding of the implications of a State religion – exemplified by the bishops' intention to see the Stranger Churches adopt the Book of Common Prayer. No one was to escape from the theological orbit of the Church of England, not even foreign

[50] Bulteel, *A Relation of the Troubles* p. 41.

immigrants. This was partly motivated by the Arminians' distrust of Calvinism. The structural implications of this uniformity are worth examining.

Anglicanism may not be an appropriate term before 1660; several authors use it for the sake of convenience, though not without some reservations. The *Church of England* may be more suitable to describe a reality which, in the early modern period, underwent perpetual revision: what a diversity of forms from the conservative schism of Henry VIII to the Protestantism of Edward's reign, to the Laudian reaction.

The refugees generally spoke of the English Church; only the learned mentioned the *Eglise anglicane*, a translation from the Latin *Ecclesia anglicana*.[51] But this geographical definition – the Church of England was the Church which happened to exist in England – quickly took on denominational innuendoes, especially in the 1630s, when the consciously insular tendency of Laudianism isolated England from the major currents of the Reformation on the Continent. We find sufficient proof of this, I think, in the attempt to replace the Calvinist discipline with a form of French-speaking 'Anglicanism'. Territorial identity then became the decisive element in the definition of Church and State.

This forced acculturation to Anglicanism met with almost total failure, at least in this first half of the century; insidiously, without any of Laud's brutal abruptness, the project was to be revived under the Restoration, with striking success as several refugees outwardly accepted religious conformity, though others proved reluctant. In fact, there were to be various degrees of occasional conformity in the second half of the century. Yet, at a very early stage, the English liturgy was adapted into French in the relatively peripheral setting of the community of Sandtoft, Lincolnshire. We do not know much about this group of men, originally Dutchmen for the most part, whom Cornelius Vermuyden had first brought over in 1626 to drain the fens of Yorkshire. Richard Neile, the Arminian archbishop of York, required the young community to conform; this was carried into effect for a brief period in 1638–9 by pastor Etienne de Cursol, who was dismissed two years later by his congregation. This set a momentous precedent: on 7 March 1638, the bishop of Norwich enjoined pastor Delmé to do the same.

The transition to would-be Anglicanism remains complex. Cursol enjoyed the support of the Reformed Churches on the Continent, especially Paris and Geneva, which distrusted the Puritans, and doubted that Laud wished to reintroduce Roman Catholicism as his adversaries claimed (or as Rome ventured to hope when they offered him a cardinal's hat). Each country was free to establish its own ceremonies and forms of

---

[51] For instance, in a letter from J. Castel to T. Beza, dated 26 August 1584, quoted at length by Schickler, *Les Eglises du Refuge en Angleterre*, III, p. 140.

worship. Passing through London, Pierre Richier showed little sympathy with the Puritan point of view in a letter to the Genevan Academy:

> If sometimes [Laud] had punished a few seditious persons who were trampling upon the discipline of this Church and attempting to introduce in its place that of France, it seems to me that they deserved it, and that they were no less reprehensible than would be those who might wish in France to abolish our discipline in order to establish that of the English Church...I have learnt, Sirs, that it is not the difference in ceremonies and regulations of the Church which prevent the Communion of the faithful, since this is only an external and not an essential thing. And since the Apostle left the arrangement of such matters to the Church...it is with good reason that the theologians hold unanimously that each Church has the power to choose its discipline and decide its ceremonies, which must in consequence be different according to the diversity of circumstances. One should not therefore find it strange if the discipline of the Church of England is different from that of France. For the *former being a Church triumphant*, and the latter subsisting and remaining alive with difficulty, the government of the two Churches cannot be alike. Besides, the disposition, temper and aptitudes of the English being different from those of the French, what is suitable for one nation is not appropriate for the other, and there is no doubt that those who took in hand the reformation of this Church would never have succeeded if they had not preserved most of the ceremonies, because the people (who are quite difficult to manage and for the most part consider only the externals) would never have suffered such a great change to be made.[52]

A Church triumphant! Laud's triumph was to be short-lived. As to the English national character, which the pastor presents with an amateur ethnographer's condescension, to this day, despite frequent visits in a professional capacity, I cannot tell if superficiality is one of its features. Every country may choose its Reformation, its Reformation 'with a human face', if I may put it that way. While refuting in advance any fixed model to be followed by all Churches, this universalist reasoning on 27 June 1639 did not offer any comfort to extremists, of whatever camp: it contrasts singularly with the vehemence of Bulteel. I shall draw the few conclusions which emerge from this opposition.

The question of the Church immediately involves the State, and vice versa. The religious controversies which permeated the century were not sectarian in essence; during these years, political rhetoric assumed a religious character. I see two reasons for this: Protestant culture, and the value attached to the Bible. This is evident. One must add a further structural factor: the inclusion of the ideological apparatus of the Church within that of the State – the 'Church triumphant', as Richier says. This overlap reached its fullest extent in England when Laud united in his

[52] *Ibid.*, pp. 195–6: letter of 27 June 1639.

hands the keys of the spiritual and temporal powers. The divine right invoked by the prelate corresponded to the divine right of the king; both king and bishops were to suffer the same fate.

A split was opening up between the Churches of the Refuge and those of the Continent. What did the French or Genevans know of England? How much did they really want to know?

But above all, it is *the community's instinct of preservation* which makes these years captivating, beyond any ideological consideration. What forces were at work to ensure the survival of the community? How did social cohesion form and disintegrate? These questions, and a few others, will be at the heart of the third part of this book, which centres on functional factors. But let us note at this stage how an outside aggression – staged by Laud – had the effect of reinforcing that immunitary reflex of human societies, consensus.

4   The Church and the body politic, 1642–1660: Godly rebellion or lay reformation?

Parliament itself is now to undertake a *Reformation*.
IVth Synod of the Foreign Churches, May 1644

God hath put *the sword of Reformation* into the soldiers' hand.
The Soldier's Catechism, *1644*

God is decreeing to begin some new and great period in his Church, even to the *reforming of Reformation itself*.
Milton, *Areopagitica*, 1644

[Pastor Jean de La Marche preached that] soon all higher powers, monarchic and hierarchical would be abrogated, and that the Saints of the Most-High will reign in this Holy General Reformation which God has begun in England. And that Christ will come to reign here.

Afore I looked upon the Scripture as a history of things that passed in other countries, pertaining to other persons; but now I look upon it as a mystery to be opened at this time, belonging also to us.
A. Evans, *An Echo to the voice of Heaven*, 1653

English scholarship has always been divided in its interpretation of the Civil War and Interregnum, which still provide historians with one of their favourite battlefields.[1] The word 'revolution', in fact, was introduced at a later date to describe the 1640s. It cropped up with Guizot in the nineteenth century, in the wake of the French Revolution, thus epitomising the similarities and deep-rooted differences which existed between the two countries.[2] This full-fledged Gallicism besides, though increasingly acceptable, still has its critics, and I should like to confess that my compatriots' exclusive devotion to the 1789 revolution has not

---

[1] L. Stone, *Social Change and Revolution in England 1540–1640*, London, 1965; R.C. Richardson, *The Debate on the English Revolution*, London, 1977. See also O. Lutaud, *Les Deux Révolutions d'Angleterre*, Paris, 1978.
[2] François Guizot, *Histoire de la révolution d'Angleterre*, Paris, 1826.

necessarily met my approval. In terms of efficiency, 1688 might be a better choice while 1642 is certainly more imaginative.

Without entering into endless quibbles, these reservations concerning the word 'revolution' should be taken into account. An impartial survey of the origin and early usage of that concept is revealing: the very word 'revolution' was not available in the 1640s or rather it had a technical and scientific meaning and was mainly applied, following Copernicus, to the cyclic movement of 'the celestial orbs'. In short, the idea of regularity and harmony prevailed over the concept of social upheaval.[3] And yet, although Cromwell's contemporaries did not use the word, they knew the thing. The trauma attending the Civil War, the rising tide of popular radicalism, the execution of the king on 30 January 1649, the proclamation of the Commonwealth are nonetheless the ingredients of a perfect revolution, according to the present meaning of the word. The proof of the pudding is in the eating. As expected, Marxist historiography, with its concern for clear-cut distinctions, reinforced that prevailing opinion and gave it wider currency still.[4] In what respect can the destiny of a minority community of a few thousand men – and, what is more, of foreign origin – allow a better understanding of the period? Indeed, it would be pointless to argue that the refugees provided a full-size portrait of English society as a whole; all such undue generalisations should be avoided with care. The 'storm over the gentry', the social composition of Parliament, the geographical distribution of Roundheads and Cavaliers could hardly be properly documented by the Church records of those aliens. Conversely, this relative paucity of first-hand documents on the most epic, not to say thorny, questions provides another type of evidence. These archives stress the pursuit of ordinary life in moments of bravery: local conflicts and petty bickerings often arose over trivial, and possibly convivial, matters. But the microscope itself may have distorting effects, and the endless strife between John, Paul and Peter, let alone the petty bickerings between a pastor and his flock, have to be put in their proper perspective.

The basic issue stems from the striking convergence of political and religious terminology in seventeenth-century England. The revolution simply accentuated the phenomenon: the banner of the Reformation, unfurled by the Puritans, shed a godly light upon social transformations. It was quite usual for contemporaries – including the refugees – to refer to these 'times of Reformation'. Such proselytising zeal was challenged, however, with a revealing determination by the younger Pierre du Moulin.

---

[3] Perez Zagorin, *The Court and the Country*, London, 1969; see also his *Rebels and Rulers 1500–1660*, Cambridge, 1982. Christopher Hill has yet retorted recently that the meaning of the word 'revolution' was not purely cyclical in the seventeenth century but could as well apply to a linear vision of time, 'The Word "Revolution" in 17th Century England', in *For Veronica Wedgwood*, London, 1986, pp. 134–51.

[4] Indispensable here is the paper by C. Hill, 'Parliament and People in 17th Century England', *Past and Present*, 92 (August 1981), pp. 100–24.

He took up in his writings Charles I's Oxford declaration against those seditious spirits who had seized upon 'the pretext of a kind of reformation' (14 May 1644).[5] This alliance of the political and the religious should not be treated, with antiquarian zeal, as some sort of quaint oddity; it remains to this day one of the basic intellectual challenges of the period, and it did in turn affect the French-speaking minority.

In this context, the word 'politics' itself is a loaded term, and should be used with the greatest of care, to avoid its secular emphasis. Conversely, the meaning of religion was much more extensive than it is today and spanned all sectors of public life. This religious monopoly was yet to undergo a drastic change with a revolution which failed to provide a lasting Church settlement. In other words religion and politics were the two sides of the same medal, and the countless allusions to the holy Writ should not be disparagingly dismissed as the feverish attempts of bigotry to assert itself. Those men were not credulous, or rather they were not more gullible than we are now, and when we come to think of it, religious terminology has not totally deserted the field of politics, at least negatively as terms of abuse: personality cults and sectarian attitudes may long remain in force. So that, more often than not, religion is a derisive word for politics.

The English seventeenth century was a case in point: religious and political labels were often interchangeable, and it would be equally misleading to insist solely upon the 'Puritan' revolution or to lay undue emphasis on worldly matters.

How far did the refugees feel personally involved in the national conflicts, the ideological debates and the revolutionary tensions which affected their daily lives? It is necessary to bear in mind the local dimension of Church, city, county or patronage. Most historians have followed a similar path, as shown by the recent vogue of the term 'community'.[6] 'Community', however, is ambiguous, because of its commonplace melancholy connotations.[7] But if we give the word 'community' a functional, rather than a purely emotional, value, then the multifarious ties of solidarity which permeated 'the world we have lost' lend an additional anthropological dimension to politics.

---

[5] Pierre du Moulin the younger, *Histoire des nouveaux presbytériens anglois et escossois...*, 1660, 'Epître au Roi'.
[6] In particular, A. Everitt, *The Community of Kent and the Great Rebellion, 1640–1660*, Leicester, 1966.
[7] A. Macfarlane, in collaboration with Sarah Harrison and Charles Jardine, *Reconstructing Historical Communities*, Cambridge, 1977. A good summary of the use of the word 'community' by historians is provided by Dr Neil Davie in his thesis 'Custom and Conflict in a Wealden Village: Pluckley 1550–1700', Oxford, D Phil, 1987.

The powers that be

Right from the beginning, the Foreign Churches felt unquestionable
sympathy for Parliament, even prior to the Civil War, which, in turn,
divided the communities. Moreover, it was most unlikely that the refugees
as a group would support Charles I. The first sign of this alignment –
tenuous as yet – can be seen in the synod organised, on an exceptionally
large scale, by the French and Dutch in London (3–21 September 1641).
The parallel with the Long Parliament, which was undertaking the reform,
if not the Reformation of the kingdom, is self-evident. The deputies of the
Churches, like the members of Parliament, decided to sit at least every
three years. Assemblies were becoming fashionable. Similarly, the Foreign
Churches cast off the bishops' tutelage, and the new-fangled ecclesiastical
discipline which they adopted no longer recognised a 'superintendent',
while off-stage, the refugees certainly rejoiced at Laud's arrest. The Crown
had proved a source of disappointment, but no one, as yet, contemplated
the abolition of monarchy. The refugees now turned to Parliament;[8] they
suggested the passing of a bill to guarantee the autonomy of their
Churches. A striking move when we realise that until then the alien
communities had mainly relied on the king's or queen's arbitration. But
Archbishop Laud, and his policy of thorough anglicisation, had taught
them to beware of their natural protectors. The application to Parliament
marked an implicit transfer of allegiance. The impeachment of Laud
clearly states, in its twelfth article:

> He hath traitorously endeavoured to cause division and discord between
> the Church of England and other Reformed churches; and to that end
> hath suppressed and abrogated the privileges and immunities, which
> have been by his Majesty and his royal ancestors granted to the French
> and Dutch Churches in this kingdom: and divers other ways hath
> expressed his malice and disaffection to these Churches, that so by such
> disunions the papists might have more advantage for overthrow and
> extirpation of both.

In fact Laud's opponents appealed to the lasting tradition of Protestant
unanimity, so many times invoked among nations, and so often flouted by
States. The revolution did not set up as a confrontation between two
distinct camps with clear-cut boundaries which could have been defined
beforehand. Men were constantly wavering in their allegiances, and so
were the refugees. 'The force of events' – a striking tautology later
invoked by Saint-Just in the midst of the French Revolution – 'cruel
necessity' – in Cromwell's own terms – multiplied the antagonising rifts

---

[8] Further petitions to the Privy Council, as late as 1640: SP Dom., Ch. I, 470, nos. 90,
109, and 478.

between men; and it was perfectly possible to object strongly to Laud and yet resent the impending rebellion. Even during the Civil War, a compromise with the king retained, or even gained, supporters. Many things remained blurred and unsettled, and the refugee communities, or their individual members, oscillated between opposite positions, in a society affected by constant seismic cleavages.

Hérault vs. de La Marche: the champion of Caesar and the millenarian preacher

The year 1642 was remarkable for the Refuge on several counts: while Charles I raised his standard in the summer, by pure coincidence, the French Church in London lost its three pastors, Ezekiel Marmet, Gilbert Primerose and Nathaniel Marie, one after the other. An intractable situation arose the following year: pastor Hérault, who was called to London, proved to be a fervent advocate of the rights of kings; while conversely de La Marche, who was also approached as a possible minister, sided with the Good Old Cause. The latter of these two men soon caused an uproar; his sanguine expectation that the king would be defeated was judged unbecoming for a Christian, as well as hazardous for a foreign community: the Lord of Hosts, in his mercy, had not clearly chosen his camp. A certain amount of moderation and self-control were deemed preferable for the time being. On 7 March, the buoyant pastor was kindly reprimanded:

> The company has taken into consideration that M. de La Marche has preached for a long time in this Church, without receiving any gratuity from the Church; it is ordered, therefore, that he shall be given £12, and that he shall be asked for the future not to refer to state affairs in his sermons. He is likewise required to pray for the King of England and the rest of the Royal Family.

On 27 April, he had to be called to order again, for apparently he misunderstood the question of the 'Church glorious', and was inclined to favour openly the great pursuit of the millennium, whereas, whatever his opinions, greater reserve would have been appropriate.

But this was nothing compared to the bewilderment which surrounded pastor Hérault's arrival from the Norman city of Alençon. With more spirit than foresight, he delivered three Royalist sermons to a dumb-founded congregation, with all the fine baroque flights of pulpit oratory which characterised seventeenth-century French rhetoric. This was in February 1643. The war had been raging for six months and while a large-scale Royalist offensive was feared against London, Hérault did not fail to preach submission to the king and public repentance. A non-committal prayer for peace in general would certainly have sounded acceptable. Who would not have agreed that 'In the present state of the kingdom, troubled with wars and division ... all men of goodwill, all true *children of God*, set their hopes in peace, long for it, and wish for it with all their minds and hearts'? Moreover, conciliation was gaining ground in February, although negotiations with the king, who had taken refuge in Oxford, unfortunately failed again. The very interpretation of Luke 20:25 was controversial. 'Caesar's due' was one of the Royalist mottoes:

> Render unto Caesar the things which be Caesar's, and unto God the things which be God's. Render unto all what is due to them; tribute where tribute is due; tolls where tolls are due; fear where fear is due; honour where honour is due. Submit to every human authority for love of God: that is, to the King, because he is placed above all others.

But how, in the middle of the City of London which had taken up arms against Charles, could men be expected to pray to 'Him who brings deliverance unto kings and heals them from the blow of the dangerous sword'? Such epic style, with its protracted effects, may delight the historian; it exasperated the audience, and so did the irrelevant reminder that the monarch was the 'Lord's anointed' – following Psalm 105. Moreover, an allusion to the king as father of his people, who owed him their filial affection in return, did nothing to mitigate the unsavoury lecture. For the time being the newcomer's provoking sincerity brought him a heavy penalty, and he returned to his flock in Alençon, bruised and wounded. He was to make his triumphant come-back seventeen years later, under the Restoration, now crowned with the honour of this first, smarting blow.

But this confrontation between the Anglo-Norman de La Marche and the French pastor Hérault is also revealing of the misunderstanding which surrounded the English revolution; at least, the Protestant Churches of France carefully avoided any show of sympathy for the Great Rebellion, while Hérault was certainly the last to defend that hotbed of sedition on his return home.

The revolution and the Second Coming

It was a sign of the times that as late as 1644, the 26th Colloquy of the French-Speaking Churches, though headed by Jean de La Marche, took place officially 'under the protection of the most puissant king of great Britain and his honourable Parliament'. Though Roundheads and Cavaliers confronted one another on the battlefields, a spurious legal pretence persisted for a time: the war was not waged against the king, but against his 'evil' counsellors. While preaching the unity of the kingdom, men came to grips and killed one another for the greater glory of the king. Friends or foes alike pretended to be the loyal servants of his Majesty, and it was in the name of the king that Parliament fought Charles I. A cynic might make much of this paradox: the service of the king, taken to the point of rebellion. J. Hexter commented, with American alacrity, upon the paradoxical situation. 'The King himself denied that anyone misled him; he accepted full responsibility for the deed the Houses tried to palm off on hidden forces of darkness. All Parliament's talk about evil councillors was patently a silly fiction.'[9]

This deceiving cover-up may sound confusing. While paying lip service to the Crown, Parliament indicted first and foremost the 'evil councillors' of the king, whose momentary loss of prestige endangered the very fabric of the realm. The forces of change have certainly been overestimated in the past; yet a character like Jean de La Marche, who demanded the king's execution, called for an irreversible process of such magnitude that it could only be expressed in semi-allegorical terms. Indeed, his congregation only accepted him with reservations, but he gained influence as time elapsed. Strangely enough, his prophecy came true: Charles I was eventually executed, thus fulfilling the predictions of the pastor. One thing remains difficult to elucidate: why did radicalism so often take the form of prophecy?

From 1645 to 1648, the Church of London underwent a 'tumult' of its own. The German-born Cisner, who lacked the glib eloquence of Jean de La Marche, realised that he had been excluded by his fiery fellow-pastor. A pamphlet, *La Complainte de l'Eglise Française de Londres* (*A Complaint from the French Church in London*), deplored this lack of Christian meekness, and indicted Jean de La Marche, whose tedious prolixity did not fall short of 'preaching to the walls'.

The Coetus – gathering French, Dutch and Italian refugees – lamented this unrestrained behaviour, and Cisner's exclusion from the ministry. An enquiry into the *cause célèbre* rests on piecemeal evidence: the consistory registers having been carefully erased, in order to remove all signs of a quarrel which, one can tell, concealed the increasingly radical involvement of Jean de La Marche and· of his followers. Hence, no doubt, the determination to remove compromising traces; yet the attempt at reconciling the divided brethren is in itself insufficient to explain this selective memory which renders the historian's task decidedly difficult. Fortunately, the deliberations of the Coetus afford a slightly clearer picture. It seems that de La Marche, together with an influential part of the consistory, exercised a form of doctrinaire dictatorship which was bitterly resented:

> He observes none of the rules of our Discipline, but governs everything
> as he pleases, having six or seven of the elders on his side: first of all he

[9] J. Hexter, *The Reign of King Pym*, Harvard, 1941, p. 106.

declares his judgement on the matter in question, and his elders follow without giving any reasons and without listening to any which may be advanced on the other side, so that the other elders are of no more account than the figure nought in a number. All those who do not submit immediately to his orders he suspends from Communion, without any delay or warning, and he often acts on his own authority, without asking the consistory to vote. And when they are thus suspended, if they fall ill and die, he will not seek to reconcile them or offer them consolation. At his suggestion, the records of the consistory are altered after the event, and some are not entered in the register at all.[10]

That long list of objurgations would be almost wearisome to summarise. These anecdotes, bordering on gossip, should not conceal the significance of a crisis which coincided with the most outspoken episodes in the revolution: the election of agitators in the army, the rebuke of Presbyterian moderation, the Levellers' plea for a wider franchise. The opprobrium cast on Jean de La Marche, however inauspicious, reflects upon that situation: he was unquestionably a man of his time. On the question of the monarchy, he remained unflinchingly obstinate, even dismissive: 'ex-pounding the 13th chapter of St Luke, concerning the parable of the fig-tree, he said that the king was the fig-tree, and not only did he bear useless fruit, but bad fruit, for it is three years now that God has awaited his repentance, but the fourth year has come, and if he bears no fruit, he will be cut down'. Once again we are allowed only to glimpse at an expurgated version of the fiery pastor's preaching:

> Concerning the doctrine which Monsieur de La Marche has preached to us at various times and from various passages, the meaning of which he twists and perverts, there would too much to relate here. We would only ask that the following be considered: he has often said that it is at present that Jesus Christ is coming to begin his temporal reign on earth, and to abolish the Beast or Antichrist which will fall in the year 1650, as he calculates.

The primary moving force of this Messianism – which is close to the thinking of other enthusiasts – is primarily the transformation of the doctrine of salvation into an impending reality – the Second Coming of the Lord is at hand. This belief definitely set apart the English revolution, and treated it as the apex, if not the end, of history. 'Here and now', Jean de La Marche seems to proclaim, 'a new era is beginning: England has been chosen, among all nations.' We feel understandably sceptical in the face of this flight of fancy, though we cannot ascertain, for lack of evidence, the number, let alone the social origin, of the supporters of Jean

[10] Schickler, *Les Eglises du Refuge en Angleterre*, II, pp. 214ff, for the remaining quotations.

de La Marche. Prophesying was indeed characteristic of the radical movements of early modern Europe: biblical imagery, with its vivid forcefulness, enabled men to express unheard-of speculations and 'might-have-beens', thus contravening the most deep-seated prohibitions. The king's death, for which Jean de La Marche clamoured several years in advance, did not simply involve a political scheme. Charles I's execution was in essence a metaphysical phenomenon, severing as it did the Gordian knot of the king's 'two bodies'. Christopher Hill's pages on Antichrist in seventeenth-century England rank among the most stimulating.[11] They clearly establish the tantalising force of that myth, before its decline after 1660. The great Marxist historian, who could hardly be suspected of irrationality, concludes his book with the following words:

> In one sense we have been exploring a trivial blind alley in human thought: but at all points it trembles on the edge of major intellectual issues. Above all, I hope I may have made good the point with which I started, that history is not an exclusively rational process; or if it is, then history's reason must include much which seems irrational to the historian, too obsessed perhaps by the standards of rationality fashionable in his own age and society.[12]

The 'blind alley in human thought' immediately reminded me of Jean de La Marche, whom one can well imagine bent over his Bible, searching there for the true meaning of the revolution, and seeking to justify, with a great many metaphors, positions which were perceived as extremist. It was clear that Joshua 8:9 condemned Charles I while the Book of Revelation spoke expressly of the English Parliament. This excess of zeal might well give cause for disquiet, and indeed it did.

Revolution in a single country

The English revolution did not succeed in creating unanimity in the Protestant camp, despite the reference to the spirit of the Reformation. New rifts appeared, both in foreign policy and in home affairs. The Protestants of France seized upon these divisions to discredit an experiment which cast disquieting suspicion on their loyalty towards monarchies.

Where was the revolution to stop? What measure would be kept in the Reformation of Church affairs? Indeed, a religious split developed among the Parliamentarians and their allies; it soon took on a political turn. The Presbyterians, who favoured political moderation, quickly came to grips

---

[11] C. Hill, *Antichrist in Seventeenth-Century England*, Oxford, 1971.
[12] *Ibid.*, p. 177.

with the Independents, who demanded an extended freedom of worship and toleration. Milton and Cromwell were Independents; there were some Independents among the refugees themselves, and the term holds many surprises for us.

From 1644 onwards, the French Reformed Churches seized upon the word to express their fears in the face of the English revolution and to exonerate themselves in advance from any undue or hasty generalisations. The synod of Charenton forcefully condemned a doctrine which postulated the decentralisation of Church government, and advocated the anutomony of individual congregations:

> It has been reported by some deputies from the coast that several men coming from foreign countries call themselves *independents*, because they teach that each Church should be governed by its own laws, without being obliged to recognise the authority of colloquies and synods for its government and direction.[13]

They feared the 'contagion of that poison', which was detrimental to the Church and State, and led to the creation of as many 'religions as there are parishes or particular assemblies'. Moïse Amyraut, Professor of Divinity at the Academy of Saumur, was hardly more lenient towards those 'who would abolish the custom and authority of synods'.[14] He clearly asserted, using the classical political categories of antiquity, that 'as on the one hand the government of the Church is neither monarchical nor entirely aristocratic so on the other hand, it is not purely and simply democratic'.[15]

But one should not imagine that the Presbyterians, who were more moderate than the Independents and less 'democratic' in Amyraut's sense, deserved the unrestricted applause of their brethren on the Continent. On the contrary, the Presbyterians' attachment to an ecclesiastical discipline close to that of the French Churches made the identification all the more dangerous and troublesome; the younger Pierre du Moulin did not miss a single opportunity to distinguish his French coreligionists from the factious spirits in England.[16] His name is equally linked to the most impassioned of denunciations of *parricide*, according to the accepted expression, when treating of the execution of Charles I.

---

[13] *The General and Particular Acts and Articles of the Late National Synod of the Reformed Churches of France…*, London, 1646.

[14] M. Amyraut, *Du gouvernement de l'Eglise…*, Saumur, 1653.

[15] *Ibid.*, p. 409. I shall quote also another passage (p. 165): 'une démocratie toute pure…tient manifestement de l'humeur sauvage des barbares' ('a pure democray… manifestly partakes of the uncivil humour of barbarians').

[16] In particular his *Regii sanguinis clamor ad coelum adversus parricides anglicanos*, The Hague, 1652, which acquired an international celebrity. But Pierre du Moulin the younger had attacked Scottish Presbyterianism (in print as early as 1640), in *A Letter of a French Protestant to a Scottishman of the Covenant…*, London, 1640.

Others joined their voices to his; Moïse Amyraut, and above all the learned Claude Saumaise.[17]

One constant element runs through all this, an argument which we have already met in the context of Henri IV's assassination: only the pernicious influence of the Jesuits could explain tyrannicide. The thesis that the Jesuits were the originators of the English revolution, or rather bore full responsibility for the king's execution, was taught, among others, by Pierre du Moulin the younger. In 1664, the Anglican churchman of Huguenot extraction was to write to Sir William Morice, who sat in the Privy Council:

> The business is this: the year before our gracious King and glorious Martyr was murdered, the Council of the Jesuits in London resolved to send a deputation of their body first to the Sorbonne in Paris, and thence to Rome, to represent that the King was altogether averse to their religion, and that the laws and constitution of the State were destructive to their party. And that therefore they desired to be resolved whether they might lawfully labour by their friends in the Council of State and Army in England to bring the King to his death, and turn the monarchy into a republic.[18]

According to a number of authors, the competition between the Catholic faith and Protestant communions therefore rested on a political basis. Which was most favourable to monarchies, Catholicism or Protestantism? Opposite answers existed side by side: some argued, in line with James I's Erastian policy, that the pope's exorbitant powers interfered with the laws of free monarchies. This is apparently the position which Pierre du Moulin advocated in his letter, remembering the friendly links his father had already entertained with the Stuarts. Yet the Puritan revolution somewhat spoilt this image, and Protestantism, especially Calvinism, was suspected of harbouring the darkest designs towards law and order. As we shall see later, some of the Huguenots themselves, when they decided to conform to Anglicanism after 1660, had mixed feelings, or possibly second thoughts, about the Presbyterian discipline of all the Reformed Churches, with its dual emphasis on the equality of pastors and participation of laymen. Indeed, if all the pastors were equal, some were more equal than others; likewise, consistories often included the senior or

---

[17] M. Amyraut, *Discours de la souveraineté des roys*, Paris, 1650; Saumaise, *Defensio regia pro Carola I* (1649), French translation, *Apologie royale pour Charles I, roi d'Angleterre*, Paris, 1650.

[18] BL Add. MSS 8880, fol 190. W. Prynne may have been one of the originators of this type of rumour. He had written, as early as December 1648: 'All the present exorbitant actings against the king, parliament [and] government and their new-modelled representatives are nothing else but the *designs and projects of Jesuits, Popish priests and recusants...*' (my italics), quoted by J. Miller, *Popery and Politics in England, 1660–1688*, Cambridge, 1973, p. 85.

most affluent members of the community. Therefore, Amyraut was certainly right when he emphasised that the Reformed Churches of his time were based on the principles of *mixed government*. If monarchy was the best polity, the mixed character of the French Protestant discipline in no way contradicted the respect due to the king. Charles I's death was used as an argument in the struggle against Protestantism: Théophile Brachet, sieur de La Milletière, a lawyer from La Rochelle who had taken up the Roman faith, saw the king's death as a punishment attending England's schism in the preceding century, and a summons to conversion.[19]

An anatomy of silence

Under the Restoration, 'sectarians' and 'fanatics' alike were the subject of indiscriminate rebuke; some twenty years before, from the 1640s onwards, the Churches of the Refuge were troubled by ceaseless divisions. In a letter of 22 November 1648, addressed to the brethren of Canterbury, the Reformed Church of Amsterdam deplored the 'scandalous and unfortunate schisms' which disturbed 'the communion of the Saints' and were 'the plague of Zion'.[20] In September, the synod of Middleburg, in the Low Countries, tried to stem the rising tide of dissent, by decreeing: 'The Churches will be required not to receive at the Lord's Supper those who come with testimonials signed by the schismatic pastors and conventicles of England, until they have shown their repentance and disavowed the schism.[21]

These international sanctions constituted a last resort; everything possible had already been done: brotherly admonishments, colloquies, complaints to Parliament. The schismatics lingered on.

Every Church of importance went through a schism, and gave rise to a separate, parallel community. One of the effects of the revolution seemed to be the birth of rival conventicles within the Refuge. The Puritan ascendancy may partly account for these multiple rifts, and the emergence of ephemeral splinter groups in constant rivalry with one another, a strange mixture indeed of doctrinal devotion and sectarian attitudes.

Besides, 'schism' was, in more cases than one, an understatement in that age of motley heresies. It expressed a dysfunction, it confirmed a rift, without explaining its origin. Very few indications allow us to grasp the nature of these alignments; besides, the oppressive insults which the rival members heaped upon one another, and the terrible war cries which they uttered, did not prevent a certain amount of peaceful coexistence; and

[19] La Milletière, *La Victoire de la Vérité pour la Paix de l'Eglise, au roy de la Grande Bretagne, pour convier sa majesté d'embrasser la Foy Catholique*, Paris, 1651.
[20] Dean and Chapter Library, MSS U-47-H 1, fol. 47.   [21] *Ibid.*, fol. 43.

attacks on reputation often prevailed over open violence, an unexpected sign of moderation. As far as I can ascertain, contempt and scorn were pretty common, while disorderly behaviour remained the exception. Hence, the importance of slander. Quite naturally, allegations concerning sexual offence or past misconduct were rife. Did pastor Poujade hold schismatic assemblies in Canterbury? In fact he was a bigamist; his wife had stayed behind at Saint-Hippolyte in Languedoc, and his unfortunate servant Magdelaine had born the fruit of his sin; he had even promised to marry the poor creature. What a character! He had to flee in dishonour.[22] Besides, his theology was not altogether beyond reproach. He had been suspended from Communion, forbidden to preach and condemned by various synods. Moreover, he held that Christ had three natures, which is at least one too many. All that remained for him, then, was to leave, while his tearful wife was officially consoled for her grief.

Thus, schismatic ministers often seemed to conform to the stereotype of the depraved seducer. They led the faithful astray to be corrupted and deceived. Jean Despagne, the pastor of a dissenting community at Westminster, was rebuked for some youthful misdemeanour, thirty years before, and an indecent measure of publicity was given to this dubious, uncertain past.[23]

The Church of Monsieur Despagne

The community of Westminster preceded the Civil War, as well as survived it. Its rivalry with Threadneedle Street was primarily a matter of location: given the growth of the metropolis, the City of Westminster needed a Reformed parish of its own, which, strangely enough, became the French Conformist Church of the Savoy after 1662. Without any doubt, an element of social disparity underlay this geographical difference: from the beginning, the survival of Monsieur Despagne's community depended on the protection of the nobility. Benjamin de Rohan, duc de Soubise, who died in 1642, had gathered a small number of the faithful in his oratory; Lady Blanche Arundell, Philip Herbert, earl of Pembroke, and John Holles, earl of Clare, lent their help to the unswerving Despagne, who was exposed to the vehemence of his compatriots in the City. Indeed, Jean Despagne's political stance is elusive: a man of the centre, he favoured conciliation; his circumspection enabled him to live through two civil wars and the Protectorate without any major hardship. As late as 1648, he expressed his wish that a compromise would be found with Charles I;[24] but this hardly prevented him from increasing his influence in

---

[22] *Ibid.*, MSS U-47-H 3
[23] William Herbert, *Reponse aux questions de M. Despagne...*, 1657.
[24] Sermon read on 11 September 1648, 'On the future treaty between king and Parliament'.

the following decade, invoking that Protestant unanimity which deserved him a pension from Cromwell in the last years of his life. He died in 1659 and his congregation was eventually to embrace the Anglican confession.

This small community, consisting of about 600 persons in the 1650s,[25] was probably characterised by its relatively distinguished and conservative leaning. Very few sources are still extant, and we must resort to conjecture and rely solely upon the consistory records of Threadneedle Street and their biased observations or possibly read Jean Despagne's posthumous works – two volumes appeared in Geneva in 1671, *Shibboleth* and the *Essai des merveilles de Dieu en l'harmonie des temps* (*An Essay on the Wonders of God in the Harmony of Times*). These books bear witness both to an incontestable pastoral zeal and to a praiseworthy concern for exegetics; they are marked, also, by a cabbalistic number mysticism which led the author to compare his discoveries with those of Menasseh ben Israel, the famous Amsterdam rabbi who visited Cromwell in 1655 to discuss the resettlement of the Jews in England. Jean Despagne was undoubtedly one of the most talented intellectuals among the refugees of the time; and the quality of his preaching partly explained the misgivings which he aroused in the Church of London. Was he not leading astray part of the congregation? We know the influence of eloquence in matters of religion in the seventeenth century. In these times of obstinacy and obloquy, how can one fail to understand the appeal of Jean Despagne, who was one of the few men to admit: 'Where is the Moses who does not stammer, even after God has spoken to him?'[26] This mildness must have seemed a distinct relief after the abrasive de La Marche, and his boisterous sermons. In the midst of the fray, Jean Despagne retained a disconcerting courtesy, as an anecdote reveals. In March 1650, Delmé, the pastor at Canterbury, applied in person to Parliament, in the name of the Churches, to lodge a new petition against the schismatics. Jean Despagne, who happened to be there for the opposite purpose, came to greet his adversary, and left him quite dumbfounded; how can one always distinguish politeness from irony? Here is how Delmé described the encounter, still in the midst of absolute amazement: 'Nonetheless, the said Monsieur Despagne, seeing me before the entrance to Parliament, on Friday, where he was waiting with his friends and soliciting support, left his company and came to greet me with a deep bow, saying that he wanted to speak to me more fully. But I have not seen him since.'[27]

Indeed Jean Despagne's moderation may have sounded extremely attractive in those times of unrest. His community, more conservative in outlook, rested on a less authoritarian basis in practice, even though it was

[25] BL, Add. MSS 32093, fol. 314.
[26] Jean Despagne, *Shibboleth*, Geneva, 1671, p. 1.
[27] Dean and Chapter Library, MSS U-47-H 2, fol. 61.

technically a 'conventicle'. Thus 9 February 1643, we find this account in the register of their Threadneedle Street rivals:

> The Coetus having met, it was found expedient to present a petition to the Lords in Parliament assembled humbly asking for their help in suppressing all the *conventicles of foreigners* which are being formed in this city, both by Cursol and by Monsieur Despagne; a copy of the petition is in the consistory, as are the rest of the papers concerning this affair, for we have demonstrated to the Lords that those litigants' plea was unfounded, and we also insisted *that the consistory was in charge of naming the consistory pastors, and not the people as they claim*...We could not secure dissolution of the said assemblies or conventicles, which gathered, one at the house of Lady Arundell, and the other – that of Cursol – at the house of Sir Arthur Haselrig.

Cursol's group is still more difficult to grasp than the supporters of Jean Despagne, and it completely eludes analysis in terms of ideology. Etienne de Cursol, a former monk, had joined the Church of England under the primacy of Laud; at the beginning of the Civil War that cleric seemed to take malign enjoyment in diverting parishioners from the temple in the City. Their protector, Arthur Haselrig, sat in Parliament; for some he was too idealistic, but to others he seemed a conservative; he has been seen by a recent historian as an 'oligarchical republican'.[28] But how can we deduce from all this any clear profile of the former monk's confederates?

The revolution in the provinces

In Norwich, between 1643 and 1650, the French-speaking community embraced the revolutionary cause, and expelled its pastor, Pierre Delaune who had been their minister for forty years. His loyalty had deserved him the protection of the king, an ecclesiastical preferment and a doctorate in divinity. Although now in his seventies, and in spite of his parishioners' commitment to the revolution, Pierre Delaune did not deny his previous allegiance to the Church and Crown. The high-spirited Pierre d'Assigny, newly arrived from the Channel Islands, ousted him. An attempt was made to reconcile the two men at the Colloquy of May 1644, but in vain. As far as Delaune was concerned, the delegates could not deny 'the scandal which he had brought upon the Church by his vindication of the bishops' (article 23). This 'Root and Branch' scorn against the episcopalian settlement was common at the time: 'prelates' appeared as the very symbol of the former establishment in Church and State. And yet the Colloquy, presided over by the fiery de La Marche whose opposition

[28] John R. MacCormack, *Revolutionary Politics in the Long Parliament*, Harvard, 1973, p. 8.

to the king's men was relentless, preached concord between the two pastors, and suggested that d'Assigny should assist de La Marche. Two years later, however, the assembly was still deploring the same disordered situation, and they requested the arbitration of the Committee for Plundered Ministers, charged by Parliament with the redress of ecclesiastical abuses. This was of no avail; the schismatic community was classified as *independent*, an indication which proves to be significant.

An agreement was reached in 1650; d'Assigny had to flee, and even though some members of the community refused to return to the fold, the affair seemed to have come to an end. Why was this? For want of explicit arguments, I would suggest that the end of the Civil War, the execution of the king, the proclamation of the Commonwealth incited the refugees to heal their wounds. Such a coincidence in time cannot be fortuitous, and shows the growing integration of refugees.

In Canterbury, on the contrary, the schism did not win unanimous support as it nearly did in Norwich. Two rival congregations confronted each other in this city, which numbered a good many Royalists among its citizens, as well as Puritan radicals. Pastor Poujade, who had arrived from Languedoc in 1638 in a state of utter destitution, quickly incurred the enmity of the other two incumbents, Delmé and Bulteel. The revolution exacerbated what was undoubtedly at first a quarrel between individuals. Poujade and Delmé came into open conflict; a spirited debate followed, which was taken to London in 1646, each camp accusing the other of the worst of doctrinal deviations: the two natures of Christ, the question of the salvation of the papists, predestination, the words spoken by Christ to the woman at Canaan. In the midst of the revolution, such, apparently, were the causes of disagreement between the rival communities; can we really take this seriously? The theological originality attributed to Poujade was no greater than that of many among his contemporaries, especially in England. There was little sympathy for the dissenting pastor, who was distinguished only by his faults: 'deceitfulness', 'perjury', 'imposture' and bigamy, as we learn from a bizarre catalogue of his 'divers particular faults and vices'.[29] Give a dog a bad name and hang him. Faced with this wave of hostile condemnation, Poujade cloaked himself in wounded dignity; he had his vocation directly from the Saviour: the elders who were persecuting him could not say the same. As Elisabeth Labrousse once observed to me, 'This Poujade of yours is a *dévot*!' There is something of the *dévot*, of the conspicuously pious in Poujade, even the baroque style of his preaching, given to interminable digressions concerning the relative merits of the blood sweated by Jesus in the Garden of Olives and of that which flowed from the wounds at the Crucifixion.

---

[29] Dean and Chapter Library, MSS U-47-H 3, fol. 32.

His parishioners, besides, found his commentaries 'too affected' to be edifying.

At this point the antipathy towards Poujade took on a political turn, as exemplified by another manuscript in the voluminous dossier entitled 'A brief account of the disorder brought about in the Walloon Church of Canterbury by the intrigues of Monsieur Joseph Poujade and his adherents since the order of Parliament against them on April 17 1648.'[30] Parliament, or rather the Committee for Plundered Ministers, having already admonished Poujade in August 1647 'not to make any disturbance in the said congregation', forced him to withdraw from Canterbury in April of the following year. It seems that the Poujadists had become embroiled in the Kentish rebellion which has been aptly described as 'the last' of the 'great local insurrections of English history'.[31] The very nature of the Walloons' involvement is difficult to assess, since at the Restoration – as we shall see – both camps pretended they had fought for the king. Yet it sounds plausible that some of the Poujadists tended to side with the rioters, while the majority party among the refugees, who had not forgotten their past strife with Laud, were favourable to Parliament. According to the 'Brief account', the 'faction' – i.e. the schismatics – had canvassed the city in May 1648, forcing all recalcitrant refugees to sign a counter-revolutionary petition: 'At the time of the uprising in this province, more than sixty among them voluntarily took up arms against Parliament – carrying a spear, the pastor of that congregation followed the drummer through the city in the guise of a sergeant raising troops – and they threatened us openly with looting.'

Yet this text is not very clear. Who is the pastor in question 'who followed the drummer through the city?' Probably François de La Prix, Poujade's nominee and successor. But how should we interpret his offensive gesture? F.W. Cross, who published an authoritative *History of the Walloon and Huguenot Church in Canterbury*, misread the French manuscript, and his mistake deserves to be quoted as it entirely changes the interpretation of the event: 'When the revolt of the *Prince* [*sic* for *province*] occurred, more than sixty of them voluntarily took up arms against the Parliament, issuing from their congregation after one with a drum [*sic* for *le Pasteur de leur congregation suivant le tambour*] who carried his halleborde as a sergeant, etc.'[32]

This Freudian slip – *Prince* for *province* – entirely changes our view of the Kentish rebellion: was it primarily a local phenomenon, which took on a national dimension, or a straightforward Royalist move? Our evidence is relatively scanty in the case of the Walloons, and we have to

---

[30] *Ibid.*, MSS U-47-H 2, fol. 42.   [31] Everitt, *The Community of Kent*, p. 241.
[32] F.W. Cross, *History of the Walloon and Huguenot Church at Canterbury, Publications of the Huguenot Society of London*, 'Quarto Series', xv, 1898, p. 128. My italics.

turn to secondary sources.[33] The Kentish 'tumult' sparked off in 1647 when the mayor of Canterbury endeavoured to proscribe the celebration of Christmas, in order to reform men and manners, and extirpate what he took to be lingering popish practices according to parliamentary regulations against feast days. But the Puritan cultural revolution failed as others have done since that date, and a crowd gathered on the market place preventing all trade on that holy day. The following spring, a petition circulated throughout the county leading to downright rebellion against Parliament. We should therefore treat Poujade's case with the greatest of caution: it would be misleading to surmise that local quarrels blindly followed the alleys of national politics, as it were. Dr Alan Everitt, in his seminal thesis on the *Community of Kent and the Great Rebellion*, has taught us to pay due attention to provincial phenomena. Cromwell's regime was indeed to mark the ascendancy of the 'nation-state over the local community'.[34] This was yet a gradual, dynamic process which displaced former contradictions between centre and periphery, or between Westminster and 'the dark corners of the land' if ever this grim description could apply to Kent and the 'garden of England'. Indeed Poujade's opponents, and especially his fellow-pastor Delmé, were branded as 'malignants' and 'roundheads' by the rioters. But did they simply realise what the revolution was all about? While the crypt of Canterbury cathedral – where to this day Protestant services are held in French – was invaded by a Poujadist commando, who reissued this offensive operation several times, should we regard this domestic feud between Walloons as an English national issue? Indeed, poor Poujade paid heavily for his involvement; on 16 July 1649, he was indicted by Parliament, or at least by the Committee for Plundered Ministers, and was obliged to quit, issuing his *Apology* to answer '*The False and injurious accusations of his adversaries*'. The schism lingered on, however, until 1654, and gathered fresh momentum three years later.

The times of the New Alliance

As expected, personal rivalries underlay the schism within the Refuge. Similarly, these alignments did not fail to echo political opinions. Yet there remains a third dimension, that of cultural shifts. An impassioned controversy started in September 1654; it had incalculable consequences,

---

[33] In particular, J.C. Cox, *Canterbury. A Historical and Topographical Account of the City*, London, 1905, contains a very good narrative of the period, using some interesting material like the *Declaration of many thousands of the City of Canterbury or County of Kent, concerning the late Tumult in the City of Canterbury, provokt by the Mayor's violent proceedings, against those who desired to continue the Celebration of the Feast of Christ's Nativity, 1500 years and upwards maintained in the Church.*

[34] Everitt, *The Community of Kent*, p. 17.

since the community of London was torn apart by a new cleavage. A rival group formed, around pastor Elie Delmé, the son of the Canterbury minister; they aimed at the abolition, or at least the reform, of the liturgical calendar: the celebration of Christmas, Easter or Whitsun was for them a matter of superstition. Far from being occasions for edification, these festivals gave rise to much feasting and other profane (and, in their eyes, licentious) amusements. On this account, Elie Delmé embodied one of the facets of the most extreme form of English Puritanism, which sought to promote a new man, completely freed from all traces of idolatry. This demand was not alien to the spirit of the Reformation in general; but without dwelling at length on the tone of the letter which Delmé sent to Cromwell in June 1656, its vocabulary betrays a sensibility more English than French. It resumes, in fact, the pamphleteering campaign of the first half of the seventeenth century, which demanded, against the king's advice, the prohibition of Sunday recreation – open-air 'sports' and Maypole dancing which were accused of encouraging vice, sloth and lasciviousness.

These terms may sound outrageous to us; from the very beginning they became the butt of anti-Puritan mockery.[35] Our surprise or irritation, however, must give way to the recognition of a new, and profoundly interesting, debate. The English revolution resulted in a remoulding of everyday life, leading, as it did, to a new perception of time and space. This is obvious enough if we compare a modern historian's predicament with Elie Delmé's own words in 1656:

> A feature which strikes one forcefully when working on ecclesiastical records is that there was a constant battle between the sacred and the profane, both in relation to *time* and *space*.[36]
> Alan Macfarlane

> We believe that Jesus Christ by his death hath taken away all that obligation inherent either to *places* or *times*, and that distinction of days which was in force under the Old Testament. We believe that all days are equal and that it is a weakness in faith to make more of one day than another.[37]
> Elie Delmé, letter to Cromwell, June 1656

The parallel between these two excerpts seems to me altogether remarkable. Elie Delmé explicitly envisaged a redefinition of time and space; and he even used these terms, thus anticipating the current concerns of historical anthropology. As always, it is well to beware of anachronism, and to avoid the nondescript annexation of the past by the

---

[35] In this connection, see Francisque Costa's, *Izaac Walton*, Paris, 1973.

[36] Macfarlane, *Reconstructing Historical Communities*, p. 195.

[37] As related in *A Justification of the Proceedings of the French Church in London, about the Suspension of Mr Elijah Delmey*, 1656, p. 26.

present. Elie Delmé reacted as a theologian; the secularisation of time and space is associated here with Christian revelation. 'Linear time', 'vectorial time', as Pierre Chaunu has written.[38] I would add immediately, 'uniform time', in Elie Delmé's conception. This criticism and rejection of the liturgical calendar implies the abandonment of the cyclical conception of time, inherited from the Ancients. The excessive celebration of festivals is akin to paganism, or at best to the Old Law. Christ's irruption into history has altered the flow of time, salvation has become a present reality. What then is the purpose of recreating in the calendar year an expectation – or 'advent' – when now there is nothing to await? In this perspective, the new-born era of the revolution saw the fulfilment of the New Alliance.

Elie Delmé and his revolutionary Messianism had a lot in common with Jean de La Marche – who had died recently. He too was the butt of criticism, even though as early as 1644 a synod had officially decreed 'the suppression of festivals, such as Christmas'. But in practice, there were many pockets of resistance, centred on deeply rooted tradition. Moreover, Christian persuasion cannot entirely do without outward signs. The impatience of the Puritans, their iconoclasm, disturbed the life of the Churches, and led to sectarianism. The arguments directed against Elie Delmé were revealing; he was neither regarded as a heretic nor accused of leading an ungodly life. He was only mistaken in matters indifferent; his intransigence had led him to call one of his critics a 'Judas'. Hence an appeal for moderation, in the same month of June 1656:

> The pastors will abstain from preaching against each other, and from giving anyone just cause for personal offence in their sermons: but each shall be free to preach as he thinks fit concerning indifferent things, that is to say such matters as do not contravene Holy Scripture, or the Confession of our Churches.[39]

A pamphlet, now in the Guildhall Library, clearly states the case: *A Justification of the Proceedings of the French Church in London, about the Suspension of Mr Elijah Delmey*, 1656.[40] Delmé (or Delmey) refused to take the advice of his consistory: several 'factious persons' followed him and held 'private assemblies'. The separatists had been in existence for about two years when the pamphlet was written – which seems to correspond with the beginning of the Protectorate.

The heart of the matter was Delmé's refusal to acknowledge the existence of 'things indifferent' – or *adiaphora*. A certain element of latitude is indeed necessary to sustain the common piety of a congregation. We have seen in the case of James I how the doctrine of 'things indifferent' was one of the pillars of the 'Anglican' *via media*. But the same would certainly

---

[38] Chaunu, *Culture et société*, p. 49.
[39] London, Guildhall Library, MSS 7412/1, p. 54.
[40] Delmé, *A Justification*: Guildhall Library, Pamphlet 5692.

apply to any Church whatsoever: along with the basic tenets of Christianity – or 'Articles of faith', – a number of private opinions remain legitimate: 'What minister is able to live with such a man, who makes all his *private opinions* to pass for so many *Articles of Faith* and condemns all the opinions of his colleagues and of almost all the Doctors of the Reformed Churches which are contrary to his, as so many heresies?'[41]

Hence, what was at stake was neither Delmé's theology, nor his way of life, but rather his tyrannical behaviour: 'If after all this we be asked what sufficient ground we have to suspend him seeing that he is neither an heretic nor an ill-liver. Truly we have not grounded our sentence against him upon any such thing. We do not accuse him of drunkenness, fornication, adultery or theft, but of rebellion against ecclesiastical order.'[42]

The real issue, in fact, was the keeping of holy days. The godly had long waged a war against the profanation of the Lord's Day, while conversely they insisted on the enforcement of strict Sabbatarianism.[43] The quietness of an English Sunday has proved a lasting feature for visitors from abroad, at least till a fairly recent date. E.P. Thompson was even to insist for a later period on the 'marriage of convenience' between 'puritanism' and 'industrial capitalism': they promoted alike 'new valuations of time'.[44] But what then was to become of Christmas, Easter and Whitsuntide? In December 1643, the Assembly of Divines, of which Elie Delmé's father was a member, raised the question of preaching on 'holy' days: if all days were equal (Romans 14:5), how could some days be more equal than others? Yet, as R.S. Paul has aptly put it, 'the Puritan suppression of Christmas was detested'.[45]

The Stranger Churches could not remain neutral and had mixed feelings about this suppression:

> In England they used heretofore to keep some days holy, and among others those of Christ's nativity, New Year's day, Easter, Pentecost, and the days that follow them; upon which there was preaching, and afterwards by an ill custom almost everyone upon those days was licentious and gave himself to games and sports. They that undertook the reformation of Church and State having abolished that scrupulous and superstitious observation of holy days, many Ministers did not think it fit to preach upon those days, hoping that by that means they would be no more considered than other common days. But it is happened through the inclination that men have to retain that which contributes to their content and delight, that although many had removed the exercises of

[41] *Ibid.*, p. 15.   [42] *Ibid.*, p. 10.
[43] C. Hill, *Society and Puritanism*, London, 1964, ch. 5: 'The Uses of Sabbatarianism'.
[44] E.P. Thompson, 'Time, Work-Discipline, and Industrial Capitalism', *Past and Present*, 38 (1967), p. 95.
[45] R.S. Paul, *The Assembly of the Lord*, Edinburgh, 1985, p. 438.

piety, they could not remove the ordinary licentiousness from that time, nay rather, whereas before that time people spent part of those days in devotion and another part in sports, now after the removing of the exercises of piety the most part spends them wholly in licentiousness; so that which was good was taken away, and the most part of the evil is left.[46]

The situation was clear enough: the stranger communities did not object to the removal of Christmas as such, but they took into account the weight of tradition. The secularisation of Christmas did not prevent the common people from indulging in profane activities on those days. The result was even worse than expected: as no preaching marked the celebration, paganism set in. Moreover, even in the midst of the Puritan revolution, the strangers insisted on keeping their own discipline unaffected by the surrounding Reformation. This separatist feeling even gained ground as years elapsed:

> Doubtless our Churches, after the example of the Dutch Churches ought to retain their ancient customs according to the privileges which they have to exercise their own Discipline. Yet one of the Ministers of our Church [de La Marche?], of his own private motion, without any commission from our Consistory, did propound to the Colloquies of our Churches in the year 1644 that holy days should be abolished thereby meaning that the exercises of piety should be left off which were used to be done in those days.[47]

Yet, in 1654, a new compromise was reached, explaining Elie Delmé's reaction:

> Since that time the Church of London in the last Colloquy held in the year 1654 moved a question whether by that act of the precedent Colloquy it was intended to brand with superstition and idolatry the Reformed Churches which use sermons upon those days. Which being resolved in the negative, we seeing our people to give over working upon those days as the other people of the land, seeing also that most part of the people wished for the sermons, thought fit of late to satisfy that just and religious desire.[48]

The Stranger Churches did not wish to sever their links with the Continent or to antagonise the most conservative of the faithful who insisted on keeping some holy days, apart from the Sabbath. But their moderation in the late 1650s may also serve to conceal their own 'experience of defeat':[49] the 'reforming of Reformation itself' – in Milton's words – had failed, or rather in those times of protectorate,

---

[46] Delmé, *A Justification*, pp. 23–4.   [47] *Ibid.*, p. 24.   [48] *Ibid.*
[49] C. Hill, *The Experience of Defeat*, London, 1984. Mr Hill's experience of defeat in the case of the English revolution starts in 1649, with the Levellers' demise.

following the turmoil of the revolution, how could one still reasonably expect a thorough change of men and manners?

Integration and xenophobia

One should maybe revolutionise revolutions and beware of fixed patterns of deference and allegiance. In that equivocal age, from *c*. 1642 to *c*. 1660, the refugees did not adopt a one-sided stance to King and Parliament, Independency or Presbyterianism. Neither did the English hosts display unguarded sympathy towards their foreign brethren. The *Moderate Publisher of Every Day's Intelligence* complained on 29 July 1653:

> There is another oppression of poor handicraftsmen, English and strangers, since the late parliament's dissolving, hotly followed by informers, set on by some monopolizing companies, who to keep all trade in their own hand, cannot be contended with their privilege of the City, but in former time got patents by friends and money, extending some miles from the City to bring all men of the same craft under their jurisdiction, and to pay to their halls, though they dwell out of their liberties: some companies suffer no man to be a Master, though he be a better workman than themselves but whom they please, under a pretence of seeing no bad ware made ... It were considerable to cause their several patents to be brought to view, that they might not tyrannize over their brethren by their unknown laws. *They are very hot in persecuting of many alien friends, who have lived many years, married Englishwomen, children born here, paid all taxes all the time of the late war here.*

The refugees' 'affection to the Commonwealth' was indeed one of the arguments used on their behalf, in order to advocate their integration. Likewise, the aliens' plight was taken up to indicate the imperfections of lingering officialdom; 'monopolies', the use of mercenary informers by patentees were among the grievances expressed by Parliament in the preceding half century. The *Moderate Publisher* presented the strangers and other 'poor handicraftsmen' as the past victims of the Court. The London Weavers' Company insisted in this same year 1653:

> Whereas divers persons born in foreign nations do dwell and reside in this Commonwealth setting up and exercising as master the trade of weaving contrary to several statutes in that case provided, some whereof were constrained to come out of their own countries for conscience sake and others have here inhabited many years and married English wives, and *in the late war have manifested much affection to the Commonwealth by adventuring themselves in the public service and contributed their estates likewise*, and others of them have lately come over into England and are not members of the church and yet do use and exercise the trade of weaving to the great damage and dishonour of the Commonwealth and prejudice of this corporation. It is therefore fit and so ordered by this

> Court that such of the said aliens as lived any considerable time and
> declared their affection to the Commonwealth and prove their service to
> the trade of weaving as aforesaid shall be admitted as members of this
> company and so become subject to the government thereof. And that
> such others of the aliens as are lately come over shall not be permitted to
> exercise the said trade of weaving any longer but be proceeded against
> according to the laws and statutes of this nation.[50]

A lasting settlement in the kingdom and good services to the
Commonwealth were therefore regarded as extenuating circumstances for
past offences. Yet local prejudices could interfere with peaceful solutions,
and the drainage of the fens by refugees was still resented by the native
English population if we are to believe the 'Petition of the farmers and
tenants of the level of Hatfield Chase, within the Counties of York,
Lincoln, Nottingham', c. 1660. The poor foreign settlers expressed their
grievances to Charles II:

> In 1642 the inhabitants of Misterton and Epworth, taking up arms
> against the King took advantage thereof to break in upon petitioners,
> took away their cattle, pulled down their houses, and destroyed their
> crops; this violence was repeated in 1652, and the inhabitants then on the
> Lord's day came to the church at Sandtoft, where petitioners were
> allowed to hold a service in French, forced away the minister and
> congregation, broke and pulled down and burnt the windows, doors,
> seats, and pulpits, stole the lead, and made a slaughterhouse of the
> church, and buried carrion in it.[51]

These few examples – the *Moderate Publisher's* testimony, the London
Weaver's Company regulations or the Hatfield Chase petition –
all seemed to take for granted a sharp Court vs. Country divide, dating
back to the first half of the century. Yet, interestingly enough, the
strangers assumed contradictory positions: local feuds were rarely one-
sided, and tended to cut across received patterns of deference and loyalty
to King and Parliament. This may in turn call into question any set
interpretation of attitudes: the refugees lived through the turmoil as well
as they could, and though massively alienated from the Crown in the late
1630s, or so it seems, they always kept an eye on their immediate interest.

The revolution revisited

Why deny the fact? When one considers the hardships encountered by
Englishmen in those years, the desultory conflicts within the Refuge may
sound derisory – a farcical comment on the outside world. More often
than not, the echoes of the Civil War and Interregnum reach us only
indistinctly, muffled by the din of internal quarrels, a pitiful caricature of

[50] Guildhall Library, MSS 4655/5: Court Minute Book of the Weavers Company, fol.
24. My italics.   [51] Historical Manuscripts Commission, *Seventh Report*, p. 110.

the great confrontations which tore England asunder; could it be that the history of the refugees has nothing to offer but a faint and partial image of England in the period of the revolution? In fact, the number of personal attacks, the heavy dossier collected against an individual such as Poujade are matched by the painful silence that surrounds the great events which were to hold the attention of Whig or Marxist historians. Little is said of the glorious battles, from Edgehill to Naseby, which marked the course of these years; the Leveller movement, the Commonwealth, Cromwell's Protectorate do not appear in broad light. At first, this led me to feel, not just impatience, but bitterness and frustration; was it that my initial assumption – that the alien communities provide one of the keys to understanding society as a whole – had led me to a blind alley? After all, the study of the refugees might prove to be of purely peripheral interest. I deciphered my archives with exasperation, in search of purple patches and heroic deeds, and found only pettiness, rancour, calumny, slander and denunciations. I had set foot on English soil in quest of a revolution, and only discovered a Puritan version of my native *Clochemerle*.

In the end, I came to rejoice at the fact; the corrective was indeed salutary. My sources provided no resounding exploits nor episodes of bloodshed. What good fortune! I was left with everyday life, and the territory I was exploring was one of the most appropriate fields of investigation to study the mechanisms of community life, the indefinite network of local solidarities and provincial resistance which English historians have recently put at the heart of their enquiries. What was lost in terms of heroism was gained in depth. A profoundly interesting problem presented itself; how was the reality of the revolution perceived by figures of secondary, or less than secondary, importance? What hidden force led individuals to align themselves with one party or another? Even in the midst of revolution, indifference may assert itself. More fundamentally still, the relationship between national politics and local feuds, bordering on private confrontation, had too often been neglected. From the start, these involved a degree of ambiguity. For, if there exists a link between the schism within the Refuge and the disorders of the kingdom, it is a complex and shifting correlation.

This parallel between the conflicts which divided the refugees and the rifts in the society around them seemed self-evident to the men of the time. Thus the consistory of Canterbury declared: 'To God we pray with all our hearts and minds that He may deliver this kingdom and our Church from these troubles and confusions, and restore peace and good order, to the glory of His great name and to the salvation and consolation of His children.'[52]

[52] Dean and Chapter Library, MSS U-47-H 2, fol. 14: Letter to P. Delmé, 3 August 1647.

Table 1. *The competition between Churches, c. 1640–60*

Official Churches	Schismatic Churches
Church of London (Threadneedle St)	*Schismatic community of London, 1642–4?*
Jean de La Marche (+1651)	Etienne de Cursol
J.-B. Stouppe (from 1652)	*Community of Elie Delmé, 1654–8*
Cisner	*Community of Westminster*
Elie Delmé	Jean Despagne (+1659) became Conformist Church of Savoy, after 1661
Church of Canterbury	*Schismatic community of Canterbury, 1645–54, 1657–62*
Philippe Delmé (+1653)	Joseph Poujade (expelled about 1649)
Le Keux	François de La Prix
	Crespin
	2nd Schism
	Jannon (from 1657)
Church of Norwich	*Schismatic community of Norwich, 1643–50?*
Pierre Delaune	Pierre d'Assigny

For the revolution, like all other visitations and trials – war, pestilence or famine – fell (and possibly still falls) within the province of metaphysics. And the lesions in the body politic, the disruption of its organic laws are manifest first of all in the dissolution of the 'fundamental solidarities' of kith and kin which – as Robert Mandrou pointed out a quarter of a century ago – are such an important element in collective psychology.[53]

While this digression into a narrative of the principal schisms seemed to be necessary, I should now like to examine what politics actually meant, at least for the refugees, in the 1640s. I have endeavoured to work out a suitable pattern of interpretation, on the basis of a few data. Let us sum up the principal rivalries which appeared in the case of the three largest communities, London, Canterbury and Norwich (see Table 1).

This table contains many uncertainties. The first of these obscurities is sociological: the sources themselves are silent in this respect – for want of sufficient information, neither social class nor age-group can be established. Would the results be conclusive, in any case? For contemporaries, on the contrary, conflicts between persons were far more important. The insidious aspects of the attacks – the immorality of Poujade – served the purpose of disestablishing an ascendancy which, one

[53] R. Mandrou, *Introduction to Modern France, 1500–1640. An Essay in Historical Psychology*, New York, 1977.

can tell, was strongly affective, even passionate, in nature. Attachment to the schismatic Churches assumed the character of allegiance, or of deviation. It shared with the revolution as a whole the character of a rebellion against natural authority in Church or State.

Another disconcerting peculiarity is that these antagonisms transcended ideologies, and the boundary which separated schismatics so distinctly from the mainstream Churches does not follow the outlines of clearly defined political camps. It would be pointless to suggest a cleavage between the King's men and Parliament, moderates and radicals. In spite of his millenarianism and his advanced ideas, Jean de La Marche supported the Royalist, Delaune, in Norwich. *Esprit de corps* with a fellow-pastor? Or Christian charity? The first of these explanations seems more convincing. Jean de La Marche may have been a radical revolutionary, he nonetheless behaved as a bureaucrat, as many revolutionaries have done since. Likewise the dissenting groups, whatever the motives of their separation, tended to flock together without any clear ideological common ground between them. François de La Prix, the successor of Poujade, who was suspected of Royalist leanings, received the lay-on of hands from d'Assigny, a supporter of the revolution, 'without his even examining the said candidate's *doctrine*, or the *conduct* of his life'.[54] And, to add to the confusion, under the Restoration, schismatics and orthodox accused one another of having lapsed. In 1662, a broadsheet testified: Poujade's schism in Canterbury was dictated by loyalty to Charles I, the martyr king.[55] There is some truth in this, no doubt, just as it is a proof of faithfulness to the Crown that the late Monsieur Despagne's community made the transition to Anglicanism. But the conflicts of the 1640s cannot be explained solely by the positions which men came to adopt at a later period; this retrospective view, this selective memory do not provide an adequate guideline. Meric Casaubon, son of the scholar befriended by James I, had the arduous task of reconciling the two rival communities in Canterbury about 1662. He clearly expressed his scepticism: were Poujade's supporters Royalists? What seems clear is that they left their Church, and joined the rank and file of sedition. And one senses that the Anglican Casaubon felt, not just reserve, but suspicion towards both of these groups. The good churchman left us an interesting document, 'The business of the Walloons in Canterbury':

> The Walloons in Canterbury who were but one Church having been divided many years (by discord) into two congregations, they did apply themselves to superior powers (according to the times), impeaching one another with divers accusations. At last to the King's Majesty by whose order a reference was made to the Dean and Chapter of Canterbury to

[54] Dean and Chapter Library, MSS U-47-H 2, fol. 42.   [55] *Ibid.*, fol. 79.

examine their complaints, and the occasions of their difference, in order to a reconciliation.[56]

But poor Meric could neither make head not tail of the various explanations he received, though he tried very hard to give a verbatim report of their quarrel:

> After some time spent in hearing both parties, it did appear (as I did conceive and do still) that the party under Mr Jannon [Poujade's ex-followers] upon a pretence (grounded upon some rash words of his) that Mr Le Keux [the majority group] did profess independentism, did make the separation; and that Mr Jannon was not legally admitted Minister, according to the Orders of their Discipline. Whereupon it was moved that the said Mr Jannon would submit to some acknowledgement, and the others received him upon it.

Indeed, like the Hebrews of old, the Walloons had stiff necks: 'But both parties showed themselves very stiff; the one, to make no kind of acknowledgement; the others, not to receive him without it.'

In fact, the Crown was much more conciliatory than the refugees, and Meric Casaubon soon gave up his attempt to determine who was who, or which was which. In his opinion, neither camp had entirely relinquished past opinions, and though he accepted a necessary compromise in the name of law and order, he still resented the leniency of the king, which gave 'the Presbyterians more advantage than it could do good'. The religious feelings of Poujade's former associates, who claimed to be so strongly drawn towards the Anglican fold, remained influenced by Puritanism, hence their rejection of the sign of the Cross or kneeling at Communion, or of the surplice. And eventually the Church of Canterbury, once reconciled, preserved its ancestral privileges and remained faithful to the Calvinist order of prayer. Charles II's declaration on 14 November 1662 demanded the reunion of the divided brethren to put an end to the disorder; but it did not pronounce in favour of either camp. In the eyes of the Restoration, there were neither good sects nor bad sects, but all sects were to blame.

Ought we to be similarly sceptical, and dismiss all 'fanaticisms' and extremes alike? Such a brief answer does not strike me as any more conclusive. And without claiming to establish a model of interpretation that accounts for all the personal variations in behaviour within the communities, I should like to put forward, as a conclusion to this chapter, a twofold hypothesis: the premium of local or individual self-assertion and the displacement of established patterns of deference and authority.

---

[56] Oxford, Bodleian Library, Tanner MSS 92, fol. 160.

Land of hope and glory

The Refuge became increasingly insular during the revolution. A petition from the Walloon Church of Norwich, addressed to the Lord Protector in October 1655, mentioned the decline in immigration.[57] A demographic analysis confirms this idea. The marriage statistics for Threadneedle Street give evidence that in the twenty years from 1630 to 1650 the proportion of newcomers among spouses was halved and dropped sharply from 75 per cent to 32 per cent. The second generation, then, was predominant within the communities during the years of revolution. Born in England, and subjects of the realm, many refugees came to adopt, through some kind of unconscious imitation, the reactions of the host population, and may have shared, for aught I know, its nationalism. Jean de La Marche conceived of England as the centre of the 'holy general Reformation' which was to set the world ablaze in the year 1650. His visionary enthusiasm might be compared with the millenarianism of the 'Fifth Monarchists' who were totally defeated at the Restoration. On a different level, Philippe Delmé's French abounds in English turns of phrase. Moreover, the Norman Hérault, the Agenois Cursol, Poujade the native of Languedoc, and to a lesser degree the Dauphinois Jean Despagne were perceived as intruders; their cultural background and political references set them apart from the other pastors. Jean de La Marche, Pierre d'Assigny, Bulteel, the Delmés (father and son) were clearly northerners, without any attachment to France. And how can one fail to see, in the suspicion attached to Poujade in particular, a growing incomprehension for the Protestantism of the south? His comparison between the blood of Christ and olive oil was felt to be altogether eccentric and outlandish to English ears. The cultivation of the olive seemed, in fact, rather suspiciously exotic, compared with that of rye or hops. In the same way, the French prophets from Cevennes were greeted with scepticism, half a century later.

This cultural distance, a certain Gallophobia and an undoubtedly ethnocentric attitude gradually became characteristic of the Refuge, which included, besides, a great number of Walloons. Rarely, in fact, was the Refuge a little patch of France transplanted on to English soil.

Accentuating this break between France and England, pastor Hérault expressed all the anxiety he felt on his return to Alençon; in 1649, following Charles I's death, he attacked 'these fanatics, who began by being *Independents* in matters of Religion and Church government, and in the end wanted to do the same in matters of State, and of civil and political government'.[58]

---

[57] SP Dom., Crom., 101, 6.
[58] Schickler, *Les Eglises du Refuge en Angleterre*, III, p. 207.

Hérault's polemical explanation summarises the connection between new concepts of the Church and new concepts of society. One has to admit, however, that every term covers a multitude of parameters. The acceleration of time which accompanied the revolution resulted in a steady erosion of the meaning of words – a further challenge to the historian. I shall give just one example: the term 'Independent' has two complementary meanings; originally, it applied to somebody advocating a broad tolerance towards the different currents stemming from the Reformation; then, as conflicts intensified, the 'Independents' became the supporters of an unrelenting war against the king. Cromwell or Milton personified both senses of the term. On the other hand, when one finds Jean Despagne described as an Independent, or, all the more so, Joseph Poujade, the word has simply an ecclesiastical meaning. Jean Despagne and Joseph Poujade were deemed Independents because they challenged the authority of the Churches; in other respects, however, the position they adopted were extremely moderate, not to say conservative. One might raise the same kind of problems for a high percentage of the terms employed. 'Puritan' and 'Presbyterian' are no exceptions to the rule, not to mention 'Royalist'. One must beware, then, of attributing a unified political philosophy to the little world of the refugees; countless shades of opinion existed, without necessarily leading to schism, while on the other hand, schism was not necessarily a matter of opinion. Even in the darkest hours, the collective interest survived, together with a sense of corporate identity which derived from a common stock of privileges and explained the refugees' submission to the authorities in Church and State. The restoration was yet greeted with a certain *malaise*, but the clouds of this uneasiness were soon dispelled by the Crown's determination not to antagonise the foreign Protestants – as Laud had done a quarter of a century before. A new division was yet to appear among the refugees between those who favoured Anglicanism, and those who opted out for nonconformity. This led to fascinating debates on Church government and its links with civil society: though obliterated as an unpleasant dream, the legacy of the revolution was still to be felt in these endless adjustments between Church and State, community and authority, politics and religion.

5 The restoration: from consensus to division, *c.* 1660–1680

The clemency of princes is often but a policy to win the affection of their people.
La Rochefoucauld

It was the Jews, Jesus' own nation, who put him to death; and the same may be said of some of those who persecuted and murdered that good king.
Pastor Piélat, *Sermons on the Execution of Charles I, Delivered in the French Church of the Savoy in Westminster* 30 January 1669

'Remembrance' and 'oblivion' would certainly sound contradictory to modern ears, yet they may serve to highlight the Restoration settlement. The blessed memory of the martyr king was revered and the Stranger Churches joined in the propitiatory fastings and prayers which were held throughout the country. But this expiatory commemoration could not altogether atone for the past, nor was the sacralised death of the late king enough to heal the wounds of the Great Rebellion.

What cause has not had its martyrs? Charles I had exchanged his 'temporal' for 'an eternal crown' as Dr Juxon had put it on the scaffold where he accompanied his master in his last moments. Who could forget that many of those who now paid lip service to the new regime had, a few years before, been singing the praises of the usurper, 'His Highness Oliver Cromwell'? In 1657, while refusing the kingship, Oliver Cromwell had accepted to be solemnly invested as Lord Protector. Indeed, as Antonia Fraser has aptly put it, 'the investiture of the Lord Protector...lacked nothing in kingliness except the person of a King himself'.[1] A few days after the ceremony, a Coetus of the Foreign Churches met on 5 July and somewhat belatedly decided not to miss the new opportunity to express their indiscriminate loyalty to the powers that be:

[1] A. Fraser, *Cromwell Our Chief of Men* (1973), London, 1985, p. 615.

> The Dutch brethren having resolved in their consistory to salute His Highness the Lord Protector upon occasion of his new establishment in the name of all the Dutch churches in England, thought fit to call a Coetus to desire the conjunction of the French and Italian churches for the fuller accomplishment of that action. To which the French and Italian brethren (having debated it apart) did give their consent. And it was agreed on all sides to write unto all the churches that they would send the deputies to assist in this solemnity or at least to give their commission that it may be done in their names, and that with all speed.[2]

Likewise, when Richard Cromwell succeeded his father, the refugees lay in his hands 'the protection of our churches' and 'by the by the tradesmen and artificers of them'.[3] Yet two years later, in June 1660, 'it was resolved that it was necessary that the King's Majesty should be congratulated' and 'a continuation of our privileges implored'.[4] One should not jump to conclusions and underline the opportunistic mood of the strangers. As a matter of fact, their good feelings towards the Lord Protector had been somewhat obscured by his endorsement of Elie Delmé's radical theology. On the other hand, they welcomed the idea, propounded by John Durie with Cromwell's assent, of Protestant unity:

> Mr Dury communicated to the Coetus the great transactions wherein he hath for many years been employed beyond the seas to work reconciliation among the Protestant churches; and to that purpose delivered several copies in Latin and English to the ministers of the several churches, desiring that they would take it into their serious consideration. The moderator did in the name of the Coetus give him thanks for his great pains, desiring God to ply his pious undertakings, and promised to contribute their best endeavours towards the advancement of so good a work.[5]

The international involvement of the Churches may have served Cromwell's policy, or rather contributed to his Protestant image, in spite of the misgivings of the Huguenots in France who feared any *rapprochement* with a regicide. The Waldensians provided a better common ground than the French Protestants of the Continent to buttress Oliver's European stature which culminated in the 1657 treaty with Mazarin. The 'Synods of the churches in the Valley of Piedmont' sent a letter to the refugees 'wherein they give the Coetus hearty thanks for their great charity towards their churches'. They wished their brethren would still 'continue the same' and 'appoint some out of [their] company to assist their deputies in soliciting the state for the arrears of the general collection which was made for their distressed churches'.[6] This was in 1659, and a few months later, some kind of agreement had to be reached

[2] Guildhall Library, MSS 7412/1, p. 69.   [3] *Ibid.*, p. 73: 26 September 1658.
[4] *Ibid.*, p. 77.   [5] *Ibid.*, p. 74: 23 October 1659.   [6] *Ibid.*

with the Restored Church of England. On 25 December 1660, a delegation officially met Dr Juxon, now archbishop of Canterbury, and Gilbert Sheldon, bishop of London, who 'both answered very favourably and promised to protect us and rather ampliate [amplify] than diminish our privileges'. Yet their lordships insisted that the 'King of late hath made an express order that all the foreign churches should be under their bishops'.[7] The conspiracy of silence was a most clever move on the part of the Crown; yet it had numerous flaws: let a dispute break out between a pastor and his flock, and the old memory would rise to the surface again. Silence often bespoke distrust, and the unspoken carried the weight of a reproach. The revolution was still there, in the back of people's mind. It negatively reinforced the fear of the fanatic and sectarian, and in the conspicuous profligacy of the Court and the reopening of the London theatres, how can one fail to see the final defiance of Puritanism, relegated to the realm of tedious morality?

The 'Restoration settlement', as it is often called, emphasises the importance of the idea of compromise for the English. Ideology played a minor role: the legal dispensation was altered to conform to a *fait accompli*. In 1660, England had returned (in a theoretical and fictitious sense) to the *status quo ante* of 1641, before the outbreak of the Great Rebellion. The eighteen years which elapsed between these two dates remained an inescapable obstacle: men endeavoured to forget them, but could never entirely do so. The revolution neither brought a new class to power, nor overturned the landed basis of the gentry, who were much more susceptible, in fact, to long-term fluctuations in landed incomes than to the upheavals of the 1640s. Indeed, the revolution swept away part of the older order, and the legal status of property, rather than its ownership, was altered: in 1660, an Act of Parliament entered onto the statute book the abolition of feudal tenures, which had taken place in 1646 (12 Charles II c. 24). The conservatism of the ruling class who sat in Parliament, their spirit of initiative, and their fear of subversion, explain the return to monarchy, which was almost unanimously greeted. In the words of Christopher Hill: 'The men who took over in the 1650s, the men who made the Restoration, were the "Realists", their main concern to preserve property and subordination.'[8]

Thus, without doubt, the 1660s were more characterised by continuity than change. Basically the radical movement had been defeated under Cromwell, and the need for social order was becoming evident – an order which the monarchy seemed most likely to uphold. The Restoration did involve some purges, but not an actual 'white terror'. The symbolic hanging of the remains of the Protector, the effective condemnation to

[7] *Ibid.*, p. 82.
[8] C. Hill, *Some Intellectual Consequences of the English Revolution*, London, 1980, p. 34.

death of a dozen regicides, the crushing of a millenarian insurrection did not endanger a consensus in which Royalists and Parliamentarians found themselves side by side, united in exorcising the past. The keyword of the period was, precisely, *oblivion*, while one of the first statutes which brought King and Parliament together again, in 1660, consisted in what was virtually a general amnesty – the sole exceptions being a few leading regicides, on whose shoulders the collective guilt was laid (12 Charles II c. 11). After all, it was easy to condemn Cromwell who had been dead for two years now, while honouring the memory of Charles I, the martyr king. On the one hand a usurper, on the other a saint; the black legend faced the icon. The portrait of the martyred king, *Eikon Basilike*, became one of the elements of the royal mystique, while Charles II, who had in theory been king since 1649, returned to his own country in May 1660, amidst all the signs of general rejoicing. Nothing was left for Milton, Cromwell's former secretary, who had miraculously escaped prosecution, but to ponder upon the fall of Adam. *Paradise Lost* was inauspiciously written under the Restoration.[9]

And yet, certain groups were quickly excluded from the consensus. In fact, the religious settlement 'turned the formerly comprehensive English Church into a persecuting one and divided the nation in two'.[10] All kinds of discriminatory measures were used to harass and isolate the nonconformists: nearly a fifth of the ministers – about 2,000 – had to leave their parishes, while at the same time assemblies were forbidden. In one sense, the profusion of sects, so characteristic of English or American piety for that matter, stems from this failure of the religious settlement, which became evident after 1662. Even some of the architects of the Restoration, the Presbyterians in particular, found themselves excluded from the compromise in spite of their moderation. The Restoration, although in a more surreptitious, less dramatic manner than the revolution, led in turn to a divided society, and some fifteen years later the appearance of the Whigs and Tories marked the empirical emergence of political parties, though not their acceptance.[11]

Here I shall end this survey. On the issue of landed property and its ownership, most refugees do not provide us with any specific clue, being drawn from the middle ranks of city-dwellers. They do, however, give us invaluable details on the nature and limits of social consensus – one of the foremost concerns of historians. Could Calvinism and monarchy coexist?

[9] R. Lejosne, *La Raison dans l'œuvre de John Milton*, Paris, 1982.
[10] Joan Thirsk, *The Restoration*, London, 1976, p. xvi; see also J.R. Jones (ed.), *The Restored Monarchy, 1660–1688*, London, 1979.
[11] The Huguenots were not indifferent to English party politics. One of them, the celebrated Rapin de Thoyras, best remembered for his seminal *History of England*, wrote an interesting *Dissertation sur les whigs et les torys*, 1717, which has been reprinted, with several other extracts, in B. Cottret and M.-M. Martinet, *Partis et factions dans l'Angleterre du premier XVIIIe siècle*, Paris, 1987.

'Most certainly they could', replied the chorus of French pastors, as they insisted on drawing a discreet veil over the Puritan episode and the execution of Charles I which served to colour the negative image of the factious Protestant, a rebellious subject whose privilege could be revoked, as Louis XIV eventually did in 1685. This point of view involved much more than the attitude of the protagonists; it concerned the very organisation of Calvinist society: was it a 'democracy', or else an 'aristocracy', as certain Protestants, among the elite of birth, fortune or scholarship, asked themselves with some dread, fearing the unruliness of the Christian flock, and their laymen's pride?

In the meantime, the life of the Churches under a restored monarchy set an example to disprove the damaging idea of a collusion between French Protestantism and the Commonwealth men. I shall quote here in full the title of a work by Pierre du Moulin the younger, published in 1660: *History of the new Presbyterians of England and Scotland. In which is shown the difference between their religious discipline and doctrine, and that of the French and other Protestants; together with the true origin of the troubles which they and those who abetted them stirred up against the King and the Church of England. Dedicated to the King. And addressed to the Gentlemen of the Reformed Churches of France, and to all Protestants who profess the christian religion and fidelity to Kings.*

The end of schisms

The general features of the Restoration certainly affected the foreign communities: the most tangible effect of this new era was, at least superficially, the recovery of the Churches, which had been disturbed by the revolution. Reconciliation was the order of the day, and the divided brethren were enjoined to reunite on political grounds. It would have been unseemly to persist with factions reminiscent of a time now abhorred. Charles II, who followed personally this new development, showed genuine clemency, displaying neither weakness nor excessive severity. One can surmise the anxiety of the Foreign Churches at this early stage. The new government would possibly unearth in the recent past tangible proof that many refugees had sided with the rebels. True to his moderation, however, Charles II chose to let bygones be bygones – although some of the refugees were more vocal in their grievances. In Canterbury, each side accused the other of harbouring hostile feelings for the king. While the schismatic followers of Jannon were among the first to embrace Anglicanism in a move to outbid the orthodox, a broadsheet *c.* 1662 presented them as the most outspoken 'independents' and supporters of the Interregnum:

> In or about the year 1647, Mr Poujade, one of the ministers of the Walloon congregations of French and Walloons in London, Canterbury

and Dover, suspended from preaching for his misdemeanours and scandalous life, drew off that part of the Walloons in Canterbury that are now of Mr Jannon's congregation; *who separated themselves, and declared themselves independents* in the Coetus at London, and broke off communion with the congregations of Walloons, French and Dutch, and set up a congregation of their own, and exercised their religion under Mr Poujade, and after by Mr Crespin in a parish church, and then in a private hall in or near Canterbury.

On the other hand, the opponents of Poujade and Jannon presented themselves in the garb of loyalty to the Crown:

> The other part of the Walloons that have not joined with Master Jannon's congregation are far the greatest number, and the most able, wealthiest, and substantiallest men, and have always been honest and loyal persons to His Majesty and his Royal Father. And in 1648 did at their own charge put themselves in arms under English commanders for His then Majesty, and contributed great sums of money to maintain the king's party then in arms for the King.[12]

Should we then conclude that the cleavage of the Walloon Church had been primarily political? One should beware of *ex post facto* rationalisations. This undignified division of sectional interests gave rise only to contempt, and Sir Thomas Peyton, who conducted an official investigation in November 1662, wisely dismissed both parties alike, refusing to grant a certificate of good political conduct to one side while withholding it from the other. The schismatic group's application to join the Church of England, flagrant in its opportunism, did not meet with a response from the authorities, who on the contrary wished to see existing customs preserved. The king's Order in Council, 'at the court at Whitehall', on 14 November, was copied meticulously into the register of the London consistory as it gave the refugees guarantees of peace of far greater consequence than the past conflict in Canterbury.

In this case as in so many others former differences should 'be forever forgotten and buried in perpetual oblivion' (article 1). Moreover, the Crown renewed the priceless privilege of maintaining a separate ecclesiastical discipline, independently of the Church of England:

> That for the time to come both parties shall unite and agree in one entire congregation of Walloons, and continue in the *exercise of the Protestant religion according to the common rites and disciplines which have formerly been exercised under the gracious protection and concession of Your Majesty's royal progenitors* [my italics].
> Article 2

It is true that this applied only to the old-established communities; new foundations were required to conform to the religion of the kingdom.

---

[12] Dean and Chapter Library, MSS U-47-H 2, fol. 89: 'The case concerning the Walloons...'. My italics.

These privileges were subject to only one fundamental limitation; they were restricted to the Foreign Churches and were not meant for the rest of the country. The religious autonomy of the refugees was reaffirmed, provided they did not interfere with the rites and ceremonies of the Church of England:

> That they shall not permit or suffer their ministers or any other member of their congregation to do or speak anything tending to the reproach or the contempt of the liturgy or any other part of the doctrine and discipline established in the Church of England or which may give cause of scandal or offence to any of your Majesty's good Protestant subjects.
> Article 4

This religious immunity, which was in no way to be emulated, extended to the primary economic duty of the Churches: the relief of the poor:

> That they shall, from time to time, maintain their own poor, without suffering them to be burthensome to any part of the City of Canterbury.
> Article 5

In perpetuating this separate administration, the Crown was, in practice, excepting the most eminent of the Foreign Churches from the application of the Act of Uniformity (14 Charles II c. 4): 'It is humbly offered to your Majesty's great wisdom ... that your Majesty would please, *for avoiding the penalties of the Act of Uniformity*, to declare this congregation to be such a part of the Foreign Reformed Churches as your Majesty is pleased to allow.'

This moderation showed the utmost clemency, and formed a happy contrast with the accumulated resentment manifest in the treatment of the nonconformists. It was dictated by political considerations but may have adumbrated one of the most fertile currents in the Anglican tradition: latitudinarianism, the forerunner of the theological liberalism which took into account the existence of differing religious sensibilities. This tension between 'comprehension' and intolerance was constantly manifest; it extended beyond the purely legal framework, and became incorporated in the underlying benevolence which willy-nilly surrounded the Protestant strangers. There would always be those, even at the highest level of the Anglican hierarchy, who were sympathetic to the Reformed Churches of the Continent – or else hostile to a form of ecclesiastical organisation which was suspected of breeding rebellion.

This was my first, initial reaction to the Crown's leniency towards the refugees as it is to be found in the original French version of this book, published in 1985. I must confess that I would add some further considerations which might suggest an alternative interpretation of Charles II's goodwill: in 1662 the Huguenots and their Churches were amongst the first to benefit from the policy of *indulgence* which the Crown wished to extend to the rest of the country. The repeated failure of indulgence led to the 1688 Revolution. Indeed, I am not pretending now that the early settlement with the refugees was devoid of commiserations, but I would certainly pinpoint the existence of another motive which rests on two elements.

1 Contrary to Laud, Charles II – or his advisers – made no distinction between recent refugees and the 'second descent'. The privilege of the Foreign Churches was confirmed even in the case of His Majesty's 'natural subjects' – i.e. of the children of immigrants born in England.

2 Many Anglican churchmen resented this latitude which, in Meric Casaubon's own words, gave 'the Presbyterians more advantage than it could do good' (see above). As a matter of fact, the oldest Refugee Churches were nonconformist, and were regarded as such, to give another example, in the 1676 religious census, ordered by Danby: 'That there are Walloons chiefly that make up the number of dissenters in Canterbury, Sandwich and Dover'.[13] Yet, unlike their dissenting brethren, the Walloons and Huguenots avoided the 'penalties of the Act of Uniformity'. In their case, the Crown had had recourse to its *dispensing power*, this 'valuable instrument of legal flexibility'.[14]

This shows the strategic importance of the 1662 Canterbury settlement: this transgression of the monopoly of the established Church was a first stage in a policy of *indulgence* which the Stuarts could never achieve for the rest of the country as it would have applied indiscriminately to the Dissenters and papists. The refugees themselves readily seized the opportunity, and implored the king's protection whenever the Anglican hierarchy tried to bring them to submission.

I shall not dwell upon these instances of harassment, which were often resolved, in any case, by the civil or religious authorities. Thus in London, on 11 March 1663, 'we were given word...that someone had gone to slander us to the vicar-general, Chaworth, saying that it was our custom in our church not to accept anyone as a member without first making them renounce the Anglican Church, and their submission to His Grace the Bishop of London – a calumny which greatly offends us'. Similarly in Southampton, in 1660, the refugees were asked 'by what right they assemble together, and when they said that it was in accordance with the

---

[13] 'The number of freeholders in England, conformists, nonconformists and papists' (i.e. in the province of Canterbury), 1676, given by A. Browning (ed.), *English Historical Documents 1660–1714*, London, 1966, p. 414. According to B. Coward, *The Stuart Age*, London, 1980, p. 253, the extent of nonconformity was certainly underestimated by the census. See also, B. Cottret, *La Glorieuse Révolution d'Angleterre, 1688*, Paris, 1988, pp. 83ff: 'Conformité ecclésiastique et dissidence'.

[14] Corinne C. Weston and Janelle R. Greenberg, *Subjects and Sovereigns*, Cambridge, 1981, p. 29.

Act of Uniformity which excepts the foreign Churches, [the bishop of Winchester] replied that *as they were all English, the exception from the Act of Uniformity did not apply to them* [my italics]'.

The Coetus held a meeting on 14 October, and their summary of the situation deserves to be quoted here:

> There was a letter received from the French Church of Southampton wherein they write us that the bishop of Winchester [George Morley] hath summoned their minister to appear before him to show by what authority he did preach in his diocese. Besides, the French brethren have related that the bishop, when their minister appeared before him, asked them to let them see their privilege under his majesty's hand...The Coetus hath resolved to write to them a letter to wish them to be quiet till the bishop sends for them again, and then if he calleth them, to desire his Lordship to let them enjoy the favours that his Majesty promised to the strangers when he was saluted by them, and to intimate him that his majesty hath lately granted to them of Norwich liberty *even to them who are born in the kingdom.*[15]

But all is well that ends well: faced with the proof of the antiquity of their privilege, the bishop yielded, and invited the recalcitrants to share his meal. This was yet an awkward position: the refugees – at least their oldest foundations in London, Canterbury, Norwich and Southampton – benefited from the exemption from the Act of Uniformity, and were therefore a pawn in the king's hand who wished to extend his indulgence to others. Nonetheless, they had their own policy to pursue, and always proved the most strenuous opponents of Catholicism. Hence, their practical links with English Dissenters. In 1683, according to a later history of Southampton:

> They were all of them dissenters, and in the year 1683 a complaint was made to the bishop by the magistrates of the town, that other dissenters made this chapel [God's house, Southampton], being a licensed one, a kind of asylum to protect them from the laws then in being against non-conformity, and the people of better sort of the islands of Guernsey and Jersey complained that their countrymen...frequently returned greatly prejudiced against the [conformist] liturgy (which was then, and I think is still [c. 1780], altogether used in those islands), praying, therefore, that the minister of this chapel may be ordered to use the liturgy of the Church of England in French, as at the Savoy in London.[16]

A few years later, in 1686, pastor Pierre Chauvin from Norwich wrote to Bishop Lloyd that his congregation 'live like as [*sic*] independents, without law, without discipline', and do not hesitate to make 'publick

---

[15] Guildhall Library, MSS 7412/1: 14 October 1668.
[16] J. Speed, *The History and Antiquity of Southampton*, c.1700, quoted by J. S. Davies, *A History of Southampton*, London, 1883, p. 410.

insurrection' against their minister 'when he checks their misdemeanour'. Moreover, it seems that the unruly flock even admitted Quakers among its ranks![17]

Monarchy in Church and State

The strangers enjoyed a liberty of conscience, a 'latitude' in matters of worship and belief which many Englishmen might envy. Indeed, some of them opted for conformity with the Church of England – for instance, the congregation meeting in the Savoy, the successor of the community of Monsieur Despagne, which adopted a French translation of the English liturgy. But, in spite of some difficulties, especially during the tensions of the 1680s, the Churches of the Refuge, at least the most prestigious of them, experienced a unique degree of freedom. In fact, the ecclesiastical compromise, which Charles II had wanted to establish, had largely failed. The Savoy conference in 1661 did not succeed in reconciling the positions of the Presbyterians and Anglicans; despite the political consensus, not all Englishmen were united in one and the same Church. England had its dissenting fringe, cavalierly categorised as 'fanatical' or 'sectarian' by its persecutors. The ideal of a single Church, uniting all the Crown subjects, seemed more remote than ever.

In this context, the refugees' privilege sounded extravagant. It implied, quite understandably, a certain reserve on their part: their minority status and their ecclesiastical exemption could not be applied to the country at large. Many immigrants chose not to conform to Anglicanism, but did not incur the severity of the body of laws, collectively known as the Clarendon Code and which turned all Dissenters into second-class citizens. As Barry Coward has put it: 'In great contrast to the days before 1640, the Clarendon Code, scant comfort though it was to those it persecuted, did give legal recognition to Protestant dissent.'[18] The notorious reference to the Clarendon Code may be misleading as the Lord Chancellor, who had served Charles I with courage, was not the only one to blame for the bigoted intolerance of the established Church and even tried to keep within bounds the Anglican reaction which developed after the revolution. The 1661 Corporation Act could force all municipal officials to take the sacrament according to Anglican rites – but this did not debar some Dissenters from 'occasional conformity' in order to qualify for the official appointment. Similarly, in the wake of the Act of Uniformity (1662), many clergymen had to leave their parishes when they refused to use the Book of Common Prayer or to 'assent and consent to everything [it] contained and prescribed'. Moreover, the two Conventicle Acts (1664 and 1670)

---

[17] Bodleian Library, Tanner MSS 92, fol. 128.
[18] Coward, *The Stuart Age*, p. 252.

forbade all assemblies in which 'five persons or more ... over and besides those of the same household' would gather 'under colour or pretence of any exercise of religion in other manner than according to the liturgy and practice of the Church of England'. Finally, the Five Mile Act (1665) endeavoured to restrain nonconformists from 'inhabiting in corporations'. The refugees were left virtually unscathed by all these measures, even though they may have occasionally been suspected on account of their similarities with the Presbyterians. The unique character of their privilege takes on its full significance when we come to realise that in matters of religious or civil government three principal types of society were recognised at the time, according to a learned distinction: monarchy, aristocracy and democracy. This classic typology, which underlay the most subtle of distinctions, presupposes that the various forms of religious society may be described in terms borrowed from the vocabulary of politics. In the same way, I believe, the State and King derived part of their mystique from religious reference. Let us examine the attitude of Charles II prior to the so-called Savoy conference which took place in Westminster from April till mid-July 1661, but failed to reconcile the Protestant subjects of His Majesty. At first, some time before the conference, the king had appointed several Presbyterian ministers as his 'chaplains ordinary', among them Richard Baxter and Edmund Calamy who were later to experience the harshness of the Restoration towards Dissenters. They strongly resented the division between Protestants, and advocated a single national Church, provided that the 'terms of Union might include nothing but necessary things'.[19] While they insisted on the qualification of clergymen who had to be 'learned', 'orthodox' and 'godly' God-fearing men who dutifully sanctified the Sabbath, they were ready to accept the existence of bishops, provided their 'presidency' was on the model of the primitive Church, and 'was balanced with a due commission of Presbyters'.[20] In no way could this warrant any form of 'arbitrary' proceeding on the part of the prelates – a clear allusion to Laud. Likewise, the most blatant 'innovations' – i.e. popish superstitions – were to be removed. Surplices, altars and crossing oneself should be prohibited, while kneeling at Communion remained optional. The lords bishops apparently did not share the same image of the ancient, apostolic times in which, according to them, no elder was ever allowed to control or censure the episcopate. As no agreement was reached, Charles II issued an important declaration, on 25 October 1660:

> The truth is, we do think ourselves more competent to propose, and with God's assistance to determine many things now in difference, from the time we have spent, and the experience we have had, *in most of the*

[19] T.B. Howell, *State Trials*, ed. W. Cobbett, 33 vols., London, 1809–26, VI, p. 1.
[20] *Ibid.*, p. 5.

> *Reformed Churches abroad*, in France, in the Low Countries, and in Germany where we have had frequent conferences with the most learned men, who have unanimously lamented the great reproach the Protestant religion undergoes from the distempers and too notorious schisms in matters of religion in England.[21]

The reference to the best Reformed Churches should have been enticing to English Presbyterians and refugees alike. The king also promised to convene a 'synod of divines', while launching his policy of indulgence, or rather promising to do so:

> In the meantime, we published in our Declaration from Breda [4/14 April 1660], a liberty to tender consciences, and that no man should be disquieted or called in question for differences of opinion in matters of religion, which do not disturb the peace of the kingdom, and that we shall be ready to consent to such an act of parliament as upon mature deliberation shall be offered to us, for the full granting that *indulgence*.[22]

Then came a most fascinating passage in which Charles II examined the links between Church and civil government:

> And upon this ground, without taking upon us to censure the government of the Church in other countries, where the government of the State is different from what it is here, or enlarging ourself upon the reasons why, whilst there was an imagination of erecting a *democratical government* here in the State, they should be willing to continue an *aristocratical government* in the Church: it shall suffice to say, that since by the wonderful blessing of God, the hearts of this whole nation are returned to an obedience to *monarchic government* in the State, it must be very reasonable to support that government in the Church which is established by law, and with which the monarchy hath flourished through so many ages, and which is, in truth, as ancient in this island as the Christian monarchy thereof.[23]

To a twentieth-century reader, this must seem an astonishing argument. And yet, it is perfectly coherent: the government of the Church and that of the State must be of the same type. James I had already declared: 'No bishop, no king.' Nonetheless, other forms of government can be envisaged: the essential requirement is logical. Church democracy may have its counterpart in civil democracy. Likewise, Charles II does not pronounce in favour either of France, or of Geneva, or of Holland; he accepts the relativity of customs, and does not claim to legislate for all Protestant countries. The prevailing principle is one of harmony: in Charles II's view, the revolution failed because it attempted to combine two incompatible forms, democracy and aristocracy, independence and presbytery, the appeal to the people and government by the best.

[21] *Ibid.*, p. 12.   [22] *Ibid.*, p. 13.   [23] *Ibid.*, p. 15.

If we accept this typology, with its three-tiered division (*monarchy*, *aristocracy* and *democracy*), where should we place Calvinism? The quest is not just theoretical: it has actual implications for the English Refuge. Moïse Amyraut, an eminent Protestant theologian, had already answered the question in his *Gouvernement de l'Eglise* (*Church Government*), 1653 (p. 409): 'For as on the one hand the government of the Church is neither monarchical nor entirely aristocratic, so on the other hand it is not purely and simply democratic.' This subtle apology of mixed government followed the *Discours de la souveraineté des roys* (*Discourse on the Sovereignty of Kings*) (1650), which I have already cited among the condemnations of Charles I's execution. Amyraut recognises the existence of three forms of government, which he calls 'popular', 'aristocratic' and 'royal', while admitting (p. 107) that 'the Scriptures speak more clearly and more favourably of the establishment of kings by the will of God than they do of any other form of Polity'.

In fact, Calvinists had found it difficult to disentangle themselves from the image of republicanism – i.e. sedition – at the beginning of the seventeenth century; Pierre du Moulin and James I's active collaboration had been able to achieve this mutation. In their turn, the English revolution, Puritan iconoclasm and the perpetuation of regicide threatened to tarnish the reputation of the Reformed Churches, however determined they might be to disclaim responsibility. These accusations lingered on till the nineteenth century and have since been fully incorporated in the strong republican zeal shown by most French Protestants who held their own meeting at the Sorbonne, of all places, to commemorate the French Revolution in 1989. Even though the election of pastors, the participation of laymen and the coopting of consistories shared none of the features of direct democracy, and were associated, in practice, with a great deal of social conservatism, they could still be construed in an unfavourable light. Indeed, some restless minds inveighed against the threat of 'democracy' in these times of restored monarchy. Two further examples could be provided. In 1674, the consistory of Threadneedle Street was obliged to defend the Calvinist discipline against the attacks of Councillor William Coventry who was particularly indignant at the election of pastors. Erroneously – so the consistory register for 1 July informs us – William Coventry 'did not believe that our government was aristocratic – as it is – but ... supposed it to be democratic'. This explanation was accompanied besides by the menacing remark 'that the King had no intention of altering our form of government; that, besides, the king is so gracious as to leave us this liberty, so also he is sufficiently powerful to make his displeasure felt, if it is not respected, and if his recommendation goes unheeded'.

The freedom enjoyed by presbyteries even irritated many of the pastors among the refugees and they were at pains to check effectively their parishioners' claims that Church affairs should be deliberated among them. This expectation may, or may not, have been intrinsically democratic, but it did not respect a sense of hierarchy which the pastors clung to nervously. This spirit of independence among the laity presented insuperable problems for pastor Hérault who in November 1674, having returned from exile ten years previously, expressed his indignation at the persistence of two types of extremists, whom he rather neatly described as *mutins mutinant* – rebels in the process of rebelling – and *mutins mutinés* – rebels who have already rebelled.

This brings us to my second example, which is even more typical of the cleavage in Calvinist society. The English experience had clearly displayed the weight of ecclesiastical emancipation and one of the most strenuous indictments of the political dangers of Calvinism proceeded from the pen of a refugee pastor, gone over to the Church of England, who complained bitterly of the insolence of his community in Rye. On 15 April 1684, pastor Bertrand described his situation in these terms: 'I do not expect to be beholden to the merchants of the French Church of London...for an explanation of the duties and concerns incumbent on a minister.'[24]

After this unprepossessing beginning, which expressed the minister's disillusionment with his lay brethren of London, he went on: 'I cannot help but marvel more and more to see to what degree of impudence *the spirit of Calvinism* is borne by its passions, in seeking to demonstrate an indiscreet zeal for a *ridiculous form of government.*'

This was hardly flattering for the Reformed Churches, whom he found even worse than the Jesuits – which in seventeenth-century England was an incitement to hatred. With equal vindictiveness, the French pastor denounced the Huguenots' disregard for the sound liturgy of the Church of England:

> To speak plainly, however right and legitimate your conformity to the Church in which you have taken refuge may be, yet there will always be honest and zealous Calvinists who by their wise counsel will spoil all the pleasure and joy you expect...For my part, I confess that this conduct only confirmed my opinion, that a *Calvinist is one of the most dangerous subjects a monarchy can have*, as everyone knows, and, to sum up the matter as His Lordship the Bishop of London [Henry Compton] did, in one of the articles which he sent to restore peace among us, all this sort of men '*are a people of more than suspected principles!*'.
>
> I take every opportunity I can to exhort them to the service of God and, accordingly, not to neglect our incomparable prayers, but all this is too un-Calvinist ever to be well received. If I were a man to betray the Church, to castigate all dangerous aristocratic principles and announce

[24] Bodleian Library, Rawlinson MSS, C. 984, fol. 51.

the happy deliverance from the ever-tyrannical yoke of the bishops, pouring upon them *ex tempore* prayers, then I would be the worthiest man in the World.

Why had not Calvinism shaken off the suspicion still attached to its name twenty-five years after the interregnum? The query eludes all simple, one-sided answers; it involves the English situation as a whole. The gloomy picture presented by Paul Bertrand, formerly a pastor in Saintonge, is rather too straightforward, and displays the fawning zeal of an Anglican convert. This intemperate and somewhat disconcerting language throws unprecedented light on the years immediately preceding the Revocation of the Edict of Nantes. Not only did the image of the factious Huguenot retain its currency, against all odds; but some members of the Protestant elite even gave vent to the suspicion attached to Calvinism. This would suggest a paradoxical hypothesis on the evolution of French Protestantism, though I am not in a position, having no other reference than the refugee communities of England, to pronounce on the French Churches as a whole. I should simply observe that a crisis probably existed in Calvinist society, *before* the Revocation of the Edict of Nantes. Moreover, there had been growing tensions between the Christian flock and their betters whom they suspected of lacking zeal.

A bishop for the Refuge?

This organic connection between monarchy within the Church and monarchy within the State is illustrated by the role of the bishops. The Restoration of the king in 1660 was followed by that of the bishops, whose office had been abolished by stages from 1642 up to 1646. 'Episcopalianism' was one of the dominant features of the Church of England and has remained so to this day. If the bishops guaranteed political security, and doctrinal stability, why not grant the refugees a bishop of their own? Such a project did exist, although it was of no avail and came to nothing in the end. The English Refuge was never to have it own mitred and appointed bishop of French Calvinist extraction, but this remained an open possibility. From the sixteenth century onwards the thorny question of episcopacy had been a matter of heated debate. As agents of the Crown, and guardians of social and religious conformity, the prelates were the object of Puritan sarcasm. Besides, their critics were not slow to point out that the bishops' role might be dispensed with, following the example of the Reformed Churches of the Continent. This consideration could prove burdensome to the Foreign Churches; moreover, the bishops had been one of the first targets of revolutionary 'Root and Branch' radicalism. Conversely their re-establishment accompanied the Restoration. The appointment of bishops among the refugees would have demonstrated beyond all doubt that they rejected republicanism altogether, and wholeheartedly supported the divine right of kings.

Besides, the abolition of the bishops had not been greeted with glee by the French Reformed Churches of the Continent who failed to appreciate the English revolution. To their eyes, the Presbyterian or Independent involvement compromised the Protestant cause. Hence Saumaise's protest in 1649:

> Their first stroke did not only consist in expelling from Parliament the estate of the clergy which had been represented by the body of the bishops, but they suppressed it altogether. I do not intend to examine here what their purpose was, or whether they were right to make this change. I shall say nothing of the antiquity of the bishops, or of the reason for their establishment, which was intended only to suppress the schisms within the Church, and I shall not mention that even at the birth of the Reformation, it was though fit not to remove the bishops in England. I shall simply observe, in passing, how important it is to re-establish them, were it only because while the authority of the bishops endured, England avoided the contagion of an infinite number of sects, and malign heresies, which have since sprung up in profusion. I have particularly in mind one recent sect, the most desperate of all, which is known as the *Independents* or *Brownists*. It was they who first abolished the bishops, and then expelled, banished and put to death the nobility of that kingdom, before eventually depriving the king of his sceptre and his life.[25]

Some influential French Calvinists like Saumaise could call for the return of the bishops in England: it would therefore be inaccurate to equate Huguenot with Puritan as we are wont to do spontaneously. The French Protestants' good behaviour explains the clemency shown by Charles II toward the Refuge. Provided they were given good pastors, the unruly flock would return to the fold. This narrow collaboration between the Protestant elite and the English Crown, which dated back to James I, was more important at the international level than the destiny of a few thousand immigrants, at least until the Revocation of the Edict of Nantes. Charles II relied on the tactical support of men such as Meric Casaubon or the younger Pierre du Moulin who both entered the Church of England. This was a family concern as Isaac Casaubon and the first Pierre du Moulin had already benefited from James I's largesse.

Likewise, the situation of the Reformed Church of London was resolved by Hérault's return. The former Royalist pastor, who had left London amid the jeers of his parishioners, returned in triumph to stage a Restoration of his own. His *Pacifique royal en deuil compris en XII sermons* (*The Pacifist in Mourning in XII Sermons*), published in Saumur in 1649, was followed

---

[25] Saumaise, *Apologie royale pour Charles I, roi d'Angleterre*, Paris, 1650, pp. 9–10.

by his *Pacifique royal en joie, compris en XX sermons* (*The Pacifist Rejoicing in XX Sermons*), which appeared in Amsterdam in 1665. Every cloud has a silver lining. Unfortunately, this *joyeuse entrée* did not lead to the supreme consecration which Hérault craved for. The scheming pastor intrigued with vehemence to allocate a proper bishop to the foreign communities in order to cure their indiscipline. There was no witch-hunt, but certain changes were implemented: Stouppe, the Swiss pastor of Threadneedle Street, was required to leave the country, being suspected of having acted as an international agent for Cromwell, which seems highly plausible.[26]

Hérault, as far as he was concerned, tried very hard to import into England something of the sacred eloquence of the *grand siègles*: his high-flown poetic diction took his listeners by surprise after the prosaic tones of the Puritan twang. The congregation of the Reformed Church of London, still remembering the confused millenarianism of Jean de La Marche, listened in amazement to the flowery rhetoric of their Royalist pastor. Indeed, the divine right of kings and God's image were now constantly interwoven. Was not Charles II for 'all the world one of the greatest Princes ever to wear a crown'? Were not the natural leaders of the kingdom made, more than other men, in the image of God? The mayor of London was congratulated, in November 1666: 'Be glad, Your Lordship, to imitate that great God of whom you are most particularly the image, in your high dignity.' Affectation invaded the consistory registers; in the midst of so many clumsy standard formulas, one comes across this pure gem of rhetoric from Hérault (28 March 1668):

> If ancient Rome..., praised and renowned for her hospitality towards the afflicted strangers who came there from all parts, and to whom she afforded asylum and refuge, was called on this account the country of all nations, your Majesty's England, has far greater claim to this illustrious reputation.

But was this eloquence really appreciated as it deserved? The small world of the refugees was regarded as philistine by Hérault. Indeed, the most talented pastors suffered from the incomprehension of these descendants of Walloons and Normans who did not always speak the king's French or the queen's English. Hence the pastor's obvious

---

[26] Stouppe is mentioned by G. Burnet in his *History of My Own Time*, 3 vols., ed. O. Airy, Oxford, 1897–1903, I, pp. 130ff: '[In the Summer of 1654] Cromwell sent Stouppe round all France, to talk with their most eminent men, to see into their strength, into their present disposition, the oppressions they lay under, and their inclinations to trust the prince of Condé.' The Swiss minister was probably instrumental in bringing about the Anglo-French alliance between Cromwell and Mazarin in those years, though he may have acted a double game, receiving money from the French and incurring the wrath of Thurloe. Osmund Airy described him as a 'very busy troublesome fellow' (p. 142).

uneasiness and frustration; his absolute loyalty to the Crown formed a convenient screen for his congregation, but they nonetheless disliked him, because of his attachment to the 'service of the King', as he himself complained in November 1674 – while in December, he likened himself to Moses, forsaken by his people. He was charitably advised, at this point, to take better care of his precarious health; his parishioners offered to find him a substitute, at least for the most burdensome of his tasks. What charitable concern! In the spring of 1675, he was even advised to retire to Canterbury, where he held a canonry. The parish could cover the expense of his journey and pay him a pension – as long as he went! He retorted by emphasising the persistence of the revolutionary spirit within the community, and quoted the reported words of one of the parishioners, who had had the good taste to flee to Jamaica (25 April 1675):

> Since the King's return, England has had cause to regret the passing of Cromwell, who was a great champion of God's law ... if the English were wise, they would rid themselves of the Stuarts – as he hoped they would, besides – and as for the service which is held in the King's chapel in Whitehall, it was scarcely different from the Mass, in a word, it was but a copy of the Mass.

The endless suspicion surrounding Hérault, whom the consistory even threatened to suspend, disclosed the lasting resentment of the refugees and the lingering rebellious mood of some of their members. In June 1675, Hérault was obliged to leave, as he had been thirty years before; he died seven years later in Canterbury.

The 'Advice for the establishing a good government in the foreign Churches of this Kingdom'

The Refuge was a focus of tensions: political disavowals, petty differences between newcomers and established refugees, a spirit of lay independence, adverse to the international elite of pastors – all were added, quite naturally, to the lasting cleavages of English society. These constant factors gained in intensity in the second half of the seventeenth century; immigration, which had fallen off since the 1630s, resumed its spate in the last three decades. The need for an effective control of this motley, undisciplined crowd became the common concern of the Crown and Church, while many pastors turned to the Anglican bishops as their natural respondents. This patronage expressed itself in two distinct ways: either through the benevolent and accommodating protection of the old Reformed Churches, allowing them to retain a relatively autonomous ecclesiastical discipline and religious life – as in Threadneedle Street – or through conformity with the established Church, as at the Savoy, Westminster. In practice, this French-speaking Anglicanism oscillated between evangelical charity and coercion, yet it achieved an unusual degree of conciliation and rallied its supporters. Hérault, although a pastor at Threadneedle Street, defended the idea of episcopacy from the beginning but his immoderate zeal finally defeated its own object. Hérault cherished the hope of becoming a bishop, but unfortunately he lacked the unruffled composure favoured by his hosts. Some years later, the Anglican clergy were to complain: 'The French ministers could learn in their exile to be as moderate as are many learned divines of the Church of England.'[27] Too unbridled in his vehemence, too French in many respects, Hérault never adopted the paucity of gestures or the jocular gravity which suited a prelate. Enthusiasm was viewed askance in England; excess of fervour, even for the right cause, remained tainted with suspicion.

Hérault had to be content with a canonry for his past services. Though he had endeavoured to set up his own bishopric, Hérault's plans for establishing a superintendent-general to the Foreign Churches – a function which he wished to exercise himself – proved of no avail, and are among the lost causes of history, along with many inventions.

And yet I decided, following Ferdinand de Schickler, to unearth the quaint document, called an 'Advice for the establishing of a good government in the foreign churches of this Kingdom'. Calvinist bishops are not too common. The pastor's bold speculations shed a crude light on the relation between episcopacy and monarchy in a Protestant country like England.

A French version of the text was sent to the king in 1662; once translated, it was passed on to the bishop of London, and to the archbishop of Canterbury, who filed the essay, twenty-five years later.[28] Accordingly, the interest of this 'secret' memorandum is not confined to the vicissitudes it underwent, or to its author's bitterness. It remained for a whole generation a credible alternative, though it threatened the privileges enjoyed by the refugees. We may peruse this document which I now give in a new English translation:

> The example of the ministers having a wondrous influence on their flocks, it can incline them favourably or unfavourably towards the State and Church, according to their good or ill dispositions towards one or the other; it is therefore of great importance to provide our Churches with good pastors, well recognised and approved as men who love peace and pursue it, and who are opposed to all faction and partialities, and to all dangerous and pernicious maxims which might trouble and injure that peace, whether in State or Church.

This preamble was no truism: it reaffirmed the unity of Church and

---

[27] London, Lambeth Palace Library, MSS Gibsoniani 933, Doc. 67.
[28] Respectively: SP Dom., Ch. II, LXVI, no. 45; Bodleian Library, Rawlinson MSS, C. 984; A.477, fol. 90; Tanner MSS, 92, fol. 73.

State. The term 'government' is common to both. Hérault went on that what applied to the English – the need for effective control – also applied to his brethren. The French Reformed Churches, he plainly admitted, 'were, in the past, troubled with many disturbances, disorders and confusion, through the bad government of some of their pastors, particularly one Jean de La Marche, who was a real firebrand, a preacher of sedition, rebellion, and parricide against the late king, in the French Church of London'.

This accurate reminder of the revolutionary past involves a discussion of the organisation of the Reformed Churches:

> For this reason, it would be necessary not to leave the choice of their pastors entirely to the whims of the people and consistories as had been the case till now... This has caused divers disorders in their midst, as seditious preaching to win the favour of the people; as the tumultuous election of ministers, by intrigues, and by other evil means; and divers other similar misfortunes, *to which I need not refer.*

I have emphasised the implicit reference to the revolution; this dialectic of remembrance and oblivion was in tune with the timely concern to erase the execrated, but constantly recurring, memory. How could a resurgence of the revolutionary past effectively be held in check? The democracy of the consistories, in Louis Hérault's view, led to demagogy. Accordingly, it was desirable to 'designate some person of well-recognised merit, well-affected to the service of God and the king, and well-intentioned towards the Church of England'. This dignity could be given the title either of overseer (superintendent) or of bishop, 'whichever is judged to be most appropriate'. The term 'superintendent' presented a twofold advantage: it referred back – as Hérault himself recognised – to the prestigious reign of Edward, and to the office held by John a Lasco. There was no suspect innovation, then, in Hérault's idea: the office of superintendent, formerly exercised by a Lasco, went back to the century of the Reformation. The title invoked the authority of precedent. But this was not its only attraction: the French word 'intendant' referred equally to civil society. It confirmed the alliance of Church and State, and implied a delegation of power. The superintendent remained an administrator: in the language of the time, he was a servant of the Crown, from which he derived his legitimacy. It followed that the principle of equality among pastors, which had already been undermined in practice, ceased to have any force. But it was above all in relation to laymen – who are described, in a revealing term, as the 'people' – that Louis Hérault found the institutions of the Reformed Churches to be far too flexible and permissive. He pointed out, with his judicious admixture of thunderous declarations and innuendoes, that the Reformed discipline seemed to lead up to religious independence. In other words, the disorders which everyone still associated with the

Cromwellian era were the logical consequence of the excessive liberty given to each Church in the administration of its own affairs:

> Whatever profession they made of rejecting independence, they are in effect independent, at least ordinarily and most of the time: for the colloquies and synods to which they are answerable meet only very rarely and with great difficulty, and only for urgent, important and extra-ordinary reasons, and during the intervening time, the consistories are sovereign and independent, ordering all things as they please, without giving any account of their government.

Hérault admitted, with all due realism, that the restoring of order among the Refugee Churches would require a decent income for the superintendent, 'an honourable subsistence' such as would enable him 'to maintain the dignity of his office with honour'.

In addition, English Dissenters, whether Presbyterian or Independent, would no longer be able to allege any formal resemblance with the French Reformed Churches: 'It would be a good means of making it known to the English Presbyterians that they are mistaken when they pretend to observe the example of the French Churches.'

There follows a list, in fourteen points, of the particular attributions of the superintendent. He is permanently invested with the supreme authority which had previously belonged to the periodic synods, over which he alone must be entitled to preside as mediator; the doctrinal examination of future pastors, and their consecration, are his province and so is the control of the consistories. Moreover, the superintendent is accountable, in the last instance, only to the king, from whom he holds his commission, or to his council.

Acculturation – or elite betrayal?

'We are feeding a traitor.' This unsavoury indictment of pastor Hérault (London consistory, 27 April 1676) may be partly justified by resentment at his secret negotiations. I shall not pass judgement on the impassioned nature of the disavowal: was Hérault a traitor, or a victim of his duty? My contention will be that the idea of elite betrayal does not simply express the common insecurity and confusion felt by the refugees from the 1660 onwards. Basically their uneasiness had cultural roots. Conformity with the Church of England involved a process of acculturation, which may have proved easier for ministers and scholars to whom the relativity of customs was a familiar fact, than it did for many among the congregations, who regarded the Anglican liturgy with a mixture of derisive bewilderment and mocking uncertainty. This concept of 'elite betrayal', in spite of its polemical undertones, cannot be entirely discounted. The destiny of a minority oscillates between two contradictory poles; the affirmation of idiosyncratic traits is mitigated by the compulsion to imitate the host society. This mimetic conformity found some of its most strenuous exponents and best advocates among the pastors and well-to-do. Hence, precisely, the heightening of tensions within the communities, which often echoed the outside world, as was the case with dissent or conformity. On the eve of the Revocation of the Edict of Nantes, Calvinism was an object of suspicion even on the part of some Calvinists themselves, who sought to tone down its Presbyterian element.

For all these reasons, it would be mistaken to treat Hérault as a fool or to regard his memorandum as a piece of opportunistic literature. This long-standing Royalist remained true to his convictions; and he was led sincerely to voice his own doubts on the 'Calvinist government' after 1660. The disgruntled morosity, which affected another pastor such as Paul Bertrand, reveals real discontent with existing institutions. As for the status of the refugees, it remained ambiguous, between the cup and the lip, the exception and the rule, the established Church and Puritan nonconformity.

Louis Hérault's initiative was not inconsistent. This former student of Pierre du Moulin followed his Master's teaching in many respects; the great pastor from Sedan had also entertained the thought of becoming a bishop. Hérault was reviving the *entente cordiale* with the Church of England, which had begun to take shape at the beginning of the century. In Chapter 3, I explained at length the significance of this convergence, which reconciled in the eyes of the world Protestantism and loyalty to the Crown. Under the Restoration, this proved no longer sufficient: the Refuge needed to offer further guarantees to Charles II. The most effective way to dissociate oneself from the Puritans was to accept fully the role of the bishops. Before 1640, French-speaking conformity had had few followers; in the second half of the century, however, the tendency was reversed. This entailed a fundamental departure from previous practices, since government by assemblies gave way to sovereign authority. The choice was often less painful than expected: absolutism seemed destined to enjoy a bright future. Two distinct models existed side by side for the refugees: Presbyterianism and episcopalianism. In the French Reformed Churches, the day-to-day administration of the communities was entrusted to individual consistories, in which pastors and laymen worked closely together. Above them, classes (colloquies) and synods were regularly summoned to debate the thorniest issues. The English Refuge has up to now provided a fairly accurate picture of this type of organisation; however, the system was discontinued after 1659 in France, and after 1660 in England.[29]

The episcopalian alternative enjoyed increasing favour in England,

---

[29] After the synod of Loudun in 1659, only provincial synods were held in France. In England, the Churches of the Refuge held their latest Colloquy in 1660.

where many Calvinist pastors from abroad lent it their support. Assemblies had acquired a dubious reputation after the revolution. One should not overestimate the element of constraint involved in the adaptation of Anglicanism. The chief attraction of conformity to the Church of England was that it demonstrated, with all the requisite solemnity, the loyalty of the French Protestants to the monarchy, and absolved them from the stigma of republicanism. In many cases, however, the refugees resisted conformity (see below). But nonetheless, this French-speaking Anglicanism prided itself on its sense of history: it met the requisites for a national, established religion adapted to the form of the State. Where their religion was concerned, the refugees could relinquish their minority status, which they had inherited from the former French situation. In a country like England, where the 'true Faith' was established, why stick to past practices? Such was the gist of the argument presented in 1705 by Grotête de La Mothe, the conformist pastor of the Savoy, in his *Correspondance fraternelle de l'Eglise anglicane avec les autres Eglises réformées et étrangères, prouvée par un dissertation historique, et par plusieurs sermons prononcés à l'occasion des réfugiés d'Orange (The Fraternal Correspondence between the Anglican Church and the Other Foreign Reformed Churches, Proven by an Historical Dissertation, and by Several Sermons Preached on the Arrival of the Refugees from Orange).* In fact, the author tells us, everything stems from the paradox that episcopacy exists by 'divine right' – just as monarchy – and yet is not necessary for salvation. One may, then, legitimately have no bishops when one is 'under the Cross', i.e. subjected to persecution. But once Protestantism has become the majority religion, once the State and its ecclesiastical servants have been won over to the cause of the Reformation, why should one do without so commendable an institution? I shall not dwell upon the arguments invoked, or upon the mention of Pierre du Moulin, who had himself admitted in 1618: 'In the time of our fathers, when God raised up servants from the midst of popery to expose the abuses of the Church of Rome, in those places where He employed the bishops of the Church of Rome for this excellent work as in England, the title and degree of bishop has remained.'[30]

The defence of the episcopalian settlement is above all historical; it refers to the specific conditions of the Reformation in each country. Yet was this precedent binding on future generation? If the Reformed Churches of the Continent had not retained bishops, this may have been the effect of chance rather than choice. There were no sound theological reasons, according to du Moulin, to preclude the eventual adoption of a Church hierarchy akin to Anglicanism. We are here treading on unfamiliar

---

[30] P. du Moulin, *De la vocation des pasteurs*, Sedan, 1681, p. 16.

ground: French Reformed episcopalianism had failed outside England, if we except the Irish or American colonies. Moreover, French Protestant historiography has often tended to be republican in character, assuming that the lay discipline of Calvinism was more democratic in essence than any other – despite Moïse Amyraut's contention that the consistories formed an aristocracy.[31] Accordingly, Huguenot episcopalianism has often been underplayed. Yet a genuine episcopalian streak emerged in the seventeenth century, starting with Pierre du Moulin the elder, and running through Hérault and the conformist pastors of the English Refuge. According to E.G. Leonard, pastor Pierre du Bosc from Caen in Normandy, one of the most famous preachers of his time, paid tribute to 'unpretentious episcopacy', though preserving the priesthood of all believers.[32] Even Pierre Jurieu, who was notorious for his Whig stance after the Revocation and Glorious Revolution, may have received Anglican orders during his stay in England *c.* 1660.[33]

High-Church Huguenots and Low-Church Anglicans

There were no High- and Low-Church parties as such till the 1701 convocation;[34] nonetheless these convenient labels deserve to be extended to prior developments. The 'High-Church' emphasis on ecclesiastical hierarchy vs. lay autonomy seems to have characterised the last twenty-five years of the official existence of the French Reformed Churches, prior to the Revocation. Among other things, no national synods were held in France after 1659, and naturally enough this tended to highlight the authority of the most conspicuous ministers.[35] This clerical trend was sometimes regarded with awe as a sheer betrayal of Calvinist principles: the rejection of Hérault by his congregation, or pastor Bertrand's recantation of a 'ridiculous form of government' (see above) display the deep-rooted *malaise* which poisoned relations between ministers and their flock.

As a matter of fact, High-Church Huguenots tended to become 'Low-Church Anglicans', as it were. Though they cannot be treated in isolation, because of constant links between England and the Continent, I should like to examine two distinct phenomena: first, the adoption of Anglicanism by refugees; secondly the internal evolution of some French Protestants towards a mild form of episcopalianism.

---

[31] E. Labrousse, *Une foi, une loi, une roi? La Révocation de l'Edit de Nantes*, Paris and Geneva, 1985, pp. 110ff: 'La dangereuse démocratie réformée'.
[32] Léonard, *Histoire générale du protestantisme*, II, pp. 344–5.
[33] On Jurieu's radical commitment, see R.J. Howells, *Pierre Jurieu: Antinomian Radical*, Durham, 1983; R.J. Howells (ed.), *Pierre Jurieu. Lettres pastorales*, Hildesheim, 1988.
[34] W.A. Speck, *Stability and Strife*, London, 1977, p. 92.
[35] E. Labrousse, 'Note sur Pierre Jurieu', *Revue d'Histoire et de Philosophie Religieuses*, 58 (1973), p. 286.

In the 1950s, Norman Sykes examined with great subtlety all the implications of the episcopal debate in early modern England.[36] Fundamentally, one concern stands out in the case of the Huguenots: the transition from minority culture to majority status. The pastors' glee when they were welcomed by bishops, the joy of being at last accepted and duly recognised are but one facet of the destiny of those men who acceded to a dominant culture and to its modes of thought after years of alienation. The Church of England offered undeniable security and moral comfort. In the last two decades of the century, when the supply of pastors outran demand, the ministers who had left forever a parish in France, could hardly be indifferent to the baits of conformity. Since 1662, an Anglican preferment entailed the humiliating process of reordination by a bishop. Things had been easier in the Elizabethan (and Jacobean or Caroline) periods when the only prerequisite for admittance to a benefice in the Church of England, when ordained 'beyond seas', was formal subscription to the 39 Articles (13 Eliz. I c. 12).

Yet several English Royalists like John Cosin, later bishop of Durham, or Sir Ralph Verney had rubbed shoulders with the Huguenots during their own exile at the time of the Civil War and Interregnum, but they may have refrained from taking the sacrament in Reformed chapels. Dr Cosin has left a remarkable letter from Paris, dated 7 January 1650, in which he clearly states 'whether you may communicate with the French Reformed Church'. He gave a measured answer to his correspondent, a Thomas Cordell who acted as tutor to several young exiles at Blois:

> I hope however that you will be allowed to receive the elements on your knees, and that certain words (words which they themselves, and even the Scots, use both in the Exhortation and in the Declaration to the people) be used to *you particularly* at the moment of delivering the elements to you.[37]

I am not at all sure that the French pastor, Monsieur Testard, complied with Dr Cosin's wish and said to his English communicants, following his recommendation: 'Prenez, mangez les viandes sacrées de notre Seigneur J. C.' ('Take, eat the holy body of our Saviour'). But whatever the good minister may have done, one thing is certain: the Huguenots could not grasp the interest of the apostolical succession. Dr Cosin hoped a solution would be found one day to cure his Reformed brethren of their Presbyterian leanings:

> Although I see that certain Reformed Churches, the Scottish especially and French, have not that which agreeth best with the Sacred Scripture, I mean the Government that is by bishops, inasmuch as both these

---

[36] N. Sykes, *Old Priest and New Presbyter*, Cambridge, 1956.
[37] C.R.L. Fletcher, 'Some Troubles of Archbishop Sancroft', *Proceedings of the Huguenot Society of London*, 13, p. 219.

churches are fallen into a different kind of regiment, which to remedy it is for the one altogether too late, and too soon for the other, during this present affliction and trouble.[38]

The revolution and Interregnum certainly widened the gap between Calvinism and what was to become fully fledged Anglicanism after 1662. The number of refugee pastors who joined the established Church is the more striking when we take into account the blemish tainting Presbyterianism. Moreover, as J. Claude, one of the major representatives of the French reformed Churches in France, objected to Compton, bishop of London, in April 1681: 'Some people complain that you do not reordain the Roman priests who join your church, while you do so in the case of French or Dutch ministers from beyond the sea.'[39]

To my knowledge no precise figures of these reordinations are available. They would involve a number of case-studies of individual pastors. In the *Hind and the Panther* (1687), John Dryden poked fun at the unfortunate French ministers who chose to conform with the established Church:

> Think you your new *French* Proselytes are come
> To starve abroad, because they starv'd at home?
> Your benefices twinkl'd from afar
> They found the new *Messiah* by the star:
> Those *Swisses* fight on any side for pay,
> And 'tis the living that conforms, not they.
> Mark with what management their bribes divide,
> Some stick to you, and some to t'other side,
> That many churches may for many mouths provide
> More vacant pulpits wou'd more converts make,
> All wou'd have latitude enough to take;
> The rest unbenefic'd, your sects maintain:
> For ordinations without cure are vain,
> And chamber practice is a silent gain.[40]

Besides these material considerations, English society offered considerable psychological comfort: the freedom of speech of parishioners must needs be restrained by their submission as subjects, and bitterness towards the Reformed consistories, and their constant changes of opinion, was one final argument that tilted the balance in favour of Anglicanism. Conformity was not necessarily opportunistic, though there were some solid reasons to conform. I should be tempted to minimise the weight of exogenous factors: the adoption of episcopalianism responded to a general ecclesiological crisis which had long affected the Reformed Churches of France. One of my contentions in this book is that some of

---

[38] *Ibid.*, p. 221.
[39] J. Claude, *Oeuvres posthumes*, 5 vols., Amsterdam, 1688–9, v, p. 269.
[40] J. Dryden, *Poems and Fables*, ed. J. Kingsley, Oxford, 1970, pp. 392–3.

the basic concepts of English history may be exported to the French case. Indeed, one should beware alike of anachronism and all-embracing generalities: nonetheless, English and for that matter French history have too often been insular in the past: the French have a passion for universality which makes them lend their idiom to other cultures; the English, on the other hand, like to think that their own experience is incomparable. Let us therefore renounce our national prejudices. As I hinted before, the High-Church/Low-Church divide may prove instrumental in the case of French Protestantism; the same would apply to the idea of 'comprehension'. One of the keys to Gallicanism could be provided by the example of Anglicanism. The concept of a single national Church was not alien to the Huguenots, though defeated by the Revocation. As early as 1670, Isaac d'Huisseau, a minister from Saumur, published his *Réunion du christianisme ou la manière de rejoindre tous les chrétiens sous une seule confession de foi* (*Christian Unity or the Reunification of All Christians under a Single Confession of Faith*). The pastor, who gave a Cartesian account of the 'essentials' of Christianity, was harshly condemned.[41] As Janine Garrisson has clearly demonstrated, the theme of religious unity became increasingly 'fashionable' in the 1670s and 1680s.[42] Yet were the Huguenots in a position to negotiate with the Catholic majority? Reunion was, and still is, a dangerous venture for a religious minority. Moreover, the Assembly of the French clergy issued on 1 July 1682 an *Avertissement pastoral à ceux de la religion prétendue réformée pour les porter à se convertir et à se réconcilier avec l'Eglise* (*A Pastoral Exhortation to Those of the So-Called Reformed Persuasion to Enable Them to Achieve Conversion and Reconciliation with the Church*). The French Protestants were no longer termed 'heretics', and became 'schismatics' instead, which as a matter of fact was not a mark of leniency at a time when separate brethren were dragooned into their parish churches. Pastor Claude rejected the offer. This was yet a troubled period for French Catholics: that same year, four celebrated articles had been issued in convocation, affirming the king of France's temporal independence from the Holy See, the supremacy of councils over the pope and the legitimacy of the liberties of the Gallican Church.[43] This Gallican charter may have raised some hopes in England; Gilbert Burnet, who later became bishop of Salisbury as a reward for his major role in the Glorious Revolution, published his *News from France, in a letter giving a relation of the present state of the difference between the French king and the Court of*

[41] R. Stauffer, *L'Affaire d'Huisseau*, Paris, 1969.
[42] J. Garrison, *L'Edit de Nantes et sa révocation*, Paris, 1985, p. 140.
[43] J. Orcibal, *Louis XIV contre Innocent XI*, Paris, 1949; B. Neveu, 'Jacques II médiateur entre Louis XIV et Innocent XI', *Mélanges d'Archéologie et d'Histoire*, 79 (1967), pp. 699–764.

Rome, London 1682, while another newsletter that same year contained *A Brief Account of the Proceedings of the French Clergy, in taking away the Pope's usurp'd supremacy.*

Pastor Jean Dubourdieu, from Montpellier, was to issue his own 'Projet de réunion des deux religions' ('A Project for the Reunion of the Two Religions'), *c.* 1684. This fascinating document is often appended to the complete works of Bossuet, the most famous Catholic preacher and controversialist of his time.[44] The text clearly refers to the 'Gallican Church', and states a number of requests on the part of the Huguenots. The belief in purgatory should be made optional, baptism and the Lord's Supper would be regarded as the main sacraments, though all debates on the real presence were to be avoided. Moreover, the laity would be allowed to read the Bible, and all services would be held in the vernacular. Some of the most prestigious religious orders – like the Jesuits and Benedictines – could be preserved. But for Dubourdieu the basic requirement remained the four articles: '(*Article xv*) The limits which the last Assembly of the French clergy set to the pope's prerogative will remain forever in force; as for his rank among the Christian bishops, he will at the utmost be regarded as *primus inter pares.*'[45]

We should further note that while this project failed as expected, Jean Dubourdieu came to England where he was one of the most outspoken mouthpieces of French Anglicanism. He was in turn chaplain to the duke of Schomberg at the battle of the Boyne, and a minister at the Savoy, where his father preached shortly before his death, aged ninety-five. This high-ranking pastor may serve as an illustration of Huguenot episcopalianism. His Gallican principles led him to favour a comprehensive, national Church.

Conformity or submission?

You are the great leader of a holy militia
Which, every day, fights for the laws of God
Chosen to this end by the greatest of kings
To rouse his people to the practice of devotion.[46]
Sonnet addressed to Sancroft, archbishop of Canterbury

[Many refugees express] their firm resolution to live in entire
conformity and orderly submission to our government both in Church
and State.[47]
Declaration by Sancroft, *c.* 1680

What could be more natural for a refugee than to conform to the religion of Church and State? And yet, I should like to avoid all undue

---

[44] J.B. Bossuet, *Oeuvres complètes*, F. Lachat, 31 vols., Paris, 1872–82, xvii, pp. 353–6.
[45] *Ibid.*, pp. 355–6.   [46] Bodleian Library, Tanner MSS 92, fol. 125.
[47] *Ibid.*, fol. 79.

simplification: the transition to Anglicanism rarely constituted a denial of the past; in most cases it involved a selective process. We shall be able to see this more clearly if we adopt a new point of view. Until now, we have insisted upon the political implications of this transfer of allegiance, while the cases of Louis Hérault and Grotête de La Mothe have illustrated the theological justifications for episcopalianism. A new aspect should now be emphasised: the cultural forms of adaptation.

Accordingly, the concept of *acculturation* will prove useful to describe this phenomenon. How, indeed, is one to define, in all its complexity, the relationship between minority and majority cultures, between the Calvinist refugees and their English hosts? The situation was, however, quite different from the colonial situation which originally inspired the concept of acculturation, nor does it correspond to one of the current uses of the terms to describe the intellectual or political ascendancy of the ruling class and the diffusion of its system of values throughout society. (The third part of this book will show a comparable phenomenon when the consistories mercilessly pursued superstition, ignorance and sexual promiscuity.) Finally we may define one further type of acculturation to suit the case of the refugees. Acculturation here is not a question of conquest, and no dominated classes could be envisaged as such. Where the Huguenots and Englishmen were concerned, I should be more inclined to speak of a dialectic between minority and majority status.

We have already encountered several types of attitudes. In the sixteenth century the minority accepted its separation – its identity was defined along particular, unchangeable lines. Yet in the 1630s, at the time of the 'Laudian persecution', this mode of thought was completely reversed. Assimilation, the planned disappearance of the foreign communities from the second generation onwards, was due to erase all previous distinctions, and turn the refugees into nondescript, abstract subjects of the king.

After 1660, French-speaking Anglicanism, that hybrid entity, constituted an adaptation to the host society; but in fact the compromise was reciprocal. While many refugees submitted to a form of French-speaking Anglicanism, they in turn modified its contours. Not all newcomers were delighted with the liturgy of the Church of England. Needless to say, our sources are relatively implicit on the subject: why should the French Protestants insist on what might prove an affront to their English hosts? But the perpetual warnings against Huguenot sarcasm and irreverence speak for themselves. Even in the most conformist French parishes, the liturgy in use remained very plain and unadorned. We have little information concerning this French Anglicanism, and often the nature of its religious sensibility has to be deduced from a small number of clues. Paradoxically, those Churches which seemed the most acceptable to the authorities by virtue of their religious conformity were also, with few exceptions, those which have passed on to us the most slender archives. The Savoy, the conformist sister-Church of the Threadneedle Street temple, has not left us its registers, apart from the baptismal records for the end of the seventeenth century. On the other hand, its worthy pastor evidently showed remarkable readiness to publish their sermons and other works.

The Anglo-Norman Jean Durel was undoubtedly the most prestigious eulogist of French Anglicanism; he adapted the Book of Common Prayer from pastor Delaune's 1616 version, and benefited from the sales of this pious work. At least, this is how I interpret the authorisation which Charles II granted him on 6 October 1662: 'And we permit the said Master Durel to have his translation printed in such place, by such persons, and in whatever form he shall think most fit, and we forbid all our subjects to use any edition other than such as may be made with his consent and by his order.' Could it be, then, that there were *un*-authorised versions of the Anglican liturgy? This rather fanciful idea – which the royal text seems to suggest – contains an element of truth. Let us imagine for a moment that a French parish, while claiming to conform with the Church of England, removed some elements of the accepted liturgy, or added some others – as had been the case during the revolution in many English parishes. I am inclined to think that there were various degrees of conformity among the refugees, and that observance was less complete than is usually believed and gave rise to frequent changes, and even disputes. This would, in any case, have been understandable in the English context: everyone was aware of the *occasional conformity* of many Dissenters who did not hesitate to attend an Anglican service in the morning, and a conventicle in the afternoon. Moreover, many refugees, apart from a few uncompromising Calvinists, had a rather hazy, exotic image of Anglicanism, which did not in the least inhibit them from moving from one Protestant communion to another.

But above all, selective use was made of the English ritual. The ministers neither wore a surplice, nor did they make the sign of the Cross, while the laity did not kneel at Communion. All the elaboration of form and gesture, which from the sixteenth century onwards had been considered by the Puritans to smack of idolatry and superstition, did not find favour with the French Anglicans who followed the very Low-Church Anglo-Norman ritual. They might not engage in controversy with the English, but they had their reservations nonetheless. We know little, however, about the numerous adjustments which existed in practice, nor can we make windows into men's souls.

For my part, I would be inclined to think that the transition to Anglicanism was selective in nature. One of the first users of the term 'acculturation' insisted on the chain of gradations separating borrowing from sheer identification.[48] Acculturation, in Herskovits' view, had to be distinguished from 'culture change', and amounted neither to 'assimilation' nor 'diffusion'. In short, it consists in differential selection. The Anglican monopoly was never total, if only because the underlying reality of the Church of England has always been heterogeneous. The institution of the consistory may serve as an example. We have seen the complaints of Louis Hérault against this form of parish government, exercised by pastors and laymen. The congregations remained, in fact, so attached to this institution that it did not disappear completely. Thus, the community of Thorpe-le-Soken in Essex conformed to the Anglican model; and yet the parishioners kept a register entitled 'consistory proceedings'. Of course, there no longer was a consistory as such; on 1 January 1684, two churchwardens had been appointed, 'both to meet the need for order, and to satisfy the constitution of the Anglican Church, to which we are obliged to conform'. Likewise, all important decisions were to be taken after the 'principal heads of families' had been convened – a procedure which remained an open possibility in the Church of England.

Thus, the common parish organisation – churchwardens and vestry – permitted, in practice, the preservation of the *status quo*, as the Anglican hierarchy was well aware. A selective adaptation of the Anglican ritual, the preservation of former customs, and local variations meant that Anglicanisation did not coincide with the disappearance of the original culture of the French Protestants. They continued to use the term *elder*, even though presbyteries had been abolished in theory.

George Morley, bishop of Winchester, issued an order on 10 August 1683 which shows his displeasure at the prolonged existence of a consistory:

> Whereas the French church settled at Wandsworth under our jurisdiction has been lately in some disorder for want of a due regulation, we do therefore appoint and ordain that henceforward there be no consistory, but for the supply thereof that they yearly choose two churchwardens, the one nominated by the minister, the other by the heads of families, who are to be regulated by the Canons and our Articles of Visitation in performance of their duty, and that they call a Vestry, consisting of the heads of families so oft as occasion shall require, according, to the usage of the Church of England.[49]

Undoubtedly, there were some obstinate critics of Anglicanism among the refugees, but, for obvious reasons, they did not commit their ideas to writing. And when they did, little survived. Louis du Moulin, the black sheep of his family, is worth mentioning for his strenuous opposition to conformity. An interesting pamphlet may help clarify his distrust, *A True*

---

[48] M. Herskovits, *Acculturation, the Study of Culture Contact*, New York, 1938.
[49] Bodleian Library, Rawlinson MSS, C. 984, fol. 213.

Report of a Discourse between Monsieur de l'Angle, Canon of Canterbury, and minister of the French church in the savoy and Lewis du Moulin the 10th of February 1678/9, London, 1679.

In the midst of the popish plot, which rested on a fake Catholic conspiracy to assassinate the king, Louis (or Lewis) du Moulin incriminated the Anglican churchmen instead of the Jesuits, as did most of his contemporaries. *They* were the real conspirators who planned to reintroduce downright popery into the kingdom in the guise of episcopalianism:

> Having had about fifteen days since some discourse with one of my friends, wherein I convinced him of this truth, that the papists had never expected nor undertook the establishing of their religion in *England* by massacres, especially by that damnable and hellish one of the most sacred person in the kingdom [the so-called 'popish plot' against Charles II], if they had not been for a long time fully persuaded, that the *Ecclesiastical Party*, who carry all things before them, were absolutely disposed to give them a most kind reception.[50]

The Anglican fifth-columnists were therefore the allies of the Church of Rome. They had long renounced the tenets of the Reformation: 'Have I sinned in maintaining that of all the Reformed Churches from popery, the *English* is the least conformable in its government and practices, and in its discipline, to the Primitive Church?'[51]

In 1680, the same du Moulin, who held principles so different from his Jacobean father and conformist brother, issued an impassioned indictment of the established Church: *A short and True Account of the Several Advances the Church of England hath made towards Rome: or a Model of the Grounds upon which the papists for these hundred years have built their hopes and expectation, that England would ere long return to popery.*

This pamphlet, which appeared the year of his death, incurred a reprimand upon the Reformed Church of London. The parish attempted to exonerate itself: they insisted that Louis du Moulin attended Communion, though he was not a regular member of the community. Moreover, the trouble-maker was advised to be more cautious, and refrain from all undue observations in future. Yet many a refugee had a glib tongue, and we may remember that pastor Bertrand had the greatest difficulty in Rye with his congregation who remained faithful to the abhorred principles of Calvinism and jeered at his endeavours to introduce the Anglican liturgy among them. Apparently, Bertrand had relinquished all links with the Reformed discipline which he regarded as subversive in itself. But how did his English hosts react to the minister's predicament which cast a shadow on the *entente cordiale* with the French refugees?

---

[50] *A True Report...*, London, 1679, p. 71.   [51] *Ibid.*, p. 72.

Heneage Finch, second earl of Winchelsea, complained to Guy Carleton, bishop of Winchester in a letter dated 22 February 1683:

> At the French congregation's first settling in Rye there hath been great endeavours and artifices used by the English fanatics there to pervert the French congregation, hoping to make them as factious against the King and Church as themselves are by endeavouring to persuade them to set up presbytery and not to comply with the Church of England, which did cause some disputes between Monsieur Bertrand and his congregation, wherein Monsieur Bertrand behaved himself very well, and by the prudence of the bishop of London they are all reconciled and have submitted themselves to the Church of England.[52]

Above all, the earl of Winchelsea feared the contagion of English 'fanaticism' on the poor French people. He therefore charitably required the protection of the law for the stranded congregation, who might otherwise ape the English and adopt their vices:

> It may also deserve your Lordship's consideration whether it may not be proper for your Lordship to write to some Justices of the Peace about Rye, and to some of the Ministers to put the laws in execution against those turbulent fanatics, who do not only every day disturb our church, but would also pervert those French that would willingly comply with the government, and when the French see these laws severely put in execution against the English, they will for fear of the like punishment acquiesce more willingly from faction.

Yet, in spite of its patronising undertones, this letter did not sound entirely optimistic. How could one impose conformity on the French refugees when some of their oldest establishments, in London and Canterbury, had retained their Presbyterian discipline? 'My Lord, in my opinion, the chief root from when all these evils spring is by permitting the French Presbyterian Church in London and Canterbury, which at his Majesty's first restoration might have been easily reduced to the Church of England.'

His Majesty's former ambassador at Constantinople did not therefore conceal his resentment against the king's indulgence for the Huguenots. Whatever his prejudices, he may have raised an important issue: how could the refugees be expected to conform when some of their congregations were exempted from uniformity?

The matter and the manner

It is not always easy to take into account the anthropological dimension of these petty vestry disputes. The Rondeau affair, however, which broke out in the spring of 1683, testifies to the interest which the history of

[52] Bodleian Library, Tanner MSS 35, fol. 210.

mentality may find in slanderous denunciation – between fear and scandal, commonplace and gossip. A former pastor in France, Jacques Rondeau quickly found himself criticised, by his churchwarden, Poulverel, for his lukewarm attitude to the Church of England. This gave rise to a 'Most humble remonstrance concerning Master Jacques Rondeau, French minister of the Church of Hollingbourne'.[53]

The unimaginative scenario is nonetheless highly instructive. Against a background of personal quarrels, it emphasises the precariousness of Anglican acculturation: for instance the pastor refused to make the sign of the Cross at a christening, 'which shows, your Grace, that the said Sieur Rondeau is a minister of the said Anglican Church only for reasons of interest, since he does not conform to what is prescribed to him'. I shall pass over other accusations: Rondeau had acquired a suspicious degree of wealth, and treated his wife harshly. We are not told whether he drank or not. In addition – another anecdote which is revealing, in all its naivety – Rondeau was found at table, 'eating a piece of roast pork', instead of conducting a service. Poulverel pointed out to him that he was 'not in a fit state to administer Communion', only to be met with the sharp rejoinder 'that it was a trifling thing' and 'that he would administer Communion, all the same'.

Nonetheless, Jacques Rondeau had to exonerate himself from these accusations, in the eyes of the Church authorities:

> I have always had all the respect for the Anglican liturgy that I should have, and I remember very well having said, on occasions, to Monsieur Poulverel that I admired its forms of worship in many places, and in particular that the order for baptism seemed to me a masterpiece, for excelling that of the French liturgy.

This purported zeal for Anglicanism was mitigated, though, by the steadfast tone of what follows:

> However, I had no thought of changing my religion when taking orders in the Church of England, and I do not see what wrong there is in saying that any learned man (I might almost have added, any ignorant man, too) will hold some personal opinion on some point of religion, *whether it concerns the matter or the manner.*

This reference to Protestant consensus enabled Jacques Rondeau to claim a right to differ in some particular. Addressing the archbishop with all due reverence, he plainly displayed his remarkable determination in matters of conscience. But a new scandal arose when Rondeau refused to wear a surplice, and tried in vain to justify his gesture in a Latin letter to his archbishop, dated 4 June 1683, in which he invoked the privileges of the Savoy.

[53] *Ibid.*, 92, fols. 145ff. All my quotations are taken from this collection of documents.

Meanwhile, tension rose, and the members of his congregation themselves expressed their reluctance to conform. An English correspondent described them as 'very rude and irreverent', and what is more 'frequently sitting on their pews' instead of kneeling. As for their other 'indecent gestures', he preferred to hold his tongue. We have no clear indications on the consequences of this affair: Rondeau was defeated and forced to put on his surplice, incurring the reprobation of some of his parishioners. He probably left the Church of England ten years later.

Should we given an allegorical value to this type of anecdote? Such topical documents raise the problem of the *fait divers*, the unconnected, apparently insignificant details of history. In truth, there are no trivial facts for observers, there are simply different levels of coherence or significance. I shall point to four of these, in order to illustrate the partial failure of French-speaking Anglicanism.

In the first place, our sources of information are extremely heterogeneous. The apology of the Church of England was an elevated genre which was entrusted to the most able pens, or at least the most renowned of ministers, from Louis Hérault to Grotête de La Mothe, and fell within the sphere of learned rhetoric. In short, it was an object of civilised argument. Altogether different was resistance to conformity, which found expression in behaviour, in mockery rather than in printed discourses, with the exception of Louis du Moulin.

Cultural barriers should be equally emphasised. Frenchmen, in those days as well as now, were supposed to gesticulate and do everything in a hurry, in the midst of sluggish Englishmen. Rondeau was no exception to these national stereotypes; an English colleague of his commended his application, 'with allowance only for that which is natural to all Frenchmen, who seem to do all things in haste'.

Moreover, in these times of Restoration, the problems of acculturation were bound up with a set of attitudes held in common by French Calvinists and Puritans. The rejection of the sign of the Cross, of the surplice and of kneeling at Communion – which were regarded as idolatrous – had been emphasised unremittingly since 1550. These transgressions of accepted Anglican practices were of cardinal importance for the refugees, even though they ran the risk of antagonising some of their English hosts.

But above all, if we take the evidence as a whole, one cannot help being struck by a curious mixture of formalism and defiance, of boldness and submission, of provocation and conciliation, of incredulity and fidelity, in short, 'of heterodoxy and rigorous observance'.[54] Jacques Rondeau scorned all dietary restrictions – or what remained of them. As early as the

---

[54] E. Labrousse, *Pierre Bayle, hétérodoxie et rigorisme*, The Hague, 1964.

sixteenth century, the French Protestants had been indicted for eating bacon in Lent time. How could the consumption of pork – the appetising roast which shocked the churchwarden – make one unfit to administer Communion? And yet the sardonic Jacques Rondeau felt profound qualms of conscience when it came to putting on the surplice. This unwritten logic of behaviour will take on its full significance when we come to analyse scandal, that enduring topic of Calvinist civilisation, in the third part of this book.

6   The impact of massive immigration, *c.* 1680–1700

In the multitude of nations lies the wealth of kingdoms...We shall represent to Your Majesty that the fame of the ancient Gauls and of the peoples of the North owed its causes, and its effects, to their great numbers.[1]
Address from French Protestants to Charles II, for liberty to settle in Ireland

[Charles R.] holds himself obliged in honour and conscience to comfort and support all such afflicted Protestants, who by reason of the rigours and severities which are used towards them, upon the account of their religion, shall be forced to quit their native country, and shall desire to shelter themselves under His Majesty's Royal Protection, for the preservation and free exercise of their religion; and in order thereunto His Majesty was pleased further to declare that he will grant unto every such distressed Protestant, who shall come hither for refuge, and reside here, His letters of denization under the Great Seal without any charge whatsoever, and likewise such further privileges and immunities as are consistent with the laws, for the liberty and free exercise of their trades and handicrafts, and that His Majesty will likewise recommend it to his parliament at their next meeting to pass an Act for the general Naturalisation of all such Protestants as shall come over as aforesaid.
Charles II, Hampton Court declaration, 28 July 1681.

The French Protestants' arrival in England was accompanied by a number of justifications. Despite their position of obvious weakness, the Huguenots had several assets and they even endeavoured to negotiate the terms of their settlement in England. They represented an un-mistakable economic force, at least according to seventeenth-century mercantilist concepts; their numerical strength, skills and 'mysteries'

---

[1] Bodleian Library, Rawlinson MSS A.478, fol. 30.

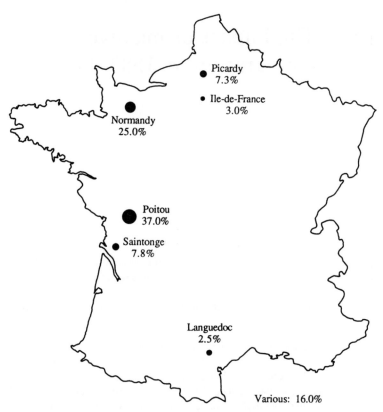

Map 2. The geographical origins of the later Refuge: the case of the Temple de La Patente at Spitalfields in London (founded 4 September 1688).

offered several guarantees to the State which welcomed them on its soil. The economic incentive to accept foreigners had long been resorted to, and ministers and laymen alike did not hesitate to adopt this type of argument in order to implore the joint blessings of Court and Country on their communities. Among several similar items, we might refer to the 'Reasons offered by the ministers and others of the French and Dutch Churches in London to the Lords of the Committee of Trade in favour of them allowing foreign artificers to settle in England', c. 1669–70:

> [We should like] his sacred Majesty to grant the same liberty and privilege to all weavers of silk, hair or worsted stuff for the quantities of these commodities that are made beyond the seas and daily imported into this kingdom are as considerable as those that are made of flax and hemp. It is true indeed that silk and hair do not grow here as flax and hemp.[2]

[2] *Ibid.*, fol. 28.

Consequently, 'those kinds of manufactures' should be 'encouraged here' in order to cut prices, and improve the balance of trade with France and other countries: 'vast quantities of raw silk, mohaire, yarn and wools are constantly fetched by the French and others from Turkey and Italy wherewith they make silks and hair stuffs which are afterwards imported into this realm'.

Moreover, the benefits to be expected from immigration were not merely economic. The ascendancy of a country and its military might were also largely related to the number of its inhabitants. The prestige of France, and the fears she inspired, both derived from the size of her population, those 20 million Frenchmen whose strength would be depleted by the demographic haemorrhage of the Huguenot exodus, or so it seemed. The adversaries of Louis XIV exploited the Revocation of the Edict of Nantes. A wide-ranging ideological campaign quickly took up the plight of the Huguenots. Protestantism was in danger. To express sympathy for the poor refugees soon became in England a mark of good citizenship and devotion to the Protestant cause. The immigrants were again able to draw advantage from this situation by affirming that they were not simply foreigners, but brethren in religion who deserved to be granted the privileges of native Englishmen.

The French Protestants' 'Magna Carta'

England had never found herself so directly involved in international affairs as in the 1680s. Undoubtedly, the preposterous atmosphere of conspiracy which hung over the decade elicited the common fear of an invasion. The period opened up in 1678 with the denunciation of a vast Jesuit plot to bring England back onto the orbit of Rome by the force of arms. Ten years later, William of Orange landed from Holland, and drove James II from his throne once and for all. In 1688 the overthrow of the king was a military, and above all a political, operation which involved the Protestant consensus of most of the population. This revolution, unanimously described as 'Glorious', began a period of military actions against Louis XIV, which only came to an end in 1697, with the peace of Ryswick. Within the space of a single generation, the Whigs and Tories emerged, James II was defeated, the Bank of England was set up. The French Protestants were closely associated with these radical trans-formations – both directly, through their action, and above all indirectly, through the polemical use made of their fate to tarnish French-style absolutism. The first waves of migration preceded the Revocation of the Edict of Nantes; this has been established by R.D. Gwynn in a remarkable article based on the lists of recantations, the 'Books of Testimonies' in which were entered the names of fugitives retracting their hasty conversion to Catholicism.[3]

It is extremely difficult, however, to set a precise figure on the refugee population. Their geographical distribution had been easier to define beforehand. The constant appearance of new temples eludes quantification, and their archives have often been lost. Were there 80,000 refugees, as Charles Weiss thought, or else some 50,000, as Samuel Mours suggests?[4] Out of a total of about 5 million inhabitants, they made up about 1 per cent of the English population. They were heavily concentrated in certain areas, as in London, where at the turn of the century about twenty communities could be traced.

If we accept these scant figures, the French Protestants were nearly as many as the English Catholics, and a quarter as many as their nonconformist brethren.[5] In short, they made up a genuine minority, despite the many divisions which tore them apart. When they conformed to Anglicanism, I am inclined to think that 'occasional conformity' partly explained their attitude.

Of course, the destiny of a minority cannot be reduced to a question of arithmetic. I do not simply have in mind the psychological mechanisms which incline men, whether for good or ill, to attribute excessive importance to minority groups. The question of minorities in the 1680s involved a real alternative. The fate of the Huguenots, which until then had been a revealing indicator, entered the domestic arena. The poor foreigners' cause was taken up, their plight became the object of general compassion. What celebrated churchman did not number among his clients an impoverished pastor, to whom he entrusted minor tasks of scholarship, and with whom he could converse on matters of piety? The English sympathiser repressed his sorrow, growing indignant, and reviled Louis XIV, while looking, out of the corner of his eye, at the king of England. One wished he would not take it into his head to follow the example of his formidable cousin. And the idea began to gain ground that absolutism led to Rome (see Document 6). A new unanimity was emerging, which had as its targets the Jesuits, the dragoons, Louis XIV and soon James II. The Glorious Revolution was all the more glorious for being carried out peacefully. A few weeks after the landing of William of Orange, the government of James II fell like a ripe fruit. The Revocation contributed its share to this discredit. While some poetasters endeavoured to 'rhyme Rome to death'[6] – though they may not have succeeded in their

[3] R.D. Gwynn, 'The Arrival of Huguenot Refugees in England 1680–1705', *Proceedings of the Huguenot Society of London*, 21, pp. 366–73.
[4] Charles Weiss, *Histoire des réfugiés protestants de France...*, Paris, 1853; Samuel Mours, *Les Eglises réformées en France*, Paris, 1958; David Hume gave the figure of 50,000 refugees in England, in his *History of Great Britain*, London, 1767.
[5] B. Coward, *The Stuart Age*, London, 1980, pp. 253, 273 and 425.
[6] E*** of R***, Dr Wilds *et al.*, *Rome Rhym'd To Death*, London, 1683.

venture – a number of pamphleteers wrote endless dissertations on the poor Protestants of France: *An apology for the Protestants of France, in Reference to the Persecutions they are under at this day in Six Letters*, London, 1683; *An Account of the Late Persecution of the Protestants in the Valleys of Piedmont; by the Duke of Savoy and the French King, in the Year 1686. Never before published*, Oxford, 1688/9; *Popish Treachery, or a Short and New Account of the Horrid Cruelties Exercised on the Protestants in France. Being a True Prospect of what is to be expected from the most solemn Promises of Roman Catholic Princes*, London, 1689; *Popery and Tyranny or the Present State of France, in Relation to its Government, Trade, Manners of the People, and Nature of the Country. As it was sent in a Letter from an English Gentleman abroad to his Friend in England. Wherein may be seen the Tyranny the Subjects of France are under being enslav'd by the two greatest Enemies to Reason, as well as to Christian or Human Liberty, I mean Popery and Arbitrary Power*, London, 1689, etc.

In fact, Louis XIV was regarded as *the* arch-enemy of the Protestant interest, fomenting the darkest designs against England and the cause of the Reformation throughout the world. The existence of a common foe facilitated Huguenot integration, or rather their ideological assimilation. All true, free-born Englishmen being Protestant, all Protestants could turn to England for shelter and assistance. Likewise, the Edict of Nantes, when it was repealed by the French king, became a symbolic equivalent of Magna Carta. Though the argument may prove deceptive, not to say specious, it nonetheless appeared in the *Memorial from the English Protestants to their Highnesses the Prince and Princess of Orange, Concerning their Grievances, and the Birth of the Pretended Prince of Wales*, which was issued in November 1688 at the time of William of Orange's landing at Torbay.[7] A number of allusions to the French situation found their way into this pamphlet: England being the 'Head of the Reformed Religion',[8] the French king's attitude towards the Huguenots served as a useful reminder for the English. What were they to expect from James II?

> The French king durst not throw off his disguise, and show himself as a ravening wolf to his Protestant subjects, till now our king [James II] had publicly espoused the Popish Design, which he had together with him long prosecuted in the dark; and until he had begun to invade the Protestant Liberties and Securities, putting the Military Power in Popish Hands.[9]

This international conspiracy aimed at the subversion of English liberties, and the persecution of the Huguenots, was therefore a first stage in a radical move to eradicate the Protestant religion throughout the

---

[7] *Memorial from the English Protestants*, in *A Collection of State Tracts*, 3 vols., London, 1705, I, pp. 1–37.   [8] *Ibid.*, p. 7.   [9] *Ibid.*, p. 9.

world. James II's policy of indulgence to the Dissenters could not be trusted; as all Catholic kings, he only meant to deceive, and stooped to conquer:

> The suppression of the Protestants of England hath been always esteemed the principal part of the Popish Design to extirpate the Protestant Religion ... and *our king proceeds in the same methods against us, wherein the French king hath been successful to destroy the Protestants of his kingdom.* His first attempt is to subvert our Civil Government and Laws, and the freedom and Being of our Parliaments; *just as the French king first invaded the Supreme Legal Authority of France, which was vested in the Assembly of Estates from whom alone he now derives his Crown.* Our king *in imitation of his brother of France,* strives to bring all the offices and Magistracy of the kingdom, that were legally of the People's choice, to be solely and immediately depending on his absolute will for their being, whether they arise by our Common Law, or be instituted by Statutes or Charters ... He seeks to make his proclamations and declarations to have as much power over our Laws, *as the French king's Edicts.* And *after his example* he establishes a mercenary army to master and subdue the People to his will.[10]

I have emphasised all the parallels between Louis XIV and James II. These cross-cultural references were extremely effective at the time, as they provided unquestionable evidence to all contemporaries:

> If [James II] can prevail in these things to overturn the Civil Government, the Liberty of the protestant Profession, and of Conscience in all forms, however seemingly settled by him will be precarious; and he may as easily destroy it *as the French king has abolished the irrevocable Edicts, Treaties or Laws of his Kingdom, confirmed by his oath, which were as good security to those Protestants as any Magna Charta that our king may make for us.*[11]

Protestant unanimity and English identity

> Now that England following the steps of Ancient Rome in her Hospitality, may likewise imitate her in her Victories and Grandeur is the Hearty Prayers of, Philopatris.[12]

The 1680s proved decisive in the life of the English Refuge: the 'shameful' Revocation of the Edict of Nantes and the 'glorious' overthrow of James II tended to highlight the sympathy of most Englishmen for the Protestant cause, and their common abhorrence of

---

[10] *Ibid.*, p. 9. My italics.   [11] *Ibid.*, pp. 9–10. My italics.
[12] *The Deplorable State and Condition of the Poor French Protestants Commiserated and Humbly Represented to all Princes and people of the True Reformed Church with Reasons for a Protestant League,* London, 1681, p. 10.

popery. However, the rising number of foreigners settling in England could have had a contrary effect as it strained labour relations in some big cities, such as London, Moreover, the identification of the English nation with Protestant election was not necessarily to the refugees' advantage: it served either to emphasise international solidarity with the Huguenots, who hence became the natural allies of their hosts and protectors, or to treat indiscriminately all foreign influences as popish in essence. This surprising attitude, which gave religion a purely nationalist character and content, was evinced by some backward islanders who feared that the Huguenots were not truly Protestant as they came from beyond the seas, and could harbour in their midst a potential popish army. This alarming threat needed to be properly circumscribed in order to allay the irrational fears of the credulous:

> The enemy had been so industrious as to waylay these poor people: and whilst they will not suffer them to live in France, they endeavour to prevent their subsisting anywhere else. Amongst some they are represented as enemies to the religion established; however, they profess the same faith, and desire to be esteemed as brethren. Amongst others they are made to appear *a mixed multitude, part Protestant, part Papist*: whereas it is impossible for any numbers of papists, or indeed almost any to thrust themselves in amongst them undiscovered; as it would be for a black among whites.[13]

The White French Protestants did yet incur the joint grievances of some bigoted upholders of the established Church, who dreaded the contagion of Presbyterian principles, and of the 'common people' who mistrusted these highly skilled competitors. The *Apology for the Protestants of France*, published two years later in 1683, still resorted to the same rhetorical devices to counter anti-Huguenot propaganda or feelings:

> Amongst some, they are represented as enemies of our religion established: though they desire to be esteemed as brethren, by professing the same faith and submitting to the same discipline. To others, they are made appear as *a mixed multitude, part Protestant, part Papist*: whereas the strict examination of their testimonials by the churches here of their own nation, makes the suggestion impossible. But that nothing may be wanting to add affliction to the misery of these poor fugitives, and render them at the same time worse than unprofitable to their brethren, it is suggested to the common people, that they come to eat the bread out of their mouths, by overstocking those populous manufacturers, which seem already to be overcharged, and by surfeiting the Land with people.[14]

---

[13] *The Present State of the Protestants in France in three Letters, Written by a Gentleman in London to his Friend in the Country*, London, 1681, 'Preface'. My italics.
[14] *An Apology for the Protestants of France, in Reference to the Persecutions they are under at this Day; in six Letters*, London, 1683, pp. 1–2. My italics.

Stereotypes have indeed a life of their own, and in 1688, a few months before the revolution, the Reverend W. Smythies, then curate of St Giles, Cripplegate, exhorted his parishioners to contribute to the general collection raised in favour of the 'poor refugees'. Nonetheless, the good minister was anxious to meet in anticipation the objections of his countrymen. On 28 March, he delivered his *Earnest Exhortation to Charity*, based on 2 Cor. 5:14: 'For the love of Christ constraineth us etc.' In order to attain a maximum degree of efficiency, W. Smythies endeavoured, with the skill of a preacher, to bring to the surface the prejudices of his congregation, in order to undeceive them from the pulpit. In spite of all its rhetorical craft, this carefully devised piece of Church oratory seems to paint with great vividness some of the genuine feelings of the English when they were confronted with their French brethren: they are not 'true Protestants', 'their garb is unsuitable to their necessitous condition' – i.e. there were several ruined persons of quality among them who had retained some of their former splendour in matters of dress, but had nonetheless to be relieved.[15] Moreover, were they not for the most part 'dissenters'? Likewise, there were probably 'papists among them' – which seems to confirm as previously the imaginary identification of 'foreigners' with 'papists', and we might also add of 'papists' with 'foreigners'. But this insular distrust of aliens and the topical assimilation of *English* and *Protestant*, in the decade separating the popish plot from the Glorious Revolution, did not hinder the eternal resentment felt by nationals towards recent immigrants: 'They hinder our trade, and take away the bread of our own poor'.[16] Even the poor English 'poor', to put it bluntly, could fear the unfair competition of newcomers, their rivals in the field of public charity. W. Smythies tried to answer this economic line of argument:

> And as to that which is said of their *under-working*; if it be true, yet it is excusable, since it can scarcely be imagined, that they can procure work at greater rates. If there be any cause of displeasure, it ought to be against our own *Englishmen*, that make a gain of their necessities, and do not give the same allowances to them, that they have done to others. It is our own covetousness, and not their industry, that is blameworthy.[17]

This moral approach may bring to mind more recent examples of Church involvement in social affairs; the charges against immigrants are the same as ever: they deplete the value of labour. Likewise, the preacher's overt insistence on the exploitation of cheap labour will sound familiar to many contemporary readers. However, seventeenth-century England was

---

[15] W. Smythies, *An Earnest Exhortation to Charity for the Relief of the French Protestants and Objections Against it Answered*, London, 1688, p. 7.   [16] *Ibid.*, p. 9.
[17] *Ibid.*, p. 10.

not a free-for-all society, and we should insist that blind market forces were the exception rather than the rule. We shall give further evidence of this phenomenon when we examine the relations between the refugees and the native craftsmen (see below, pp. 195–9).

Fear was often the root of xenophobia. We may perhaps interrupt our narrative to recall how, a few years after the Glorious Revolution, the vision of the Huguenots even became associated with the dread of a Jacobite invasion. Among the Finch manuscripts is a remarkable affidavit, dated 21 April 1692: 'Some heads of what Mr Taafe told me'. One Captain Blount, alias Widdrington, had told the informer's wife that 'king James would be in England within a few days.'[18] This was shortly before the French fleet was defeated at the battle of the Hogue by Admiral Russell, and in this context, Daniel Finch, second earl of Nottingham, who was then secretary of war, could not reasonably leave a single stone unturned, even though this denunciation rested on hearsay. In essence, the Huguenot 'conspiracy' was a remake of the 1678 popish plot – which proves the lasting potency of nationalist, insular imagery:

> That there were 20,000 men in this town ready to take arms for him [James II], most of whom were Frenchmen; that there were several thousands of the French *who passed here for Protestants and go duly to the French Protestant churches, who indeed are good catholics and would show themselves to be so upon King James's landing.*[19]

Several locations were explicitly mentioned:

> [Captain Blount] told her they had consults or meetings every day at several houses assigned them for that purpose in the City and other parts of the town, where they were to receive orders to be all in arms at an hour's warning, and he named the Royal Oak in Drury Lane, the Blue Anchor in Wild Street and a tavern in Holborn whose sign she has forgot; that there were 150 French officers lately landed in the West and other ports who came under the notion of *refugiés* who had escaped from France; that they were now in town and among them a general officer who was to head the forces that were to rise for King James; that they would kill man, woman and child that would not be quiet and befriend their design, but that their orders were not to break so much as a glass window of those that would not be quiet and give 'em no opposition.[20]

Like the Catholic Irishmen, the French Protestants were therefore accused of harbouring the dark design of 'cutting de Englishmen's

---

[18] Historical Manuscripts Commission, Finch MS, IV, 1965, p. 107.

[19] *Ibid.*, On the Jacobite scare, see in particular Eveline Cruickshanks and Jeremy Black (eds)., *The Jacobite Challenge*, Edinburgh, 1988.

[20] Historical Manuscripts Commission, Finch MS, IV, pp. 107–8.

throats'. Fortunately, this disgraceful reputation was to prove purely mythical, and contrary to the popish plot, the Huguenot conspiracy was too unlikely ever to be deemed plausible by an important cross-section of the English population. The Huguenot epic, on the contrary, attained wide respectability, and became incorporated into the positive image of Britannia. In the late eighteenth century, an apocryphal pamphlet, supposedly written by Jean-Jacques Calet, a French Huguenot, epitomised the differences between the two countries: 'Monsieur Calet is a French gentleman by birth and education: by religion a Protestant: in his ideas of liberty an Englishman.' I am afraid that in spite of his great admiration for Britain, Jean-Jacques Calet never existed. This spurious character owed his name to Calais, one of the first cities which the English visited on their grand tour of the Continent, while Jean-Jacques reminds one of Jean-Jacques Rousseau.[21] Jean-Jacques Calet evinces a natural gradation between gentility, Protestantism and the English sense of liberty. Having been delivered from the Bastille on 14 July 1789, the hero finally settled in England, as his coreligionists had done a century before, and his choice proved significant: in spite of its declaration of human rights, the French Revolution could not completely sever its links with tyranny:

> Poor France! Wast thou cruel and perfidious more than two centuries ago? When wilst thou resume thyself from slavery and superstition? Condemned and convicted of meanness and treachery from the mouth, and recorded as base by the pen of thy native, learn honour and integrity from thy enemies. Compare with the candour and dignity of a British Court suffering thy Navy at the present crisis to lay secure in its harbour: thine own pitiful proceedings during the American war! Can Britain so far forgive as not to * * *. But I will say no more of my country: my country! I disclaim the appellation! Beggar and vagabond as I am, France shall never have the honour of relieving me: I will secure to myself my person under the very standard of Liberty itself, the British Scepter...
>
> Where was I to fly but to this land of Liberty and Peace: a land which heaven has thrust from other lands in order to bless it beyond comparison.
>
> Blessed in its climate, in its productions, in its liberty, religion and laws: blessed in its inhabitants, in its constitution and king.[22]

---

[21] J.-J. Calet, *A True and Minute Account of the Destruction of the Bastile: by Jean-Jacques Calet, a French Protestant: who had been a prisoner there upwards of twenty years, and who recovered his Liberty on, and who assisted at the DEMOLITION of that INFAMOUS PRISON. Translated from the French by an English Gentleman*, London, 1789, There were at least two further editions of this text, one in Norwich in 1796 where it was 'sold a few rods west of the meeting-house' and one at Medford, Massachussets in 1800. On the myth of the Bastille, see Monique Cottret, *La Bastille à prendre*, Paris, 1986.   [22] *Ibid.*, pp. 58–60.

The rising patriotism which marked the 'apotheosis' of George III,[23] the enmity with revolutionary France, equally served to magnify the past achievements of England as a land of Refuge. The manifold blessings which the Lord had auspiciously granted to his people – among other marks of his bounty, the English weather – proved the election of Britannia in the concert of nations. Who could better than Jean-Jacques Calet plead the cause of English superiority?

Economic integration and rivalry

You Weavers all I pray give ear
A story true I will declare,
Our masters they do much repine,
Saying that the French them undermine
And get their trade away from them.
Our weaving trade is grown so dead,
We scarcely can get us bread...
Because the French are grown so ill,
In selling their work at an under-price,
Which makes the tears run from our eyes
And Weavers all may curse their fates
Because the French work under rates.[24]
The Valiant Weaver (1681)

Encroaching upon the privileges of native subjects or engrossing certain specific activities had been a common accusation levelled at foreigners in the 1620s, along with the scarcity of silver. The Domestic Series of the State Papers contains a number of petitions in those years which clearly demonstrate the obvious link between economic depression and xenophobia. Sir Robert Heath, who then acted as solicitor-general, received several complaints from the Goldsmiths' Company – against foreign counterfeit jewels (January 1622) – from the Coopers of London, from the Clockmakers, from the Leatherdressers of Southwark or from the Company of Joiners (March 1622). In turn, the aliens often retorted that they had been molested by their English hosts.

However, the question of aliens would still require further research into specified company registers before we could come to a full-blown picture of their situation in London alone. Moreover, to make matters still more intricate, not all foreigners belonged to one of the Stranger Churches. The greatest single occupation of the Franco-Walloon community was weaving, and W.C. Waller published in 1931 some very useful *Extracts*

---

[23] Linda Colley, 'The Apotheosis of George III: Loyalty, Royalty and the English Nation', *Past and Present*, 102 (1984), pp. 94–129.
[24] Quoted by E. Lipson, *The Economic History of England*, 3 vols., London, 1915–31, III, p. 61.

from the Court Books of the Weavers' Company of London. These deserve to be studied carefully, along with the original manuscripts, now at the Guildhall.

In fact, the attitude to the French Protestants, especially after 1660, was far from one-sided, and no undue emphasis should be laid on social tensions with the foreign population. While in 1662, ten years of residence were still deemed necessary to be admitted into the company, this figure was brought down to three years in 1668, though greater flexibility still may have existed in practice: 'This court will be very tender, but do absolutely resolve that from henceforth no alien shall be admitted unless he have been here for one year past at least, reckoning from this time.'[25]

Indeed, 'membership' of either the French or Dutch Church, 'accompanied by guarantees of proper qualification acquired here or abroad, was a sure passport into the guild, for both master and journeyman'.[26] Religion, though it could never be treated separately, remained an important concern; and the elders of the French and Dutch congregations often interceded on behalf of their brethren, as was the case that same year 1668: 'Some of the gentlemen of the French and Dutch congregations appeared at this Court declaring that by reason of a persecution in France they prayed the kindness of this company as heretofore to admit such as shall come.' To which it was answered:

> The foreign members have and do invite more strangers over (and they do come) *under pretence of a persecution.* But if that calamity shall really happen and this court sensible thereof being satisfied that [the newcomers] were brought up and have right to this trade, this Court will as heretofore continue their favour and kindness to them and as they doubt not will be satisfactory to both Churches.[27]

Yet the following year, the French community had to intervene again in the case of four Frenchmen who had been indicted by the yeomen of the Weavers' Company and sent to Clerkenwell. This was not the sole incident of this type as in December 1668 one Louis Saunier had already been imprisoned in Fleet Street, following the brushmakers' complaint against him. But the arrest of four French weavers, the next autumn, was to prove even more decisive. On 24 October 1669, the Threadneedle Street consistory was informed of the prosecution of Adrien Dancre and François Boulleaux, who belonged to the Church, along with two other compatriots, Samuel Desbordes from Paris – who also pretended he was a Protestant – and Pierre Blondeau, from Tours, himself a papist. The

[25] W.C. Waller, *Extracts from the Court Books of the Weavers' Company of London,* *Publications of the Huguenot Society of London,* 'Quarto Series', XXXIII, 1931, p. xiii.
[26] *Ibid.,* p. xii.
[27] Guildhall Library, MSS 4655/5: 'Weavers Company, Ordinance and Record Books', fols. 22–5.

four men had been caught redhanded: they had exercised the honourable trade of weaving without serving their seven-year apprenticeship, 'according to the laws of the kingdom'. The consistory immediately decided to send two deputies to confer with 'Messieurs de la Halle des Weavers', and defend their two brethren, thus leaving aside their papist countryman and their would-be coreligionist. Moreover, Lord Arlington was also pleased to receive the delegation advising them to send their petition to the king's council. Apparently, the poor weavers were to recover their liberty on bail only at Christmas time, but again, we have to note the positive role assumed by the Crown. In November, the king's council had insisted that the Weavers' Company should clearly state their conditions for the admittance of aliens, and even threatened to issue a *Quo Warranto* against their charter and privileges if they did not comply. In June 1672, the elders and deacons of the French Church entreated 'la Compagnie des Weaivers' to treat newcomers with moderation and 'enlarge, rather than diminish the liberties which the king had been so good as to grant them'. Moreover, they required further delays for all destitute masters or journeymen who had to pay their entrance fees.

Apparently a settlement was found in those years, as on 1 September 1672 the Ordinance and Record Book of the Weavers' Company gives the French text of an oath which foreign masters or journeymen were to take in order to be admitted either as 'ouvrier estrangier' or as a 'maistre estrangier'.[28] Yet not all misgivings disappeared, and in 1676–7, new restrictions were issued: 'No alien or stranger born shall be admitted master, except it be debated and agreed by a full Court, and *in that case also to be ever sparing in admitting any master but upon some weighty grounds or reasons.*'[29]

In fact, the English weavers certainly had mixed feelings about their French hosts. One might possibly argue that the fear of competition was at its highest down the social scale. In his history of the London Weavers' Company, Alfred Plummer suggests that master weavers tended to be more hospitable than journeymen, as they valued the acquisition of new skills (silk, damask, or velvet).[30] As in other cases, the presence of the refugees or aliens may act as a powerful catalyst and revealer of the tensions within the host society. This would account in turn for the heterogeneity of attitudes evinced by the Weaver's Company. For example, in March 1685, a complaint was lodged against the foreign masters who employed more French than English journeymen. Yet, that same year, Jean Larguier was admitted without paying his entry fee, thanks to his great skill in making 'à la mode' silk.

[28] *Ibid.*, 4655/7, fol. 1.   [29] *Ibid.*, 4655/8, fol. 81.
[30] A. Plummer, *The London Weavers' Company 1600–1970*, London, 1972, in particular ch. 7: 'Strangers and Settlers', p. 147.

Table 2. *Petitions against foreigners, London 1675–99*

Date	Trade or occupation	Source
Oct. 1675	Fishmongers	Rep. 80, fol. 283
July 1675	Handicraft tailors	Rep. 80, fol. 258
Sept. 1675	Handicraft tailors	Rep. 80, fol. 274
Oct. 1681	Handicraft tailors	Jour. 49, fol. 254
Jan. 1682	Fellowship of porters	Rep. 87, fol. 51
Nov. 1682	Feltmakers Co.	Rep. 82, fol. 10
Nov. 1682	Needlemakers	Rep. 88, fol. 29
May 1682	Needlemakers	Rep. 87, fol. 160
22 Nov. 1683	Journeymen dyers	Rep. 89, fol. 14
29 Nov., 1683	Journeymen dyers	Rep. 89, fol. 24
21 Oct. 1684	Shipwrights	Rep. 89, fol. 24
13 Oct. 1685	Journeymen barber surgeons	Rep. 90, fol. 146
June 1686	Tailors	Rep. 91, fol. 110
1 July 1686	Tailors	Rep. 91, fol. 116
27 July 1686	Tailors	Rep. 91, fols. 141–2
26 Jan. 1687	Carpenters and joiners	Rep. 93, fols. 58–9
19 March 1693	Musicians	Jour. 51, fols. 300–1
5 June 1694	Plasterers	Jour. 51, fols. 313–14
11 Sept. 1794	Musicians	Jour. 52, fols. 15–17

Source: Guildhall Library, Court of Aldermen 'Repertories', and 'Journals' of the Common Council.

One should not surmise, however, that all complaints were groundless or the effect of pure malevolence towards the strangers. In 1696, the consistory of the French Church in the City urged its members to observe the regulations of the Weavers' Company, and not to forswear their oaths of loyalty – as became good Protestants. This incentive to comply could also proceed from the 'general decay in the policy of regulation' which marked the end of the century, and which, as a matter of fact, 'had less to do with any burgeoning concepts of economic liberalism than with the increasing practical difficulties of applying an ancient policy to a changed structure of output'.[31] The sheer diversification of economic activity, the urge to reduce costs, coincided with the afflux of foreigners who acted as a powerful symptom of the crisis of long-established practices. The 'visible hand'[32] of the guilds should not therefore be treated indiscriminately as a mark of xenophobia: it rested on tradition and privilege.

[31] D.C. Coleman, *The Economy of England 1450–1750*, Oxford, 1977, p. 179.
[32] While Adam Smith had spoken of an 'invisible hand' to describe his liberal idea of *laissez-faire*, S.L. Kaplan has inverted the metaphor to describe traditional labour regulations, 'La Lutte pour le contrôle du marché du travail à Paris au xviiie siècle', *Revue d'Histoire Moderne et Contemporaine*, 36 (1989), p. 361.

Yet there were some cases when the strangers' presence was resented as such. When we go through the City of London records, we are struck by the strenuous determination of the several companies to avoid the general naturalisation of Protestant strangers. As early as March 1657, the mayor, aldermen and commons, 'in Common Council assembled', intimated that once naturalised the strangers would enjoy greater advantages than native subjects, due to their alliances abroad. Besides, in 1660, the prospect of naturalisation was deemed both unprofitable to the State and contrary to precedents. In the 1670s, 1680s and 1690s, the same arguments were used, with greater obstinacy still.

In the last quarter of the century, several petitions were directed against strangers and foreigners (see Table 2). Yet, the word 'foreigner' was ambiguous at the time, as it retained some of its old meaning – i.e. an Englishman from another part of the country. We would therefore expect a binary opposition between 'freemen' and 'foreigners', 'strangers' and 'natural subjects'. The distinction was probably less consistent at the end of the century than it had been a hundred years before; in 1693, the London musicians launched an offensive against the dancing masters of the metropolis whom they suspected of rude and disorderly behaviour. Though there were probably few Huguenots among those 'Foreigners, Papists and Aliens', the general distrust of 'foreigners' certainly extended to all those born beyond the seas. Moreover, in more cases than one, this discontent, though not a class phenomenon in the present sense of the word, confirmed the social division between masters and journeymen. Unless one could achieve a painstaking reconstruction of all the Huguenots involved in each sector of activity, we are left with piecemeal evidence, and the fluidity of actual practice contrasts with segmented regulations.

Banishment and moral majority

Worldliness has wrought greater effects among us than persecution, with all its violence and artifices, has been able to achieve among our brethren. Irreligion, atheism, and several dangerous errors assail our souls with all their might, to gain a foothold within the Church. The use of God's Word, which is the sole foundation of our faith, is perverted, and wasted on men who listen to it listlessly while turning their affections to worldly things with a critical discontented spirit. Vanity, luxury and scandal nearly hold sway over us. Everyone submits to their inducement, and proud ambition creeps in the midst of our misfortunes. The lack of sincerity and good faith, the inconstancy of men's hearts continually giver righteous men cause to grieve; lies prevail among those who profess to suffer for truth's sake. Some wallow in ribaldry, while many of their brethren sigh sometimes in vain for their daily bread. Some there are, lastly, who abandon themselves to gambling, dancing and other *worldly distractions*, as if they had quite forgotten those holy Churches which begot them through our Lord and Saviour Jesus Christ, and whose sad state so tenderly implores the assistance of their most keen and bitter repentance.

West Street Register, 27 February 1699

Was this a society of saints, or of reprobates? As elsewhere one needs to make allowances for the role of stereotypes. God's visitation in times of affliction invite to repentance, and the recreations which the consistory condemned were often innocent merriment. Dancing, in particular, was accused of corrupting the moral sense of the people. Moreover, foreign was often synonymous with irregular or illicit, and out of mimetism, confirming the 'laws of imitation' identified by Gabriel Tarde,[33] some prominent members of the Refuge secretly internalised the fear of immigrants, and transferred it to their coreligionists. Yet, to all intent, few of the refugees adopted the mores of Sodom and Gomorrah. However, this moral *malaise* should not be overlooked; it expressed in bombastic language a real trauma due to the fragmentation of former ties of solidarity, consequent on the unprecedented scale of immigration. The men of that century, who distrusted innovation and change, found themselves suddenly confronted with the instability of geographical, political, religious and social boundaries. The uprooting of individuals from · their place and rank, mobility and restlessness, the change of circumstances, the loss of identity, even, undoubtedly explain the moral ascendancy of the 1690s which derived, as usual, from insecurity. There is a marked correlation between the demographic explosion of the communities in the wake of the Revocation and the difficulty of containing and checking the motley and disparate flood of refugees who, having fled from persecution, the dragoons and the galleys, submitted with bad grace to the intrusive testing of their orthodoxy or moral conduct.

The newcomer's first act, in the majority of cases, was the recantation of a reviled and detested Catholicism to which he or she had had to submit in haste, and under duress. Certain Catholics in France were even disturbed to see the Roman sacraments administered by force to the 'New Converts'. But suspicion persisted, often for several weeks. The distribution of relief to the poor, for instance, inclined towards greater severity. In these times of crisis, faced with the influx of fugitives in a state of utter destitution the consistories demanded the recipients of relief to give correct answers on the most important points of doctrine – provided they were still able-bodied. This temporary examination was subject to renewal. The consistory of London reiterated the following order in April 1685, then in December 1697 and March 1698:

[33] G. Tarde, *Les Lois de l'imitation, étude sociologique*, 7th edn, Paris, 1921.

No pauper – unless he be prevented by illness – shall be granted assistance unless he come first to declare his state of poverty to the consistory, and be examined to give account of his instruction in the faith by making reasonable answers to the questions he is asked. Those who receive assistance shall appear before the consistory every six months for the same purpose, and the deacons shall also take care to have them instructed.

From fear to fright

England is assuredly doing a very good thing for the country, in ridding it of those people who are called *Jesuits*, as men scandalous, very pernicious and dangerous within a State... My Lord, no one has yet remarked another sort of ruffians staying in the city of London, who are no less dangerous than the Jesuits. These are the people called *proselytes*, who are downright scoundrels, and true Jesuits at heart and in their profession, and all the more dangerous as they insinuate themselves into families.[34]
Letter to Compton, bishop of London, 15 June 1679

If we resume our narrative, we can emphasise the various shades of fear which weighed upon this last quarter-century, from the 1678 popish plot onwards.[35] The Huguenots themselves were affected by this bout of collective hysteria; on 15 June 1679, G. Bonvallet wrote to Compton from The Hague to inform him of the presence of several pretended converts in London who obtained tutorships in certain affluent families in order to corrupt the young. He even disclosed the name of Gilbert Gerrard, in Pall Mall, who employed one such papist in disguise.[36] The Glorious Revolution, that triumphant episode, was played out against a background of plots, real or counterfeit, which blackened the image of the Crown.[37] James II, the fallen Catholic king who was forced to flee when William of Orange rallied the support of the country, was indeed subjected at the hand of Whig historians to that curse of the defeated, which is to

[34] Bodleian Library, Rawlinson MSS C.982, fol. 11.
[35] Here I have of course, made use of Jean Delumeau's *La Peur en Occident, XIV–XVIIIe siècles*, Paris, 1978. On the English Catholics there are several excellent books: John Bossy, *The English Catholic Community, 1570–1850*, Cambridge, 1973; John Miller, *Popery and Politics in England, 1660–1668*, Cambridge, 1973. The nonconformist Protestants have been studied by G.R. Cragg, *From Puritanism to the Age of Reason*, Cambridge, 1950, and more recently by M.R. Watts, *The Dissenters, from the Reformation to the French Revolution*, Oxford, 1978. Lastly, on a particularly striking aspect of the period, see J.P. Kenyon, *The Popish Plot*, London, 1972.
[36] Bodleian Library, Rawlinson MS C.982, fol. 11.
[37] W. Speck, *Reluctant Revolutionaries. Englishmen and the Revolution of 1688*, Oxford, 1988; B. Cottret, *La Glorieuse Révolution d'Angleterre, 1688* Paris, 1988; D.L. Jones, *Parliamentary History of the Glorious Revolution*, London, 1988.

have always been wrong. The reader will grant me that the Revocation of the Edict of Nantes by Louis XIV was of little help to the English sovereign.

The 1680s elicit an undeniable synchronism between the two kingdoms: the escalation of anti-Catholic feeling in England was coeval with the visitations of the French dragoons upon the subjects 'of the so-called reformed religion'. In 1681, George Hickes, the king's chaplain, attempted to rule out any confusion, by advocating the right kind of persecution:

> [The French Protestants] have no quarrel at the Church, because it is episcopal, but because it is popish; for though they have no bishops, yet their and other reformed writers have approved the office, and protested that they would, if they could, have retained them, and desired that their rejecting of them might be imputed to necessity and not to their choice.[38]

If Protestants were the victims of persecution in France, one could not deduce from their example that Dissenters and Catholics were to be tolerated in England. The nonconformists were justly punished, being in error. This terse denial shows, in fact, the fundamental similarity between the situations of the different minorities. However, the idea proved hardly acceptable in the seventeenth century; it found expression in the visionary plea which an anonymous refugee wrote in favour of James II's policy of indulgence *c.* 1687. I have already drawn the attention of scholars to this text, which rises above accepted codes of behaviour to demonstrate the similar treatment of all minorities by the State: the French Protestants and English Catholics had encountered the same reprobation in their respective countries.[39] (I have, in addition, provided an extract from this text in the Documents at the end of the book – Document 7.)

However, the comparison between the two countries has its limits. It has too often given rise to the hypothesis of political contagion: a puppet James II would have secretly followed his cousin's example, wishing to compel his English subjects to adopt Catholicism by the force of arms. The correspondence of the French ambassador, Paul de Barillon, may even seem to lend some credit to this idea when it is not read properly. On 17 January 1686 he wrote to Louis XIV, who had just revoked the Edict of Nantes:

> The king of England knows well, *in his heart*, that nothing is so great, nor so sound, as the work which Your Majesty has undertaken. He sees that its success has surpassed any human hopes or expectations, but *he is obliged* to act with great circumspection towards all that surrounds him,

---

[38] G. Hickes, *The True Notion of Persecution*, London, 1682, p. 24.
[39] B. Cottret, 'Révocation et prodromes de la tolérance: le parallèle des protestants français et des catholiques d'Angleterre', *Bulletin de la Société de l'Histoire du Protestantisme Français* (1980), pp. 559–66.

and *not always to express his meaning* in accordance with his true sentiments.[40]

I have set in italics the elements which seem in fact to mitigate this thesis: the diplomatic correspondence, with its sense of oblique statement, betrays James II's obvious reluctance to commit himself. The rather summary polemical interpretation, which tends to merge the Sun-King with his pale and ineffectual imitation across the Channel, is no longer acceptable, and I have attempted elsewhere to qualify this judgement.[41]

The hatred of James II stemmed from several causes: the absolutist trend, the standing army, the attacks on privilege. But one word seemed to sum up the situation with artless cunning: *popery*, which incurred the two contradictory charges of leading to State despotism and to foreign domination. The wandering Jesuit, as he appeared in propaganda, epitomised the dread of a cosmopolitan take-over.

Verging on hypochondria, the identification of Protestantism with England, had two corollaries: every papist was a foreigner, and every foreigner a potential papist. This singular association may help explain the distrust which surrounded the French refugees: at times the English could even wonder if the Huguenots were not, in reality, Jesuits in the garb of Protestants, when it was not the Churches themselves which, internalising this fear, mercilessly pursued, behind the 'spurious' refugee, the agent of Louis XIV. The Jesuits, besides, were everywhere: the protean spectre of conspiracy raised its head in the most unexpected places. On hearing of the setting up of a new conformist Church – at Hungerford Market, under the direction of Pierre Alix – Jean Dubourdieu, pastor at the Savoy, reacted sharply to this unfair competition.

> The Jesuits are endeavouring with all their might to drive us from the Savoy... We are now in a more unhappy state than we were in France, since we are equally exposed to the persecutions of these ministers and of the Jesuits. Perhaps, Sir, this expression will seem a little strong to you, but what else should we say to describe these people who want to establish their congregation just between our two Churches [the Savoy and Threadneedle Street], and who are already going from house to house, to lure away the parishioners whose contributions support our Church? For do not suppose that it is for the refugees that they are working: they have nothing to give, and sheep without fleece would not suit their purpose at all.[42]

[40] *Recueil des instructions données aux ambassadeurs*, vol. XXV: *Angleterre, vol. 2, 1669–90*, Paris, 1929, p. 316, 1 October 1685.

[41] B. Cottret, 'Glorieuse Révolution, révocation honteuse?' in *Le Refuge Huguenot*, Paris, 1985.

[42] Bodleian Library, Tanner MSS 92, fol. 171, 5 December 1687. Pierre Allix had previously been pastor at Charenton; Jean Dubourdieu came from Montpellier. There were in fact Jesuits in the Savoy district of Westminster at this period.

Should we believe the good shepherd? Could there be wolves in the sheep-fold? However absurd in its conclusions, this frenzy was not altogether groundless: Louis XIV's spies endeavoured to insinuate themselves amid the refugees.

Freedom of conscience between king and Parliament

> Huguenot Princes cannot show the same tolerance to Catholics in their States as Catholic Princes can to Huguenots: for Protestant Princes cannot be assured of the loyalty of their Catholic subjects, because they have taken an oath of loyalty to another Prince whom they consider to be greater than any king, namely the Pope.[43]
> Pierre Jurieu, 1681

The definition of freedom of conscience took on an acute dimension in the 1680s. The debate was not confined to learned circles: it involved the political future of English society as a whole, and was conducted on the lines of modern philosophical thought. John Locke's first *Letter concerning Toleration* appeared in Latin, and then in English, in 1689 in the Netherlands. 'In accordance with the gospel and with reason', the philosopher excluded Catholics and atheists, at least in theory. The concept of toleration has already been the subject of several useful works.[44] I shall tackle the problem from a different angle. The question of toleration in seventeenth-century England did not so much concern the individuals' right to differ, as the destiny of minorities in their relation to the country at large.

The refugees, who constituted a highly privileged minority, felt deeply involved. They found themselves embroiled in the specific situation of England. On the periphery of the established Church, originally the only full recognised Church, there existed not one, but two religious minorities, diametrically opposed: the Catholics on the one hand, and the Protestant Dissenters on the other. If the risks of seeing the refugees take sides with the English 'papists' were fairly slight, on the other hand the non-conformist temptation remained a constant. Not every Huguenot cheerfully accepted the supremacy of the bishops. The divisions within the host society were transposed to a large extent among the refugees, who could not long remain unaffected.

How, then, was a compromise to be reached between *the* established

---

[43] Pierre Jurieu, *La Politique du clergé de France, ou entretiens curieux de deux catholiques romains, l'un parisien et l'autre provincial, sur les moyens dont on se sert aujourd'hui pour détruire la religion protestante dans ce royaume*, Cologne, 1681, p. 121. This text appeared in an English version in the same year: *The Policy of the clergy of France, to destroy the Protestants of that Kingdom*, London, 1681.

[44] Joseph Lecler, *Histoire de la tolérance au siècle de la Réforme*, Paris, 1955; on England: W.K. Jordan, *The Development of Religious Toleration in England*, 4 vols., London, 1932–40.

Church and the different religious minorities? In theory, three solutions could be envisaged, at least by seventeenth-century Englishmen: 'comprehension', 'indulgence' or 'toleration'. All three rested on different forms of alliance between the official Church and nonconformist groups, between majority culture and minority status.

The first possibility, 'comprehension', always failed. It involved the union of the scattered brethren in the same fold. The ideal of a single national Church, 'comprehending' different currents of the Reformation, remained unattainable. This plan reappeared periodically in the great phases of national consensus: under the Restoration in 1661, and again at the time of the Glorious Revolution in 1689. Such Protestant unanimity remained hypothetical.

The policy of 'indulgence' also suffered resounding and repeated setbacks. Initially, at least, it did not involve doctrinal unity or a single Church, but rather seemed to endorse officially the several forms of worship. The term 'indulgence' is revealing; it belonged to the vocabulary of Stuart absolutism. Charles II kept using the word in 1662 and again in 1672 as part of his prerogative. The Crown intended to retrieve its power of dispensing its subjects from obedience to the Church of England. The long-established Walloon or Huguenot Churches of the kingdom had been the first to benefit from this leniency. Indulgence, or in other words the sovereign's clemency, involved an extension of the royal prerogative to the whole of civil society. Such ostensible magnanimity was perceived as the Trojan horse of absolutism: this excessive generosity confirmed the idea that the king was above the law, and could exempt anyone he wished from its provision. Puritan sectaries and Roman Catholics would obtain by a sovereign decree the civic dignity which the laws enacted by Parliament still denied them. This power of suspending the application of the penal laws – which affected nonconformists of every hue – was felt to be a dangerous innovation on the part of James II. A fundamental ambiguity was attached to the policy of indulgence. Did it foreshadow freedom of worship? Or else, on the contrary, should this royal assertion be seen as a shift towards an authoritarian conception of the State? If we emphasise the avowed aim – tolerance – or the manner in which it was to be achieved – through the arbitrary use of power – James II's gesture can lend itself to fundamentally different interpretations. Have we not here an instance of the opposition, which has become proverbial, between the end and the means? History has given an unfavourable verdict on James II, while the majority of historians have emphasised the unavoidable nature of his failure: how could the English have tolerated an absolutism fit, at best, for Latin countries? And yet when in April 1687 James II, addressing his 'well beloved subjects', guaranteed their 'freedom of conscience', his aims were not clear. The royal policy had its intrinsic coherence; the Crown was attempting to draw support *both* from the Catholic minority and from the Protestant Dissenters, to overcome the resistance of the established Church.

This unnatural alliance between extremes was, indeed, unrealistic and gained the support of a few Quakers, a minority among minorities, but without leading to an effective historic compromise. On the contrary, a sort of united front of Protestants was formed, transcending the old divisions. Old wounds were salved, the Anglicans turning towards their dissenting brethren whom, till recently, they had eyed with disdain. Solidarity was restored in the face of the peril of a Catholic re-conquest which seemed imminent. Toleration was to be established, not with the Catholics, but against them. Halifax, the 'great trimmer', addressed his *Letter to a Dissenter*[45] in the summer of 1687. How could James II's friendship be trusted? The 'liberty' which he claimed to impose on his subjects was contradicted by the 'infallibility' which he arrogated to himself. Halifax makes a point of the distinction between end and means which I referred to above, except that it is invested with anti-Catholic sarcasm. The king cannot bind or unbind his subjects from the observance of the laws of the realm – any more than the pope can. By this expedient, absolutism is cast out into the outer darkness. And when in April 1688 James II renewed his Declaration of Indulgence, and demanded the Anglican clergy to read it out from the pulpit, a serious crisis ensued. The bishops, who were wont to obey, rebelled against this command. Six months later, James II was swept away in the midst of little resistance.

The French-speaking Protestant minority played a definite role in these events. The Churches of the Refuge were indeed the hostages of the royal policy. What would happen in the context of a reintroduction of Catholicism in England? James II, engaged in his subtle balancing of Catholics and Protestants, added contradiction to contradiction. He did not like the Huguenots, how could he? The English translation of pastor Claude's famous book *An Account of the Persecutions and Oppression of the Protestants in France* (1686) was burnt by James II's order as soon as it was published. Even Louis XIV considered the gesture to have been inept, 'since such books usually lose the influence they might have had, by being but little considered, and are only sought after because of the pains which are taken to suppress them'.[46] And yet, finding himself at a deadlock, James II tried one last gesture of reconciliation towards the Huguenots on 4 September 1688. He granted a letter patent for the erection of a new nonconformist chapel at Spitalfields, thus giving the

---

[45] Halifax, *A Letter to a Dissenter* (1687), printed in Miscellanies, London 1700. Henry Savile, the brother of Halifax, was a regular churchgoer at the services held in the Reformed temple of Charenton, while ambassador in Paris from 1679 to 1682.

[46] *Recueil des instructions*, p. 315.

refugees, rather late in the day, his royal protection.[47] This reversion, which corresponded to a general retreat in the face of growing unpopularity, made no difference. James II tried to disentangle himself from the situation. The refugees, the natural victims of Louis XIV's absolutism, were a trump card in the campaign against the Crown. In the context of the Revocation of the Edict of Nantes, it could hardly be otherwise. As expected the *dragonnades* were frequently alluded to in the struggle against James II. In 1689, the English edition of the *Sighs of France in Slavery*, that best-seller of the Huguenot diaspora, asserted that 'this Portrait of the present French government will give an idea of what ours would have been, had King James continued upon the throne'.[48]

The Dutchman William of Orange was fully aware of the advantages he could draw from the Revocation of the Edict of Nantes, to assert his own image. As early as 25 April 1689, the new king addressed a solemn declaration to his French coreligionists:

> Whereas it hath pleased Almighty God to deliver our Realm of England, and the subjects thereof, from the Persecution lately threatening them for their Religion, and from the Oppression and Destruction which the subversion of their laws, and the Arbitrary Exercise of Power and Dominion over them had very near introduced; we finding in our subjects a true and just sense thereof, and of the miseries and oppressions, the *French* Protestants lie under; for their relief, and to encourage them that shall be willing to transport themselves, their families and estates, into this our Kingdom; we do hereby declare that all *French* Protestants that shall seek their Refuge in, and transport themselves into this our Royal Protection for themselves, families and estates within this our Realm [will be welcome], but we will also do Our Endeavour in all reasonable ways and means to support, aid and assist them in their several and respective trades and ways of livelihood, and as their living and being in this Realm, may be comfortable and easy to them.

This text was even secretly distributed and sold in Louis XIV's France, and eventually seized.[49]

The issue of toleration accompanied the Glorious Revolution from beginning to end. The failure of the policy of indulgence left a legal vacuum, soon to be filled by the Toleration Act of May 1689. Toleration was distinct from 'indulgence' for two reasons. Having been passed by Parliament, it did not have the character of an exception which attached to the measures advocated by James II. The new government was indeed a

---

[47] London, French Reformed Church, MS 294; On the king's prerogative and dispensing power, see in particular C.C. Weston and J.R. Greenberg, *Subjects and Sovereigns*, Cambridge, 1981.   [48] *The Sighs of France in Slavery*, London, 1689.
[49] BN, MSS fr. 7044, fol. 278.

mixed monarchy, whose supreme authority was the King-in-Parliament.[50] But this regime of toleration was, at least in theory, more restrictive than indulgence; it included only 'their majesties' Protestant subjects' whom their 'scrupulous consciences' alienated from the established Church. At first sight, the Catholics remained outside the pale of compromise, although in practice the thirteenth article of the Act was more lenient and encouraged 'popish recusants' to renounce the power 'ecclesiastical or spiritual' of the pope 'within this realm'. The law also emphasised the necessity of believing in the Holy Trinity if one was to benefit from toleration. At the end of the seventeenth century, many questioned the two natures of Jesus Christ, including some of the refugees, who were regarded with disquiet by their countrymen. Their former persecution did not necessarily make the refugees more humane, and high-ranking Huguenots endeavoured to separate the wheat from the chaff. One year later, in 1690, the French-speaking community swiftly reflected this fear of the antitrinitarian heresy. The deviants who were pursued were generally described as *Socinians*, thus attributing the paternity of their error to the Siennese Sozzini who had lived in the previous century. Yet what was the meaning of the accusation of Socinianism in the early 1690? Why did this learned term take on such sudden importance among the refugees, who had been ignorant of it until then? I shall suggest two explanations; the first relates to the circumstances of the time. The massive immigration which resulted from the Revocation of the Edict of Nantes, the disturbance brought about by the Glorious Revolution, were accompanied by a feeling of insecurity and moral negligence which gave rise to impassioned debates. Moreover, we cannot entirely exclude the hypothesis that periods of grave crisis have the curious effect of producing, by a kind of compensatory mechanism, a hardening of doctrine. In its darkest hours, the French Protestantism of the second half of the seventeenth century was preoccupied with highly technical debates on the question of grace.

But the fear of the Socinian also had its structural causes. The last decade of the seventeenth century saw the upsurge of an increasingly rational, if not rationalist, religion which applied to an elite of scientists and ministers. The 1690s are an approximate date; in matters of belief, how can one claim to establish any strict chronology? Nonetheless, the end of the century was characterised by a new equilibrium between faith and reason, above all in England.[51] The term 'Socinian' undoubtedly covers the emergence of this new spirit. We may then turn to Pierre Bayle's definition: the Socinians are those who refuse 'to believe whatever seems to them contrary to the Light of Philosophy, and to submit their faith to

---

[50] B. Cottret, 'Le Roi, les Lords et les Communes. Monarchie mixte et états du royaume en Angleterre (XVIe–XVIIIe siècles)', *Annales ESC*, 41, (1986), pp. 127–50.
[51] B. Cottret, *Le Christ des Lumières, Jésus de Newton à Voltaire*, Paris, 1990.

the inconceivable mysteries of the Christian religion'.[52] More recently George Gusdorf explained:

> Despite the scarcity of data, one can see, across time and geographical boundaries, an antitrinitarian international taking shape... The absence of a defined body of dogma favoured the diffusion of ideas, for it was not altogether clear where Socinianism began and where it ended. It was an association of tendencies rather than a positive profession of faith. The dominant themes of this liberalism were the humanisation of Christ, who became a man of inspiration, a prophet; the affirmation of free will and the rejection of original sin... These various aspects, which might be more or less pronounced at times, corresponded to a simplification and a rationalisation of Christianity.[53]

An anonymous document in the archives of the archbishop of Canterbury at Lambeth[54] disdainfully flouts the refugees' zeal to extirpate Socinianism from their ranks: while they held a correspondence with Holland to identify the black sheep among the flock, a 'Committee of Twelve' was set up to check the orthodoxy of the pastors, who would have been required to sign a declaration against the offending articles. Similar methods had been in use in Holland since 1686, following the synod of Rotterdam.[55] And yet, in the England of Locke and Newton, such procedures were on the wane. The increasingly rational tendency of English Protestantism was clearly formulated by Stillingfleet, the latitudinarian bishop of Worcester, who set out a summary of his faith which no longer referred either to *sola scriptura* or predestination, but emphasised only the enlightened aspect of the religion he professed, in order to contrast it with the darkness of Roman superstition. In 1695, Locke endeavoured to show that authentic Christianity, according to the Scriptures, was in agreement with Reason, while a year later John Toland denied the existence of mysteries. If these rationalist arguments, taken to extremes, did not win unanimous agreement in England, this theological liberalism was nonetheless shared by part of the elite in Church and State, who regarded with increasing suspicion Jurieu's ratiocinations and defence of orthodoxy.[56]

---

[52] P. Bayle, article 'Socin', *Dictionnaire historique et critique* (1696–1701), Hildesheim and New York, 1982, II, p. 236. Bayle's point of view is discussed by E. Labrousse in *Pierre Bayle, hétérodoxie et rigorisme*, The Hague, 1964, p. 439.

[53] G. Gusdorf, *La Révolution galiléenne*, 2 vols., Paris, 1969, II, pp. 55–6.

[54] Lambeth palace Library, MSS Gibsoniani 933, fol. 67; on the same affair, Bodleian Library, Rawlinson MSS D.480, pp. 1–109: 'Opposition de la confession de foi des Eglises Réformées aux erreurs des sociniens...' (1693).

[55] P. Jurieu instigated the measure; cf. R.J. Howells, *Pierre Jurieu: Antinomian Radical*, Durham, 1983, p. 52.

[56] J. Locke, *The Reasonableness of Christianity as Delivered in the Scriptures*, London, 1695; J. Toland, *Christianity not Mysterious*, London, 1696. See also B. Cottret, 'Hégémonie du discours et discours hégémoniques...', *Recherches sur le XVIIe siècle*, Paris, 1980.

The Socinian contagion affected the community of Canterbury, which numbered among its members 'several heterodox persons' who professed 'perverse doctrines' concerning the Trinity, and wanted '*covertly to introduce sects which lead men to perdition*, by denying, directly or indirectly the Lord who redeemed them' – 20 February 1696. Excommunication and – from 1693 – exclusion proved ineffective against these heretics who had to be avoided 'like so many pests'. The 'new sect', as it was called, was in keeping with the 1690s when an Act against 'impiety' and 'immorality' tried to curb the excesses of toleration (IX Wm. and M., c. 35).

Refugees or renegades?

But in order to describe, in a single word, the cunning and affectation of my persecutors, you should know that immediately after I changed my condition they tried to paint me as a spy against England, in order to ruin me among the English, in such an odious character. And two or three years later, they were claiming that I had spied for England against France, to draw down upon me the hatred of the Frenchmen who are here. I thank God who has always preserved me in the sentiments that I owed to these two kingdoms, both of which I regard as my own country, since I was born in the first and prepare myself to die in the other.

Breval, *Le foi victorieuse du monde…(Faith Victorious over this World…)*, London, 1670

François Durant de Bréval, a former Capuchin who had become pastor at the conformist Church of the Savoy, was here describing the calumnies which his former Catholic coreligionists poured upon him in England. Loyalty to two different kings did lend itself, in advance, to slander, and the flowery rhetoric of the French queen mother's former preacher did not quite conceal his unease. The question of secrecy, conspiracy and dissimulation deserved increasing consideration in the years preceding the Glorious Revolution.

This atmosphere of general suspicion, this climate of fear, were partly justified. Fear transposed, into a world of fancy, a real threat. By treating the Stuart sovereigns as his pensionaries, by assisting them with his funds, Louis XIV defeated his own object: sooner or later, this compromising association was bound to become public. Besides, the French monarch's friendship had its limits: the objective was to help the kings of England to withstand Parliament, without enabling them to assert themselves. A certain weakness was desirable; Louis XIV stated his objectives plainly, on 23 November 1680:

Provided the English monarchy can preserve itself in the unsteady state in which it is at present, and does not degenerate into a real republic under the name of a monarchy – as would happen if Parliament established fixed and regular sessions which the king were unable to suspend – there is no ground to apprehend that this Crown may soon find itself in a position to form powerful alliances against my interests, and *I could not wish that it were in a much better situation than the confused state in which it is at present.*[57]

The Refuge was by no means immune from the underhand dealings of secret diplomacy. The questions of loyalty or allegiance took on extremely complex forms for these Huguenots uprooted from their native soil. One cannot entirely exclude the hypothesis of double agents among the faithful, the famous 'proselytes' who had to be neutralised.

From the beginning, some prominent refugees, who acted as cultural mediators between England and France, did not resist the temptation of international involvement. Pierre du Moulin the younger set an example: in May 1669, while staying in his old country, he supplied the English with a detailed list of the French fleet, giving the number of ships and crew, together with their firepower.[58] This made a change from academic controversies on grace; in the seventeenth century, churchmen proved excellent statesmen. The theologian had more than one string to his bow, and his nephew, too, was suspected of putting his pen in the service of the Dutch, in 1673.[59]

The French Crown, as one might suspect, was no less efficient and it attempted to infiltrate the ranks of the immigrants, in particular after the Revocation. Bonrepaus was Louis XIV's authorised emissary, in charge of delicate affairs at the French embassy in London. In the winter of 1685–6, he discussed the purpose of his journey with the ambassador:

> I have explained the object of my journey to M. de Barillon. He thinks that nothing will prove difficult, except for the return of *those of the 'Reformed' religion to France.* There are many in this country. I hope that it will not be as difficult as M. de Barillon assumes to bring back the greater part of them. What causes the greatest difficulty is a few merchants who have come lately from France, among other places from La Rochelle, who say that great severity is being used there against the Protestants, and give examples of people who had their feet scorched by the dragoons, although in all likelihood that did not happen.[60]

Thus, Bonrepaus' mission was perfectly clear: he had to win over the fugitives and convince them to return. He came up against the negative

---

[57] *Recueil des instructions*, p. 268, letter from Louis XIV to Barillon, 23 November 1680. My italics.   [58] Bodleian Library, Rawlinson MSS A.477, fols. 171ff.

[59] [Pierre du Moulin?], *England's Appeal from the Private Cabal at Whitehall...* (1673), reproduced in *State Tracts*, London, 1689, pp. 1–25. Attributed to Pierre III du Moulin.

[60] Weiss, *Histoire des réfugiés protestants*, II, p. 419. On François Usson de Bonrepaus, see D. Dessert, *Argent, pouvoir et société au Grande Siècle*, Paris, 1984, pp. 699–700.

image of cruelty which the persecutions, and especially the *dragonnades*, had fostered. He therefore resorted to what he called 'the ways of gentleness and instruction'. His task was far from easy; the public campaign had already become so extensive, two and a half years before the Glorious Revolution, that James II forthrightly expressed his fears:

> His Britannic Majesty could not forbear to tell me that he considered all Protestants as republicans, and particularly those who are fleeing from France, but that as the rumours which are put abroad here about the violence used against them have a harmful effect, and give people cause to say that *he might one day treat his subjects in the same way*, he would wish this affair to be treated more gently, so as to put an end to these rumours.[61]

Bonrepaus' activity was not, however, fundamentally ideological in its motivation. His aim was less innocuous: in a mercantilist perspective this leakage of men and techniques was thought to have disastrous consequences for France:

> A few seamen are leaving today to return to France, with a few other fugitives, but I am sorely grieved to see that our best manufactures are being established in this kingdom. It is not just people of the so-called Reformed religion who come to work in these manufactures, but several Catholics join them.
>
> They had begun in Ipswich by manufacturing cloths which the English have been accustomed to buy in France for the West Indian trade... I found means to draw hither two of these Catholic workmen, under the pretext of wanting to buy some of their cloths, which I was well pleased to see, in order to ascertain their quality. They have agreed to return to France. I am keeping one of them here until the return of his fellow, who has gone to Ipswich to try to bring back several of his companions, as I have promised him ten pistols for each journeyman whom he could induce to follow him, whether Catholic or Protestant.[62]

These forms of economic counter-espionage depended on money, the sinews of war as well as of diplomacy. They derived their rationale from a global geopolitical analysis: the haemorrhage of French workmen was not confined to the Huguenots alone, as many Catholics from Normandy and Brittany were involved. For Bonrepaus, accordingly, it was a question of driving the Huguenot manufactures to bankruptcy, as he states plainly, by bribing craftsmen away. His attention, however, was drawn equally to the financial consequences of the exodus. Bonrepaus estimated the deficit in the balance of payments at 2 m livres for 1685.

One initial fact is evident: as early as 1685, the economic consequences of the Revocation of the Edict of Nantes caused some disquiet in the

---

[61] *Ibid.*, p. 420.   [62] *Ibid.*, p. 423.

corridors of power. Vauban's plea of October 1689, 'For the recall of the Huguenots',[63] the memoranda of *intendants* which, from 1698 to 1700, emphasised the depopulation of the French provinces,[64] has been anticipated long before. The economic effects of the abolition of the 'so-called Reformed religion' had caused concern from the beginning, or nearly so, and were to bring a useful corrective to the enthusiasm expressed in the union of Church and Crown in France.[65]

The thesis of the disastrous consequences brought about by the Revocation has been tempered by the researches of an American revisionist historian who showed that its negative effects on the French economy had undoubtedly been exaggerated.[66] This vast question remains a subject of controversy; it extends beyond the scope of the present study. Although I cannot pretend to conclude one way or another, the history of mentality would certainly highlight the weight of experience and shared belief. From the sixteenth century onwards – as we have seen in the case of Norwich – and later under the regency of Marie de Medicis in France,[67] or finally in the 1680s, the transfer of skills, the technical drain preoccupied successive governments. The results of the Revocation of the Edict of Nantes did not concern the French economy alone; they assumed a portentous European dimension: England, Ireland, the United Provinces – the great Ark of refugees – and the states of Germany were equally concerned. The Protestant diaspora strained international relations as a whole. Moreover, any approach to this question is impaired by a paradox: the detractors of the Huguenots and their ardent defenders alike tended to attach excessive importance to the Protestant factor, which consequently was overvalued right from the beginning.

Henri Daguesseau, the father of the future chancellor, was to pose the problem in revealing terms:

> As for the craftsmen, there are many established in London who are considered the best workmen there, and live very comfortably. They have imitated perfectly our gold and silver braid and other gilt work; they have introduced our manner of glove-making, they are imitating our silk brocade, our glazed taffetas, and French workmen of every kind are to be found there...It is to be feared that all these workmen scattered throughout the north, working there without control, both as concerns workmanship and dyeing, etc., will produce many inferior goods, bring them into France, and dazzle the people by the low prices at which they

[63] BN, MSS fr. 7044, fols. 289ff; Vauban, *Mémoire*, ed. P. Vassaux, Carrière-sous-Poissy, 1985.   [64] BN, MSS fr. 22205–22.

[65] Here I have drawn upon a seminar conducted by E. Le Roy Ladurie at the Collège de France in 1982–3 entitled 'Le système Louis XIV, la Révocation'.

[66] W.C. Scoville, *The Persecution of Huguenots and French Economic Development, 1680–1729*, Univ. of California Press, 1960.

[67] Antoine de Montchrestien, *Traicté de l'Oeconomie Politique* (1615), Paris, 1889.

will sell them, to the great detriment of our workmen, who are obliged
by our regulations to produce honest work.[68]

One should not belittle an economic challenge which required the
personal attention of an envoy of Louis XIV like Bonrepaus. If we take
his testimony for granted the English Refuge was an extremely complex
reality. It would seem that he maintained a veritable network of spies. An
anonymous letter from the same period informs us: 'I left behind...in
London, in Rotterdam and Amsterdam some of these fugitives who have
been converted, and whom I could see to be sincere, who miss no
opportunity of soliciting their compatriots to take the same course as they
have taken.'[69] And a manuscript memorandum of 1688 reveals:

> During my stay in England, there was always a minister of the so-called
> Reformed French Church in London who kept me informed of
> everything that went on in France concerning the false converts, and
> those who have not yet abjured. There was also a clerk of the customs
> in London, and several other persons, who gave me notice of all the
> fugitives who arrived in England, and of what means they had used to
> leave the kingdom.[70]

I have not been able to establish the identity of the suspected pastor; it
is difficult, three centuries later, to unravel a covert network. But, whether
true or false, this piece of information is a symptom of the prevailing
climate of chronic insecurity in late seventeenth-century England.

Allegiances, old and new

Loyalty is without doubt one of the cardinal values of social life. In the
seventeenth century, this truism held a particular significance: the respect
of one's word of honour and spoken testimony still retained all their
meaning. In England the use of oaths was even institutionalised, from the
reign of James I onwards, as an instrument of government, confirming the
subjects' allegiance to their king, exclusive of any papal dominion.

This connection between religion and politics favoured the Huguenots:
the king of England, defender of the (Protestant) faith, appeared as their
natural ally. In exceptional cases, such as the siege of La Rochelle in
1627–8, he could intervene on their side, against their rightful sovereign,
the king of France. However, Protestant unanimity was often a mask for
Reason of State. Two notable changes intervened in the last two decades
of the seventeenth century: the Revocation of the Edict of Nantes, and the
rise of Anglo-French antagonism. Indefinitely transposed onto every

---

[68] BN, MSS fr. 7044, fols. 279ff: 'Mémoire sur la Conduite des Princes du Nord à
l'égard des réfugiés François'.
[69] *Ibid.*, fol. 239, anonymous letter, 13 June 1686.
[70] *Ibid.*, fol. 273: 'Mémoire de Bonrepaus sur les huguenots de Londres, 1688'.

theatre of operations, the rivalry between France and England was to play a decisive role up to 1815: the War of the League of Augsburg, the War of the Spanish Succession, the War of the Austrian Succession, the Seven Years War, the American War of Independence and finally the wars of the French Revolution and the Napoleonic wars followed one upon the other, though not without intervening lulls. In short, the refugees could hardly claim that they remained loyal to both sides. A whole generation of Huguenots – who had sucked in the tradition of loyalty to the monarchy along with their mother's milk – found themselves suddenly at a loss, at least initially. It is difficult to write the history of men's consciences, and I do not claim here to sound hearts and minds. But this transfer of loyalty is worth considering; our records though, with their insistence on outward behaviour, provide little information on that deepest of feelings, apart from a few stereotypes on the duty of obedience. It was with keen interest, therefore, that I came across a letter of allegiance to Charles II, from a group of aristocratic refugees. I shall quote this text *in extenso*.

> To the King's excellent Majesty.   26th July 1683
> Sire,
> Here at the feet of Your Majesty are twenty-Five French gentlemen, all Protestants by the grace of God, who, seeing themselves stripped for their Religion's sake of their employments, which were of some consequence, have come to offer their Hearts, their swords and their whole persons to the august defender of their Faith. The offering, sire, is of slight importance in itself, and it is the zeal with which they dedicate it to Your Majesty which lends it all its worth and all its merit; for in a word, the supplicants have now in their hearts that same fire and that same ardour which burnt so constantly in their fathers for their kings, so long as it pleased their kings to avail themselves of it without striking a blow at the sacred rights of their consciences. They have the same loyalty, and the same tender veneration for crowned heads as their ancestors so signally showed when the Great Henry, the maternal grandfather of Your Majesty, was to be borne onto the throne of his predecessors, and when this same throne had to be defended against those who wished to overthrow it in the civil wars, in which, in spite of the difference of religion, they sacrificed everything to the service of their monarch, with such success that they may boast of having saved the state, without having ever failed or slackened in the least. It is with these sentiments, sire, that they present themselves on bended knees before Your Majesty resolved to live and die at your feet, for the glory of your Sacred Crown, if Your Majesty thinks fit to take them into his service for so great and dear a cause. You shall speak, Sire, you shall give orders, and they will go, sword in hand, to carry them out through all the Earth. They will fight like the people of God against your Amalekites, and at the same time, Sire, like Moses they will raise their hands and their eyes to Heaven, to call down with their prayers every Blessing on the Sacred

Person of Your Majesty, on his Royal House, on his designs, and lastly on his kingdom, Sire.

P. Fannet; A. de Lengaine; Ph. de Lengaine; Ph. Fournel; J. Naugine; C. Coverdon; J. de Jouisse; D. Deharques; D. Pacards; P. Duchêne; M. Soy; D. Lacoste; Isaac   Planque; P. Grand-champ; C. Hoquel; D. de Beauvoir; B. Souzet; A. Aroux; P. Chameau, etc.[71]

This piece of spirited eloquence joins the purest aristocratic style to Huguenot rhetoric. The memory of Henri IV, blood propinquity and biblical imagery are strikingly interwoven. One singular aspect should be emphasised: the outrageous disclosure of resentment towards the French Crown, its affective tone. The absolutist mystique was infused with a passionate element; the fury of rejected servants, the flaw of trust betrayed, in short disillusionment and disdain undoubtedly explain the transition to a new allegiance – which in this case occurred at a very early stage, two years before the Revocation. The Huguenot element in the English army was conspicuous, in particular after the Glorious Revolution. Many French Protestants, such as Henri de Massue de Ruvigny, later earl of Galway, were to help the new regime and transfer to William of Orange hopes which had been disappointed in Louis XIV. The Irish odyssey, the battle of the Boyne, the eviction of the Catholics: these were so many episodes long considered glorious. The unpublished narrative of Lacoste affords us a remarkable testimony of this epic, unencumbered by all the impositions of historians.[72] He fled from Casteljaloux in the south-west of France, after addressing one last gibe to his curé: 'Monsieur le curé, here I am booted to go to a country where I shall taste more liberty than I have here.' After a good many troubles, he arrived at The Hague. He was drafted into a regiment which was being assembled 'to make a descent to England'. As an ensign, he disembarked under the order of the Prince of Orange and the duke of Schomberg. Then, with the revolution accomplished and William crowned king of England, new regiments, 'the finest in the army', were brought together to cross over to Ireland: 'All the French officers that were there were packed into it, so that there were fifteen officers in each company: five captains, five lieutenants, and five ensigns. I was one of these. I believe we could boldly have faced the phalanxes of Alexander and the Roman legions.'

After the Irish campaign, which took him to Londonderry, came the warrior's rest, and Lacoste's two favourite pastimes,

> hunting and love-making, not having any other occupation. In the neighbourhood were some very comely ladies, and that was almost all

[71] Bodleian Library, Rawlinson MSS D.18, fol. 44.
[72] *Ibid.*, D.452: 'Détail de mes études, voyages, campagnes et aventures qui me sont arrivés pendant le cours de cinquante-deux années' (1730).

they had to their name. We had no particular attachment to one more than to another, although there were some who would have pleased the most exigent men of taste.

The lively clergyman's son speaks little of the dispositions of his soul. He married his landlady in Ireland, became a blacksmith; his wife then died, he took a commission again, and went to fight in Portugal in the War of the Spanish Succession. He married again – this time the daughter of a citizen of Dieppe. Attachment to the English cause, which soon became identified with Protestantism, did not present the slightest problem for this true born Frenchman. The exiled Huguenots' bitterness towards their old country, which Louis-Sébastien Mercier, in his turn, was to note around 1780, seems to have been a relatively common feeling.[73]

If Protestantism constituted one of the axiomatic features of English national consciousness, as it emerged in the century separating the Invincible Armada from the Glorious Revolution, Protestant foreigners occupied a place apart. They could almost be pardoned for not being quite English by birth, since they were already entitled to salvation. A number of them were granted the naturalisation for which they craved; the promise of a *general naturalisation* of all religious refugees remained an open alternative. This would have require an Act of Parliament. From the 1670s onward, several plans were put forward, without any success.[74] Thus, in 1673, while Charles II's Declaration of Indulgence caused an uproar in the Commons, a campaign was launched for the naturalisation of foreign Protestants. In all likelihood, this counter-proposal intended to challenge Charles II on his own ground, lenity to the nonconformists. The causes of English Catholics and Dissenters, albeit dissimilar in essence were jointly associated in debates. The wish which was expressed, of granting 'freedom of conscience' to all Protestants and naturalisation to the Huguenots, served to curb the king's intention to recognise the Catholics. What reason was there, indeed, to trouble those who 'differ from the Church of England only in matters of discipline, while they are in agreement concerning peace with the civil government, and respect the government of the established Church'?[75]

On the political chessboard, four variables can be identified. The majority Church, the nonconformists, the Protestant refugees and lastly the Catholics. The rules of the game were fairly simple: unanimity presupposed exclusion.

---

[73] L.-S. Mercier, 'Une des causes de la haines des Anglois', in C. Bruneteau and B. Cottret (eds.), *Parallèle de Paris et de Londres* (1781), Paris, 1982.

[74] Here I have made use of the fine work edited by Joan Thirsk and J.P. Cooper, *Seventeenth-Century Economic Documents*, Oxford, 1972, pp. 741ff.

[75] *Ibid.*, p. 743, extract from *The Grand Concern of England* (1673).

In February 1673, a bill on the naturalisation of foreigners, much akin to the Test Act, provided for the following oath:

> I A.B. do swear that I will bear faith and true allegiance to our sovereign Lord the King, his heirs and successors; and shall likewise subscribe this declaration: I A.B. do declare that I do not believe that there is any transubstantiation in the elements of bread and wine in the sacrament of the Lord's supper upon or after the consecration thereof by any person whatsoever.[76]

A Catholic could not take such an oath, which went against his conception of the eucharist, without repudiating his faith; on the other hand, this rather evasive definition of Communion could be unanimously accepted among Protestants. But the bill failed, in 1673 as in 1677. A new fear was expressed: that of a standing army of mercenaries, bound to the government by its advocacy of liberty of conscience. Quite clearly the insular fear of an invasion dominated the scene; 'It was urged that it would draw on the pretence of a standing army to keep so many strangers quiet, and would endanger the religion established, by introducing liberty of conscience.'[77]

In 1685, anti-Huguenot propaganda took on an obvious Tory tone. The French Protestants were clearly accused of Whig leanings, and occasional conformity:

> 'Tis much feared that the late great confluence of strangers hither was in order to no good end for that these people were invited over and encouraged here by them only that were the conspirators in the late [Rye House] plot and were observed to crowd the Lord Russell's and Shaftesbury's door; and that that faction were the only patrons is apparent in that Papillon and Dubois, both Walloons, were the greatest sticklers in this affair and both members of the French Protestant church, yet took the sacrament to serve a turn.[78]

The notorious Thomas Papillon, a merchant by trade, was the son of a Huguenot architect and military engineer who had settled in England in his youth. He warmly embraced Whig ideas and stood with John Dubois in the disputed 1682 elections for the positions of sheriffs of London and Middlesex. They thereby defeated the two Court candidates and incurred the rage of the Tories. The next year, they were summoned before the lord mayor, who expressed his hopes that the king would 'take a course' to send back the Huguenots 'to their country'. The two men had had to listen patiently to a scurrilous, arrogant statement of their foreign

---

[76] *Ibid.*, p. 745, House of Lords Record Office.   [77] *Ibid.*, p. 746.
[78] *Ibid.*, p. 747: 'Reasons humbly offered by the inhabitants of the City and Liberty of Westminster … to the knights, citizens and burgesses in this present Parliament assembled against the passing of a bill entitled An Act for the enabling of Protestant strangers to exercise their trades in the places in the Act mentioned.'

ancestry, which bluntly referred to the 'French Walloon Protestants that came into this nation for refuge, and had got estates, and would overthrow the government and cut our throats'.[79]

The Rye House plot, which came to light in June 1683, was another fake conspiracy against the king, bearing some resemblance with the former 'popish plot', though this time the Whigs were the victims. Joshiah Keeling, 'a man of anabaptist sympathies and a decaying business',[80] who clearly belonged to the same class of desperados as Titus Oates, came up with the trumped-up story of a scheme to kill the king which perfectly suited the Court. Some major Country opponents were prosecuted, among them William Lord Russell and Algernon Sidney, who were executed. While Essex committed suicide in the Tower, Monmouth and several other Whigs were able to flee to Holland, where Shaftesbury had already found shelter. Papillon was to follow them in their exile in 1684, the same year as John Locke, thus reinforcing William of Orange's French connection with the Huguenots.

The French Protestants were visibly embarrassed by the disclosure of the plot. Even though they rejoiced at 'his Majesty's most happy and signal deliverance', they evidently hesitated to commit themselves too strenuously in favour of a thesis which ruined the Whigs. Along with the Dutch brethren, they adopted a moderate course on 25 July 1683:

> The Coetus being met to consider if it were not expedient to congratulate his Majesty upon his happy delivery of the late horrid conspiracy, after a long mature deliberation (though very desirous it might be done yet), considering no English churches have done it before, *thought it too great a presumption, and a matter of too high a moment for our Churches.*[81]

But this non-committal humility displeased the bishop of London, and on 5 August, the Foreign Churches wrote to the king, throwing themselves at his feet to implore his gracious protection. They likewise discarded all relations with 'riotous people' – *gens remuans* – and reassuringly stated their unconditional attachment to monarchies. They even seemed to share the arch-Tory belief in passive obedience and non-resistance. In February 1685, they likewise congratulated James II on his accession, and carefully paid homage to the late king's memory who had gone to rest like the sun: 'le coucher de ce grand soleil'. Yet the emergence of party politics was nonetheless to exercise a major influence on the life of the 'poor refugees' whose cause was taken up with great gusto and dynamic vigour by the Whigs. It was not, in fact, until the reign of Queen Anne that, in 1708, an 'Act for the Naturalisation of Foreign Protestants' was passed – VII Anne c. 5. It required attendance at Communion, either in the Church of

---

[79] Gwynn, *Huguenot Heritage*, p. 123.
[80] D. Ogg, *England in the Reign of Charles II* (1934), Oxford, 1967, p. 647.
[81] Guildhall Library, MSS 7412/1, p. 112.

England, or in a Reformed chapel. This conciliatory text, however, was repealed in 1712. The rage of parties was largely to blame. The Whigs, who always drew support from the nonconformists, tended to protect the Huguenots, while the Tories made no secret of their misgivings and attempted by every means to reduce the influence of Dissenters. In fact, the Huguenots were not the sole target of this inhospitable move: about 8,000 foreign Protestants from the Palatinate had entered the country, raising widespread hostility. Many of these poor destitute people who had fled their native Germany were eventually to migrate to Ireland and America.

Jonathan Swift provides a fairly accurate picture of the High-Church Tory reaction to the Naturalisation Act and its repeal. He gave the following summary of the event in his *Four Last Years of Queen Anne's Reign*: 'On the 9th of February was repealed the Act for naturalising foreign Protestants, which had been under the last [Whig] ministry, and, as many people thought, to very ill purposes.'[82] The Irish dean explained his resentment:

> By this act, any foreigner who would take the oaths to the government, and profess himself a Protestant, of whatever denomination, was immediately naturalised, and had all the privileges of an English-born subject, at the expense of a shilling. *Most protestants abroad differ from us in the points of church-government; so that all the acquisitions by this act would increase the number of dissenters*; and therefore the proposal that such foreigners should be obliged to conform to the established worship was rejected.

The first argument was therefore ecclesiastical: the foreign Protestants tended to mix with the Dissenters and raise the numerical importance of nonconformity. Jonathan Swift does thereby confirm the diverging evolution of Anglicanism and Continental Protestantism; the disagreement in points of 'Church government' assumes a wider meaning: it divides good, lawful subjects from potential extremists. But this King (or rather Queen) and Country attitude, which was clearly inherited from the Restoration, lingered on in the eighteenth century. It was even to reach a climax in the last years of Queen Anne's reign when occasional conformity and schism – at least in matters of education – were equally banned, though such discrimination was of no avail as it was repealed in 1719. The enduring stigma of nonconformity, which outlasted all the efforts of the French Anglican congregations, was in fact closely related to the economic and political involvement of some wealthy refugees: the Houblon brothers, John and James, were respectively governor and deputy-governor of the incipient Bank of England, set up in 1694. The commercial

[82] W. Cobbett, *Parliamentary History of England*, 12 vols., London, 1806–123, VI, p. 1089. My italics.

and financial assets of some members of the Franco-Walloon community were regarded with suspicion by the Tories, in their bitter denunciation of 'stock jobbers' and war speculators.[83]

Yet, even though he was well aware of the established relationship between the Whigs and Protestant refugees, Jonathan Swift paid even more attention to the ingrained fear of an invasion, which had long been a feature of anti-alien propaganda. The churchman tried to defeat the mercantilist equation between the sheer number of inhabitants and the wealth of a nation:

> The maxim, *That people are the riches of a nation*, hath been crudely understood by many writers and reasoners upon that subject. There are several ways by which people are brought into the country. Sometimes a nation is invaded and subdued; and the conquerors seize the lands, and make the natives their under-tenants or servants. Colonies have been always planted where the natives were driven out or destroyed, or the land uncultivated or waste.

After this fair appraisal of the imperial drive, with his eyes fixed on Ireland and possibly America, the good clergyman went on: 'Sometimes, in governments newly instituted, where there are not people to till the ground, many laws have been made to encourage and allure numbers from the neighbouring countries. And, in all these cases, the newcomers have either lands allotted to them, or are slaves to the proprietors.'

While foreign settlements or 'plantations' could be necessary to reinforce the English presence in colonies, immigration and naturalisation had to be more selective at home: 'The true way of multiplying mankind to public advantage, in such a country as England, is to invite from abroad only able handicraftsmen and artificers, or such who bring over a sufficient share of property to secure them from want.'

In fact, the palatines were the prime target of Dean Swift, who grudgingly compared them to an 'unsightly' and 'troublesome' excrescence.

Liberality and constraint

From the sixteenth century onwards, the relief of the poor in England had not been confused with mercy. Individual benevolence, and philanthropy, continued, although one cannot suggest a generally accepted quantification.[84] But the social management of pauperism, its moral government, its rationalisation and assessment were entrusted to the parishes, or, in the

---

[83] P.G.M. Dickson, *The Financial Revolution in England*, London, 1967; F. Crouzet, 'Walloons, Huguenots and the Bank of England', *Proceedings of the Huguenot Society*, 25 (1990), pp. 167–78. A longer version of professor Crouzet's article is still due to appear in the *Landes Festschrift* (forthcoming).
[84] W.K. Jordan, *Philanthropy in England*, London, 1959.

case which concerns us more particularly here, to the Foreign Churches. The pauper was entering the age of double-entry bookkeeping, or at least of its more general adoption; England was indeed the home of what, at the end of the seventeenth century, came to be called 'social arithmetic'. Hence, the sense of harshness which strikes us when we come to consider this period: charity was already a sector of budgetary expenditure and the Churches managed their resources as rigorously as accountants. I shall later show what importance monetary relationships held within the foreign communities and their extra-economic role.

A third type of financial levy and distribution existed: voluntary collections. According to the American historian Roy Sundstrom,[85] the contributions for the 'poor refugees' were four in number: from 1681, 1686, 1688 and 1694 onwards, alms flowed in from all the parishes and bishoprics of the kingdom on the Crown's initiative. The sums collected were considerable: in round figures, they amounted to £14,600 from 1681 to 1689 and £63,000 from 1686–8 to 1695, falling to £11,800 from 1694 to 1701. The fortunes of these collections paralleled the misfortunes of French Protestantism. The charitable exhortations pronounced in each parish in favour of the Huguenots, the accounts of the *dragonnades*, and the horror of persecution, probably gave rise to demonstrations of anti-Catholic feeling which incriminated Charles II, and more particularly his brother James II. This explains why the Crown took the initiative of these collections, in order to exonerate itself from any collusion with the persecuting king Louis XIV. In his capacity as head of the Church, the king issued, each time according to the same fixed procedure, a *brief* calling upon his people to show compassion. On 10 September 1681, Charles II emphasised this was not only a matter of relieving 'distressed strangers', but 'persecuted Protestants'.[86] The funds raised were transmitted to the archbishop of Canterbury, the bishop of London and the lord mayor, who deposited them in the City; they were later distributed by the representatives of the Savoy and the Reformed Church.

Some fundamental changes, however, were quickly to occur, and embitter this charitable administration. First, a specialised board emerged in order to distribute the good manna equitably. The trustees were accused, as expected, of every kind of corruption. The Comité Français were not slow to incur the enduring resentment of many refugees. To make matters even worse, in November 1685, two months after the Revocation of the Edict of Nantes, and at the request of the conformist Church of the Savoy, James II confined this assistance to those French Protestants who adopted the Anglican confession. This English version of

---

[85] Roy A. Sundstrom, 'Aid and Assimilation: A Study of the Economic Support Given French Protestants in England, 1680–1722', PhD thesis, Kent State University Graduate School, 1972.   [86] Bodleian Library, Rawlinson MSS C.984, fol. 43.

a fund for converting Huguenots aroused some scorn, and one can well imagine that the administrators inflamed popular hatred.

Besides, the division persisted even after the Glorious Revolution. Though William and Mary invoked 'the cause of our common religion' at the beginning of the brief which they issued in 1694, the refugees suffered more than ever from the rift between conformists and nonconformists. At the turn of the century, a manuscript protest described the authoritarian practices of the Comité Français:

> In 1686, Monsieur Alix having established a conformist Church [at Hungerford Market], the Committee gave him large sums of money out of the collection, for the support of this Church, and to help the poor of the said Church. He was admitted himself as one of the distributors on the Committee.
>
> [On the other hand] Monsieur Daillon having, with his colleagues, established a Church in 1688 [La Patente, Spitalfields] he addressed himself to the grand Committee with one of his colleagues from their Communion, to claim some money for the maintenance of the ministers of their corporation, who had already begun their ministry, and to request that one of them be admitted as a member of the French Committee, or that they be allocated a sum for the relief of such poor persons as might apply to them for assistance, offering to give good and faithful account of these funds. Their application was rejected, and none of their other requests was granted, as a result of the opposition of the French Committee, viz. Messrs Primerose, Piozet, La Mothe, ministers; Chardin and Moreau, elders. [See also Document 8.][87]

The funds administered by the Committee did not derive solely from the collections; to these must be added the Royal Bounty, established by William and Mary *c.* 1689 and which amounted to £15,000 in 1696. The archives of the Comité Français would deserve extensive computer treatment. From June 1687 to August 1688, I reckon about 10,000 persons were given assistance, including women and children.[88] This register would suggest one immediate observation: charity often took the form of practical assistance to provide a livelihood; Pierre Astruc, for example, 'has had £12 to establish himself as a hat-maker in Ipswich' or again Jean Ailleau received '£5 for his apprenticeship'. The allocated sum varied according to social class: pastors and gentlemen were better treated than people of middling rank or humble origin. As expected, the crucial problem remained religious conformity. I should be inclined to think that the Committee was more inflexible with the pastors, requiring them to be effectively reordained by a bishop, than it was with the congregations, although one of the account books for the same period (April 1687 – July 1688) mentions certificates attesting that Communion had been received

[87] *Ibid.*, D.641, fol. 94.   [88] London, Huguenot Library, Aa, MSS 1.

according to the rites of the Church of England. But was it always possible
to keep an effective check on conformity?[89]

One Jacques Fontaine describes the procedure in his *Mémoires*. On his
arrival, he was offered £30 a year, although he was not yet a pastor. As a
comparison, £45 was an average income for an Anglican minister. Jacques
Fontaine tells us:

> God had vouchsafed me the esteem and the favour of all the members of
> the Committee, the evidence of which was clear to see, since they had put
> me on the same footing as the ministers, – there was, I say, in their letter,
> a condition which required that before I could receive another quarter's
> allowance, I must take Communion after the manner of the Church of
> England and send a certificate to the Committee, which I could remit to
> them or to any of my friends. – I, who had just escaped the Tempter, felt
> alarmed at this manner of offering charity, and although I had already
> been to Communion very cordially with Englishmen and with French-
> men after the manner of the Anglican Church, without any misgivings,
> and in the spirit of charity ... I felt some doubt as to the virtue of receiving
> Communion in order to qualify for a pension, and it seemed to me that
> this was just like the behaviour of the Papists: 'Come to mass and you
> will be spared the dragoons, and you shall have a pension like us.'[90]

A lasting dispersion

Once again, after two or three generations, the fate of Protestantism
seemed to depend on the Lord of Hosts. The wars of religion had an
archaic flavour; they had been relegated to a distant past by the reign of
Henri IV, with the exception of the 1620s. At the end of the century, there
was widespread speculation as to the outcome of the conflict between
France, England and her allies. Would Louis XIV's 'likely defeat', and
William of Orange's providential victory portend the triumphant return of
the Huguenots to their former country?

And yet, neither the day nor the hour of this heavenly prospect were
known; the time of trials exhorted to conversion and repentance. Jurieu,
a former professor at Sedan, now pastor in Rotteram, read the Scriptures,
and significantly the Book of Revelation, with feverish intensity in order
to decipher the present. In the midst of hardship and adversity, he uttered
an immense cry of hope in 1686: *The accomplishment of the scripture
prophecies, or the approaching deliverance of the Church. Proving, that the
papacy is the antichristian kingdom, and that the kingdom is not far from its
ruin. That the present persecution may end in three years and a half ... after
which the destruction of antichrist shall begin.*

[89] *Ibid.*, MSS 2.
[90] Jacques Fontaine, *Mémoires* ... (1722), Montpellier, Presses du Languedoc (forthcoming).

This was the title of the English translation published in the following year. Jurieu foresaw the beginning of a new era in 1689, to be followed by the final defeat of Antichrist *c.* 1710–15. Then was to begin the great Millennium, the thousand-year reign of Christ, marked by the conversion of the Jews, ushering in the end of the world. In short, the eventual return from exile led into the Messianic expectation of the return of Christ. Under such good omen, was not the Glorious Revolution the prelude to a new age? The personality of Jurieu – the offending Jurieu, the 'injurieux Jurieu' – his authoritarianism and his eschatology did not meet with unmitigated approval. Jurieu irritated his contemporaries, played on their nerves and even exasperated them at times. The harmony of biblical chronology and world history was commonly accepted.[91] Yet how far did Jurieu's visions prove convincing? Emmanuel Le Roy Ladurie has found traces of Messianic belief in Protestant Languedoc,[92] though men were slightly more cautious in England where the elite of Church and State were increasingly steeped in rationalism. Christopher Hill has noted the retreat of Antichrist after 1660.[93] Neither have I found any trace in my records of any formal adherence to Jurieu's apocalyptic thesis. I would not question, however, the symbolic value of the *Accomplishment of the scripture prophecies* which sustained Huguenot resistance. This portentous challenge, this feverish bitterness account for the elaboration of the wildest plans. The first will be the last, the vanquished will be the victors. The expectation of an impending re-establishment was to be continually frustrated. Charles Piozet, the pastor of Threadneedle Street, anticipated the return to France; but he did not predict it. In a letter to Bishop Compton he described the fate of the 'Churches of our dispersion', envisaging the day when the 'flock' would again 'gather together'.[94] Yet this wish remained conditional; it depended on the Lord's determination, 'by an extraordinary dispensation of his providence, to re-establish them'.

The peace of Ryswick, which in 1697 brought provisionally to an end England's military engagement against Louis XIV, proved extremely disappointing to the Huguenots.[95] The fortunes of arms did not permit them to return to their old country. However, some secret meetings had been held a few months before, in October 1696, in the nonconformist temple of Leicesterfields. Unfortunately, we know of their existence only through the testimony of an opponent who published in Cologne a resounding indictment of the Comité Français in 1699: *Mémoires envoyés de Londres à M * par M * au sujet de l'établissement d'un conseil pour*

[91] P. Hazard, *The European Mind 1680–1715*, Harmondsworth, 1973.
[92] E. Le Roy Ladurie, *Les Paysans de Languedoc* (1966), Paris, 1969, p. 330.
[93] C. Hill, *Antichrist in Seventeenth Century England*, Oxford, 1971.
[94] Bodleian Library, Rawlinson MSS C.982, fol. 153.
[95] Robert Mandrou, *Louis XIV en son temps*, Paris, 1973, pp. 484–504.

veiller sur la conduite des protestants réfugiés en Angleterre (*Memoranda Sent from London by Monsieur * to Monsieur *, Concerning the Establishment of a Committee to Watch over the Conduct of the French Protestant Refugees in England*). The anonymous author explains, regarding the Committee (p. 10):

> What was, at the beginning, only a fortuitous and temporary administration of the funds from a special donation became, as far as they were concerned, a kind of office and established commission, which these Gentlemen now find so much to their advantage that, whatever semblance they may show of complaining of their burden, they would assuredly be greatly displeased to be relieved of it. Far from it, there is nothing which they would not gladly sacrifice to their determination to hold their position.

This unaccommodating portrayal of the ills of bureaucracy explains how the administration of charity could give rise to censure. And, expectedly in a Huguenot author, comparisons with the Roman Church abound: the 'Council of Trent', the 'papal legates' and even the 'Inquisition' are called to mind. Further still, the Comité Français would have been manipulated by a secret council, from 1695 onwards. Instead of the 'form of government prescribed' by the Calvinist discipline, 'despotic government' prevailed (p. 58). The great principle of consultation was thereby violated (p. 70): 'It appears an act of temerity, that private individuals should have undertaken of their own accord to set themselves at the head of a great body, without its participation.'

In short, they were an 'assembly of worthies', which had begun to deliberate without consulting the 'nation'. The tone of this denunciation foreshadows the Enlightenment.

The secret council is said to have included some of the most prestigious pastors and noblemen, though its membership cut across the conformist/nonconformist divide. They may have enjoyed the support of the great Huguenot general Ruvigny, earl of Galway. Although undoubtedly polemical, this pamphlet sounds relatively objective. The unpublished disclaimer which followed it, while refuting the idea of secrecy, admits nonetheless that respectability and the concern for orthodoxy came uppermost. The 'Memorandum in defence of the French Committee' explains:

> It was of the utmost importance that none but suitable persons should enter the French ministry. Some time afterwards, the existence of scandalous preachers among the French was an established fact, though there were no means of bringing them back to their duty, as they belonged to no Church in particular.[96]

[96] Lambeth Palace Library, MSS Gibsoniani 941, fol. 87.

This sense of elite betrayal remains relevant in the anonymous denunciator's complaint. But, even if the idea of secret manipulation looks excessive, some underhand confidential discussions were nonetheless organised. Besides, this secrecy is after all logical when one considers the obsession with conspiracy and espionage which oppressed the refugee communities. Let us allow our polemicist to speak once more (p. 30): 'Their great purpose was to work for the recall of all Protestants to France, without concerning themselves over-scrupulously to ensure the restoration of the Edict of Nantes.'

Were there, in fact, any grounds, in the best of hypotheses, to envisage a return to the situation prior to 1685? Several dissentient views were held. Our author exclaims (p. 39):

> It would be shameful indeed for the French refugees to give up an edict like the Edict of Nantes, which nothing in the world could equal in value; our adversaries could ask for nothing better, in order to silence us forever concerning the irrevocability of the edict; it would be, besides, a subject of eternal reproach against us, if we were voluntarily to abandon the purity and the simplicity of a form of worship which will always be an honour to our Reformation.

A minority of refugees were apparently prepared to compromise on this principle. What alternative was there to the Calvinist discipline, which was suspected of republicanism? An episcopalian Church, without any presbyteries, on the Anglican model. The idea 'of a new plan' was apparently put forward (p. 35):

> The king of France could be entreated directly, and asked for permission to practise our religion publicly following Anglican usage. Our Churches would be governed by bishops, nominated by King Louis XIV. The ministers wishing to be granted a living would be ordained by bishops, and without introducing any fundamental innovation in our belief, or in our form of worship, we could be satisfied by a solemn edict, which would be given with all due guarantees, without any interference with the king of France's prerogative or the least offence to the clergy, who could no longer question the minister's legitimacy of vocation.

In the event, neither the Edict of Nantes nor this Reformed form of Gallicanism was to have a future. Another solution would have consisted in toleration but this was an unattainable ideal in France. Moreover, toleration was still regarded with suspicion by many of the refugees, as Elisabeth Labrousse wrote:

> Not until a good ten years had passed did an ideal of tolerance begin to gain ground among the refugees, and progressively cease to seem scandalous and impious to them. But by then, having abandoned the political theory of absolutism, and adopted a programme of toleration,

the Refuge would have moved decisively away from the seventeenth-century mentality, and have inaugurated the neo-Protestantism of the Enlightenment.[97]

[97] E. Labrousse, 'Absolutisme et protestantisme' 1685–1985, *Centre protestant d'études et de documentation* (Dec–Jan. 1982–3).

III STRANGER COMMUNITIES AND MINORITIES

7 An alternative form of social life?

Reforming oneself often means reforming others. Calvinism involves a transformation of social life, and the force of consensus, the great moments of fraternisation, the altogether scriptural emphasis on *reconciliation*, were as essential as the break with the past; the unanimity which at certain moments prevailed among individuals who had come from varying backgrounds was as important as the sense of differences: immigration tightened these multiple ties of solidarity within a minority group. The social life of Calvinism was not to be equated with conviviality: entertainment in all its forms was suspect; dancing, the ale-house and other festive occasions handed down by custom were the objects of constant admonitions.

Likewise, the highest value was set upon community life. It would be unfair to overestimate the moral rigour permeating the grand design to let men administer their own destiny according to the Word. Calvinist pessimism, unlike Jansenism, did not lead to a withdrawal from the world. For Calvin, society was not rooted in nature: it came to be regarded as an 'institution'. The dissociation of culture and nature was not yet invested with any nostalgia. The idea that an initial compact lay at the origin of the City was to form a prominent element in the later evolution of a body of secularised political thought which had its roots in Protestantism, from Hobbes to Locke, or Rousseau.

And yet the historical appraisal of Calvinism is beset with difficulties.[1] Henri Hauser attempted to demonstrate that in the Protestant Reformation 'social revolution' and 'religious revolution' were linked.[2] In 1904–5, the German sociologist Max Weber skilfully delineated the

[1] This complexity is brought out admirably in the collection of papers edited by P. Joutard, *Historiographie de la Réforme*, Paris, Neuchâtel and Montreal, 1977.
[2] H. Hauser, 'La Réforme et les classes populaires en France au XVIe siècle', *Revue d'histoire moderne et contemporaine*, 1 (1899), pp. 24–34.

connections between 'the Protestant ethic and the spirit of capitalism'.[3]
Richard Tawney, although qualifying this thesis in the case of Luther,
gave it wider historical currency.[4] However, Herbert Lüthy wished to alter
the terms of this 'ill-formulated question':

> All practical forms of action bear an equivocal relationship to faith, and
> even, in secularised societies, to ideology; every absolute concept,
> whether it be religious in nature or part of a substitute for religion bears
> an equivocal relationship to practice; to subdue one to the other is to
> condemn it to atrophy.[5]

I should like to show the political ambiguity attached to Calvinism for
the men of the early modern period. Did the reformed discipline lead to
republicanism or monarchy? This uncertainty was constantly present; it
can be felt, indirectly, in the mistrust which surrounded the Huguenots,
almost unremittingly, in seventeenth-century England. The evidence of
men's behaviour may be contradictory and inconsistent – protestations of
loyalty to kings occurring side by side with uncompromising demonstrations of lay pride. What was most suspect, in fact, was not the
Calvinists' avowed ideology, but their social organisation, which was held
to be unduly democratic. Hence the urgent need, in the present case, for
a study of the 'forms of social life'.[6]

It had long been recognised that Calvinism involved an organisation of
society; some hostile spirits had even seized upon this pretext to deny the
strictly theological importance of Calvin's works. But Emile G. Léonard,
who cannot be accused of any such extravagance, nonetheless introduced
Calvin positively as the 'founder of a civilisation'.[7] Calvinism was, indeed,
a social, just as much as a religious, phenomenon: it implied in practice a
redefinition of men's relationships in society. The Calvinist Reformation
involved a discriminate selection of old practices, while legitimising new
ones; in a word, to the dissemination of its message it added the institution
of a code. Hence the necessity, which Maurice Agulhon has emphasised,
of investigating the 'life of forms'.[8] In this respect, the simple analysis of
explicit statements, though a good starting point, proves unsatisfactory in
the long run. Although written testimonies were often used for themselves,
I aimed at the recreation of men's behaviour. I had several assets: the
consistory registers are extraordinarily eloquent and informative about

[3] M. Weber, *Die protestantische Ethik und der Geist des Kapitalismus*, (1904–5). I have
summed up this debate in 'Max Weber Revisited', *Americana*, 4 (1989), pp. 75–96.
[4] R.H. Tawney, *Religion and the Rise of Capitalism* (1926). Pelican, 1938, and numerous
subsequent editions.
[5] H. Lüthy, *La Banque protestante en France, de la révocation de l'Edit de Nantes à la
Révolution*, Paris, 1959, p. 752.
[6] M. Agulhon, *Pénitents et francs-maçons de l'ancienne Provence. Essai sur la sociabilité
méridionale* (1966–8), new edn, Paris, 1984.
[7] Léonard, *Histoire générale du protestantisme*, I, pp. 258ff.
[8] Agulhon, *Pénitents et francs-maçons*, ch. 15: 'Une vie des formes?', pp. 357ff.

the doings of the refugees; in the sixteenth century in particular, body and soul went together and physical attitudes are constantly referred to. But this reconstruction is hampered by conspicuous silence on many points. Our records do not mention what contemporaries took for granted. Implicit concerns are the least obtrusive form of evidence. Moreover, certain attitudes were not even apparent to the actors themselves: thus, exogamy was discouraged in practice, but not in theory. It would have been unseemly to cast discredit officially on marriages contracted *outside* the community. Similarly, financial relationships assumed more than simple economic significance: for the Refuge Churches, the independent management of their affairs involved the preservation of their distinct identity. World pictures also changed during this century and a half; in the absence of thunderous declarations, an increasingly rationalist turn of mind developed. I have accordingly constantly interpreted the evidence in the light of specific historical concerns. Other researchers may insist on different phenomena. I have on purpose paid particular attention to functional, systemic elements: the laws of adaptation or survival, the transmission of identity, the definition of a minority have preoccupied me more than individual biography. But I hope that I have never sacrificed the picturesque elements or the everyday concerns of the refugees.

Police and 'polis'

We are entrenched in ambiguity: in these centuries there was a constant interpolation of the religious and political. *Monarchy, aristocracy, democracy* are terms which come to mind continually even when speaking of Churches. Conversely, *Presbyterian, Puritan* or *Independent* refer to social movements at least as much as to religious ideologies. This confusion of two separate spheres, according to our twentieth-century categories, was less blatant than it seems. And, having shown the constant connections which linked religion and politics, we will need to dissociate them again, in order to bring out the specific character of the Church.

By one of the quirks of Reason, the 'democracy of citizens',[9] with its lay, secular character, has one of its obvious origins in the life of religious groups. This 'potential democracy'[10] was equally characteristic of the consistories. To a large extent, lay participation provoked the opposition of ministers: the adoption of Anglicanism was a response, often betraying a measure of embarrassment, to this Presbyterian challenge.

Turning back now to the development which led from the congregation

---

[9] R. Descimon, *Qui étaient les seize? Mythes et réalités de la Ligue parisienne (1585–1594)*, Paris, 1983, p. 297.

[10] Agulhon, *Pénitents et francs-maçons*, p. iv; on the question of the transference from religious to political forms, see Monique Cottret 'Aux origines du républicanisme janséniste: le mythe de l'Eglise primitive et le primitivisme des Lumières', *Revue d'histoire moderne et contemporaine*, 31 (1984), pp. 99–115.

to the community of citizens, we may consider the notion of law as it prevailed in the Refuge. The life of the Churches was regulated by a twofold jurisdiction: the customary authority of the consistories, which will be examined in the following chapter; and the statutory rights embodied in the *ecclesiastical discipline*. This text defined in anticipation a division of tasks, if not a balance of powers within the group. One can easily imagine the virtues and the limitations of such normative prescription: an idealised vision entails a gap between law and current practice. The discipline of the reformed Church of London, to give but one example, went through four successive versions, drawn up *c.* 1550 in the reign of Edward VI, in 1561 and 1578 during the Elizabethan period and finally in 1641, on the eve of the Civil War. This last version is still in use[11] and should be briefly summarised. According to common Reformed constitutions, it recognises four distinct offices within the Church: pastors, doctors, elders and deacons. The pastors expound the gospel and administer the Sacraments – baptism and the Lord's Supper. The doctors teach, without, however, being confined to catechism; they are also responsible for instruction in 'letters and sciences, which are the aids to greater learning'. The elders are the backbone of the community; together with the pastor, they make up the consistory, which is entrusted with the management of the Church and its moral supervision. As for the deacons, they are in charge of poor relief. The role played by this body of officers, half-pastoral, half-laymen, is considerable and deserves to be fully illustrated with the help of concrete examples. The discipline also draws attention to the main rites of passage: christening, marriage and burial. It provides for sanctions: admonishment, or, in the case of obdurate 'delinquents', excommunication. It is, moreover, a colourful text; it draws a clear distinction between 'vices which are not to be tolerated in a minister' and other 'vices which are more tolerable in a minister, provided that, on being warned, they do not prove incorrigible'. Thus simony, lewdness, drunkenness and fighting are more serious than a 'strange manner of teaching', frivolity, 'scurrility', 'meanness', susceptibility to flattery, or anger, to name some of the failings which, apparently, pastors might be vulnerable to. In short, the term 'police', which was sometimes used to designate the discipline, is illuminating. In accordance with the etymology of the term, the Church had to be set up on the pattern of the City.

Yet this judgement should be qualified: the Church was not coextensive with the body politic. Consisting of refugees, the members of a linguistic minority, the Stranger Church constituted a religious vanguard, or a 'little flock', to adopt the customary metaphor; being a society of saints, at least ideally so, its sense of democracy implied a restricted society. In short, the

[11] *Ecclesiastical Discipline of the French Protestant Church of London...*, London, 1915.

Churches of the Refuge were contractual associations, whose members had, more or less, chosen to be there and stick to the admission rules. One either 'joined in' or 'cut oneself off' from the community by scandalous behaviour. Admittedly, the consistories showed a certain flexibility in practice; very few people were officially cast out into the outer darkness, though many refugees left the community voluntarily. But ostracism remained a possibility:

> When some individuals have been expelled by the Magistrate's authority, on account of their disreputable conduct, or have withdrawn of their own accord, having led a scandalous life, it will be well for the Churches to warn one another, so that such persons do not find their way into other flocks, contaminating them and causing further scandals.

During the Restoration, the consistory of London was called upon to renounce democracy. They replied that the term was inappropriate, since their government was in fact aristocratic; this claim was partly true. This was, indeed, a form of democracy, though a democracy of the best. The 'people' were invoked on great occasions, in particular on the appointment of a pastor, to ratify the consistory's decisions. The manuscript version of the 1578 discipline is illuminating in this respect: the new pastor is 'firstly examined and approved by the ministers, elders and deacons, then nominated to the people, and finally he is accepted with the consent of the whole church, or *the greater and sounder part thereof*'. This concept of representation was subject to one practical restriction: the consistory had the last word. Thus, if the appointment of a minister remains unsettled, the 1641 version states clearly that 'the consistory will decide whether the objection shall be made quietly and whispered in the minister's ear, or else openly'. The consistory finally passes judgement 'according to the true interest and mutual edification of the Church'.

The refugee community was based on partnership. It rested upon prior consent and involved a conscious choice, sustained by specific rites of entry – the examination of credentials supplied by another Reformed Church, or the recantation of Roman Catholicism. In other words, individual membership rested on a voluntary decision. This alternative form of social life entailed clear-cut boundaries. Newly elected pastors had to take an oath to adhere to the constitution, promising to 'observe the Ecclesiastical Ordinances and the Discipline', in which no one could 'change anything or make any innovation on his own authority'. In a way, the social contract was a systematisation of the Calvinist form of society, its transposition from the one to the many.[12] The cooperative dimension of the Churches, which also characterised their financial

---

[12] M. Baridon, 'Lumières et enlightenment, faux parallèle ou vraie dynamique du mouvement philosophique?', *Dix-huitième siècle, Qu'est-ce que les Lumières?* 10 (1978), pp. 45–69: a remarkable essay on contractualism and its Protestant origins.

management, is lost to us if we do not bear in mind the prior (although often implicit) commitment of each member of the Church.

The art of prophesying

'Christian liberty', in John a Lasco's own words, led in fact to moral control. Some ordinary members of the community were not afraid, if need be, to confront the pastor or indeed the whole consistory. In matters of conscience, faith or conviction, how could one ever rely on majority rule? Between 1578 and 1641, a remarkable development occurred: the abolition of 'prophesying'. What are we to understand by this term? John a Lasco provides the following definition: 'prophesying...consists in examining well the mysteries of the Scriptures, to interpret them correctly'.[13]

John a Lasco's remark rests on a scriptural element, on a rhetorical approach, and last but not least on a definite vision of history. By mentioning prophesying along with the gift of tongues, John a Lasco clearly indicates his model, the apostolic Church founded simultaneously on the rise of Christ and on the expectation of his Second Coming.[14] Moreover, by associating prophesying with 'erudition', 'exhortation' and 'incitement', the reformer links it plainly to eloquence. Finally, the meaning of the term remains restrictive in John a Lasco's usage: no new revelation should be contemplated; 'the era of visions' is over, as Richard Stauffer has aptly put it in the case of Calvin.[15] Christian prophesying can only revert to a message already contained in the Bible, as God has fully revealed himself to man. More radical reformers, outside the pale of mainstream Calvinism, thought differently and admitted the possibility of continuous revelation. Yet in spite of a Lasco's moderation, prophesying constituted a potential danger. The 1578 discipline still mentions it, with the greatest of cautions:

> Whenever it shall please God to allow the use of prophesying, through the disclosure and agency of those to whom God has given the gift of interpreting the Scriptures, it will be meet to permit the practice of the same as it has been followed hitherto in the Church.
>
> None shall be allowed to speak in public save those who shall be deemed capable and competent to do so. The judgement of which shall rest with the ministers and elders of the Church.[16]

[13] John a Lasco, *Toute la forme et manière du ministère ecclésiastique en l'Eglise des étrangers dressée à Londres*, Emden, 1556, p. 10.

[14] P.-M. Beaude, *Jésus oublié. Les évangiles et nous*, Paris, 1977.

[15] R. Stauffer, *Dieu, la création et la Providence dans la prédication de Calvin*, Berne, 1978, p. 70.

[16] London, French Reformed church, MSS 297: 'Police et discipline ecclésiastique' (1578), fol. 9.

Even subject to this control, however, prophesying died out, undoubtedly on political grounds. In a letter of 7 May 1577, addressed to Grindal, archbishop of Canterbury, Elizabeth I irrevocably condemned 'disputations and new devised opinions upon points of divinity far and unmeet of unlearned people'. She went on: 'which manner of invasions they in some places call prophesying and in some other places exercises'. In short, such (un)inspired exercises could lead to schism and division, even within the family.[17]

The archbishop refused to yield and was suspended. This crisis could not fail to affect the Refuge: prophesying, although still mentioned in 1610, sank into oblivion. At the beginning of the eighteenth century, the prophets from Languedoc were to be viewed with obvious anxiety by the consistories. I shall mention these conflicts more fully in my conclusion; obviously, prophesying was a restricted phenomenon which came to be envisaged with growing suspicion as a sectarian challenge.

The Word and the Sword

The minister, by the exercise of his office, shall make the people obey God and the magistrate. The magistrate, by his authority, shall cause the people to observe and conform to the Word of God and the Ecclesiastical Discipline.[18]
Pastoral resolution, *c.* 1574

Religion and politics were constantly linked. The refugees' micro-society and the history of their English hosts clearly show that the forms of ecclesiastical organisation and the role assumed by the congregations exerted an influence on conceptions of the *body politic*. In early modern England, any view of the Church could not be altogether separated from a vision of society. However radical, this thesis should be envisaged more critically.

The investigator is subjected to an optical delusion. To a large extent, we are inclined to *overvalue* the distinctive features of past societies. The bonds of interest between religion and politics seem all the stronger to us as our century has tended to dissociate them, by atomising religious observance. Except for a few dispirited individuals, religion is a private matter for our Western contemporaries. Our modes of thought have undeniably become secularised. Some sociologists in an enquiry into 'Churches and religious groups in French society', came to the following conclusion: 'The general phenomenon of secularisation which has been proceeding in the West for several centuries has consequently created a rift between civil society and religious society. This rift has continued to

---

[17] G.R. Elton, *The Tudor Constitution*, Cambridge, 1960, and numerous later editions, p. 443.   [18] Schickler, *Les Eglises du Refuge en Angleterre*, III, p. 87.

deepen. The Churches have been pushed towards the periphery of social life, religion has become privatised.'[19]

However true, this sociological survey should not lead us to project unduly into the past an idealised image of Christian unanimity. In the sixteenth century the links between 'civil' and 'religious society' were already perceived as equivocal. In England anticlericalism was a constant phenomenon: the Laudian reaction which threatened the refugee communities in the 1630s would not otherwise be intelligible. The 'beauty of holiness', the Arminian emphasis on the sacraments, the role of the clergy were a response to the lay, Puritan challenge. All men were aware of the dialectic between Church and State.

As their faith was at the heart of their identity, the Protestant refugees afford one of the best illustrations of the links between religious and civil society. In fact, despite the avowed aim of moralising social life to the extreme, religion and politics did not entirely coincide. Theocracy – the complete fusion of civil and religious authority – was rejected all the more vigorously as it was identified with Anabaptism. How can one fail to note that it was precisely in the reign of Elizabeth that the foreign communities became fervent advocates of the separation of the civil from the religious orbs? It is not always easy to disentangle the motives which led the Churches to distance themselves from civil authority and accentuate their purely spiritual role precisely in the years between 1570 and 1580. Tactical considerations may not have been entirely absent.

During these years, two communities, Norwich and Canterbury, appointed a new body, which had not been initially envisaged: the 'hommes politiques' – politic men who were distinct from the elders of the consistory. Their function was to keep law and order: they took note of offences and misdemeanours and helped to settle disputes which arose among the alien population. One of their registers has been preserved in the case of Norwich, for 1605–15, but it is most difficult to handle as it is written in four languages, French, English, Latin and above all Dutch.[20]

This newfangled institution sprang from the open need to distinguish the spiritual role of the Churches from their social function. As early as 25 July 1576, the consistory register in Canterbury contains a revealing sentence: 'that the consistory would not interfere in matters of pure policy, in order not to confuse *Church matters* with *matters of police*, the administration of which is different'.

In July 1589, it was decided to follow the example of Norwich which had had its twelve 'politic men' since 1567: 'All the guilds have decreed with the consistory that a group of twelve politic men would be

[19] Université des sciences humaines, Strasbourg, *Eglises et groupes religieux dans la société française. Intégration ou marginalisation*, Strasburg, 1977, introduction by R. Mehl, pp. 9–10.   [20] BL Add. MSS 43862.

established to help the consistory to deal with several misconducts and disorders which it could do nothing to prevent'.

The 'politic men' and consistories worked closely together. In fact the 'politic men' provided the consistories with a 'secular arm'. When all admonishments had proved of no avail – which happened fairly regularly – the 'politic men' were called upon to deal with the malignants. If all settlements failed, the consistory turned to the *magistrate*, that key figure in the Calvinist City. The word *magistrate* did not only refer to law courts as in present-day usage. The magistrate was anyone endowed with temporal authority. Accordingly, the magistrate could either refer to the king or to any justice of the peace, in a distant shire. Originally, the use of a single term to describe all holders of civil power, whatever their rank, may have sounded impudent. The *Right of Magistrates*, published by Theodore Beza in 1573, clearly evinces the radical potentialities of the term.[21] Moreover, the magistrate was defined by a function – the administration of justice – rather than by an immutable, dynastic right to govern his subjects. He was a legislator.

One should interpret in this light the determination, clearly evinced by the Colloquy of refugee Churches, to define a distinct division of tasks between pastors and magistrates. Their resolution, dated from the same period – June 1582 – affords an excellent summary of the situation:

> Since a number of strangers take refuge here, and are received by the kindness of Her Majesty and of the Gentlemen of the Council on grounds of Religion – in spite of their impiety and dissolute life – some others – although they have been admitted into our Churches – nonetheless live in a disorderly manner scorning all warnings and censures from the Church – we decide that it will be expedient to refer such persons to the *magistrate*, so that those who cannot be governed by the ministry of the Church should be curbed by the authority of the said magistrate, whom God has ordained to this end.

This warning is remarkable in more respects than one. It infers the existence, on the fringe of the Churches, of a rather drifting population who did not submit to any ecclesiastical censure. It is difficult to deduce, from such a general reference, any well-defined religious profile, but one cannot altogether exclude the hypothesis that religious indifference partly accounted for this disaffection which was facilitated by the geographical uprooting of individuals. I would say indifference, and not atheism, nor even, necessarily, unbelief.[22] The foreigners who did not conform to any Church could well have been Catholics, in the case of the French, or even

---

[21] An admirable edition of this essential text is that by R.M. Kingdon, *Du Droit des Magistrats*, Geneva, 1971.

[22] G.E. Aylmer, 'Unbelief in Seventeenth-Century England', in *Puritans and Revolutionaries*, Oxford, 1978.

Jews for the Spanish or Portuguese communities. This possibility – that they professed a religion which was not authorised by law – remains plausible, but I would incline towards the first hypothesis: faith was not shared equally by all men.

The second interesting aspect of this text is the balance of powers which it suggests. Calvinist society rested on a theory of distinct authorities: the pastors and the magistrates remained separate. One can well imagine that this relative autonomy of ecclesiastical and civil government was subjected to constant revision, that the limits of their respective spheres were not entirely fixed. There remained the possibility of arbitration between the Word and the Sword, in the case of conflicting interests.

Church and society, in the refugees' view, were to a large degree *coextensive*.[23] Yet it would be mistaken to regard an era of Reformations and revolutions as the purely 'theological age' of nineteenth-century rationalism. Our evidence seems to contradict this positivist approach: with the possible exception of radical, fundamentalist sects, the Reformation implied a secularisation of society: even though they overlapped continually, politics and religion were distinct spheres. Yet, though pastors and magistrates were not confused – at least in mainstream Calvinism – what remained unsettled was their ascendancy: either the Church was the servant of the State, as in Erastian Anglicanism, or religion entailed the reform of society, as the godly insisted.

[23] C. Hill, *Economic Problems of the Church*, Oxford, 1956, p. 348.

8   Moral enforcement: the obligation of dignity

A social fact is to be recognised by its actual or potential power of external coercion over individuals, and the presence of this power may be recognised in turn either by the existence of some specific sanction or by the resistance offered against every individual effort that tends to violate it.[1]

Emile Durkheim

The 'genesis of a Protestant society' highlights the particular interest presented by Calvinist consistory registers from the sixteenth century onwards.[2] Meeting regularly as they did once or twice a week, the consistories have left us a very accurate picture of the refugees' everyday life. Their role was far from passive: the consistories were not content to reflect the events around them, but they intervened at every stage. They constituted the most influential of protagonists in the Churches' ascendancy over public life. An American specialist in the history of crime also pointed out that consistories illustrated 'the considerable importance of infra-judicial agreements' in early modern societies and 'the existence of an astonishing number of amicable settlements reached before legal proceedings were taken'.[3] Indeed, we have already emphasised how formal prosecution before a magistrate served as a last resort when all 'admonishments' had failed. Last but not least, Pierre Chaunu has also surmised that the 'Protestant Reformations' involved a great degree of acculturation.[4] The question of acculturation, which was raised originally

---

[1] Emile Durkheim, *Les règles de la méthode sociologique*, 9th edn, Paris, 1938, p. 15; English translation: *The Rules of Sociological Method*, Chicago, 1938.

[2] J. Estèbe and B. Vogler, 'Protestants languedociens et palatins vers 1600', *Annales ESC*, 31 (1976), pp. 362–88.

[3] Alfred Soman, in collaboration with E. Labrousse, 'Le registre consistorial de Coutras 1582–1584', *Bulletin de la Société de l'Histoire du Protestantisme Français* (1980) pp. 193–228. This quotation is taken from p. 194.

[4] P. Chaunu, *Le Temps des Réformes*, Paris, 1975, p. 295.

by social anthropologists,[5] takes on its full significance in the study of past social life, and particularly in the case of religious history.

The French or Walloon Protestants belonged to a minority in terms of language, culture and geographical origin, but also on account of their religion. The implantation of Calvinism in sixteenth-century England had not resulted in a single Protestant Church: the Refuge remained a separate element retaining its own specific identity. This did not prevent fraternisation with the English – but even though these contacts were fruitful, on both sides, an astonishing difference of sensibility persisted. The consistories, far more than the pastors as such, acted as natural trustees, defending the religious and cultural identity of the minority. The feeling of *otherness*, albeit mitigated by familiarity with the surrounding population, was a way of asserting oneself. There is, indeed, as one writer put it, some 'pride in being different – a difference accepted as a victory'.[6] Of course, this competition did not take on the same character as in Catholic countries like France; confrontation was less open, but nonetheless remained a constant. This implied a great deal of circumspection both in relation to English society and to the refugees. This fundamental preoccupation did not, however, relate only to questions of doctrine; it extended to the whole of collective life, and was often concerned even with attitudes. Thus in London, on 18 February 1690, it was made clear that entertainments, meals and other sources of merriment, might 'scandalise the English nation which it is so much in our interests not to offend, and cause our nation to be held in poor esteem by them, which could lessen their compassion towards our poor refugee brethren and stem the flow of their charity and alms'.

Arbitration within the community

Relations between individuals were undoubtedly marked by great harshness, at least according to present-day standards. Admittedly, I cannot attempt to quantify the everyday violence which ran through the life of the community. Brawls and scuffles of various kinds were common currency among the refugees. Brutality, rage, irascibility were everpresent.

This negative image needs, however, to be mitigated; the vigour of men's confrontation was counterbalanced by the moral authority of the consistories, which were called upon to decide on petty bickerings or more serious offences. The administration of justice ensured, more or less, the preservation of order, with an emphasis on reconciliation. The available sanctions were limited. Paul Testelet, who was suspected of having beaten

---

[5] M. Herskovits, *Acculturation, the Study of Culture Contact*, New York, 1938, ch. 5.

[6] J. Garrison-Estèbe, *L'Homme protestant*, Paris, 1980, p. 8.

his journeyman to death, was simply suspended from the Lord's Supper, on 17 June 1564 in London. He left us the following account:

> [*For having spoilt six ounces of silk*] *I gave him two or three blows with a little stick, one of which fell on his head, and caused him to bleed a little.* The latter was healed after three days, thanks to a little urine which was put on his wound. Then, his wife having died of the plague a short time before, the said servant happened to catch the plague, which he died of. As he was in his grave, hearing that he was said to have died from this blow with a stick, the English vicar and the neighbours had him disinterred twice and examined.

Manslaughter remained extremely rare though, whereas wound and swollen heads were rife. They often followed insults, attacks on honour and reputation, or the promptings of vanity. One reads between the lines when in Norwich, on 6 May 1628, Philippe Longuesnée is 'reprimanded for several foul and infamous remarks, casting discredit on the wives of other men'. Sexual insults, despite their rich and varied repertory, revolved in fact around a limited number of situations, and marital honour was the foremost target.

In London, on 10 October 1571, 'having gone to the tennis-court on the Monday after the Lord's Supper', Thomas Grain and Bocquet came to blows, as a result of doubt being cast on the virtue of mistress Bocquet, while in 1577, Godefroy, a native of Rouen, reached for his sword to strike Nicolas, who had 'insulted him and called him a pimp'.

Some rather hot-blooded individuals seem even to have involved in fights for their own sake, without any clearly stated pretext, such as the Nicolas Lance from Norwich, who took a malicious pleasure in drubbing Englishmen in the 1630s. These physical exchanges could take surprising forms; in the same city on 14 March 1629, Pierre Bouteleu had to admit to 'having bitten Daniel Durieu on the ear'.

Fortunately, in more cases than one, the trouble soon blew over, and the consistories managed to reconcile the divided 'brethren' readily, at least until a new dispute arose. On 8 October 1635 Isaac Casé was summoned in Norwich, as he 'boasted that he enjoyed the favours of the good women of this Church'. He quickly admitted that he had said more than he meant to say, and declared that he 'repented of it'.

Besides, the elders were often insulted and vilified by the offenders in their enforcement of law and order. Nicolas Descolle, of Norwich, appeared before the consistory of 3 July 1634, for having declared that 'the elders performing their functions...are to be compared to little dogs that go about stirring up bigger dogs'.

Arbitration from without

> It will never be deemed reasonable, either by law or by example, that
> strangers should share the same privileges and rights as citizens. Sound
> fellowship commands us to do good to all men, but especially to our
> own. In this point we could do well with a little of the *English mood.*[7]
> Antoine de Montchrestien

This praise of English liberty, written by a Huguenot in 1615, emphasises
in particular the judicious use of aliens in the economic rivalry between
States. From the sixteenth century onwards, England undoubtedly
managed to turn Protestant immigration to her advantage. On the whole,
the alien master craftsmen or journeymen, who had settled in that land of
refuge, were inclined to stay permanently.

We need not review here the role which the consistories played in the
refugee communities' relations with the Crown, the bishops, or the
Corporations. I shall concentrate rather on labour conflicts; though
common at all times, petty quarrels and confrontations tended to follow
economic fluctuations. Now, as ever, distrust of foreigners is greater at
times of crisis than in periods of prosperity. The depression of the 1620s
was a case in point: a series of petitions from the London guilds came
before the Crown. They expressed various grievances: illicit exportation
of bullions, unfair competition, overabundant demography – the aliens
had too many children. Goldsmiths and watchmakers took up the refrain,
casting discredit on the quality of the foreigners' work; in the workshops
of Daniel Tibergen and Pierre Cozie (Cousin?) adulterated dystuffs had
been used.[8] From time to time, the refugees became the object of growing
popular suspicion; if their numbers grew abruptly, or when an economic
slump occurred, the blame was laid at their door. In such circumstances,
Protestant unanimity was of little help; from 1675 to 1680 onwards, when
Huguenot immigration gathered momentum, the different London guilds
expressed their disquiet: fishmongers, tailors, barbers, surgeons, dyers,
carpenters complained about the French influx. These episodes of unrest,
these outbursts of discontent, need, however, to be set in perspective (see
Ch. 6, Table 2).

Generally, the refugees' skills and thrift were highly commended. Their
utility and prosperity were also a blessing for the English who benefited
from the employment they sustained: the Churches thrived thanks to this
reputation, though they were not economic agents as such. In July 1638
the consistory of London defended the establishment of these refugee
craftsmen in England:

> In the year 1574, the growing persecution in Flanders and in France
> having forced a greater number of strangers than previously to come to

[7] Antoine de Montchrestien, *Traicté de l'Oeconomie Politique* (1615), Paris, 1889.
[8] SP Dom., James I, CXXVII, 114, 20.

London, and among them many silk-workers, and various other craftsmen, Queen Elizabeth, on the advice of her council, ordered that they should choose such towns in her kingdom as they though best, to practise their religion, discipline and manufactures, forbidding all persons to give them hindrance, notwithstanding any laws to the contrary.

Thus the aliens' establishments, the consistory went on, 'depended only on the king'. This formulation sounds inappropriate – in the case of Norwich (Ch. 2), we have seen the selective regulations which hindered their activity. Yet from the sixteenth century onwards, there was constant praise for the techniques of weaving and other arts and mysteries which they implanted, or at least which they helped to develop, in England: damask, satin, silk, serge. One can consult the glossary of technical terms recently compiled by A. Lottin.[9] The process involved in textile production undoubtedly formed the main sector of the refugees' economic activity: between a third and a half of the active population were weavers, corders, wool-combers, dyers. This was probably the case in Norwich or Canterbury, though we have no statistics. In the later Refuge, the contrasts became more marked: in Spitalfields, 54 per cent of the congregation of La Patente were directly dependent on spinning or related activities at the end of the seventeenth century – in accordance with the district's avocation. On the other hand, in the parishes of Westminster, there was a greater diversity of occupations: apothecaries, doctors, surgeons, jewellers, tailors, hatmakers and wigmakers served a varied clientèle, and undoubtedly imported the French fashions which appealed to aristocratic taste. But to the north of Westminster, the predominant activity was again textiles, centred on silk, that most desirable of commodities.

This immigration was marked by three essential characteristics. In the first place, the refugees were, on the whole, a highly qualified workforce. The Huguenots, like the Walloons before them, were not the under-privileged auxiliaries of English economic development, and they thereby aroused constant jealousy. But it is better to inspire envy than pity, and these aliens were appreciated for the skills which they brought with them. A linguistic observation helps to explain the fact: in accordance with medieval usage, sixteenth-century English made use of several terms to designate crafts and trades; 'art' and 'mystery' recur incessantly. The word 'mystery' conveys perfectly the premium of oral transmission. The refugees were able to benefit from this advantage; they held – and sometimes guarded jealously – techniques which others envied them. This applied to many fields; thus, on 6 March 1560, a revealing anecdote came before the London consistory:

---

[9] A. Lottin, 'Lexique Etoffes', in *Chavatte, ouvrier lillois*, Paris, 1979, pp. 382ff.

> On the sixth day of March *anno* 1560, in the consistory which was held after the sermon, Robert Laloé, Jean Pitéot and a young man, the brother of the said Pitéot, appeared in order to complain that the said young Pitéot, having learnt their trade of making moulds for buttons with his brother, did not want to work with his brother nor with those of his own nation, but was going off to work for an Englishman and teach them the trade, which, they say, will be the cause of great scandal and disorder.

The transient character of skill, the extreme importance attached to secrecy, explain the considerable role played by human migration in the transference of techniques and the acquisition of crafts. Mobility was for an artisan the best way to complete his training: conversely, the English had the highest expectations of the aliens whom they permitted to settle on their soil. The instrumental value of the human factor explains that in the fellow-Protestant who sought refuge, the English also saw an economic auxiliary. The consistories were aware of their public utility for the common weal, which was reinforced by prevailing mercantilist theories, and they were to use this argument to the full.

Scandal, from moral norm to social observation

Woe to that man by whom the offence cometh!
Matthew, 18:7

Of all topics, that of 'public offence' or 'scandal' is the most widespread and the most significant in the life of the Refuge. When a scandal occurred, its author would be summoned before the consistory. The procedure was identical in the majority of cases: the culprit was called upon to mend his ways, there followed his reparation for the past offence. This atonement was given a greater or lesser degree of publicity depending on the seriousness of the misdeed. Alternatively, suspension from the Lord's Supper, excommunication or denunciation to the magistrate should have been sufficient to overcome any resistance.

Let us take a case at random; on 26 November 1595, in Canterbury: 'Simon Bebarel was censured for being found in bed with his sister-in-law during her illness. He made it known that it was for his own rest and for the relief of his wife. Promised, since people were drawing conclusions from it, that he would refrain from doing so.'

Or again, in Norwich, on 31 March 1631: 'Pierre Dauvin and Jeanne Lance appeared, admitting their offence of carnal association with *scandal*. Declare their regret, and wholehearted repentance, being agreed that it should be made public from the pulpit, at the discretion of the consistory, to *remove the scandal* it has caused.'

The offence, besides, might be a collective one. In London, on 23 July

1684, several refugees admitted: 'there are several members of this church who persevere in their excesses and dissolute conduct, spending days and nights in the taverns'. What follows is revealing; this behaviour proved detrimental to the 'refugees' and tarnished the reputation of the 'persecuted', thus 'scandalising' the English. Hence a firm resolution was passed:

> The company, in order to prevent so great an evil, and to avert the grievous consequences which might ensue, exhorts accordingly all the members of the Church, of whatever condition to renounce their licentiousness, and to put aside *the bad customs which they might have adopted among those of the Roman Communion*, and to cease to profane the Lord's Day by their amusement and wantonness.

Apparently, the festive animation of the tavern induced to 'gambling and swearing' while men 'being carried away by dancing and profane songs' made all the 'commotion' which is the likely outcome of revelling and carousing.

This last example illustrates the weight of stereotypes, which clearly limit the value of the consistory registers as a reliable source to reconstitute the actual mores of the past. Moral deviation was perceived through a preexisting code: lewdness, drunkenness, gambling violence, Church/ tavern. Should one, then, attempt to quantify the various offences, examining their fluctuations, in order to determine whether the flesh was a greater source of trouble in London in 1580 than alcoholism in Norwich in 1640? I have not pursued this possibility for want of conclusive results, but this sort of investigation can be fruitful on a very large scale. Professor Janine Garrisson has recently examined in this light the consistory registers of about thirty parishes in the south and south-west of France, comparing the list of transgressions with the injunctions of the provincial and national synods. She came to some interesting conclusions which a study of the English Refuge would certainly confirm: insults (33 per cent of all cases) were the most common trespass, followed by gaming (11 per cent), dancing (8.5 per cent) and violent misdemeanour (7 per cent). Sexual misconduct only obtained 12 per cent of the total, though the figure would certainly be much higher if we added domestic and family strife (7 and 2 per cent).[10] But moral control was not the sole value of the consistory registers, even though they contained a number of cases which could be regarded as so many precedents to judge an offence. Indeed, by its recording of successive periods, the consistory register gave the refugees a sense of belonging. Growing in an organic way, along with the community, it constituted a permanent reference, binding future gener-

---

[10] J. Garrisson, *Les Protestants au XVIe siècle*, Paris, 1988, p. 72.

ations. In 1712, the most important judgements were reviewed, one by one
in London, in a systematic catalogue.[11] The repetitive nature of the
accusations is thus an indication of coherence; and, in fact, the sense of
continuity and permanence clearly prevailed. The major part of the
consistories' activity was directed towards everyday life – hence the
historical interest of their registers which record the most trivial
occurrences, and often convey, in all its vividness, the speech of these men
who lived and died three centuries ago. Without wishing to concentrate
unduly on the picturesque, I shall certainly quote for the reader a few
examples of this vigour and raciness of expression, which come down to
us with the same immediacy now as then. Permanence and continuity,
however, do not imply immobility. While outward attitudes continued to
be governed by persisting features grounded in common experience, the
same did not apply to men's view of the world. Indeed, the consistory was
also the guarantor of an orthodoxy. And, during this century and a half,
from 1550 to 1700, opinions shifted considerably. We have several
indications of this; the governance of the congregation's morals,
undertaken by the consistories of the various churches, did not concern
behaviour or social ethics alone – it involved a constant reappraisal of the
Christian faith. Resistance – readily interpreted as heresy – was frequent.
The forms it took reflected in turn the great controversies which shook the
Protestant world and its learned circles; the question of the Trinity in the
sixteenth century, which gave rise to fears of contagion from the ideas of
Servetus, the debates concerning predestination in the seventeenth
century, which bore witness to the influence of Amyraut, or the
Socinianism of the 1690s. These theological disputes, which are well
known to specialists, affected some of the refugees; I shall simply point
out the connection, without dwelling on it.

Concerning heresy – and the world picture which it sustained – I should
like to make one preliminary remark. The consistories did not so much
pursue heresy, as the heretic who spread his ideas, not so much misguided
conscience, as scandal. One could almost say that the individual member
of the Refugee Churches had the right to persist in his error, provided he
did not contaminate others. Though often uncompromising, the consistory was never inquisitorial.

In addition, the concept of error, along with that of truth, underwent
a drastic change; while often scriptural in character in the sixteenth
century, heresy and dogmatics moved, a century later, into the realm of
rationality. Spiritual reference became a hymn to reason. In the earlier
period, enthusiasts of all kinds – 'fantastical' persons, according to
Calvin – allegedly entertained relations with the devil; finally after 1660,

---

[11] French Reformed Church, MSS 295.

the suspected enthusiasts, and then the prophets from Languedoc, were regarded as 'fanatical', and no longer as 'possessed'.

One no longer finds any trace, after, say, *c*. 1600, of the demonology which flourished in the sixteenth century, and had been taken for granted by Jean Bodin and James VI of Scotland. Though, as Robert Mandrou taught us, a compendium of witchcraft survived well into the seventeenth century,[12] among the refugees I can see no trace of its persistence. Error was increasingly categorised as a kind of contagion, or indeed plague. This drift towards pathology has already been pointed out, in the case of Arminianism, about 1620 (see Ch. 3).

In the reign of Elizabeth I, on the other hand, reference to the devil remained a common feature. Thus Philippe Le Roy, on 5 September 1571, in London 'says that he has given his soul to the devil'. In fact, he was essentially charged with holding materialistic views which struck at the very foundations of Christian revelations, discarding in advance any reference to the Bible, that focal concern of Protestantism, since 'the Word of God is not the word of God, but that of men'. Neither the remission of sins nor the resurrection of the body found favour in his eyes. As to Denis de Boningham, who was accused of 'lewd conduct', he answered, in exasperation, on 6 October of the same year, that if that were true, he would give himself 'to the devil, or to all the million devils'.

Yet unbelief was not the sole cause of doctrinal concern. Conversely, a highly developed Christocentric piety could give rise in turn to a sense of personal prophetic revelation. The deacon Jean Gérard inundated the Refuge with his own writings, to which, according to him, 'one should give credence as entire as is given to those of Moses, Elisha, Jesus Christ and the apostles'. On 1 August 1594, he was asked if 'it is not the spirit of Satan which is guiding him'. Reconstructing a whole theodicy preceding even the Creation, he came to maintain that 'the Son does not originate in the Father, in so far as he is a Son'. Having been reported to the magistrate, Jean Gérard had to sign a written recantation, and abandon his 'imaginary personal revelations, by means of which Satan led him to believe that God was speaking in his ear' (see Document 2).

Gasparo and the magic spells

A deep-seated transformation of systems of belief took place in the early modern era. It concerned the relationship between magic, science and religion. Indeed, the secularisation of knowledge, and 'departmen-talisation' of thought,[13] have too often been interpreted as a linear

---

[12] R. Mandrou, *Possession et sorcellerie au XVIIe siècle*, Paris, 1979.
[13] C. Hill, *Economic Problems of the Church*, Oxford, 1956, p. 348.

process, attending the scientific revolution. Yet, as Christopher Hill
pointed out, the English evolution was much more complex as 'all ideas
tended to be religious ideas, even those which challenged the clerical
monopoly and its system of thought'.[14] Owing to our positivism which
tends to treat religious phenomena with a Voltairian sneer, we in France
have a great deal to learn from English historians. In particular, the
opposition between reason and faith proves largely inadequate to
understand the scientific let alone the political revolutions of the
seventeenth century. The English situation was much more complex, and
challenges this interpretation. In fact, secularisation was at least a three-
tier process, involving magic, scientific or technical achievements *and*
religion. Keith Thomas has admirably expressed the link between
'religion' and the 'decline of magic', which heralded rather than followed
the scientific revolution:

> We are, therefore, forced to the conclusion that men emancipated
> themselves from these magical beliefs without necessarily having devised
> any effective technology with which to replace them. In the seventeenth
> century they were able to take this step because magic was ceasing to be
> intellectually acceptable, and because their religion taught them to try
> self-help before invoking supernatural aid. But the ultimate origins of this
> faith in unaided human capacity remain mysterious.[15]

Though the resilience of popular culture *cum* belief in wonders was
certainly stronger in Catholic countries, Professor Jean Delumeau has
come to similar conclusions recently, discarding the plain dichotomy of
reason vs. paganism.[16] The Christian faith, in its Calvinist or Puritan
expression, certainly wrought a genuine cultural revolution, which
embarked on the secularisation of the world. The dissociation between
God and second causes, which was so effective in Bacon's philosophy,
belongs to a general trend of thought emphasising a new code of action.
As an illustration, I shall cite the revealing story of the Italian Gasparo di
Gatti, a dyer by trade, whose insistence on consulting with a sorceress
brought him some celebrity. In 1574, the Foreign Churches of London
were called upon to pronounce jointly on his fate. His story is as follows.[17]
He possessed 'a dyeing caldron which was very fine to look at, but
thoroughly bad in fact'. For, 'wanting to dye some silk, he found that it
was of no use, which greatly astonished him, and trying once again to dye
some cloth, he still found that the same dye had no effect'. How could the
spell be removed? A certain Giacometti, a Rochester glassmaker by trade,
knew a woman who 'disenchants things that have been enchanted'. When

[14] *Ibid.*
[15] K. Thomas, *Religion and the Decline of Magic* (1971), Penguin, 1973, p. 794.
[16] J. Delumeau, *Rassurer et protéger*, Paris, 1989, p. 190.
[17] Guildhall Library, MSS 7413, fols. 15ff.

taken to task by one of the elders, who reviled his unchristian attitudes, Gasparo went into a violent rage, and became 'obstinate and obdurate', in spite of the mildness with which he was treated. In his defence, he cited other examples in which the intervention of the witch had been equally beneficial, recalling Giacometti's case, or that of the baker who had put his bread into a hot oven only to find it uncooked when he took it out. Besides, she could not be a witch, since her intercession was beneficial; she was a 'good woman', who had rid his cauldron of 'the Evil Spirit'. In short, she 'does what she does publicly according to God and Christ'. He was told that she was acting at 'the instigation of the devil', but he would not listen to reason. He was accordingly suspended from the Lord's Supper.

The story is typical. It demonstrates, together with other indications, the persistence of magical beliefs among the refugees, at least in the sixteenth century. It was still quite common in London in the years between 1560 and 1570 for God's chosen people to consult soothsayers and disenchanters, to the great displeasure of the consistory or Coetus. It also proved necessary to combat the influence of almanacs and their claim that 'all things, both general and particular, are revealed in dreams', or else that 'dreams are signs and tokens of the Word' (London, 19 January 1576).

Though all indications are elusive, I should yet be tempted to think that the refugees were on the whole much less gullible than the surrounding population in the seventeenth century. Magical healing or astrology, to which many Englishmen still clung at the time, had met the sharp rebuke of Calvin. Moreover, the consistories exercised a tighter control over the strangers than did the English parishes over their flocks. But this does not mean that all irrational practices had disappeared. A certain propensity to read, or open the Book at random to decipher past prophecies, especially during the Civil War, may be interpreted as the same genuine need to find solace and comfort as superstition. Jean de La Marche or Poujade (see Ch. 5) still relied on analogy as a way to truth, while Jurieu, in the 1680s, encountered Pierre Bayle's sarcasm for his predictions.

These episodes suggest a threefold observation. On the one hand, manifestations of the supernatural, apart from those recorded in the Bible, were discarded, or even considered as the works of the devil rather than God. At bottom, Huguenot arrogance and disdain, their desacralisation of the world, their scepticism concerning spells and bewitchments, did not spring from unbelief but from faith. The rejection of witchcraft and sorcery hinges on a common refusal of all intercessors. It was pointed out to Gasparo that 'all those who profess to pray and fast for others, and for many, without their having, or being able to have, any public vocation in the Church, cannot and must not be approved, nor considered to be

Christian persons'. Thus the same accusation was levelled both at witchcraft and at the Catholic priesthood: simony, trafficking in metaphysical powers, arrogance and superfluousness. Accordingly, cases of magic appeared in the sixteenth century, precisely at the moment when the remaining traces of 'Roman idolatry' were forcefully eradicated. Catholicism was often inveighed against as paganism by the same men. But moreover – and this is my third point – this religious imperative involved a cultural strategy: there was to be no separation between the piety of the common people and that of the elite. In this perspective, there could not be a popular religion and an enlightened one – as Gasparo discovered to his cost. The minority community thus launched a real strategy of acculturation towards its members; the consistories served as the most effective of instruments for this conquest. Immemorial codes of behaviour, supernatural phenomena, sexual promiscuity and innocuous sources of merriment such as dancing were all brought under rigorous scrutiny, with varying degrees of success. The consistory registers lend themselves readily to different interpretations: is one to conclude from the sheer number of investigations which the consistory unremittingly pursued that the micro-society of the refugees, subjected to a close control of its beliefs and behaviour, witnessed the emergence of a new man? Conversely, could we not infer from this survey that the authority of the consistories was imposed only with difficulty? Demonstrations of strength, indeed, are often tantamount to an admission of weakness. I shall suggest, accordingly, a qualified conclusion: the attempt to institute a uniformed moral law was never completely successful; it often involved a dialectic of cultural confrontation, between submission and disobedience, prescription and proscription, consensus and division.

From the relief of the poor to economic solidarity

> Those who become bankrupt shall be exhorted, once they have come to a composition, to make every effort to satisfy their creditors, and to promise in front of the assembled company to acquit themselves of their debts as much they shall be able to.
> London, 31 December 1690

The control of public morals extended to the financial sphere. Solvency was the counterpart, in the economic order, of social respectability; the fear of 'scandal' was at the root of the rigorous, day-to-day supervision of finances. If one leaves aside exceptional levies, collections for refugees or miscellaneous contributions,[18] the regular resources of each Church were subject to a judicious distinction between 'necessity' spendings –

---

[18] French Reformed Church, MSS 62.

bourse des nécessités – and the poor funds – *bourse des pauvres*. In the case of London, the budget for regular expenditure was entrusted to the elders – support of the pastor, maintenance of the temple, etc. – and remained clearly distinct from the sums allocated to the poor, which were administered by the deacons.

The fund for 'necessities' follows the rules of double-entry accountancy: from 1650 onwards,[19] the ledger was kept carefully, revealing an excellent balance of income and expenditure. Apparently, neither deficits nor surpluses impaired this sound management; assets and liabilities were exactly matched. This strict coincidence indicates constant appeals to the community to cover momentary needs. This budget underwent considerable fluctuations from £337 in 1651, it rose up to £1,203 in 1694. As expected, between those two figures lay a constant progression.

The functional division between 'necessities' and poor-chest was occasioned by the scale of the tasks to be undertaken, but it also served to provide additional guarantees of honesty and fair-dealing, and to cut short any suggestions of mismanagement. The carefully checked and audited accounts of each company would undoubtedly deserve more systematic analysis, extending beyond the period considered here, and taking the eighteenth century as a reference.

Before 1650, indeed, any attempt at reconstruction is haphazard. We could yet assume that gradually an autonomous financial function emerged from the budget for the relief of the poor. Caring for the most destitute led in the long run to more complex monetary operations. The most elementary form of charity consisted in gifts in kind, that survival of barter in a mercantile society. For instance, in order to relieve pressing hardship at the onset of winter, warm clothings were distributed – as recorded in the 'List of garments' kept from 1666 onwards.[20] But mutual help soon replaced this basic charity: increasingly, the Churches took on an economic role akin to that played by banks. The aptly named 'Capital books'[21] enable us, from 1648 onwards, to see the complexity of the operations undertaken by the deacons.

Loans with interest, commonly around 6 per cent, undoubtedly facilitated the establishment of the refugees. But, as well as providing credit, the deacons commonly acted as trustees for orphans and widows. This evolution led, in the eighteenth century, to straightforward investment, such as the purchase, in 1720, of shares in the ill-fated South Sea Company.

The same dexterity in the handling of money was shown by the elders who conducted similar operations – which were recorded from 1669 onwards in the 'Notes of the City District'.[22] The sums involved could be

---

[19] *Ibid.*, MSS 90.   [20] *Ibid.*, MSS 73, 74, 75.   [21] *Ibid.*, MSS 258, 129, 35.
[22] *Ibid.*, MSS 94.

substantial; around 1680, Stéphane Beaumont left £1,400 to his nephew Stéphane Allemand. The interest of 4 per cent was paid out for the child's education.[23]

It would be mistaken, however, to assume that profit was the sole motive. The administration of the consistory or deacons was governed by social imperatives. Charity, in the strictly distributive sense of the term, was reserved for hopeless cases. It was thought better, in general, to help those who helped themselves, by granting them facilities to set up independently. The provision of apprenticeships met these criteria. In February 1674, the deacons of Canterbury paid £9 for James Laman to take on Jeanne de Lescluse, on the understanding that he would teach her weaving and keep an eye on the girl's morals, who was to indulge neither in 'fornication' nor 'marriage', nor was she supposed to 'play cards' or go to 'taverns'[24] (see Document 4).

Herbert Lüthy has brought out the implications of this work ethic: 'With largely unforeseen consequences Calvinist morality involved the necessity to tackle the paramount issue of pauperism not through plain charity, but through work discipline, social organisation, apprenticeship and education in general.'[25]

Face to face civilisation[26]

A young *Englishman* was questioned concerning Gilles Desportes and declared that about last Christmas (a year ago) he saw the said Desportes, around ten or eleven at night, with a sailor's wife and a boy walking with a lantern, going into the said Desporte's dwelling; and when the boy had gone, they closed the door, and both undressed, and blew out the candle... And, the better to see the proceedings, the said young Englishman put two stools one upon the other. Has nothing else to relate, and is willing to stand by what he has declared upon oath.
London, 12 April 1607

Said that he lived for quite some time at an inn called the 'Ville de Bordeaux' situated, opposite the house of M. Granisset – who lived on Finch Lane and that from there, he had seen M. Granisset put his hands on the breasts and under the skirt of a girl of about sixteen, and that a *Papist* cook who served in the said inn had seen this as he did.
London, 7 June 1691

The gaze of observers or intruders was always to be felt, interfering and insinuating itself, disclosing and reporting: the eyes of kith and kin, of neighbours and presbyters. And finally, the scrutiny of strangers to the

---

[23] *Ibid.*, Misc. MSS 18.   [24] Dean and Chapter Library, MSS U-47-H 4, fol. 10.
[25] H. Lüthy, *La Banque protestante en France, de la révocation de l'Edit de Nantes à la Révolution*, Paris 1959, p. 7.
[26] J. Delumeau, *La Peur en Occident, XIV–XVIIIe siècles*, Paris, 1978, p. 52.

community, Englishmen or else Catholics, prepared to watch for the slightest misdemeanour. The testimony of others aggravated every failing – as in the two cases cited above – and caused further scandal, divulging in a crude light trifling or ludicrous details. This lack of privacy has been brought out forcefully by Philippe Ariès in one of his pioneering studies.[27] This was not a peculiar feature of Protestant societies; rather, Calvinism systematised under the name of 'scandal' this constant exchange and interplay between the household and the street, the individual and the crowd.

Public and private space continually overlapped. This openness sets the inquisitiveness of the consistories in its historical context. The sixteenth century did not share our modern sense of domestic independence, and the 'indecency' of many examinations conducted by the presbyters, their prolixity and lack of propriety when discussing private behaviour, were in keeping with the publicity which surrounded every family event. The boundaries of the household were not as yet sharply defined, and the privacy which was to become so sacred to the English was slow to establish itself. It presupposed the emergence of a new type of family, centred on 'affective individualism'.[28]

Without attempting to set any precise date, a blatant shift of emphasis occurs in the consistory registers after 1650. A new tone appears. While private attitudes might still be mentioned, or the life of couples sanctioned, the consistories' observations become on the whole less obtrusive. The pastors and elders were less inclined to expatiate; their comments tended increasingly to envisage general applications behind individual cases. In short, the idea that 'one should not wash one's dirty linen in public' was gaining ground.

The consistories participated in the 'birth of the modern family'.[29] If one assumes that the closing off of the family, its new-found impermeability to outside scrutiny, presupposed a new distribution of domestic space, one cannot fail to emphasise the constant attempts to suppress *promiscuity* and enforce sexual morality. The arrangements of the home, the specialisation of the different rooms, the seclusion of the master's bedroom from that of his servants or children, the disapproval of nudity and 'villainous and immodest' physical contacts: these are some of the major themes of the campaign undertaken by sixteenth-century consistories.

On 10 July 1561, the head of a family, Jean Mékynon, was summoned before the consistory in London. His servant, Paul Beauvais, 'is too familiar with his mistress', whom he had been kissing conspicuously.

---

[27] P. Ariès, *L'Enfant et la vie familiale sous l'Ancien Régime*, Paris, 1973, p. 460.
[28] L. Stone, *The Family, Sex and Marriage*, London, 1977.
[29] E. Shorter, *Naissance de la famille moderne* (1975), Paris, 1977.

Moreover, he had been found in his master's bedroom 'in his shirt, at six o'clock in the morning', ostensibly looking for his breeches. Tolerant husband that he was, Jean Mékynon refused to take offence, apparently accepting that youth must have its fling. He was advised or rather entreated to show greater firmness in the name of the manly 'honour' so important to the rest of masculine society. On 22 June 1564, a sharp rebuke was administered to Maline Toutvaille and Nicolas Lance, who, having sworn undying love to one another, had spent a fortnight tasting the delights of the connubial state. They had gone so far as to share their bed 'for two nights' with an English friend, William Cavin, who was passing through. Maline's protestations of innocence did not prevent a severe reprimand. Likewise, the consistory categorically forbade, on 6 January 1575, the liberties which were commonly taken when washing together, especially when doing so in a group. Thus, several young people of both sexes, taking a bath together, evidently indulged in rather ribald playfulness, in which 'there was no decency, but only villainous baseness'.

A certain suspicion also attached to widows, who were suspected of contributing to the amorous education of the young, either by their attentions, or by harbouring secret love-affairs. The most remarkable fact, in my view, is the tolerance shown by some of the adults, who quite plainly provided young people with opportunities to see one another, to meet regularly, or to live together, sometimes for several days. It would be mistaken to see marriage purely as a matter of convenience or as a domestic association, arranged in advance by families. Examples of such marriages can be found, but other kinds of union remained possible. We might even surmise that in more cases than one, the celebration of wedlock followed, rather than preceded, physical relations. A simple exchange of mutual consent, without any witnesses, and the couple felt united for life. Official marriage intervened only at a later stage, to regularise the situation. At least this was common practice in the sixteenth century, if we are to believe the consistories' strenuous efforts to rule out cohabitation. On 14 November 1564, a warning was issued in London to 'those who hold all their affairs in common and think that in the eyes of God they are married'. There was a tendency to admit without any restriction unions which were sanctified by custom and neighbours' acceptance. But this concern to establish moral standards in the home amid countless innuendoes, rested on the fundamental fear of incest. Though rare in the extreme, some cases were heard in the consistories.

The reorganisation of space was by no means confined to the household, which no longer called for such pungent commentaries from the consistories after 1600. The campaign against promiscuity, in particular in the bedchamber, had no doubt borne its first fruits. In the seventeenth century, these regulations were directed away from the home and towards the outside world. The tavern had always appeared as a den of iniquity, which gave rise to every kind of debauchery and presented unfair competition to the Sunday sermon, especially in the afternoon.[30] The growth of Puritanism revived these long-standing reservations. Sunday, which in the meantime had become the Sabbath, called for increasingly rigorous observance, thus acquiring its legendary solemnity. The 'English Sunday', in its rather stiff dignity, was an invention of the seventeenth century although it was only imposed with some difficulty. In the 1680s, in the final stage of this development, the moral reform of space was extended to the street, which until recently had been given over to endless games, social gatherings, gossips and sauntering, in short to strolling and entertainment. Thus, in London, on 27 June 1682: 'It was decided to give warning that, as there are children who make a noise in the streets, the parents shall be warned that if they do not take care to restrain their children, there is an officer of the city who must undertake to chastise them.' Or again, on 19 September: 'the Congregation are exhorted not to leave the temple before the blessing, and not to stop in the street after leaving the Church'. That last survival of the more open form of social life, the theatre of the street, receded, while the family became established in its aloof separateness, cutting loose the old ties of solidarity once exercised by the surrounding community which was so oppressive or so warm at times.

The disintegration of the communities

As for those who shall withdraw from our Churches in order to join the English Churches, our brethren have determined that it shall be expedient for such persons to be referred both to the Magistrates and to the ministers of the said English Churches, and for them to be advised that since such persons are no longer of our communion, they are no longer considered to belong to us, and we regard ourselves as being relieved and excused of the care and responsibility both for their souls and for their bodily necessities, theirs and their children's.
Article 4, Canterbury Colloquy, 1590

As the demographic analysis presented in the Introduction showed, the communities' survival depended directly on new arrivals. In other words, natural growth alone was not enough to compensate for the losses caused by mortality and to replace those who left. We should then enquire how the refugee community was absorbed into the surrounding English population. Strangely enough, this problem was practically never mentioned as such. If we except the crisis of the 1630s, and the sharp

---

[30] P. Clark, 'The Alehouse and the Alternative Society', in *Puritans and Revolutionaries*, Oxford, 1978.

reactions which accompanied the Crown's clearly expressed intention of planning, within the space of a single generation, the extinction of the Foreign Churches, the forms of resistance to anglicisation are fairly difficult to determine. This phenomenon invites an obvious answer: it would have been unseemly to warn the refugees officially against the solicitations of English society, which sheltered them. And yet the homoeostatic balance of the communities, and their financial adminis-tration, required some remedy for the haemorrhage which condemned the Churches, in the medium term, to decrease and ultimately disappear. Accordingly, it was necessary to decree a code of behaviour, sufficiently flexible not to offend the host population, but offering at the same time a guarantee of effectiveness.

These implicit constraints, which are not stated directly in any register, are elicited both by the importance of regular financial contributions and the discouragement of exogamy. Conversely, the Anglican clergy's favoured tactics for attracting the aliens to the parish Churches took up these two points. Clandestine marriages were facilitated, and attempts were made to levy contributions for the benefit of the Church of England.

Recent studies have shown that the question of Christian marriage oscillated between two poles: *sacrament* and *contract*. While repudiating the sacrament of marriage, did Protestant civilisation move closer to the idea of contract? In fact, the term 'contract' was itself ambiguous as it could apply either to the exchange of mutual consent between the spouses, or to the agreement between their families. The Refuge was characterised throughout by this duality: the accent was laid alternatively on the nuclear, consensual commitment of the couple, or on that of their families. Moreover, this ambivalence, which is so clearly marked in *Romeo and Juliet*, seems to be characteristic of modern societies in general.[31]

An anecdote will make this more explicit. On 15 February 1573, Pierre Passé and Elisabeth Udric appeared before the London consistory. They had 'married on their own by exchanging a promise', and then lived together in the Netherlands, sharing 'one and the same house', 'one table and one bed and all other things in common', 'eating, drinking and sleeping together, in the knowledge and sight of their servants, neighbours and acquaintances'. The judgement delivered by the consistory is revealing; the promises exchanged were 'valid and sufficient'. They were accordingly declared husband and wife; a solemn celebration in the temple would only confirm the union which had already been contracted, since there was 'a promise of marriage between them legitimately given'. One can deduce from this example that there were a number of concubinary couples within the Refuge; moreover, it is likely that a prior

[31] R. Pillorget, *Le Tige et le rameau. Familles anglaises et françaises 16e–18e siècles*, Paris, 1979.

promise of marriage authorised *de facto* a certain degree of cohabitation between the future spouses, although they were often curbed by the consistories.[32]

But the notion of a contract, which may lend itself to a liberal interpretation, could conversely involve a twofold constraint. Promises of marriage were almost as binding as marriage itself; they could only be broken for extremely serious reasons. And the influence of families asserted itself directly and with some weight. Thus, we are told, in London on 14 February 1611, Daniel Abraham has 'been greatly at fault in marrying without having the banns published in our Church'. It appears also that 'in order to be married in the [Stranger] Church he would have needed his parents' consent'.

Therefore several couples fled to the Church of England, which was accused of condoning clandestine exchanges. On 1 August 1571, the consistory of London issued a warning to those who 'without reflection join this Church with levity to marry elsewhere, without having their banns read, which persons will not be admitted again, save through public repentance'. On 8 November, the 'list of those who have married clandestinely' was sent to the bishop. In Norwich, on 7 November 1632, the same terms were used to condemn those who, in order to escape from parental supervision, reinforced by the authority of the consistories, married in a neighbouring parish Church. This exogamy could take two complementary forms: elopement on the part of two young lovers, both the children of refugees, or else marriage to an Englishman (or Englishwoman). In every case, there was virtually no remedy: the solidarity of the group was challenged, and along with it the authority of families. Sometimes duplicity was involved; in Norwich, on 23 September 1628, the consistory admonished Arnold Lecoq and Déborah Martin who, *with the complicity of the girl's mother*, had fled to an English parish. Likewise, Esther Saint-Loyer had apparently been abducted by Jean Lamothe, and had married him without informing the Walloon community, 'not without suspicion of unchastity before their marriage'. The host society played the role of a frontier for the Refuge. The accusation of simony, or even of bigamy, which was levelled at marriages contracted in the Church of England says a good deal about the communities' distrust of their hosts.

Financial administration also played a major role in the definition of the minority community. The Churches' administrative autonomy enabled them to assume their spiritual independence. But monetary relationships put on an extra-economic significance: the cash nexus marked a visible tie

---

[32] For instance the mention, on 14 November 1564, of those 'qui font toutes leurs affaires ensemble et estiment que devant Dieu ils sont mariés' ('who hold everything in common and consider that in the eyes of God they are married').

with the community. Even when they were minimal, financial contributions assumed a symbolic value: they expressed a basic sense of solidarity, and allowed the individual to expect a number of advantages in return, from economic assistance to plain relief. To bring this contribution to an end or to contract a clandestine marriage outside the community, without publishing the banns, were considered as complementary disorders, which both ruined from within the credit and credibility of the Foreign Churches. Thus in London, on 24 March 1594, Jeanne Choquet was sharply rebuked, 'because she had married an Englishman against the order of the church' after having 'always been assisted out of the poor-chest'. She had thus 'defrauded and misused the poor-chest'. Accordingly, she was expelled from the community.

Such insistence on economic compulsion may, in fact, have derived from an underlying fear of dissolution into the English population. In Norwich, on 6 May 1628, the consistory castigated the increasing number of 'those who neglect to pay their contributions'. The established Church invariably tried to seize the opportunity by pressing foreigners to contribute their mite to the English parish. For the most part, this financial competition did not involve the episcopal hierarchy; it went on at a local level and was accentuated by the jealousies which sprang from proximity. The churchwardens or overseers of the poor wished to fill their charitable purse by taxing these foreigners who fought shy of paying the poor rates. In 1663, the established Church deplored the strangers' refusal to contribute to the support of the English parishes in Canterbury.[33] Fifteen years later, in June 1677, the parish of St Peter's finally managed to make some of these foreigners pay, assessing their wealth as one third of the total. But time and the force of inertia are invaluable allies, and that same month, the churchwardens and overseer of the poor of the parish of St Alphage issued their own warrant to the constable of the North Ward to 'imprison those that did not pay for the English poor'.[34]

I should like to conclude this brief survey by mentioning, by way of illustration, the Depon affair. This sad case acts as a useful reminder of the legal imbroglio which accompanied the thorny question of public relief. The French Reformed Church in Canterbury found itself in conflict with the English, from 1679 onwards, concerning an infant who was still sucking at his nurse's breast, his mother having fled.

Who, in fact, held the financial responsibility for the young Depon, or possibly Dupont? The matter, which would have suited a comedy, occupied everyone's energies and gave rise to interminable lawsuits. This was, indeed, a question of principle. In the eyes of the English, the

---

[33] Dean and Chapter Library, Burghmote Minute Book, No. 5, fol. 82.
[34] *Ibid.*, MSS U-47-H 4, fol. 16.

Duponts of all discretion were by necessity members of the French-speaking community. Not in the least, replied the latter, Jacques Dupont is the son of a papist; we have nothing to do with those people, and we have warned you against them often enough. Several pages of dense argument have been preserved in the Dean and Chapter Library at Canterbury.[35] I have gathered the following pieces of information from them. In June 1677, Matthieu Dupont, the father of the child, settled in England, where he worked for an English Catholic by the name of Berry. At the time of the popish plot, two years later, both men had to flee, abandoning the child to the care of a nurse, Elise Smart. The infant was duly baptised in the English parish of Westgate, and then the English attempted to put the onus for his support on the foreign community. The Court of Quarter Sessions and the County Assizes entrusted the child to the Walloon Church in the summer. And yet attempts continued to be made to have the decision reversed:

> *The case.* That one Matthew de Pon [Dupont?] being a foreigner and Frenchman, about June 1677 came into the parish of Westgate and was settled as an inhabitant there, is lately run away and left a child to the said parish, who have at Midsummer sessions 1679 holden for the said county obtained an order to charge the child on the Walloon congregation, although it was then proved on the behalf of the said Walloon congregation that the said De Pon was a Papist and none of the Walloon congregation, and that the said Walloon congregation had in the month of June 1677 given notice to churchwardens and overseers of the said parish that there were divers foreign [papists], not of the Walloon congregation come to inhabit in their parish, and that the said parish would take care to remove them or to secure themselves, lest any charge might happen to the said parish and the said De Pon was then an inhabitant of the said parish.[36]

For our twentieth-century sensibilities, these disputes may sound somewhat squalid and devoid of any magnanimity. However, I have decided to make use of this dossier, with all its inglorious features, because it provides extremely valuable information on the workings of public relief, and throws some light on the often tacit organic laws which governed relations between individuals. This storm in a teacup reveals the uncertainty shared by the English concerning the status of the refugees. They did not always see, or want to see, what distinguished a French Catholic from a Protestant. After all, these people spoke the same language, they were equally foreigners and had to settle their accounts between themselves.

The Dupont affairs was also the culmination of several years of wrangling over contributions to the Anglican Church. But more

---

[35] *Ibid.*, fols. 19–35.   [36] *Ibid.*, fol. 19.

fundamentally, the French-speaking community in Canterbury was led to analyse in precise terms the fears which prompted it. It constituted, we are told, 'a voluntary congregation' and not 'a parish'.[37] Its annual budget of £470 was also based on 'voluntary contributions', and there was practically no recourse to be had against those who failed to pay. Moreover, many members among the wealthiest had become definitively assimilated into the English population. This pessimistic summary was evidently justified. The sectarian reflex, the tendency to turn in upon oneself, distrust of the surrounding world, were to be a constant temptation; many genuine refugees were to feel uneasy with their institutions.

[37] *Ibid.*

Conclusion

Towards a typology of minorities?

Aliens, minorities and fringe groups should be distinguished in order not to run the risk of 'lexicological confusion'.[1] These three representative cases are indeed defined primarily in terms of difference. But there the similarity ends. Foreigners or strangers never exist as such, but only in the eyes of the surrounding population. This legal formalism, in its abstractness, eludes any precise identity: for the refugees whom we have been studying, the major concern was certainly to avoid appearing as mere foreigners.

One is a foreigner by chance, as a result of circumstances, misfortune or banishment. On the other hand, one chooses to belong to a minority or to a fringe group. Yet minority status and underground culture are far from coextensive. The refugee communities' primary concern was always to prevent such confusion, at the cost of reinforcing moral control. The vindication of difference and unconformity was no excuse for laxity or negligence. I can think of no better illustration of this righteousness than a text of July 1698 which deserves to be quoted *in extenso*:

> *An act for the suppression of scandals among the French refugees.* The French Churches in and about the City of London, in order to respond to the best of their abilities to the pious and Christian endeavours of His Majesty and his Parliament to suppress profanity and the dissolute morals of the people, considering with sorrow that they cannot fully repress such scandals as arise amongst themselves because those who commit them move from one Church to another, whenever an attempt is made to correct them, and because those who are not attached to any

[1] J. Freund, 'La Notion de marginalité', *Eglises et groupes religieux dans la société français*, Strasburg, 1977, p. 27.

Church mean to live independently, they have thought it their duty to seek for some effective means to remedy so great an evil. Having, therefore, called upon the name of God, to obtain His help and inspiration, the said Churches agreed that they should remain united in the enforcement of discipline alone and that from henceforth no person will be received at Communion in a Church of which he is not a member, unless he be known there, or unless he show a certificate of good conduct, signed by one of the ministers and elders of his Church.

It has been agreed also that when some scandalous person have been judged and censured in one of the said Churches, and refuse to submit to the judgement of his consistory, it shall be made known to all the said Churches, so that he shall not be received as a member, nor admitted to Communion, until he shall have edified his Church by his submission and repentance, and, since there are among the French divers persons who are not attached to any Church, if in the future one of them commit some scandalous action, the Church nearest to his dwelling shall examine the matter, and address its censure to him in the same way as it would towards one of its members.

And if, on the aforesaid points, there be some difficulty which the individual consistories cannot resolve, the consistory which has charge of the matter shall inform the other consistories, which shall assemble, in the persons of their deputies, in order to give one another the necessary advice and assistance, leaving, however, all the said Churches the free and entire exercise of all the rights and privileges which they have at present and so that the members of the said Churches shall be informed of the contents of this act, it has been decided that it shall be read, on Sunday July 3rd, in all the said Churches, and then registered in the books of all the consistories. Decreed in the assembly of the said French Churches held at Hungerford, July 3 1698.[2]

We need to allow for the particular circumstances which lay behind the drafting of this text: the scale of immigration in the last twenty-five years of the seventeenth century caused obvious disquiet, and the protracted concern to uphold a high standard of public morals, or to avoid the slur of public scandal, is revealing. In fact, the demographic challenge led the communities to express their most specific characteristics. A few central themes stand out: the tendency towards mimetic assimilation to the host society; the homoeostatic balance of the group; the ambivalent nature of its insertion.

The imitation of English society was obvious. The refugees had always been alert to the world around them, isolating and incorporating its most salient features. What aspects of English society did most strikingly impress them in the 1690s? The role of Parliament; in their assemblies the representatives of the Churches aped the King-in-Parliament, and entitled

[2] Huguenot Library, Ja MSS 2, 'Livre des actes du consistoire de l'Eglise qui s'assemble à Hungerford', fol. 33.

the result of their deliberation 'An act for the suppression of scandals'. The Churches were adjusting their principles to the officials' ideals of English society and echoed the 1698 Act of Parliament against 'impiety' and 'immorality' to curb licentiousness. This symbiotic trend was a constant feature of the Refuge. One needs to recognise, however, that absorption did not necessarily lead to a loss of identity – on the contrary, imitation is necessary to adapt oneself. In extreme cases, this mimetic urge extended to prejudices, and after a few years, some of the refugees looked upon their coreligionists with the condescension which the English had taught them. The deep-rooted feeling of elite betrayal formed the counterpart of the cultural melting-pot, which was more marked, perhaps, among gentlemen. As far as we know, the common people of the Refuge were probably more conservative than their betters, who, thanks to their education, regarded local variations as negligible. Quite evidently, the adoption of Anglicanism was a clear choice on the part of all those who did not wish to maintain the 'Presbyterian' forms of French Calvinism, which were marred in their eyes by potential republicanism. Moreover, there was to be a widening gap with the native Protestantism of the Huguenots who had remained in France. At the beginning of the eighteenth century, the earlier refugees and their sons were to look with an anxious eye upon their newly arrived brethren who had survived the epic of the Camisards: on 23 July 1707, the Threadneedle Street consistory charged with 'fraud' and 'fanaticism' the prophets from the Cévennes, who 'dishonour Religion and draw down censure upon our Refuge'. Marion, Fage and Cavalier were banished from the churches, and condemned by the English authorities; sectarians and enthusiasts were to give the French prophets the support which the refugees denied them.[3] A pamphlet published in 1709 took things to their logical conclusion and identified every kind of contagion from France with Catholic attempts to discredit the protestants: *Politique du papisme en Angleterre, avec les moyens d'en arrêter le progrès, ouvrage très utile à tous les états protestants* (*The Papists' Policy in England, with the Means of Arresting its Progress. A Work most useful to all Protestant States*) (Rotterdam, 1709).

This distrust of French enthusiasts was articulated around several major themes: anxiety in the face of guerrilla warfare; an increasingly rationalist frame of mind; and the rejection of prophesying. This rift had been impending from a much earlier period; the Franco-Walloon establishment had always had a passion for decency. Indeed, their minority status even accentuated their social conformism and loyalty. Respectability is one of the forms of imitation (see Document 8).

---

[3] H. Schwarz, *The French Prophets – The History of a Millenarian Group in Eighteenth-Century England*, Berkeley, 1980.

The minority identity was extremely restrictive. It operated in a selective manner: the newcomer had to go through a rite of admission. No one could be accepted unless he supplied a letter of recommendation – or 'testimony' – from his former community. When persecution raged, in the period of forced conversions to Roman Catholicism, recantation of popery marked the entry into the new Church – as was the case in the 1680s. Moreover, membership entailed financial obligations covering contributions both to the maintenance of the Church and to the poor-chest. Many refugees evaded these demands: the result was a confused situation, brought out clearly by the 'Act for the suppression of scandals' of 1698: some of the refugees were beyond the Churches' control either out of laziness, indifference or exasperation on their part; hence the allusion to 'divers persons who are not attached to any Church'. This had far-reaching consequences in terms of demography: the number of recognised members of the Churches was less than the refugee population as a whole. On the margins of the Churches, though in their zone of influence, there always existed a group of French-speaking people, ill-defined in outline and ready to merge into the Church of England or the dissenting sects. This shifting population makes the statistical patterns yielded by baptismal records of purely relative value, and accounts for their irregularity. This constituted, beyond any doubt, the principal 'scandal' which the Churches deplored in the 1690s: these people were difficult to control and hence they were accused of all sorts of disorders.

The foreign communities exercised some self-regulating mechanisms to contain these unruly elements. Consistories, 'politic men', pastors or simply heads of families were invested with the responsibility of preserving, reproducing and controlling the minority identity. We have seen how a whole set of precedents could be extracted from the most notable cases examined by the consistories.

Part of the rules which governed the workings of the community belonged, however, to an implicit, inarticulate code. A whole system of fiduciary signs served to express the cohesion of the Church. The celebration of the Lord's Supper was one of the great demonstrations of social cohesion; on the other hand, excommunication – which proved, in fact, extremely rare – was the most dreaded expression of rejection. During the weeks leading up to Communion, the elders distributed, district by district, symbolic tokens, called 'méreaux', which authorised the bearer to receive Communion. Monetary relations also assumed, as we have seen, an extra-economic function: the few shillings one received when in need, the contribution one paid to the poor-chest, even if minimal, involved on each occasion a genuine sense of partnership. This cooperative spirit, and the importance attached to the family, are far removed from the possessive individualism with which Protestantism has too often been associated, while the Reformation itself was deceptively treated as a bourgeois movement, if not the beginnings of *laissez-faire*.

The refugee communities were not, therefore, centres of agitation in which an alternative society was developed. The Foreign Churches always disowned the sectarian spirit of conventicles. Even when they refused to conform to the established Church, they never entirely shared the characteristics of dissent. Indeed, the refugees did not live in self-sufficient isolation but they entertained an ambivalent relationship with the host society. The communities survived only in so far as they adapted, but, at the same time, the more they complied, the less autonomous they became, the more they appeared to lose their idiosyncratic character. Therefore, they were in a perpetual state of instability, and, with the renewal of each generation, or as a result of geographical mobility, they were confronted with the danger of losing their identity. Such are the multiple paradoxes of minority status, between compliance and rejection, similarity and difference, pride and resignation, the universal and the singular. Comparison with other minorities in other countries, under other skies, and in other times, would be worth pursuing. I do not pretend to have come to a fixed, permanent model. Though I do believe in comparative history, yet, I should be equally wary of anachronism and the tendency to conflate distinct phenomena. While I was writing the French version of this book my most fruitful contacts were with some Jewish friends; I think that this is not entirely a coincidence. The figure of the Jew – an often mythical figure, indeed – constantly appears in my records: along with the related theme of dispersion or the crossing of the Red Sea. The use of biblical imagery brings home the typical convergences and dissimilarities surrounding minorities in north-west Europe when England and the United Provinces had been equally won over to toleration.

Let me not be misunderstood: I have not intended to write an abstract analysis, or reduce the life of men to some stereotypes. I wish to preserve the attractions of aphorism. Accordingly, I should pay tribute to the late Robert Mandrou, who used to say (I do not believe that he ever wrote these words): 'time, for us historians, is more than a mere variable'. That time is the measure of all things, that the passage of succeeding generations, the transmission of an identity beyond death, the ebb and flow of human lives are more important than any preconceived view of history: such was one of the principal experiences of the anonymous refugees whom I have followed through a century and a half of this history, in an endeavour to avert the loss of memory.

DOCUMENTS

1 The charter granted by Edward VI, 24 July 1550

Source: John a Lasco, *Toute la forme et manière du ministère ecclésiastique en l'Eglise des étrangers dressée à Londres*, Emden, 1556: quoted in Schickler, *Les Eglises du Refuge en Angleterre*, III, pp. 3–6.

Edward the Sixth, by the grace of God, king of England, France and Ireland: defender of the faith and supreme head on earth under Christ, of the Church of England and Ireland. To all those who shall receive the present letters, Greetings.

Since great and grave considerations have induced us especially at present, and regarding also with what affection and charity it is fitting for Christian Princes to make prompt endeavour in the service of God's holy and sacred Gospel, and the apostolic religion begun, instituted and given by Christ himself, without which civil government, and police cannot long endure, nor preserve its honour, unless Princes and other mighty persons, whom God has set in government over kingdoms, seek above all things to establish religion in its purity and entirety throughout the body of the republic; and unless the Church, instituted and increased in truly Christian and apostolic manners and opinions, be preserved by her holy ministers, dead to the flesh and the world: for as much as we decree that it is the office of a Christian Prince, among other very great cogitations, in order to administer his kingdom well and nobly, to provide for religion and for calamitous and afflicted persons banished because of their religion. Know ye that considering not only the aforementioned things, and wishing to preserve the Church, which we have restored to her former liberty, from the tyranny of the pope; but also taking pity upon the condition of the exiled and foreign persons, who have lived already for some time in our kingdom of England, being condemned to voluntary banishment for the sake of religion and of the Church; for we have by no means thought it worthy of a Christian man nor of the magnificence of a Prince, that his liberality should be constrained or closed to poor foreign persons, ill-used and driven from their country, who have sought refuge in our kingdom, having need of the help necessary to life in such a condition. And notwithstanding, several of the Dutch and other strangers, who have come, and daily come into our kingdom, both from Germany and from other distant countries, in which the freedom of the Gospel, under the dominion of the papacy, have begun to be impaired and oppressed, have no sure place in our kingdom where they may hold their assemblies, and where among men of their nation and their language they may treat intelligibly of matters of religion, and of things ecclesiastical, according to the custom and the manner of their country. Accordingly, by our especial grace, and of our certain knowledge and by our sovereign will, and also following the judgement of our Council, we wish, grant and command, that from henceforth there shall be a temple or consecrated house in our City of London, which shall be called the temple of the Lord Jesus: in which the congregation and assembly of the Dutch and other strangers may be held and celebrated to this end and intention, that by the ministers of the Church of the Dutch and other strangers, the holy and sacred Gospel shall be interpreted purely, and the Sacraments administered according to the Word of God and apostolic ordinance. And we hereby establish, create, ordain and found this temple or consecrated house, with a superintendent, and with four ministers of the Word. And so that the said superintendent and ministers shall be in fact, and in name, a body incorporated and politic in itself, under the name of the superintendent and ministers of the Church of the Dutch and other strangers, by the foundation of King Edward the Sixth: we hereby incorporate them in the City of London, and hereby create, establish, ordain and constitute really, and in fact, a body incorporated and politic, by the same and that there shall be descendence.

And moreover, by our especial grace, and of our certain knowledge and entire volition, and following the judgement of our Council, we have given and granted, and hereby do give and grant to the said superintendent and ministers of the Church of the Dutch and other strangers in the City of London, all of the temple or Church of the Augustinians, who were formerly in our City of London, and all the ground, foundation and floor of the said Church, except all the choir of the said Church, and the ground, foundations and floor thereof. The said superintendent and ministers and their successors shall have and enjoy the said temple or Church, and the aforementioned things, save those things which are excepted, and hold them from us, our heirs and successors, as a simple and entire donation.

Moreover, by the aforesaid counsel, and of our certain knowledge, and our aforesaid sovereign will, we hereby grant to the said superintendent and ministers, and to their successors, full licence, power and authority to increase, and make greater number of ministers, to name them, and appoint from time to time such and similar ministers, to serve in the said temple, as it shall seem to be necessary to the said superintendent and ministers. And all these things shall be according to the sovereign pleasure of the king. Moreover, we wish John a Lasco of the Polish nation, a most honourable man, by cause of his integrity and purity of life and conduct, and of his singular erudition, to be the first superintendent of the said Church in our time and Galterus Deloenus, Martin Flanders, François de La Rivière, and Richard François to be the first four ministers in our time. Moreover, we give and grant to the said superintendent and ministers, and to their successors licence, authority and power, upon the death or vacancy of any of the said ministers, from time to time to choose, appoint and substitute another in his place, a capable and suitable person: providing always that the person so named and elected be presented and brought before us, our heirs and successors, and that they shall be appointed to the said ministry by us or our heirs and successors. We confer also upon the said superintendent, ministers and upon their successors, authority and licence, upon the death or vacancy of the superintendent, from time to time to elect, appoint and substitute another in his place, a learned and sober person. Provided always that the person thus named and elected be presented and brought before us, and our heirs and successors, in the said office of superintendent.

We instruct and firmly enjoin and command the mayor, councillors and aldermen of our City of London, the bishop of London and his successors, all other archbishops, bishops, justices and officers, and all the other ministers to permit the said superintendent and ministers freely and peacefully to enjoy, use and practise among their people, their own manners and ceremonies, and their own particular ecclesiastical discipline, notwithstanding that they are not in conformity with our own manners and ceremonies used in our kingdom, without hindrance or disturbance from them, or from any of them, by any statute, act, proclamation, injunction, restriction or contrary usage which they have formerly held: any act, edicts, or proclamation to the contrary notwithstanding...

In witness whereof, we have caused these our letters patent to be made. Witness myself at Leighes, the twenty-fourth day of July, in the fourth year of our reign: given under the privy Seal, and by the authority of Parliament.

J. Southwell,   W. Harrys

2 Jean Gérard recants his errors, 4 February 1595

Source: Consistory register, London.

During the months of October, November and December past, the two Flemish and Italian Churches have had several disputes and arguments with Jean Gérard, because of his holding various opinions which are foreign and contrary to the Word of God and the ordinance of the Church, notwithstanding the endeavours which the brethren of the French Church have made before, and continued to make on his behalf, but since it is of no avail with him, and there is nothing assured in the best of his retractions, which are very dubious and convoluted, the brethren with whom he is associated, and among whom he holds the office of deacon, have therefore accepted that he should be removed from his office as being unfit for it, and that they should remedy this scandal, with such moderation as they shall judge to be necessary.

When the matter was declared to the congregation, and likewise in the two public assemblies which were held, the said Gérard rebelled against all discipline, causing an uproar and thereupon the magistrate, hearing of his insolence, referred him to the three Churches, to submit to their judgement, after several prayers, exhortations, remonstrances and conjurations to repudiate all his writings, heresies and blasphemies, and with them his imaginary private revelations, through which Satan has made him believe that God was speaking in his ear. He implores the mercy of the Lord for his faults, with tears and lamentations, and is ready to make amends for his offence against the Church. He has been required to sign with his own hand the following articles, in order to give firm and assured proof of his repentance. [The text follows:]

> As it has pleased the three Churches to summon me before them, in order to lead me back to the straight path from which I have shamefully strayed, I have been induced and persuaded in my conscience, and of my own accord inclined by the reasons which they have shown me, and the remonstrances which they have made, to confess my faults and to show greater conformity in my repentance, in the following manner.
>
> Firstly, I condemn and abhor, before God and men, all my writings sent to His Excellency the Ambassador, to the consistory of the French Church, to individual persons of that Church, and others, and to which writings, being led astray by Satan, I gave the name of the Everlasting, of the living God, of the Son of everlasting wisdom, of the Spirit and angels of Heaven. I consider them full of impious notions and heresies of the Devil's making, the father of lies, and that in attributing them to God, I have uttered a horrible blasphemy, and I renounce with all my heart any revelation contrary to the Word written in the books of the prophets and apostles.
>
> Secondly, I recognise before God and men that the said brethren who

have care of the Churches, ministers, elders and deacons, sought me out eight months ago, both in private and in church, with as much care as they could to induce me to do my duty, and that they have done everything to relieve, admonish and persuade me, in order to bring me back into Christ's flock, and I am sorry to have scorned and abused their solicitude, kindness and patience, and not to have abided firmly by the recantation which I signed in the consistory on the Second of August last.

Thirdly, I promise before God and men for the public scandal which I have caused repeatedly in the French Church, rebelling insolently against its discipline, and for several subjects of offence given to many good people by my presumption, obduracy, calumnies, and in any other way, that I will submit to the judgement of the brethren, and shall make such reparation, and at such time and in such manner, as they shall order me to make for the good of the Church.

3 Francis Bacon and Edward Coke on the status of aliens, 1608

Source: 'The Case of the *Postnati*, or of the Union of the Realm of Scotland with England', Howell, *State Trials*, II, pp. 581–638.

(a) *Francis Bacon*

Naturalization is best discerned in the degrees whereby the law doth mount and ascend thereunto...The degrees are four.

The first degree of persons, as to this purpose, and that the law takes knowledge of, is an alien enemy; that is such a one as is born under the obeisance of a prince or state that is in hostility with the king of England. To this person the law giveth no benefit or protection at all; but if he come into the realm after war proclaimed, or war in fact, he comes at his own peril, he may be used as an enemy: for the law accounts of him but, as the scripture saith, as of a spy that comes to see the weakness of the land...Nevertheless, this admitteth a distinction. *For if he come with safeconduct otherwise it is*: for then he may not be violated, either in person or goods. But he must fetch his justice at the fountain-head, for none of the conduit pipes are open to him: he can have no remedy in any of the king's courts; but he must complain himself before the king's privy counsel: there he shall have a proceeding summary from hour to hour, and cause shall be determined by natural equity, and not by rules of law; and the decree of the counsel shall be executed by aid of the Chancery...

The second person is an alien friend, that is, such a one as is born under the obeisance of such a king or state as is confederate with the king of England, or at least not in war with him. To this person the law alloteth this benefit, that as the law accounts, that the hold it hath over him, is but a transitory hold, for he may be an enemy; so the law doth indue him but with a transitory benefit, that is, of moveable goods and personal actions.

But for free-hold, or lease, or actions real or mixt, he is not enabled, except it be in *autre droit*...

The third person is a denizen, using the word properly, for sometimes it is confounded with a natural born subject. This is one that is but *subditus infitivus*, or *adoptivus*, and is never by birth, but only by the king's charter, and by no other means, come he never so young into the realm, or stay he never so long. Mansion or habitation will not indenize him, no, nor swearing obedience to the king in a leet, which doth in law the subject; but only, as I said, the king's grace and gift. To this person the law giveth an ability and capacity abridged, not in matter, but in time. And as there was a time when he was no subject, so the law doth not acknowledge him before that time. For if he purchase free-hold after his denization, he may take it; but if he have purchased any before, he shall not hold it; so if he have children after, they shall inherit; but if he have any before, they shall not inherit. So he is but priviledged *a parte post*, as the schoolmen say, and not *a parte ante*.

The fourth and last degree is a natural born subject, which is evermore by birth, or by act of parliament; and he is complete and entire. For the law of England, there is *nil ultra*; there is no more subtle division between these.

(b) *Edward Coke*

There is found in the law four kinds of ligeances; the first is, *ligeantia naturalis, absoluta, pura et indefinita* and this originally is due by nature and birth-right, and is called *alta ligeantia*, and he that oweth this is called *subditus natus*. The second is called *ligeantia acquisita* not by nature but by acquisition or denization, being called a denizen, or rather donaizon, because he is *subditus datus*. The third is *ligeantia localis*, wrought by the law, and that is when an alien that is in amity cometh into England; because as long as he is within England, he is within the king's protection; therefore so long as he is here, he oweth unto the king a local obedience or ligeance...The fourth is a legal obedience, or ligeance which is called legal, because the municipal laws have prescribed the order and form of it; and this is to be done upon oath at the town of leet...

Every man is either *alienigena*, an alien born, or *subditus*, a subject born. Every alien is either a friend that is in league &c or an enemy that is in open war &c. Every alien enemy is either *pro tempore*, temporary for a time, or *perpetuus*, perpetual, or *specialiter permissus*, permitted especially. Every subject is either, *natus*, born, or *datus*, given or made...

Alien friends cannot acquire, or get nor maintain any action, real or personal, for any land or house, unless the house be for their necessary habitation. For if they should be disabled to acquire and maintain these things, it were in effect to deny unto them trade and traffick, which is the life of every island.

4 Indenture of Jeanne Delescluse, 19 February 1674

Source: Canterbury, Dean and Chapter Library, MSS U-47-H 4, fol. 10.

The said Jeanne de l'Escluse as well of her own free will and accord as by the consort of Peter le Hooke Junior and Samuel Cornar collectors and deacons for the poore of the walloon congregation in Canterbury hath put her selfe in servis as an apprentis to and with the said James Laman to dwell and serve from the day of the date heereof unto the full end and terme of ten yeares from thence next ensuing and fully to be compleated and ended during which said terme the said apprentice her said Master and Mistresse well and faithfully shall serve, their secrets shall keepe, their commandements lawful and honest every where she shall gladly doe, hurt to her said Master she shall not doe nor consent to be done by an other, but shee to her power shall prevent and forthwith give notice to her said Master or Mistresse. Of the same shee shall not committ fornication nor contract matrimony within the said terme. Att cards, dice or any other unlawfull games shee shall not play. The goods of her said Master she shall not inordinately wast or consume nor them to anybody lend without her Master and Mistresse licence. Tavernes or Alehouses shee shall not hant except if it be about their businesse, from the servis of her said Master by day or night shee shall not absent herselfe but as a true and faithfull servant and apprentice she shall carry and demeane her self during the said terme.

In consideration whereof as also that the said deacons or overseers and collectors for the poor do paye at the ensealling thereof unto the said James Laman the summe of nine pounds of good and lawfull money of England, the said James Laman and Mary his wife covenants that they shall teach or cause to be taught and instruct theire said apprentice good house wifery and all such works as the said apprentice shall be able to performe and do according to their best skill, wite and understanding with due and lawful correction and not otherwise, finding and allowing unto the said apprentice sufficient meat, drink, lodging and apparell linen hose, and theese and all other things needful during the said terme. And at the end of the said terme, shall provid, allow and give unto the said aprentice double apparell, that is to say a sute for the working dayes, and a new sute for the holy dayes, meet and convenient for such an apprentice to have and weave with sufficient shifts and changes and other linnen as shee had at her comming to be an apprentice.

And further it hath been covenanteth and agreed upon that if in case the said apprentice shall die or decease before shee has served a yeare of her said apprentiship, that then the said James Laman shall returne fower pounds of the sayd money unto the said deacons and collectors for the poore or their successor.

5 Freemen and foreigners, 31 August 1681

Source: Canterbury, Dean and Chapter Library, Bughmote Minute Book, vol. v, fols. 233–4, 31 August 1681.

Whereas the ffrench or walloone congregation in the said citty upon their first reception and afterwards by severall articles made betweene them and this citty and by severall ancient orders of Burghmote were to use onely certain arts and misteries in the said articles and orders mentioned and no other although they were denizen borne and whereas this court is informed by the humble petition of the company of mercers and other ffreemen of this citty and upon inquest hath found that notwithstanding the said articles and orders the said congregation have of late years used most of the arts, misteries and trade in the said citty, and have sould and dayly doe sell as well by retail as in gross most of the wares belonging to the said all trades and misterys used within the said citty to the great damage, prejudice and almost utter ruin of the English Nation, freemen and inhabitants of this citty, and that for the most effectual carrying on of their designes of enriching themselves by the ruine of the English freemen and inhabitants of this citty, some of the said congregation doe pretend that they have heretofore obtayned the freedome of this city (although contrary to the intent and true meaning of the said articles and orders) and by meanes thereof doe hope to make their children and servants free of this citty which (unless some truely remidy may be provided) will prouve the utter ruine of the English freemen within this citty for that the people of the said congregation doe to this day remaine a separate body from the English of this citty, and doe distinguish themselves as people of another nation and doe live according to their owne laws and constitutions, and by a strict confederacy between themselves, do endeavour to procure and advance the wealth and interests of their own people without any respect and regard to the interest of the English freemen and inhabitants of this citty and that such of them who pretend to be free of this citty doe under colour thereof sell and vouch the wares and comodities of others of their congregation who are forreyners and straungers to the freedom of this citty. And also that the people of the said congregation having relacions and correspondents beyond the seas, by that meanes have opportunity to import and doe dayly import uncustomed goods into this kingdom where they can and do sell at lower rates than the freemen of this citty (who pay customes for their goods) can doe, and that the said congregation doth dayly increase by the continuall resort of strangers to this citty who, for the most part, are received and admitted into the said congregation and doe usually bring with them uncustomed goods or prohibited goods ... By which means not onely the English freemen inhabiting within this citty are very much impoverished but the citty itself is in danger to be wholly overspread and possessed by fforeyners.

It is therefore ... thought fitt and so ordered and decreed by that court that no person or persons whatsoever of the ffrench or walloone congregation within this citty nor any other forreyner or forreyners whatsoever that now are or at any tyme hereafter shall inhabite, dwell, reside or be within this citty or the liberty or freedome of the same, shall from hereforth be admitted to the freedome of this citty. [The freedom] shall not at any time hereafter be granted unto any person of any sort whatsoever of the said ffrench or walloone congregation or any other fforeyner or fforeyners whatsoever, although any of them now doe or at any time or times hereafter shall or may pretend to serve or to have served an apprentiship with any freeman or freemen of the said citty or the liberties thereof, or to have married the daughter of any freeman whatsoever of the said citty. And it is also thought fitt and so ordered and decreed by this court that no freeman of the said citty shall at any time hereafter take any of the said ffrench or walloon congregation or any forreyner or forreyners nor any of their children to be his apprentice or apprentices or to serve with him as an apprentice, and that the Chamberlain of the said citty for the time being shall not inroll the indenture of apprentisship of any such apprentice or apprentices in the Chamber of the said citty.

6 The *Dragonnades*: the circulation in manuscript form of newsletters relating the fate of the French Protestants

Source: Oxford, Bodleian Library, Rawlinson MSS, C. 984, fol. 62r.

Copy of a letter written by the Sieur Thomas Bureau of Niort in Poitou on 30 August 1685, to his brother, a bookseller in London.

It is now that we are put to the test, my dear brother, this poor province is inundated with dragoons who are laying everything waste. Returning from Poitiers with my brother-in-law, passing through Saint-Maixent, we saw the excesses which were being committed there, and how the Intendant had given order that no one should be permitted to leave the town, and to this end set thirty musketeers at each gate. I feared that they would do the same at Niort, which obliged me to take horse and go there, but the dragoons were there already, committing the most extraordinary outrages. This prevented my entering the town; my brother-in-law did so, because, being the head of a household, it would have been criminal for him to have absented himself; as soon as the dragoons were in the town, four of them were sent to our house: they began with the shop, throwing all the books on the ground, then with axes and hammers broke into pieces all the framework of the shop, the shelves, the glass and the woodwork, brought their horses in and let them use the books as their litter. They went next into the bedrooms, and threw everything into the street, so that within a short time there was such a clutter that one could not pass through. The mayor watched all this from his doorway, delighting in it all.

I am resolved to leave today for Paris in order to go and seek leave there for us. I am now half a league from the town at the house of a friend. My mother has sent me word by a messenger that she can endure it no longer. These wretches are treating her in the most appalling manner imaginable, and she is assuredly an admirable example in her constancy. She sends word to me that she can no longer meet the costs of their excessive spending, for apart from the 4 Crowns which she gives them each day, they have consumed all her silver plate. I am writing to her to tell her to find some means of hiding wherever she can, with my sister – which is almost impossible, for Roman Catholics are forbidden to give refuge to any Protestant on pain of the galleys. The commander of the dragoons, coming to our house last night, called my mother and said to her 'What, you bitch, you have not yet changed your religion, nor your whore of a daughter'. To which my mother answered that she hoped by the grace of God never to deny Him. 'Well then,' he said, 'damned bitch, you shall soon be hanged along with eight or ten other stubborn persons in this town who are no more willing to change than you.'

The dragoons said that it would be better to fasten their horses' halters around their necks, and drag them through the streets like mad dogs to serve as an example. I was told in a letter that today they are to double the guard on our house, that is to say send another four dragoons there, and that the mayor and ten other persons are searching for me everywhere, but I'm going to take horse and set off for Paris. The mayor told my mother that if she left her house even for six hours, he would have her hanged, and that they were going to take all the books which are in our shop to the square in front of the Château to burn them. I am exhorting my mother not to be daunted by all this, and to continue as she has so well begun.

The time is pressing on me now when I must leave, and I am so grieved that I can only give a faint picture of the most horrible scene, that has ever been witnessed. My brother-in-law has three dragoons who are doing much the same to him; you may judge of our state from that. I will not tell you what others are suffering. Monsieur Pérot Senior, and Messrs Mérichau and Valvod are imprisoned in dungeons, with irons on their feet, for having said merely that they were good and faithful subjects of the King, but that they would never change their Religion.

God be with you, my dear brother,
    Pray for us,
        Thomas Bureau.

7 The destiny of a minority: French Protestants and English Catholics

Source: London, BL Add. MSS 32095, fols. 363–80 [anon., *c.* 1687].
*Parallel between the penal laws of France against the Protestants and the
penal laws of England against those of the Roman religion (extracts).*

This comparison between the penal laws of France and England is a
demonstration that the majority of men are scarcely wise. In this I make
exception of no religion. The mass of the Roman Church has applauded
the great number of decrees which have overwhelmed the Protestants of
France. And yet, ask the doctors of the Roman Church if they approve of
the penal laws of England, and they will reply that they were dictated by
the devil. On the other hand, if you suggest to most Englishmen that the
penal laws should be revoked, they will be sure to tell you that they serve
as a barrier to popery, and that they would not be abrogated without
opening the door to it; but if you then ask them what they think of all
these declarations of the king of France, they will answer that they are
inhuman, unjust and worse. And yet these penal laws of England and
France are in perfect conformity with each other. It is as if the same spirit
had dictated them. How comes it then that what is sacred in Paris is
impious in London and that what is just in London is not legitimate in
Paris? Could it be that the sea serves as a boundary to confine equity and
justice, as it serves as a frontier for the two states? No, but rather that men
judge things only according to their own interests; they sacrifice everything
to them, truth, justice, religion and God himself. This is what creates the
pitiful contradiction between their feelings and their words. The
Protestants say that the French declarations are a work of darkness.
Those of the Roman religion say the same of the penal laws of England.
They are both to be believed, both are right, for since they are similar, that
is to say that they are, by their common admission, the fruit of passion and
iniquity.

Let us be just, however, to our century. If in our day most men are
scarcely to be accounted wise, no doubt they were hardly more civil in
those centuries which are considered to have been the purest and most
felicitous. The early Christians protested terribly against their persecutors,
but once God had given them emperors of their own religion, they found
that there was no harm in persecuting others. In their Apologiae, they
declaim against pagan laws which tended to force men's consciences, but
they compensated for this well enough, some time afterwards, and caused

a great many similar laws to be enacted against pagans and heretics, by Valentinian, Theodosius, Marcian and Justinian...

In our day we are reduced to discovering a writer's chronology in order to know his sentiments, because they do not follow justice and truth, but the circumstances in which they find themselves. When the Jansenists were condemned and their works censured, they wrote some excellent books on the way of criticism as against the way of authority; some time afterwards, having attacked the Protestants in order to rid the public of the suspicion that they were in accord with Geneva, they re-established the way of authority and showed that the way of criticism was illusory and impossible...

8 French-speaking Anglicanism, or nonconformity?

Source: London, Lambeth Palace Library, MSS Gibsoniani, vol. I, 929, fol. 53.

The underwritten French Ministers actually officiating in four french churches united to one another & wholly conform to the Church of England are forced by their wants to represent to your Lordships and worships that though their churches be the first established here in London by publick authority, since ye last Persecution in France and by a Patent under the great seal of England, in which they are called by ye name of ye Refugiees, yet they are ready to fall and their Ministers to starve for want of a competent subsistence. It is true y^t ye most part of ye Persons of quality among the Refugees, very well affected to ye Church of England and its Liturgy, doe ye best they can according to their ability to maintain them. But some french Meetings, raised up & encreased lately by the help and money of the Nonconformist English Party take away many of ye people, who beeing poor, have rather to lett a place at a small rate in these Meetings than to gett one in our Churches, y^t are forced to lett them at a higher rate because of ye great charges we lay under; Nay, lately one of the said Meetings hath taken away from us one of our Ministers, who was forced by his wants to leave us. But if your charity would put us in such a condition, y^t we could lett our pews, which are all our subsistence, at a smaller rate y^n we can doe now: we doubt not but our people would come to us again, and conform themselves gladly to ye Church of England, wherefore we most humbly desire your Lordships and worships to take into their consideration ye sad condition we are reduced to, and to doe what you can in order y^t confirming to ye Church of England, for which we ever had & will ever have a great respect and to which we are much addicted, be not priudicial to our interest, and to that you could easily doe if you were pleased to subscribe every one of you for a small summ yearly: But we will prescribe nothing to ye charity to wch we doe onely humbly recommand our persons, our familyes, our Ministery and our churches, and so we remain...

Lombard, de Galenière, de Sicqueville, Jouneau, P. Roussillon, de Rocheblave, Doules.

(On the back)

| I do give to this request | £3. H. London |
| I do give | £2 Wm Sherlock |

9 The condemnation of the prophets from Languedoc

Source: London, Threadneedle Street Consistory, 23 July 1707, 'Announcement to be read the following Sunday'.

You are aware, apparently, that there are in this city three persons of our nation who claim that the spirit, or the angel, of God inspires them to make certain pronouncements which others hear with respect, as truly divine oracles. We have cause to praise God for the fact that after the diligent enquires which we have made, no member of the Church has been found to have fallen into error in this respect, and that on the contrary the members of our Church have generally made it plain that they in no way approved of these supposed inspirations. The things which we have learnt from several persons who had occasion to see or hear those who claim to be inspired, together with a few copies of what they call their prophetic declarations – which we were shown initially and which few people are now unaware of, having read a collection of similar pronouncements which they have had printed – make us sufficiently inclined to believe, to speak mildly, that if they are not impostors, knowingly blaspheming the holy name of God, then they can only be reckoned among the class of visionaries, and of those sick minds which delude themselves.

Had we been able to do so, we should have examined them more closely, in order to speak with greater certainty in this matter as eyewitnesses, but, as they first refused to appear before our deputies, and as they withdrew to another district of the City, this examination was conducted by those of our brethren who are there; until this matter was brought before the magistrate, we have not been able, under any reasonable pretext, to acquire direct knowledge of it. We believe, however, that such knowledge as you and we have of the matter should be sufficient to put you on your guard against those people, who certainly (whether it be imposture or fanaticism on their part) bring down dishonour on Religion and censure upon our Refuge.

But you must also take heed that your zeal be worthy of true Christians, and that it does not degenerate into an unrestrained fury that would border on sedition and might disturb the public peace.

We hope, therefore, that none among you will join with others to throng the streets as people did on account of these misguided unfortunates. We expect, on the contrary, of your wisdom and Christian moderation that each shall stay calm and endeavour to see that those of his household, children and servants do the same, leaving it to the judges and magistrates to take what precautions they shall judge to be necessary concerning the toleration or destruction of this new sect, which, indeed, seems unlikely to be able to endure for long, such is its impious character, or its extravagance.

And a further consideration which should induce us even more powerfully to avoid any outward violence in this connection, even if it had but the appearance of a tumult, is the clemency which our sovereign has shown us, but which gives us no right to expect any further proof of it, if we abuse the first which she had given us by stopping the proceedings started against some Frenchmen who had been accused, even though wrongfully they protest, of supporting or even stirring up popular unrest against the supposed prophets.

God grant that we be not as children drifting and carried hither and thither by every wind of doctrine, through the deceipt of men, but that following truth with charity we may grow in all things through Jesus Christ. Amen.

AFTERWORD

EMMANUEL LE ROY LADURIE

Glorious revolution, shameful revocation

I

Bernard Cottret's book first appeared in a French version in 1985, the year of the three hundredth anniversary of the Revocation of the Edict of Nantes which provided some justification for my afterword. Without overlooking discrimination elsewhere on the Continent, I shall be considering in particular, in a 'bi-national' spirit, the respective attitudes of the Bourbon kingdom and of its counterpart across the Channel towards certain religious minorities which alike became the victims of oppression or simply exclusion.[1] Though in England such exclusion ultimately proved to be benign in character, this has not always been so, by any means. Let me emphasise first of all, in line with a remarkable paper given by John Bossy,[2] that I do not pretend to put the two phenomena on the same footing, nor to equate the one with the other: the English Catholics fared much better than the Huguenots in France after 1685. It is a question, rather, of moving away from a purely French perspective, and comparing in the same light great states in which there existed, in various degrees, a certain level of intolerance, whether verbal or real, symbolic or actual. Since it is out of the question to deal with every possible case (from the Spain of the expulsion of the Jews and Moriscos to Avakkum's Russia and the Japan of the first anti-Christian Tokugawas), it might be interesting to contrast, with a similar problem in view, two great territorial entities comparable in size and historical importance – northern and southern France, on the one hand, and the British Isles, or England and

---

[1] Bernard Cottret, 'Glorieuse Révolution, Révocation Honteuse? Protestants français et protestants d'Angeleterre', in M. Magdelaine and R. von Thadden (eds.), *Le Refuge huguenot/Die Huguenotten*, Paris/Frankfurt, 1985.

[2] Unpublished paper presented at the International History Conference held in Stuttgart in the summer of 1985.

Ireland, on the other. In the 1680s, which proved crucial, three decisive events occurred which we may regard here as closely interlinked: the 1682 Assembly of the French clergy with its strong Gallican and anti-Protestant tendency; the Revocation of the Edict of Nantes in 1685; and the Glorious Revolution three years later. The last of these was not unrelated to the Revocation, even though its immediate origin lay in causes peculiar to England.

The Revocation, as we know, did not come out of the blue. During the wars of religion, between 1562 and the end of the sixteenth century, a succession of edicts alternatively decreed tolerance and persecution, according to the government of the day and the prevailing balance of power. Among the liberal texts, we may cite those of 1562 and 1575–7. Conversely, the royal legislation of 1568 and 1585 (under the influence of the Catholic League) 'revoked' as it were before the event the more or less theoretical liberties which the monarch and the regent, Catherine de Medicis, had previously proclaimed. Yet the first revocations in the 1560s and 1580s failed for lack of sufficient coercive power – contrary to the might of the Sun-King a century later. Louis XIV's army – a force of 300,000 men in time of war, which was still considerable in peacetime – was to constitute a means of repression such as the agents of Henri III could not have dreamt of. In this respect the Revocation sprang, among other things, from advances in military organisation.

In 1598, the Edict of Nantes had launched a new and distinct phase, which proved most dissimilar from the last four decades of the sixteenth century – as also from the years after 1685. The Edict did not provide for explicit tolerance, but simply for a simultaneous, peaceful coexistence between the two varieties of Christianity, the Protestant minority and the Catholic majority. This peaceful coexistence could, of course, turn to cold war, as Elisabeth Labrousse has shown in a recent work.[3] The achievement of such coexistence, however limited it may seem was by no means negligible. It carried the personal stamp of Henri IV; this uncommon king symbolised a certain national reconciliation, or as his biographer, Janine Garrisson, has put it, a 'Henrician synthesis',[4] the equivalent of which was scarcely to be seen again in France, let us say until de Gaulle, that other fighting man and restorer of unity. The Edict of Nantes, with its annexes, and the body of law to which it soon gave rise, guaranteed the Huguenots various authorised places of worship in the midst of areas where their services were otherwise proscribed, together with civil and civic rights, specific jurisdictions, military strongholds and, in practice, the right to hold national political assemblies regularly.

The situation thus created was without precedent, or virtually so. This

[3] Labrousse, *La Révocation de l'Edit de Nantes*.
[4] Janine Garrisson, *Henri IV*, Paris, 1984.

pragmatic solution depended on the existence of a body of middle-of-the-road moderates composed for the most part of accommodating laymen, of either religion, who were little inclined towards fanaticism. This device, however admirable, had long awaited its theoretical justifications. Among its exponents, we may mention the Protestant scholar of Saumur, Moïse Amyraut, who died in 1664, and who stood in the line of descent of the militant 'Politiques' of the sixteenth century, and of the theories of natural law; and, above all, Bayle, who did not write his decisive texts on the question until the 1680s, already overshadowed by persecution: the concept of tolerance was to find its full expression only at the beginning of a dark period, preceding the 'dawn' of the Enlightenment. A brief geographical survey makes clear the exceptional, even privileged, nature of the socio-religious compromise, with its dualistic tendency, which, for less than a century, let us say for two generations at the most, was to prevail in France during the period of *non-revocation*, from 1598 to *c*. 1685 or in fact to 1670 at the very latest. In the first third of the seventeenth century, Edo Japan, a distant contemporary of the beginnings of the Bourbon dynasty, was preparing to exterminate its Christians, who already formed a large minority in the south of the archipelago. Spain, in 1611, expelled its Moriscos, and we know to what an extent the persecution of the Iberian Jews at the beginning of the Renaissance constituted a model for all subsequent discrimination in Western Europe. Russia, in the middle of the seventeenth century, was suppressing Avakkum and his supporters. Austria ill-treated its Czech and Hungarian Protestants. In England, the 50,000 Catholics remained subject to penal laws, albeit with varying degrees of intensity. 'Popish' Ireland was to lose nothing in the mean time. Scandinavia was generally allergic to a Catholicism which by now was no more than residual in Sweden, Iceland or Denmark. The undeniable pluralism of Poland was remote indeed. Germany, after 1555, and even more so after the treatise of Westphalia, manifested a stable religious pluralism in a chequered pattern (*Cujus regio ejus religio*), but this great country with its patchwork of semi-independent states and free cities does not lend itself to comparison with the proto-centralised kingdom of France. As for the Dutch, they admittedly practised a modest *de facto* tolerance, but neither wished, nor were able, to propagate it abroad.

After 1598 France combined in an original measure religious pluralism with the (still loose) control of a monarchy whose vocation it was to unify. This mixture was both unstable and productive: the Protestants in their 'fertile crescent' in southern France formed substantial minorities among the peasantry and in the cities like Montpellier, or La Rochelle and even in the royal treasury, which was infiltrated by Protestants – Sully, and before long, Herwart – although according to Dr Dessert's recent work,[5] less markedly so than historians of earlier generations had believed.

Over the long term, in the light of a certain fervour, and of the intensity of Huguenot devotions, it does not seem, *pace* Emile Léonard, that French Calvinism was spiritually in decline during this period: at the most, one can observe shades of difference between a more fundamentalist southern Protestantism and a more opportunist north.

On the whole, the faith of the French Protestants, under Henri IV, Louis XIII, and the Louis XIV of the first twenty-five years of his reign, remained a deep-rooted and active faith, but this optimistic observation holds true equally for the French Catholic Church, then strongly in the ascendant, in that 'century of the saints' marked by the invasion of devotion. This intense dynamism on the part of the competing *papist* majority was accordingly prejudicial to 'heresy': even when they originated with the Crown, anti-Huguenot initiatives would have been less threatening if they had not been sustained by the rejuvenated vigour of a Catholic conviction which was on the whole strongly shared by the Christian masses at large.

In a society formed of 'Estates', intolerance emanated from the 'bodies' which made up the kingdom, or from some of them. Thus, the 'national' Assembly of the French Clergy represented a more effective lobby than, for instance, the Compagnie du Saint-Sacrement or the Oeuvre de la propagation de la foi which had been actively militant against the Huguenots since 1627–34. These two typical organisations of the 'dévot' party were extremely active, though their size and scope of action remained limited. Louis XIV, in any case, was to show little sympathy for cabals, even and above all for devout cabals. The Assembly of the Clergy had its origins in the struggle against Protestantism at the time of the Colloquy of Poissy (1561) and of the levying of voluntary contributions from the Church; 'dons gratuits' and tithes both proved indispensable to the Crown in the prosecution of the 'wars of religion', and became established exclusively in the Catholic camp, at least until the time of the League. In 1615, faithful to this old 'genetic code', the Assembly of the Clergy took up the cause of Catholic liberties in the Béarn, imploring the king to restore them. They were, in fact, locally reduced or non-existent, as a result of the lingering Protestant monopoly in the region. This 'popish' request addressed to the Crown soon produced its effect. Louis XIII yielded to the 'affectionate solicitations' of the clergy. In 1620 he decided during a stay at Pau, that the Bearn should be completely absorbed into French territory with the favourable

[5] D. Dessert, *Argent, pouvoir et société au Grand Siècle*, Paris, 1984, p. 197.

consequences which this entailed for the local Catholics[6] – the usual correlation between the centralisation of power and support for the established Church. We shall meet with this 'correlative' effect often again, up to the Revocation and beyond. Thus, from the beginning of the century, we can clearly see the hegemonic consensus which united Church and Crown in an historic identification of interests – the object being to restrain the influence of Protestantism, a limitation which later turned to eradication. The two powers involved, Church and State, acted jointly each in its own interest, and in the interest of the other; this strategy provided too many shared advantages, both spiritual and social, not to sound attractive.

Before long this collaboration was to assume a continuous character. In 1621 the Assembly of the Gallican Clergy, persevering in its trajectory, called for the destruction of Huguenot strongholds, thus adumbrating the victorious policy of one of its members, who was shortly to reach the summit of power: I mean Richelieu, then bishop of Luçon and soon to be cardinal.

The cardinal's policy was to destroy the Protestants as a political force, still allowing their religious communities to survive. Moreover, he favoured by every means the Protestants of Germany and Sweden and eventually proposed the reunification of the Churches – which, indeed, caused some disquiet to some of their ministers. The Huguenots, after the humiliating peace of Alès in 1629, were nonetheless to enjoy a generation's respite: a respite which, with hindsight was to appear favourable to the minority Churches.

The demands put forward by the Assembly of the Clergy in 1636, and the *cahier* which it drew up, prove to be equally significant: both express the wish that the *parlements*, which acted in appeal, should pass judgements on conflicts arising from the application of the Edict of Nantes, which still gave rise to endless controversy and legal wrangling. In the heated debate surrounding the Revocation – whose origins lay in a distant past – one should emphasise the alliance between the established Church and *parlements*: the Assemblies of the Clergy naturally thought in monopolistic terms while the *parlements*, long since purged of their Calvinists, were filled with pious magistrates. These fierce Gallicans were hostile to the preservation of a Huguenot identity; and resented the competition of the half-Catholic and half-Protestant chambers, established by the Edict. They would have liked to govern the Protestants with the carrot and the stick, conjuring up the image of anti-papal

---

[6] My account follows P. Blet, *Le Clergé de France et la Monarchie*, Rome, 1959; see also *idem, Les Assemblées du Clergé et Louis XIV (1670–1693)* Rome, 1972; and his article in *Bibliothèque de l'Ecole des Chartes*, 130 (1972).

Gallicanism, in order to constrain the Huguenots to re-enter the fold of the Church. Yet all this was of no avail.

During the interlude of the Fronde, the Huguenots benefited from a tolerance which was all the more effective for being profitable: on all sides; Mazarin could not afford to antagonise the Protestants or their Cromwellian friends in England. But fundamentally Mazarin, like his queen and the state servants themselves, remained ill-disposed towards the Huguenots in conformity with the attitude of the Church. A royal declaration of 1652, issued in the midst of the crisis, and consequently favourable to the Huguenots, had appalled the prelates[7] who regarded it as a 'work of darkness'. In 1654, soon after the coronation of Louis XIV, the bishop of Montauban expressed the clergy's frustration, and presented their grievances to the sovereign in the usual manner: they merely asked for the application – the full application – of the clauses of the Edict of Nantes. The Edict, and nothing but the Edict! In 1655–7, the Assembly of the Clergy, always acting as an extremist lobby, obtained the cautious approval of Chancellor Séguier and Cardinal Mazarin, who no longer feared his English allies. While some commissioners were appointed to examine the state of heresy, national synods were brought to an end. A united front emerged; the king, the chancellor, the *parlements*, the Church were reverting to a harsh interpretation of the Edict (systematic attacks were above all to become official policy after 1679). The coalition against the *Religion Prétendue Réformée* – the 'supposedly Reformed religion' – brought together the clergy and the legal administration (Chancery and higher tribunals), while the king himself was moved by a concern for his royal dignity. The financial administration, under the Colbert clan, was to prove distinctly more lenient than the legal administration. In the face of this historic alliance of interests, the situation of the Protestants took a turn for the worse: they had always been suspected of republicanism, owing to their links with Geneva and Holland, and to the relatively democratic organisation of their Churches. But the beheading of Charles I in February 1649, following a revolution begun by the Scottish Presbyterians, seemed to comfort the gory republican reputation of the French Calvinists, despite their ultra-royalist zeal. As a result the State became at least as hostile to them as the Church had been. This may help explain Louis XIV's excessive zeal.

The foreign wars did not come to an end until 1659, still affording some respite to the French Huguenots. The treaty of the Pyrenees (1659), and the beginning of Louis XIV's personal reign, ushered in an era of systematic discrimination against the followers of Geneva. The interplay of the various social and political factors which were to produce intolerance in

---

[7] For what follows, see the accounts given by Blet.

the years leading up to the culmination of 1685 appears from now on in a stark light.

Anti-Huguenot measures, from the 1660s onwards, were issued by the king's council. It acted as a court, rather than as a modern cabinet. They also sprang from the decisions of identical *parlements* (Toulouse), or from votes taken by regional assemblies (the Estates of Languedoc). In Languedoc the truce of the Fronde years was not even respected. The king's council did not always act spontaneously nor necessarily on it own: it often followed the requests of Church authorities (general assemblies or agents of the clergy, and diocesan syndics). Protestantism had to face the dual challenge of Church and State, though the clergy acted with greater foresight than the Crown. The Crown, which was to fly into a temper, remained docile to the clergy and soon came to anticipate their promptings. The collaboration which developed at the highest level between a few great prelates (Harlay, Le Tellier, Bossuet) and the organs of the legal administration (king, Chancery, secretaries of state) had an equivalent, or rather a counterpart in rank-and-file anti-Protestant militancy: the ideologists who prepared the Revocation might be Jesuits, sometimes Gallicanised, contrary to the vows of their society: Father Meynier and Maimbourg, for instance. Or else they sprang up among the minority provincial clergy, under the auspices of Maître Bernard, a councillor in the presidial of Béziers, who published in 1666 an *Explanation of the Edict of Nantes* (*Explication de l'Edit de Nantes*) which was violently hostile to the Huguenots, in Languedoc and elsewhere. Admittedly the measures decreed against the minority were far from being universally applied, or even applicable. They treated it as a schismatic entity, destined simply to be reintegrated within the Church, whereas in fact what was involved was an heretical group which could not be reconciled, owing to fundamental differences over rites and dogmas. However, these repressive measures undermined the legal workings of the Reformed Churches, and more generally of the Protestant communities, at every level; they entailed the speedy suppression of the national synods and bi-partisan chambers (*chambres mi-parties*), while bringing about the destruction of *temples*, whatever their origin – *exercises de fief* (restricted to some Huguenot manors); *bailliage* concessions (corresponding to judicial units); or simply *possession* (which implied continuous existence since 1598). They limited, with a greater or lesser degree of success, the number of Huguenots who could take part in symbolic acts performed in the streets or in the open air (processions and funeral corteges, etc.). They imposed, on those of the 'supposedly Reformed religion', an outward show of respect for public manifestations of the Catholic faith, such as the exposition of the host or the worship of the Virgin Mary. They eroded Calvinism in those regions which had been incorporated into France after the Edict of Nantes, and in which, on legal grounds, the Edict was not supposed to apply retrospectively.

The implementation of anti-Huguenot policy, on the other hand, involved widespread exclusion from some professions or occupations, a *Berufsverbot* in the broadest sense of the term. This may be regarded as a common denominator with the English papists who encountered similar restrictions, at least in the public sector; the said papists, however, were often less harshly treated than the Huguenots. The Conseil du Roi, from Versailles, barred Protestants from corporations or from purchasing royal or seigniorial offices. Such prohibitions, promulgated between 1661 and 1685, were difficult to apply in any case, owing to the lack of competent, or suitable, Catholic specialists in some areas of the south of France. They came into effect, nonetheless, in an ever greater number of communities. In the private, or semi-public, sector, the disqualification which struck the Huguenots affected some guilds (tinplate workers or laundresses) and the professions (advocates or doctors). There might be complete debarment, or simply a *numerus clausus*. Finally the life-cycle of the individual was placed under supervision, in successive stages: whenever a child was born, it was 'recommended' and therefore prescribed to call in a Catholic midwife, even if the mother was Protestant. Likewise the schools of the dominant Church aimed at eliminating Huguenot education. Even his last agony was denied to the Protestant, visited on his deathbed by judges, who came to enquire whether a desirable last-minute conversion might be forthcoming. Transfers of allegiance to the competing faith were checked, punished and then forbidden, whenever they benefited the Calvinist Churches. But they were subsidised by means of monetary rewards or tax exemptions, when they operated to the advantage of Catholicism. Some purely theoretical clauses were added, forbidding Muslims to adhere to the doctrine of Geneva, or encouraging a change of religion when a child had reached his years of discretion.

II

These measures did not issue forth all at once, or fully armed, from the brow of Louis XIV. They appeared successively, taking on an increasingly harsh character, over a quarter of a century (1661–85). They highlight the period, tracing the lines of a clear strategy, on the part of the entities or institutions which devised them. In this way, the bane of the Revocation was progressively instilled. It was not just a question of eliminating outwardly a deviant, untypical or troublesome minority, for the benefit of a monopolistic clergy. The king and his ministers heartily wished to offer this fine gift of doctrinal and pastoral unanimity to the Church; but they also obtained, in exchange, the clergy's complete subservience to the authority of the Crown. Everyone – at least within certain spheres –

derived some advantages from the operation, beginning with the upholders of the social order, which was to be less and less threatened by rebellion, since the population was from now on held in check by priests loyal to the sovereign. These were, at least, the results obtained by opportunist politicians who failed to grasp the future ill-effects of this intolerance. In this respect, as far as their principles were concerned, Louis and his advisers were quite close to the religious absolutism of James I or Hobbes, let alone the supporters of the set of doctrines which are described, rightly or wrongly, as 'Erastian'. Catholics and Protestants, when in power, could hold certain attitudes in common.

Mutual flattery was illustrated by the 1670 Assembly of the Clergy which granted the king a considerable financial subsidy. They expected in return that His Majesty would take some drastic measures towards the Protestants. Subsequently, the play of interests becomes less easy to reduce to the elementary terms of these rather unedifying transactions. The 1669 'peace of the Church' had set aside the dispute over Jansenism for the next thirty years. In these circumstances a certain harmony prevailed on the momentary basis of Catholic unity. From the 1673 conflict over the *régale* to the 1682 Assembly of the Clergy, which passed the notorious Four Articles, a common interest reconciled for the time being three forms of Gallicanism centred respectively on the king, Church or *parlement* to the anti-Huguenot persecutions, which grew in intensity from 1679 onwards. The peace of Nijmegen (1678) had just put an end to the foreign wars, thus leaving the sovereign complete freedom of action within his own kingdom. From then on, he would be able to comply with the wishes of this Church, and even exceed their expectations by dealing a final blow to his dissenting subjects. This glorious, mock-heroic attitude deserved him to be regarded as a second Constantine, or a new Theodosius, the champions of official religion to the detriment of other creeds.

From the period of the Dutch war onwards, however, the dutiful defender of the (Catholic) faith obtained vast bargaining powers with the French priesthood who were only too grateful to thank him for his attentions. There was no need for the Roman pontificate to be convinced of the expediency of this policy, provided that the prelates of the kingdom were the creatures of Louis the God-given, by the very conditions of their appointment. As Christian priests, however, they preserved a great measure of spiritual autonomy in relation to their temporal master. But this inclined them precisely to grant this devout king what they would have plainly refused to Henri IV, an ex-Huguenot and the son of a Huguenot mother.

Indeed, the affair of the *régale*, in the midst of the conflict with Holland, highlights the unexpected bonds of mutual sympathy which united the State and clergy: self-interest prevailed on either side as the Protestant minority and the pope provided a dual albeit contradictory scapegoat. The king's declaration of 1673, which was inspired in particular by the Gallicanism of the *parlements*, extended the *régale* to the southern bishoprics, where, incidentally, the Calvinist population was most strongly concentrated. These areas had until then escaped the Crown's claim to the *régale*, which was widely established among the northern dioceses. From now on, in virtue of this claim, the king would be able to collect certain Church revenues from the diocese, and to make some ecclesiastical appointments, when the bishopric was vacant. These new developments were part of a general offensive of integration of the southern region, which the monarchy led on two fronts, 'Papist' and Huguenot. The *régale* in itself had few practical consequences and was more symbolic than real. The revenue, which from now on was collected by the king during the interval between bishops, was eventually returned to the prelates (after a short diversion) and was significantly used to fight Protestantism. As for the ecclesiastical preferments which were thus handed over to the Crown, the French Church managed to keep the situation under control, by surrendering only a modest number of appointments to the king's initiative. The pill of the Crown's right to the *régale* was the less bitter to swallow for the bishops as it gave them an opportunity to combine with the Crown. They could indulge in their favourite pastime of assailing the papacy with typically Gallican issues. Besides, the Sun-King was so well disposed in the 1670s to lead a campaign against Protestantism that the bishops could hardly deny him their blessings. The notion of barter or exchange, which we referred to above, remained an underlying element. It was of little avail for Pope Innocent XI – urged on to an astonishing degree by Caulet, the bishop of Pamiers (himself a Jansenist in persuasion) – to react as best he could against the encroachments of the *régale*, which were too secular in spirit for his liking. Louis XIV had, in this connection, an irresistible counter-argument, which left the Pontiff absolutely speechless. In 1678, the king had only to remind the Vatican authorities of his resolute interventions in favour of religion, i.e. against the Huguenots. Reciprocally, he felt all the more entitled to control the bishoprics during the intervals between prelates, and could not admit the least objection on the part of the pope. The bishops for their part were not to be outdone: in the spring of 1680, at a time when the anti-Huguenot escalation reached an intensity which had been unheard of since the wars of religion, the French Cardinal César d'Estrées reproached the Vatican for its opposition to the *régale*. To complete his argument, he praised the king's efforts against heresy, which Louis XIV had attacked constantly since 1661. 'Now it is succumbing!', the prelate declared, 'under the blows of the High Council.' And he proceeded to point out that the revenues from the *régale* would serve to convert the Huguenots.[8] 'If the pope', added d'Estrées, 'knew what the Crown plans for the sake of Religion [that is, against the Protestants], tears of gratitude would fall from his eyes.' Was César d'Estrées privy to the secrets of the sovereign? Janine Garrisson has shown in a recent book that the Revocation in its legal or practical aspects was premeditated by the king and his associates a few years in advance.[9] This testimony shows a remarkable correlation between the Gallican *régale* and anti-Huguenot feelings, prior to the Revocation.

The correlation continued. In July 1680, the instructions which d'Estrées received for his embassy to Rome were equally inspired by a double justification: the cardinal was to remind the pope of the king's actions against heresy, and of the French Crown's sovereign rights over the *régale*. The Paris *parlement*, through its procurator-general, Harlay (in September 1680), also set the severe anti-Protestant attacks in a Gallican perspective, with all the heat of a lay jurist. Harlay criticised the Vatican's interference with the administration of the convent at Charonne, which should have remained under the control of the French episcopate. He went on to condemn the pope's disrespect for the Sun-King. Louis XIV's triumphs at the expense of the Calvinists should have inspired greater respect and gratitude on the part of the Supreme Pontiff. This same summer, 1680, two French cardinals, Le Camus and the same d'Estrées, demonstrated plainly that any papal censures directed against Louis XIV on the subject of the *régale*, would only serve to diminish the king's zeal against the heretics, whereas His Majesty 'was the only monarch from whom help for the [Roman] Church in England could be expected'. This illustrates the 'communicating vessels' principle – or, in more elevated terms, the reciprocal links – between Gallicanism (of whatever denomination, *parlement*, Church or Crown) and the ensuing Revocation. This complementary dialectic came vividly to the fore during the bishops' Paris meeting in May 1681.

Though informal at first, this camarilla paved the way for the famous Assembly of the Clergy in 1681–2. On this occasion, a figure of some consequence entered the stage: the archbishop of Rheims, Maurice Le Tellier, had been imbued from the cradle with the principles of Gallicanism, which were further instilled in his head at the Sorbonne. The son of Chancellor Michel Le Tellier, and the brother of Louvois, the prelate of Rheims was loyal to Louis XIV, even though he managed to preserve – despite his unseemly wantonness – a sense of prelatical autonomy. His behaviour was in no ways comparable to that of the archbishop of Paris, François Harlay de Champvallon, an obsequious Versailles courtier. Le Tellier's intention was rather to act as a mediator: he wished

---

[8] Blet, *Assemblées*, pp. 174–6.
[9] Janine Garrisson, *L'Edit de Nantes et sa révocation. Histoire d'une intolérance*, Paris, 1985.

to arbitrate between pope and king, and mitigate, rather than suppress, the ultra-Gallican intemperance of the *parlements* and lawyers as a whole (we know the extreme position they were to adopt a century later at the time of the Civil Constitution of the clergy, when events finally gave free rein to their ambition to exercise authority in 1790). Accordingly, in his address of May 1681, Maurice Le Tellier expatiated on Louis' efforts to banish the Huguenot faith from his dominions, in order to defend and justify the king his master against the pope, on the subject of the *régale*. In the same vein, he dismissed other Roman claims, upholding the rights of the episcopate against the monasteries. Finally, he vindicated the attitude of Gerbais. This priest had incurred the hatred of the Vatican for his support of the temporal authorities and Assembly of the Clergy in their joint disputes with the Holy See. Throughout Maurice Le Tellier's weighty and penetrating remarks, there runs the triple ornamented thread of anti-Protestantism, Crown and Church Gallicanism. Le Tellier went on to propose – what will come as no great surprise – the holding of a national council, or, at least, he called for an extraordinary Assembly of the French Clergy, held in 1682, whose influence has already been assessed.

In the meantime, the links between Gallicanism and anti-Protestantism remained strongly in evidence: in October 1681, Louis XIV took possession of Strasburg and re-established the practice of the Catholic religion in that city, to the confusion of the local Lutherans. He wished to capitalise on the merits of his action in favour of the faith, and attempted, accordingly, to obtain from the pope, as a special reward, an *indult* (or special grace) conceding French claims over the *régale*. Should the Sovereign Pontiff refuse to make this concession (as he did in the event), Louis' authority would be combined with a special Assembly of the Clergy following Maurice Le Tellier's requirements, in order to counterbalance the claims of Rome. The 'delutheranisation' of Strasburg, as it were, was only a first step, in a scenario combining Church and King Gallicanism and the common distrust of Rome. The threefold or fourfold strategy of the 'Bourbon' Church and State, was still in force; the Protestants had only to wait.

The celebrated Assembly of the Clergy of 1681–2 did not depart from this accepted pattern. When in November 1681 Bossuet – a loyal Gallican – suggested in convocation that the pope's power be limited in relation to the Church and Country he lay due emphasis on Louis XIV's merits and fortitude as demonstrated by 'the conversion of Calvinists, the destruction of the *temples* and the seizure of the cathedral of Strasburg from the followers of Luther'. Was it a question of exchanging one benefit for another? A few days later, Harlay, archbishop of Paris, echoed Le Tellier and Bossuet. Louis XIV's anti-Protestant policy had been so fruitful to the Church 'that all the treasures of this Church were not sufficient to acknowledge it'. The archbishop hoped, therefore, that the pope would choose to recognise and reward this royal service 'rather than wish to infringe upon the liberties of the Gallican Church'. The terms of this implicit bargain appear very clearly; that same month, Cheron, who had a power of attorney in the diocese of Paris, brandished anti-Calvinist references and praised the king's success in the struggle against heresy; he immediately combined this rhetoric with the extolling both of Crown and Church Gallicanism ('the priest-king', or 'the bishops re-established in their sees'). Many texts could be added, but let it suffice to say that the common Gallicanism of Monseigneur Le Tellier, Louis XIV and their associates appears as a strictly internal French affair, allowing the king and bishops to achieve their reciprocal end. It was thus logical to leave the pope 'on the sidelines' and oppress the Huguenots. The same people who twisted the Vatican lion's tail took care simultaneously to wring the necks of the Protestants.

Until the end, the debates and decisions of the 1682 Assembly hinged likewise on two fundamental texts: the *Four Articles*, drawn up by Bossuet, and the *Pastoral Admonishment to the Protestants*. The Bossuet of the *Four Articles* was exactly, as Pierre Blet has shown, the same Bossuet who had converted Turenne from Protestantism in 1668, and had written for this purpose an *Exposition of the Catholic Doctrine*. Well before 1682, this text already challenged papal infallibility, possibly to remove a major stumbling-block on the way towards Christian unity. We may say, in the light of Pierre Blet's scholarly works, that the Gallican *Four Articles* were thus, according to Bossuet, the price to be paid to persuade the separated brethren to return to the fold, even though this happy prospect was to be accompanied in the near future by a few *dragonnades*. This is how we are to understand the famous *Pastoral Admonishment of the Gallican Church Assembled in Paris [in 1682] to Those of the Supposedly Reformed Religion, to Induce Them to Become Converted and Reconciled with the Church*. This text is linked on the one hand to the Gallican resolutions of the Assembly which had exalted the power of the Crown in an effort to make this unpopish Church more palatable to the Huguenots. But we should also bear in mind the numerous destructions of temples, which were carried into effect in those years as a means to reward the clerical lobby for its obedience and consolidate the monopoly shared by Church and King. The conjunction of Gallicanism and repression caused a serious rift in the course of the following months and years: the Protestant revolt of June 1683, organised by the Huguenot lawyer Brousson, was significant in this respect. Rebellions in the predominantly Catholic regions had in fact exerted great influence until 1675, when the last uprisings took place in Brittany and in the Bordeaux area. Without disappearing entirely, these tumults, originating in 'papist' communities, subsided after that date, when anti-Protestant measures were on the increase. The French Catholics became more tractable, and obedient, bedazzled as they were by the 'godly wonders' of 'decalvinisation', which were to reach their climax with the massive 'conversions' of 1685.

In the short term, the events of 1683 had led directly to those of 1685. Brousson intended simply to organise reprisals against the eradication of the temples. But the overall success of the popular demonstrations of Huguenot dissent which he triggered off in June 1683 served to justify in turn, albeit mendaciously, more rigorous repression still. This culminated in the use of military force entrusted to Louvois to eradicate the Huguenot faith. After the magistrates' litigations came the season of plain violence in the hands of the soldiery, or *dragonnades*, leading up to the Revocation in 1685.

Independently from all factors and actors, causes and effects, any assessment of the Revocation should avoid anachronism in keeping with Elisabeth Labrousse's recent work.

I shall ask the reader's leave to state the obvious: in terms of abstract morality, the Revocation proved reprehensible. This was already so in 1685 for an observer like Bayle, for instance, who transcended the miseries of his age and rose to a concept of tolerance – which has progressively become our own since the Enlightenment. The Revocation, on the other hand, could be vindicated – however contemptible it is for us today – if we stick to the requirements of Church, King and Country unity – which had become obsolete in France by the following century; 'une foi, un roi, une loi', this motto supposedly guaranteed the cohesion of the kingdom. The social pact between the monarchy, on the one hand, and the overwhelming Catholic majority, on the other, was indeed strengthened by the Revocation, which also sustained alliances with Spain and other peripheral powers. In the 1700s the French army operated in Catholic Spain like a fish in water, and a comparison with the cruel fate encountered by the 'impious' Napoleonic armies in the peninsula more than a hundred years later would be eloquent enough in this respect. The 1685 religious and political settlement was to last at least until the 1770s. Among other factors conducive to social homogeneity, imposed from above and accepted from below by the great mass of subjects with some exceptions, this compromise safeguarded social peace throughout the country; whatever its motives, such tranquillity had been postponed either by the ultra-Catholic League at the end of the sixteenth century or by the endless internal wars and popular tumults, which made up a long-drawn *Fronde* from 1620 to 1675. The Revocation brought to a close an era of major upheavals among the Catholic masses – despite a few later exceptions. This is not mere coincidence. (Neither were there any

Protestant revolts after 1710 – an achievement which is by no means glorious.) Even though apparently checked by the papacy from the 1690s onwards, Gallicanism confirmed in practice, around 1682–5, the close association of the two swords, lay and spiritual, clerical and royal. This fusion acted as a strong deterrent and induced all French subjects – now that they belonged almost unanimously to the established Church – to accept an ethic of submission and discipline which Henri III and even Louis XIII had failed to impose in a country still divided by questions of religion. If not conducive to economic prosperity, the Revocation brought about a pervading consensus from which only dissenting minorities were excluded by definition. Their misery acted as a foil and paradoxically it enhanced the religious or national integration of a vast majority of Frenchmen – albeit they were not necessarily a 'silent majority'.

The bishops and priests were all the more ready to preach social harmony, and even patriotic unity, to their flocks that they commended the religious zeal of the monarch. Catholic *petty bourgeois*, so well depicted in the memoirs of Borrelly, a notary of Nîmes, made strenuous efforts to pay their taxes to the king who gave such signal proof of his favour towards the 'true' faith. Only a precursor like the Huguenot Bayle could envisage, contrary to Bossuet or Jurieu, a brand of unrestrained tolerance and freedom which defended the rights of individual conscience against the forced unanimity of the Revocation. One has to be an historian and stand at a certain distance in time to realise that the Revocation and the surrounding legislation were to prove lethal to the ancien régime. With the advice of the Church, the French monarchy rushed headlong towards its fate, as a result of long-fermented hatreds. This growing enmity, which was Huguenot in the first place, turned towards the Church, and fairly soon against the king. But in 1685, the reckoning was still far off.

III

In addition, early modern France was not the only country to enforce religious uniformity and buttress the alliance of Church and State to the detriment of a religious minority. I have mentioned Spain, Russia and even Japan, and finally Scandinavia, though other names should be added. The situation of our English neighbour is of exceptional interest. The Protestant power, which became one of the centres of tolerance in Europe, deserves to be compared with Catholic France. Moreover, the French Revocation – influenced as it was by the 1682 convocation – also played an important role in the genesis of another decisive event in the decade, the Glorious Revolution of 1688. The comparative history of the period should be resolutely Anglo-French. As in the case of France, one needs to envisage the situation over a number of years: the anti-Catholic legislation of the Elizabethan period is well known. Yet Elizabeth Labrousse's recommendation concerning the French measures against the Huguenots is also relevant in a British context: it is the practical application of these laws which matters. In fact, according to Alan Dures' recent assessment, the real turning point in the repression of the Catholic minority in Elizabethan England corresponded to the years from 1568 to 1572: they marked a breach between England and the papacy, soon to be followed by Spain and the France of the St Bartholomew. After this date, the penal laws which struck at the property, and sometimes the lives, of the recusant papists were applied a little less laxly than in the past: the number of executions in the last twenty years of the sixteenth century was well over 100; more than half the Catholic priests who entered the country between 1581 and 1586 were killed or imprisoned. Such measures were scarcely more liberal than those which Louis XIV was later to adopt against Reformed ministers. Indeed, Whig history has been more lenient to the Virgin Queen than to the Sun-King. This is because the tendency of Protestantism was, without any doubt, in agreement with the movement of history, and led towards genuine human progress. Conversely, the Church of Rome has long been considered as reactionary and there is an element of truth in this appreciation.

In the second half of James I's reign, the situation seems to have eased considerably in practice: the treatment of papists underwent considerable fluctuations. The common denominator of this policy remained the imposition of fines, accompanied sometimes by confiscations of land – both of which, whether real vexations or simple pinpricks, were particularly disagreeable to the Catholic gentry.

The tax assessment of the Recusants appears to have intensified under Charles I. On the other hand, the number of Catholics executed[10] remained remarkably low during his reign, at least until the 1640s, when that figure rose again. The other forms of persecution became markedly less severe and the Catholic population rose from 35,000 to 50,000 between 1603 and the 1640s.[11]

The anti-Catholic tendencies persisted under Cromwell, though not without some astonishing gestures of indulgence on the Protector's part. But from then on, it was outside England that the most crucial episodes took place: in the wake of Cromwell's victories in Ireland and following drastic expropriations, the proportion of land in Catholic hands fell from 60 per cent to 20 per cent, in round figures, to the advantage of the Protestant landowners.[12] The expulsion of the native Irish may be

[10] Alan Dures, *English Catholicism 1558–1642*, London, 1983.
[11] In France, on the other hand, executions of pastors and lay preachers were to take place after 1685–6.
[12] Toby Barnard, *The English Republic*, London, 1982, p. 72.

regarded as a sort of agrarian Revocation which lasted more than a century. This was a social or colonial venture rather than a purely religious phenomenon: it could be interpreted, accordingly, as a clash between two nations. Indeed, French Protestantism itself has been presented not only as a spiritual conviction, but also as a local, quasi-national reaction. May I refer here to the seminal studies by Janine Garrisson, one of our great experts on the Revocation, who insisted on the 'Occitan challenge'?[13] Without going so far, we may observe that in Ireland, as in the south of France, religion can hardly be separated from regional particularism.

In any case, in the middle years of the seventeenth century, especially from 1649 to 1658, English Protestantism acquired a disquieting image, instilling fear into the heart of the Catholics of the Continent who resented the expropriation of the Irish and more particularly the execution of Charles I. As I recalled earlier Elisabeth Labrousse has brought out the role played by the shocking image of this regicide in the origins of the Revocation. There is, indeed, an English, or even an Anglo-Irish, dimension to the history of the Revocation: it cannot be confined to the French context alone.

During the Restoration, the situation of the Catholics (who had never been entirely excluded) improved irregularly, though not without bouts of repression; the former anti-Catholic legislation was not completely applied, if one excepts the *Berufsverbot*, reinforced by the notorious Test Act. These laws were strenuously applied at the time of the popish plot, the 'Jesuit' pseudo-conspiracy forged by Titus Oates. The 'plot' aimed at discrediting Catholics in England. For a few years, in an atmosphere of paranoia and hysteria, the Oates affair resulted in the voluntary or forced exile or arrest of hundreds of Catholics, who were sentenced, fined and submitted to endless confiscations and discriminations. Several priests, secular or regular, were executed.[14] Some qualifications should be made for the anti-Jesuit paranoia of the English which brought into play the belief – widely held by Protestants throughout Europe around 1680 – that England was a beleaguered island, while France was identified with arbitrary and papist absolutism.

There still remains, in terms of comparative history, the interesting case of the Glorious Revolution: its roots lay in the British context. Yet for the rest of Europe, it could be regarded in several respects as the (natural) outcome of the Revocation of the Edict of Nantes, three years earlier. As Maurice Ashley has recalled,[15] the question of English Catholicism in all aspects – international and insular, Jesuit and secular – and the problem

[13] In A. Armengaud and R. Lafont, *Histoire d'Occitanie*, Paris, 1979, pp. 440–72.
[14] J.P. Kenyon, *The Popish Plot*, London, 1972.
[15] Maurice Ashley, *The Glorious Revolution of 1688*, New York, 1966.

of its reintroduction, or on the contrary of its symbolic 'revocation' as it were, are among the causes of 1688. Conversely, as far as its beneficial liberal consequences are concerned, this episode proved to be more political than religious in character. To confirm Ashley's interpretation, besides, one has only to point to James II's well-known initiatives in favour of Catholic emancipation, albeit the king's secret motives, whether sincere or Machiavellian, are open to question. Among these interventions, of a general or a more specific nature, should be cited the unwarranted abeyance of the Test Act, Godden vs. Hales, and finally the two Declarations of Indulgence in 1687 and 1688. On the other hand, one should also mention the violent reaction of the establishment against the Crown. We may surmise, whatever our private opinion on the king, that such measures were anti-discriminatory, and therefore assumed, at least in theory, a positive character. They were clearly untimely, though, given the passions they aroused in England. The way to hell, after all, is paved with good intentions, even in the case of James II. Historical assessments of the period are often misleading in this respect, were it only because of its emotional appeal even in our day. Some of our colleagues, among the most enlightened, rightly condemn Louis XIV's abrasive policy against the Protestants of his kingdom, while finding it difficult to achieve an indispensable degree of detachment from the anti-Catholic wave which affected their own country at the time. Whatever the pride and prejudices of present-day historians, if we take a close look at the seventeenth century, the benevolent intentions of the Crown, however confused and confusing, combined with the ingrained anti-Catholic reaction of the English elites. Their defiance of the Court led to the 'revolutionary' seizure of power by William of Orange, who insisted in his own words on the 'Protestant religion' and the 'liberties of England'. As a matter of fact, this political *coup* produced a wider degree of freedom, whatever its own starting point. In 1689, the Toleration Act exempted 'their Majesties' Protestant subjects, dissenting from the Church of England, from the penalties of certain laws', which seemed to imply that the Catholics were excepted from its provisions. The old penal laws, as well as double taxation, though not always applied, could be enforced against the Catholics, by virtue of a logic which derived from the very essence of the revolution of 1688. Likewise, in 1701 the Act of Settlement excluded Catholic princes from the succession, a wise decision, no doubt, in practical terms, though highly revealing of the significance of James II's overthrow.

If we say simply, along with Bernard Cottret, 'shameful revocation, glorious revolution', this may serve to emphasise a profound contrast between these two events, and a certain symmetry, resulting from a closely interwoven mesh of causality across the Channel. Moreover, and to

balance whatever one-sidedness there might be in our estimate, Professor
John Bossy has reminded us that even when debarred from office like the
French Protestants, the English Catholics of the eighteenth century
benefited in many areas from a flourishing demographic situation,
undeniable economic prosperity and unofficial permissiveness for their
assemblies – even though they were held in barns. They also enjoyed, all
in all, good working relations with their Protestant neighbours. We may
note incidentally that the Protestant historian Emile Léonard in a book
published fifty years ago[16] reached fairly similar conclusions concerning
the Protestants of the pays de Vaunage, in Languedoc, once the wave of
anti-Camisard repression had abated, if we except a few subsequent
storms.

In fact the comparison might be more relevant still in the case of
Ireland, which epitomises the 'negative' results of 1688. The Cromwellian
expropriations of land were carried on apace, shortly after the battle of the
Boyne; they continued on a massive scale in the west in the eighteenth
century (in so far as there was still any papist land left to expropriate). The
Irish Catholics held 59 per cent of the land in 1641; following all kinds of
procedures, some of which were violently discriminatory, they retained
only 22 per cent in 1688, 14 per cent in 1703 and 5 per cent in 1778.[17] As
in the case of the Huguenots in the south of France, one cannot separate
the initial thrust of centralisation undertaken at the end of the seventeenth
century by the French monarchy from the efforts to achieve denominational unity – in terms of Catholic observance in France, and in an
agrarian mode, which all in all proved more efficient, around Dublin and
Belfast. This suggestion on my part does not underestimate the undeniable
prosperity of eighteenth-century Ireland, which has been so clearly
brought to light by Professor Cullen in his research; and I am equally
conscious of the genuine attempts at national emancipation which were
later made in their turn by the Protestants of the green isle of Erin. At all
events, neither the Irish tragedy nor the Huguenot drama should be
ignored. In keeping with the ideals of comparative history, could we
suggest some common ground of comparison and understanding between
the two experiences? This would be all the more legitimate, even on the

---

[16] Emile G. Léonard, *Mon village sous Louis XV, d'après les Mémoires d'un paysan*,
Paris, 1941.
[17] See, on the subject of the expropriations of land in Ireland, T.W. Moody and F.X.
Martin (eds.), *The Course of Irish History*, Cork, 1977, reprinted several times between
1967 and 1978. In 1641, before the Cromwellian expropriations, the Catholics still
owned 59 per cent of the land in Ireland; in 1688, after these expropriations, 22 per
cent; in 1703, after the expropriations carried out in the reign of William of Orange, it
was no more than 14 per cent. This percentage subsequently fell to about 5 in 1778.
This dramatic fall was due, among other causes, to discriminatory legislation. The
fundamental data, in Moody and Martin's book are on pp. 201 (maps) and 202–20, in
particular pp. 219–20 for the eighteenth century.

British scale, if we insist that phenomena of moral or cultural isolation and victimisation came forcibly into play against the English papists, who were alike despised by the learned, and eventually reviled by the people. On the contrary, the Huguenots experienced the compassion of the enlightened, especially around Voltaire.

If we stick to the *long-term* consequences of the 1680s, and more generally of the seventeenth century, with its later repercussions, we are struck by the remarkable parallel between the vast territories of present-day France (principally the Protestant south) and the British Isles (above all in the Celtic and Catholic zone).[18] In both cases, certain Christian minorities were crushed or oppressed, dispossessed or discriminated against – a process which served to consolidate the respective interests of the nationally dominant varieties of Christianity – Gallican and Protestant – and to strengthen the position of the existing or remodelled monarchy, be it the Bourbons of France or the Protestant successors of James II. An efficient, albeit objectionable, compromise was established, which lasted until the complete emancipation of the Huguenots and English Catholics.

The 'verdict of history' was nonetheless very different in the two cases: as far as the Glorious Revolution, and its sequels, are concerned, historians have sometimes been a little inclined to overlook the regrettable fact of anti-Catholic discrimination and above all anti-Irish repression – which coincided in some areas.

Such disregard can be explained, and partly justified, if we insist on the favourable achievements of the Glorious Revolution for Great Britain and even for the rest of Europe. On the other hand, the Revocation of 1685, which was approved, albeit reluctantly at times, by the intellectual elite of France (La Bruyère, Bossuet) was to become, quite understandably for future generations, the most dishonourable part of Louis XIV's long reign. This revengeful and well-founded condemnation had for a long time been threatening. The Sun-King was very soon to meet with a pitiless and clear-sighted judge within his own cultural sphere: in the 1680s Bayle was to invent in the midst of the French-speaking world the conceptual paradigm of tolerance against the Bourbon monarch.[19]

The Revocation was not to be revoked altogether until the time of Louis XVI and above all of the Constituent Assembly. But the very relevance of the Act of 1685 was subject to legitimate suspicion from the beginning of the Enlightenment, when gradually the ideas of the apostles of religious pluralism – Bayle, first of all, and soon afterward Voltaire – gained the ascendancy. Thus there came to an end among men of advanced intelligence – until such time as their philosophy became enshrined in law

---

[18] In both cases, there was, of course, at least partial bilingualism, Anglo-Gaelic among the Irish Catholics, the clergy in particular, and Occitan-French among the Huguenots in southern France.

[19] A. Morvan, *La Tolérance dans le roman anglais de 1726 à 1771*, Paris, 1984.

– one great cycle of intolerance in the modern period, consubstantial with the monarchy of the classical era. The cycle began in 1492, at the time of the persecution of the Jews in Spain. It continued without remission throughout the endless wars of religion. The events of 1685, in France, with their English and above all Irish counterparts (these last initiated, for the most part, by the middle of the seventeenth century) were to form a fitting culmination. The eighteenth century, on the other hand, was to popularise a pluriconfessional ideal. This new-found enlightenment did not signify, for all that, the death of the national clergies: beyond the years from 1750 to 1800, they were to survive the advent of a new spirit, and the happy, or dramatic, end of intolerance. On the other hand, monarchies were driven by choice or necessity to rely on the sacred and on religious monocracy. The English monarchy made a transition with its usual panache. The Bourbons were far from being so successful, and had some unpleasant moments ahead of them.

SELECT BIBLIOGRAPHY

Primary Sources

Manuscripts

Canterbury

Dean and Chapter Library
MSS U-47-A (1–7): consistory registers (1576–8, 1581–4, 1595–9, 1623–37, 1663, 1680–2, 1693–9).
MSS U-47-H (1–4): correspondence.
MSS A/C (1, 2, 4, 5): Burghmote Minute Book.

London

British Library
Egerton MSS 2568, 2734, 2982.
Stowe, MSS 109, 151, 156.
Add. MSS 43862: register of the 'hommes politiques' in Norwich.
Add. MSS 32093, 32095.

French Reformed Church, Soho Square
Archives of the community in London, from 1550 onwards.
Manuscript series A: charter, successive versions of the Church discipline, lists of pastors, etc.: consistory registers (1560–5; 1571–1708).
Manuscript series C: financial administration, loans, etc.
Manuscript series D: deacons' books, relief of the poor.
Manuscript series F: conferences, in particular the register of the Coetus (assembly of the Foreign Churches) from 1575 to 1598, and the book of Colloquies for 1591 to 1654.
Manuscript series G: correspondence.

Guildhall Library, City of London
MSS 4629–46: registers of the Weavers' Company.

MSS 7412/1–2: Coetus Registers 1649–1850.
MSS 7413: various papers (duplicates of lost registers).

Huguenot Library, University College
Manuscript series, A, B, C: collections for the refugees from 1686 onwards.
Manuscript series J: consistory proceedings from the 1680s onwards: the later
   Refuge.

Lambeth Palace Library
MSS Gibsoniani 929, 930, 933, 935, 941, 942.
MSS Miscellani 953, 1029.

Norwich

Norfolk Record Office
MSS NRO, 31/G IX: consistory register (1628–1828).
MSS NRO, 17/D: Book of Orders.

Oxford

Bodleian Library: in particular
Rawlinson MSS A.477–8, D.641, C.983–4; second half of the seventeenth century.
Tanner MSS 30–2, 34–6, 44–5, 82, 92; petitions and ecclesiastical correspondence
   c. 1680.

Paris

Bibliothèque Nationale
MSS fr. 7022: reports on French refugees, *c*. 1680.
MSS Dupuy 104: correspondence between Calvin and England, *c*. 1550–*c*. 1560.

Bibliothèque de l'Arsenal
MSS 3847: on refugees in England, *c*. 1572.
MSS 10422–3: papers seized from fugitives, *c*. 1680.

Printed

Hessels, J.H., *Ecclesiae Londino-Batavae Archivum*, 3 vols., Cambridge, 1889–97,
   describes archives which have since been dispersed (after the Second World
   War).
Howell, T.B., *State Trials*, ed. W. Cobbett, 33 vols., London, 1809–26.
Journal of the House of Commons.
Proceedings of the Huguenot Society of London.

Publication of the Huguenot Society of London.
State Papers, Domestic series.

SECONDARY SOURCES

Agnew, David, *Protestant Exiles from France*, Edinburgh, 1866.
Armogathe, J.R., *L'Eglise catholique et la Révocation de l'Edit de Nantes*, Paris, 1985.
Baird, Charles, *History of the Huguenot Emigration to America*, New York, 1885.
Browning, W.S., *History of the Huguenots, from 1598 to 1838*, London, 1839.
Burn, John S., *History of the French, Walloon, Dutch and Other Foreign Protestant Refugees Settled in England*, London, 1846.
Butler, Jon, *The Huguenots in America. A Refugee People in New World Society*, Harvard, 1983.
Caldicott, C.E.J., Gough, H., and Pittion, J.-P. (eds.), *The Huguenots and Ireland. Anatomy of an Emigration*, Dublin, 1987.
Campbell, John, 'The Walloon Community in Canterbury, 1625–1649', unpublished thesis, University of Wisconsin, 1970.
Carré, Albert, *L'Influence des Huguenots français en Irlande aux 17e et 18e siècles*, Paris, 1937.
CNRS, *Le Refuge huguenot en Allemagne*, Paris, 1981.
Denis, Philippe, 'Les Eglises d'étrangers à Londres jusqu'à la mort de Calvin', unpublished dissertation, University of Liège, 1974.
Garrisson, Janine, *L'Edit de Nantes et sa révocation. Histoire d'une intolérance*, Paris, 1985.
Gwynn, R.D., *Huguenot Heritage*, London, 1985.
Histoire des Protestants en France, Toulouse, Privat, 1977.
Joutard, Philippe (ed.), *Historiographie de la Réforme*, Paris, Neuchâtel and Montreal, 1977.
Kershaw, S.W., *Protestants from France*, London, 1885.
Labrousse, Elisabeth, *Une foi, une loi, un roi? La Révocation de l'Edit de Nantes*, Paris and Geneva, 1985.
Léonard, E.G., *Histoire générale du protestantisme*, 3 vols., Paris, 1961–4.
Lindeboom, J., *Austin Friars. History of the Dutch Reformed Church in London*, The Hague, 1950.
Magdelaine, Michèle, and von Thadden, R. (eds.), *Le Refuge huguenot/Die Huguenotten*, Paris/Frankfurt, 1985.
Magen, Beate, *Die Wallongemeinde in Canterbury*, Frankfurt, 1973.
Mayo, Ronald, 'Les Huguenots à Bristol, 1681–1791', unpublished thesis, University of Lille, 1966.
Mours, Samuel, *Les Eglises réformées en France*, Paris, 1958.
Pettegree, A. *Foreign Protestant Communities in Sixteenth-Century London*, Oxford, 1986.
Poisson, Isabelle, 'Etude d'une communauté de huguenots à Londres. Threadneedle St. 1685–1705', Mémoire de maîtrise, Paris IV, 1988.
Prestwich, Menna (ed.), *International Calvinism 1541–1715*, Oxford, 1985.

Quéniart, Jean, *La Révocation de l'Edit de Nantes. Protestants et catholiques français de 1598 à 1685*, Paris, 1985.

Schickler, F. de, *Les Eglises du Refuge en Angleterre*, 3 vols., Paris, 1892.

Schwartz, Hillel, *The French Prophets – The History of a Millenarian Group in Eighteenth-Century England*, Berkeley, 1980.

Scouloudi, Irene, 'Alien Immigration and Alien Communities in London, 1558–1640', MSc. dissertation, London, 1936.

Returns of Strangers in the Metropolis 1593, 1627, 1635, 1639. A Study of an Active Minority, Publications of the Huguenot Society in London, 'Quarto Series', LVIII, 1985.

(ed.), *Huguenots in Britain and their French Background 1550–1800*, London, 1987.

Smiles, Samuel, *The Huguenots, their Settlements, Churches and Industries in England and Ireland*, London, 1867.

Spicer, A.P., 'The French-speaking Reformed Community in Southampton, 1567 – c. 1616', forthcoming thesis, University of Southampton.

Sundstrom, Roy A., 'Aid and Assimilation: A Study of the Economic Support Given French Protestants in England, 1680–1727', PhD thesis, Kent State University Graduate School, USA, 1972.

Weiss, Charles, *Histoire des réfugiés protestants de France...*, Paris, 1852.

Yardeni, Myriam, *Le Refuge protestant*, Paris, 1985.

Zuber, R., and Theis, L. (eds.), *La Révocation de l'Edit de Nantes et le protestantisme français en 1685*, Paris, 1986.

Index of names

Abbott, George, archbishop of
  Canterbury, 104, 106
Abraham, 83–4
Abraham, Daniel, 259
Agulhon, Maurice, 46n, 232–3n
Ailleau, Jean, 223
Airy, O., 165n
a Lasco, John, 10, 20, 26–7, 33–44, 47–50,
  168, 236, 271, 273
Alba, duke of, 55–6
Albiac, Accasse d', 29
Alexander the Great, 216
Alexandre, Pierre, pastor, 26, 48–9
Alix, Pierre, pastor, 203, 223
Allemand, Stéphane, 254
Amyraut, Moïse, 128–30, 161, 172, 248,
  287
Anne, Queen, 219–20
Ariès, Philippe, 255
Arlington, Henry Benmet, 1st earl of, 197
Armengaud, A., 301n
Arminius, 99
Aroux, A., 216
Arundell, Lady Blanche, 131
Ashley, Maurice, 301–2
Assigny, Pierre d', pastor, 133–4, 144–5, 147
Astruc, Pierre, 223
Avvakum, Russian archpriest, 285–7
Aylmer, G. E., 239n

Bacon, Sir Francis, 52, 102, 250, 275–6
Baridon, Michel, 235
Barillon, Paul de, French ambassador,
  202, 211
Barlow, W., 94n–5n
Barnard, Toby, 300n
Baxter, Richard, 159
Bayle, Pierre, 6, 208–9n, 251, 287, 298–9,
  304

Beaude, P.-M., 236n
Beaumont, Stéphane, 253
Beauvais, Paul, 255–6
Beauvoir, D. de, 216
Bebarel, Simon, 246
Bellarmine, Robert, SJ, cardinal, 88, 90
Bellemain, Jean, 28
Ben Israel, Menasseh, 132
Bennassar, B., 61n
Bernard, Maître, lawyer, 291
Berry, 261
Betrand, Paul, pastor, 162–3, 170, 172,
  180–1
Beza (or de Bèze), Theodore, 25, 47, 72,
  83, 85, 87, 239
Black, Jeremy, 193n
Blet, Pierre, 289–90n, 295n
Blondeau, Pierre, 196
Blondel, David, 91n
Blount, alias Widdrington, captain, 193
Bocquet, 243
Bodin, Jean, 249
Bolingbroke, Henry St John, viscount,
  81–2
Boningham, Denis de, 249
Bonrepaus, François Usson de, 211–12,
  214
Bonvallet, G., 201
Borne, William, 5
Borrelly, notary, 299
Bossuet, Jacques Bénigne, bishop of
  Meaux, 176, 291, 296–7, 299, 304
Bossy, J., 201n, 285, 303
Boulleaux, François, 196
Bourcier, Elisabeth, 74n
Bouteleu, Pierre, 243
Braudel, F., 3–4n
Brent, Nathaniel, vicar general, 105–6, 112
Bréval, François Durant de, pastor, 210

Lightning Source UK Ltd.
Milton Keynes UK
23 April 2010

153258UK00001B/21/P